Europe's Postwar Periods
1989, 1945, 1918

Europe's Postwar Periods
1989, 1945, 1918

Writing History Backwards

Edited by
Martin Conway, Pieter Lagrou and Henry Rousso

BLOOMSBURY ACADEMIC
LONDON · NEW YORK · OXFORD · NEW DELHI · SYDNEY

BLOOMSBURY ACADEMIC
Bloomsbury Publishing Plc
50 Bedford Square, London, WC1B 3DP, UK
1385 Broadway, New York, NY 10018, USA

BLOOMSBURY, BLOOMSBURY ACADEMIC and the Diana logo are trademarks of
Bloomsbury Publishing Plc

First published in Great Britain 2019

A catalogue record for this book is available from the British Library.

A catalog record for this book is available from the Library of Congress.

ISBN: HB: 978-1-4742-7650-4
ePDF: 978-1-4742-7651-1
eBook: 978-1-4742-7652-8

Typeset by Newgen KnowledgeWorks Pvt. Ltd., Chennai, India
Printed and bound in Great Britain

To find out more about our authors and books visit www.bloomsbury.com
and sign up for our newsletters.

Contents

Preface

This book is the outcome of a series of workshops organized by the 'European Network on Contemporary History' (EURHISTXX), created in 2007 and benefitting from funding by the French *Centre national de la Recherche scientifique* (CNRS) as a *Groupe de recherche européen*. The network was formed in a specific intellectual and political context. A decade after the fall of the Berlin Wall, academics from the eastern and western parts of Europe were still searching for the means to create a common basis which would unite the historical discipline. Contemporary history, as a sub-discipline, was also facing significant additional challenges. The end of the twentieth century and the beginning of the twenty-first century were characterized by intense battles over the memory of the recent past, and the European continent remained divided into different historical traditions, separated by the legacies of the two world wars, the Holocaust, the Cold War, decolonization, and above all the experience of communism. In this context, while historians were – and still are – constrained by ever-increasing social and political demands, there was an urgent necessity to launch a transnational reflection on how to write about the recent past.

The network brought together a group of historians belonging to research institutions and universities all over Europe who were preoccupied with the legacy of traumatic events, the presence of the past, the social role of historians and their transformation into 'experts', including those in the legal sphere. Most of them had been involved in the previous years, in major national or international debates over history and memory. The network, coordinated by Henry Rousso at the Institut d'histoire du temps présent (CNRS) in Paris, included scholars based in Amsterdam, Bologna, Brussels, Budapest, Dublin, Edinburgh, Jena, Oxford, Paris, Potsdam, Vienna and Warsaw.[1] Sorin Antohi, Péter Apor, Vincent Auzas, Muriel Blaive, Donald Bloxham, Paolo Capuzzo, Martin Conway, Norbert Frei, Stefan-Ludwig Hoffmann, John Horne, Constantin Iordachi, Konrad Jarausch, Michael Kopeček, Pieter Lagrou, Marie-Claire Lavabre, Thomas Lindenberger, Guillaume Mouralis, Malika Rahal, Peter Romijn, Maria Salvati, Dariusz Stola, Annette Weinke have all actively contributed to the debates condensed in this book, regardless of whether they authored a chapter or not. Our discussions have also much benefited from our exchanges with, and help from, Fabrice d'Almeida, Stéphane Audoin-Rouzeau, Annette Becker, Kenneth Bertrams, Donald Bloxham, Ciaran Brady, Patricia Clavin, Alberto de Bernardi, Christian Delage, Julia Eichenberg, Christian Gerbel, Robert Gildea, Libora Oates-Indruchová, Christian Ingrao, Conny Kristel, Thi-Ngeune Lo, Gabrielle Muc, John Paul Newman, Pawel Machcewicz, Andrzej Paczkowski, Cristina Petrescu, Dara Price, Annelie Ramsbrock, Marjan Schwegman, Anne Simonin, Teena Stabler, Patryk Wasiak and Nicolas Werth.

Even before the formal constitution of EURHISTXX, the partners in the project had engaged in extensive discussions about the challenges facing the writing of European contemporary history, in the framework of an ultimately unsuccessful application for the 6th European Framework Programme of the European Commission for Research. As part of a larger network, EURHIST initiated by the École des hautes études en sciences sociales (Paris), a subgroup of contemporary historians focused on the legacies of the major conflicts that shaped Europe's twentieth century: the First and Second World Wars and the Cold War. We organized various conferences and workshops: 'Thinking Europe. Towards a Europeanization of Contemporary Histories' (Potsdam, Zentrum für Zeithistorische Forschung, 6–8 May 2004); the Memory of Communism (Paris, Institut d'histoire du temps présent, 17 December 2007) and 'Demobilization in Europe after the Cold War' (Warsaw, 16–18 October 2008), both available on the EURHISTXX website;[2] 'Rethinking Violence in Communist Dictatorship in East Central Europe' (Budapest, Central European University, with the Institute of Contemporary History of Prague and the University of Cluj-Napoca, 22–23 October 2009) and 'Veterans Internationalism and the Culture of Victory and Peace' (Trinity College Dublin, 23–24 October 2009). In 2007, the network published the first collective work edited by Konrad H. Jarausch and Thomas Lindenberger (*Conflicted Memories. Europeanizing Contemporary Histories*, Oxford/New York: Berghahn Books). It was part of a new series 'Studies in Contemporary European History', directed by Konrad Jarausch and the author of this preface, and which is another lasting outcome of EURHISTXX. The present book shares the same ambition of promoting 'Europeanization' of contemporary histories, against historiographical traditions which stress either national singularities or a teleological view of the history of Europe.

Last but not least, when the group decided, thanks to John Horne's intuition, to raise the question of the three postwar periods – including the post–Cold War period – within a long-term perspective, it adopted not only a 'regressive method' as explained in Martin Conway's introduction, but also a reflexive perspective: the research itself, the institutions where it was based, the historians and the social scientists who drove it are fully part of the analysis.

Henry Rousso

Notes

1   The Centre for Historical Studies from the Central European University in Budapest, the Centre for the Study of the two world wars at the University of Edinburgh, the Department of History of the University of Bologna, the Institut d'Études européennes at the Université libre de Bruxelles, the Institut des sciences sociales du politique at the Université Paris-Nanterre, the Institute of Contemporary History from the Czech Academy of Sciences in Prague, the Institute of Political Sciences at the Polish Academy of Sciences in Warsaw, the Jena Center Geschichte des 20 Jahrhunderts at the Friedrich-Schiller-Universität Jena, the Ludwig Boltzmann Institute for European History and Public Spheres in Vienna, the Modern European History Research Centre at the University of Oxford, the NIOD Institute for War, Holocaust and Genocide Studies in Amsterdam, the School of Histories and Humanities at Trinity College Dublin, the Zentrum für Zeithistorische Forschung in Potsdam

2   http://eurhistxx.de

Contributors

Péter Apor is a research fellow at the Research Centre for the Humanities, Hungarian Academy of Sciences.

Paolo Capuzzo is professor of contemporary history and director of the Department of History and Cultures at the University of Bologna.

Martin Conway is professor of contemporary European history at the University of Oxford and a fellow of Balliol College, Oxford.

John Horne is a historian, emeritus professor of European history at Trinity College, Dublin, and a member of the Royal Irish Academy.

Pieter Lagrou is professor of contemporary history at the Université Libre de Bruxelles.

Guillaume Mouralis is a historian, researcher at the Centre national de la recherche scientifique and a fellow of the Centre Marc Bloch in Berlin.

Malika Rahal is a historian, researcher at the Centre national de la recherche scientifique and a fellow of the Institut d'histoire du temps présent in Paris.

Henry Rousso is a historian, senior researcher at the Centre national de la recherche scientifique and a fellow of the Institut d'histoire du temps présent in Paris.

Dariusz Stola is professor of history at the Institute of Political Studies, Polish Academy of Sciences, and director of the Polin Museum of the History of Polish Jews.

Annette Weinke is assistant professor of history at the Friedrich Schiller University of Jena and co-director of the Jena Center 20th Century History.

Introduction

Reading 1989 Backwards

Martin Conway

Historians always have an ambiguous relationship with the present. The present is the land we inhabit, but not that in which we were born and were formed; similarly, the present is the vantage point from which we view the past but which we seek rather deliberately to exclude from our perception of that past. Nothing, as books of historical methodology never tire of repeating, is as bad as writing history from the perspective of the present, imposing anachronistic forms of identity onto the people of the past, or constructing facile teleological narratives which interpret the past as a road leading, for better or for worse, towards the present day.

Yet, the present is of course always with us. Whatever our resolve to escape from present-minded concepts and narratives, historians cannot avoid the world in which we do our work. This poses problems that we can perceive and denounce in the writings of historians of past generations, but do not always confront in ourselves. This has perhaps been especially so for historians of twentieth-century Europe since the events of 1989. We live in a different Europe – one that is larger and more unified, at least in its political structures, but also more global and less self-sufficient in its society and economy than before 1989; yet we persist for the most part in devoting our energies to the study of the history of twentieth-century Europe as if the era since the fall of the Berlin Wall forms part of a separate story. Indeed, the scale of the changes which took place in Europe, east and west, over the decade following 1989, seems to provide a rationale to ignore the shadow of the present. If the present is indeed so different, it leaves us free to study the past simply as the past, liberated from the way in which, prior to 1989, the major milestones of the twentieth century – be they the Russian Revolution, the Third Reich, the Holocaust or the Cold War – were instrumentalized and mobilized to justify the political causes, state regimes and international alliances of the present. This is the seductive invitation apparently offered by the concept of the 'short twentieth century'. First articulated by Eric Hobsbawm in his influential *Age of Extremes*, it presented the twentieth century as a period of intense ideological, economic and political conflict that had reached its terminus in the period around 1989–91.[1]

However, as Hobsbawm himself was always at pains to emphasize, the recognition that the years around 1989 marked a decisive turning point in Europe's recent history cannot be used by historians of the twentieth century to exempt themselves from the challenging task of comprehending the present-day nature of Europe. To ignore the present is to fail to be alert to the ways in which the assumptions of our own time can infiltrate themselves, however unconsciously, into the study of the past. Moreover, for all of our professional insistence that the events of the past must be studied in their own right, and without reference to 'what happened next', how can historians of twentieth-century Europe exclude from their analyses the fall of communism, the demise of the Soviet Union, the expansion of the European Union (EU), the wars in the former Yugoslavia and the changes in state boundaries that followed more or less directly from the events of 1989? That year was simply too important, too replete in consequences and too emphatically European, to be absent from the history of Europe in the twentieth century. Above all, the writing of the past without reference to the present diminishes the scope and importance of history as a discipline with an intellectual and political relevance to the wider society. We are, of course, all aware of the way in which the works of major historians of the past, from Marx and Tocqueville to Bloch and Meinecke, and indeed Furet and Hobsbawm, were strongly marked and enriched by their engagement with the present; and yet the nature of the historical profession and in particular its corporate ethos have encouraged in recent years an inward-turning mentality, which asserts the autonomy of the past in order to block out the noise of the present.

This book is therefore the fruit of a collective endeavour on the part of a group of historians of twentieth-century Europe to bring the post-1989 present into our past. In that respect, the collective biography of the authors of this volume is in itself significant. We are drawn from different regions and states of Europe, both east and west, and we encompass a range of ethnicities, languages and political mentalities. But we are also, almost all, male, and white, and all operate within a professional historical world, and its institutions of universities and research institutes. We come from different generations, but we are also all historians whose personal roots lie in the pre-1989 world, for whom the post-1989 reality of Europe constitutes the world around us, but remains different from the world we remember.

Our purpose in writing this volume and engaging in the collective reflection which underpins it is therefore to confront quite directly the nature of the European present, but to do so in terms of the implications which it presents for our understanding of the past. This is not an easy or an uncontroversial task, and we do not expect to convince everybody, not least among our fellow twentieth-century historians, either of the validity of our project or of the theses we advance. We are, however, all motivated by a shared conviction that the gap – or perhaps more exactly the dissonance – that exists between the present and the recent twentieth-century past is harmful and needs to be diminished.

Broad-sweep histories of the European experience of the twentieth century have not been lacking in recent years, and for good reason. In addition to that of Eric Hobsbawm (*Age of Extremes*) already mentioned, there have been important utions by Mark Mazower (*Dark Continent*) and Tony Judt (*Postwar*), each of which was conceived and written in the years following 1989.[3] In each case, a changing present acted as a stimulus to explore the complexities of the recent past. However, the direction of flow in all three of these works was always clear. As the titles of their works demonstrate, they take as their centre point the violent middle years of the century – which Enzo Traverso has recently characterized as a 'European civil war'[4] – exploring how Europe succumbed to such intense conflict and how, subsequently, it found a path to the revolutions of 1989. This out of ashes conception of the history of Europe in the second half of the twentieth century, to borrow the title of another recent such volume by Konrad Jarausch,[5] has underpinned much of the energy invested by historians in recent years in exploring the post-1945 period in Europe. But this approach brings with it its own chains of causes and consequences, by which Europe proceeded from its nadir in 1945 towards an implied resolution at the end of the century.

Our approach in writing this volume is not to supplant these accounts but instead to see what happens when one changes the questions, and more especially the direction of flow. The consequence is emphatically not a revisionist history, but perhaps to some extent an anti-narrative one. In particular, in order to structure our thinking about Europe in the twentieth century, we have made two decisions, which in large measure determine what we have included in the volume and what we have excluded. The first of these is to base our analysis around a comparative analysis of three postwar moments of 1918, 1945 and 1989. The second has been to approach our discussion of them through a regressive methodology, which starts from 1989 and then goes back in turn to the other two postwar moments.

Both of these choices can of course be challenged. To study three postwar moments raises questions both about the moments we have selected and the emphasis on particular wars and their outcomes which it privileges. Neither the First nor the Second World War was, in anything other than specifically military terms, a unitary event. They were plural wars that took different forms on different fronts and within different states. This was perhaps especially so regarding the Second World War, which at one and the same time encompassed a conflict of empires, of European states, of ideologies and, at the more local level of political movements, of communities, and indeed, as Jan Gross has emphasized with reference to wartime Poland, of violence between neighbours.[6] To approach these wars as discrete events, with particular outcomes, is therefore in some respects a misleading simplification that neglects national diversity, but also the essential fact that war happened within communities as well as being visited upon them. Moreover, as a collection of essays with a similar purpose edited by Carl Levy and Mark Roseman well demonstrates, any attempt to compare three particular moments in history has a somewhat arbitrary character.[7] The moment of transition from war to peace was rarely clear-cut, and whatever the precision of the armistice declared on the eleventh hour of the eleventh day of the eleventh month in 1918, there was no single moment when war ended in 1918 or in the two subsequent conflicts. Modern European wars – with their continental scale and their diverse combatants – have ragged ends, and to seize upon a specific endpoint of these conflicts risks neglecting the after-wars that were such a prominent element of all three conflicts.[8] It also necessarily marginalizes more gradual and less chronologically specific forms of change, for example, in socio-economic structures and class or gender relations, or intellectual beliefs. Finally, our choice of a conventional triptych of rather too famous dates raises questions too about why we should focus on these three wars rather than other conflicts which had a European resonance, such as the Spanish Civil War from 1936 to 1939, or the many wars of decolonization engaged in by European imperial powers from the 1940s to the 1970s. The First and Second World Wars, as well as the Cold War, were not the only wars which occurred in twentieth-century Europe, and the tendency of historians to privilege them as European (and global) cataclysms often disguises the extent to which they were primarily German-centred conflicts. All three were to a large extent wars about who ruled Germany, and who Germany should rule, as well as what its borders should be; and, though our ambition in writing this volume has been emphatically to adopt an inclusive and Europe-wide approach, our choice of conflicts tacitly accords a centrality to the history of Germany, and its relations with neighbouring European states.

The decision to begin from 1989 is, if anything, even more open to question. Placing it alongside 1918 and 1945 presents 1989 as a postwar moment, and yet the Cold War was not in any conventional sense a war (at least not in Europe), and had become in many respects an armed peace long before the events of 1989. Comparing it with the two previous postwar moments does therefore suggest a similarity which in many respects was illusory: After all, why shouldn't the events of 1989 be regarded instead as a revolutionary process, for which the upheavals of 1917–19, 1936 or 1968 would provide a more appropriate framework of comparison?[9] The difficulty of course lies in the Janus-faced nature of the events of 1989, facing back into the Cold War and forward into a new era of European unity. As experienced by populations, and narrated by the ubiquitous media commentaries of the time, 1989 was above all an ending. It was the year when, in the words of Göran Therborn, 'the "postwar" period in Europe ended'.[10] But, alongside the visible demobilization of the structures of Communist political rule, and the accompanying networks of Soviet-directed military, political and economic control, the events of 1989 and their immediate aftermath also marked the emergence of new structures of control. The liberation of the states of East-Central Europe from Soviet over-lordship (and in the early 1990s of the western borderlands of the Soviet Union from more long-standing structures of Russian imperial control) was rapidly followed by the integration of the new post-communist states within the institutions of the North Atlantic Treaty Organization (NATO) and of the EU, with a consequent assertion of American and German diplomatic and economic influence. Moreover, while 1918 and 1945 were – the histories of some neutral states, notably Spain, partly excepted – emphatically European events, 1989 was perceived at least at the time as an exclusively regional phenomenon: the 'return' of the states of East-Central Europe to the wider community of Europe. This was in many respects a manifestation of the myopia of the West. 1989 had profound consequences for the whole of Europe, notably through enabling the reunification of Germany and the construction of a German-centric definition of European unity, and more particularly of its economic organization. But, whatever these wider consequences, to define 1989 as a postwar moment raises awkward conceptual questions about how far the states of Western Europe were engaged in a war prior to 1989 and to what extent they experienced an equivalent process of postwar demobilization.

The ambivalent nature of 1989 – both as an event and as a convenient label for ... roughly decade-long process of political, social and economic changes that followed the demise of the late-socialist regimes – therefore renders it difficult to use it as the jumping-off point for our regressive analysis of the previous postwar moments. While certain themes, such as state structures, borders and justice, lend themselves most readily to comparison with 1945 and 1918, there are other themes, such as changes in gender relations and economic structures, for which 1989 does not obviously provide a point of departure. The comparison of 1989 with 1945 and 1918 must, therefore, to some extent be a rather awkward triple jump across the twentieth-century history of Europe, in which the first longest leap is from 1989 to 1945. The intervening years encompassed what Göran Therborn described as 'an amazing concentration of social historical turns', which reshaped the patterns of almost all European lives.[11] To compare 1989 with 1945 might simply pass over too much of what had changed in between: both within Europe and in Europe's relations with other areas of the world, such as the Global South and the United States.[12]

However, as this project has advanced, we have become increasingly convinced that, for all of these shortcomings and challenges, the perspective provided by approaching the history of twentieth-century Europe from the vantage point of 1989 is a valuable one. Not only does it rightly join the history of present-day Europe to that of its recent past, but it also enables us to ask new and provocative questions about the changes that took place in 1945 and 1918. For historians, explaining the present in terms of the past is a familiar task and also a demonstration of the social utility of their discipline: When Europe changed in 1989, its leaders called for their historians (though they did not always choose wisely) to advise them on the new reality.[13] But our purpose is the inverse: We have chosen to place the past in the context of the present.

This reversal of the normal flow of historical narratives and ways of thinking does, we believe, offer a number of benefits for analysing the history of twentieth-century Europe. It is an exercise that is also to our mind overdue. Since roughly the 1970s, we have lived through what in retrospect can be seen to have been a remarkable era of historical investigation of the twentieth century, reflecting the way in which, as the events of the mid-century decades receded into the past, their relevance to the present seemed to be more real and the historical investigation of them to be more urgent. This created a strange sense of time: Europe was changing (at least in its social and cultural structures) more rapidly than ever before, and yet, especially in Western Europe, there was a dominant sense of living 'afterwards', of living after the upheavals of the years of the Second World War and, from the 1960s onwards, of living after the shadow of the Jewish genocide, memorialized as the Holocaust.[14] This invested the project of contemporary history with a particular energy and focus. In Western Europe, a predominantly younger generation of historians not directly implicated in the events of the 1930s and 1940s used their historical skills to investigate a canon of dominant topics – interwar fascism, wartime collaboration, state violence and societal complicity in forms of violence – that acquired a second wind so to speak when, after 1989, their colleagues in central and eastern Europe began to explore not only the Communist era, but also its prehistory in the violence of the Second World War.[15]

However, with that outpouring of historical energies has come inevitably the definition of a conventional agenda of themes, of which the works of Mazower and Judt provide the most impressive expression.[16] That era is now at an end. The political and moral momentum that led historians to explore the collective complicity of European citizens, and indeed of European history *tout court*, in the horrors of the mid-twentieth century has lost its power to shock. Indeed, as Pieter Lagrou has argued in a recent article, the project of contemporary history in present-day Europe has ceased to be a means of holding European society to account for its past failings and present shortcomings, and has become all too often a tool by which the present derives legitimacy from a rather complacent comparison with the recent past.[17]

In its limited way, this volume is therefore intended to contribute to the necessary rejuvenation of thinking about the European history of the twentieth century: its shape, periodization and frontiers. Here again lie obvious dangers, notably of diminishing themes, such as mass violence and genocide, which are less central to 1989, and of privileging others, notably the ascendancy of a liberal and free-market definition of democracy that came to the fore after 1989 but which had relatively limited historical antecedents, at least in the first half of the twentieth century. But there are also advantages in such an approach that, by enabling us to connect the history of the twentieth century with that of the present day, focuses attention on the defining characteristics of the European political order that had taken shape by the end of the twentieth century: a unified political framework across the large majority of the European continent; a resilient structure of nation states, based around variants of parliamentary and presidential democracy; a capitalist economic system, deeply integrated into a global trading culture and a complex network of social provision and welfare structures, operating under state aegis but with the participation of a range of local and parastatal partners.

Francis Fukuyama famously declared 1989 to be 'the end of history' in an essay more often cited than read, which he wrote in the immediate aftermath of the events of that year.[18] This book is not intended as a refutation of Fukuyama's thesis, which was a more mature reflection on the Hegelian dynamics of history than its many detractors often suggest. Instead, it seeks to take up the challenge presented by Fukuyama's presentation of 1989 as a terminus to the historical conflicts of the modern era, and to think not so much about the manifold ways in which the events of 1989 were shaped by prior events, but about how we can rethink the past in the new light of that present.

Notes

1 Eric Hobsbawm, *Age of Extremes: The Short Twentieth Century 1914–1991* (London: Michael Joseph, 1994).
2 See, for example, his reconceptualization of the era 1973–2008 as the '*reductio ad absurdum* of market forces', in Eric Hobsbawm, 'Marx and Labour: The Long Century', in *How to Change the World: Marx and Marxism 1840–2011*, ed. Eric Hobsbawm (London: Little Brown, 2011), 411–19.

3 Mark Mazower, *Dark Continent: Europe's Twentieth Century* (London: Allen Lane, 1998); Tony Judt, *Postwar: A History of Europe since 1945* (London: William Heinemann, 2005). See also Judt's valedictory reflections on the historical context of *Postwar* in Tony Judt (with Timothy Snyder), *Thinking the Twentieth Century* (London: William Heinemann, 2012), 249–83.

4 Enzo Traverso, *Fire and Blood. The European Civil War, 1914–1945* (London and New York: Verso, 2016).

5 Konrad Jarausch, *Out of Ashes: A New History of Europe in the Twentieth Century* (Princeton: Princeton University Press, 2015).

6 See Jan Gross, *Neighbors: The Destruction of the Jewish Community in Jedwabne, Poland* (Princeton and Oxford: Princeton University Press, 2001). But the concept of the Second World War as a war within communities has been a common theme of much of the recent historiography of the war, sometimes linked to discussions of how far the war should be perceived as a civil war. See, for example, Claudio Pavone, *A Civil War: A History of the Italian Resistance* (London and New York: Verso, 2013); Tzvetan Todorov, *A French Tragedy. Scenes of Civil War, Summer 1944* (Hanover: University Press of New England, 1996); Timothy Snyder, 'The Causes of Ukrainian-Polish Ethnic Cleansing 1943', *Past and Present* No. 179 (2003): 197–234; Stathis Kalyvas, *The Logic of Violence in Civil War* (Cambridge and New York: Cambridge University Press, 2006).

7 Carl Levy and Mark Roseman, ed., *Three Postwar Eras in Comparison: Western Europe 1918–1945–1989* (Basingstoke: Palgrave, 2002).

8 Robert Gerwarth, *The Vanquished: Why the First World War Failed to End* (London: Allen Lane, 2016).

9 See Martin Conway and Robert Gerwarth, 'Revolution and Counter-Revolution', in *Political Violence in Twentieth-Century Europe*, ed. Donald Bloxham and Robert Gerwarth (Cambridge: Cambridge University Press, 2011), 140–75.

10 Göran Therborn, *European Modernity and Beyond: The Trajectory of European Societies 1945–2000* (London: Sage, 1995), 351.

11 Therborn, *European Modernity*, 351.

12 On the latter, see recently David Ellwood, *The Shock of America: Europe and the Challenge of the Century* (Oxford: Oxford University Press, 2012); and Victoria de Grazia, *Irresistible Empire: America's Advance through Twentieth-century Europe* (Cambridge, MA, and London: Belknap Press of Harvard University Press, 2005).

13 Norman Stone, 'Germany? Maggie Was Absolutely Right', *The Sunday Times*, 23 September 1996.

14 See the influential works of Henry Rousso, notably *The Vichy Syndrome: History and Memory in France since 1944* (Cambridge Mass. and London: Harvard University Press, 1991) and Eric Conan and Henry Rousso, *Vichy, an Ever-Present Past* (Hanover: University Press of New England, 1998).

15 Henry Rousso, *The Latest Catastrophe: History, the Present, the Contemporary* (Chicago: The Chicago University Press, 2016).

16 Mazower, *Dark Continent*; Judt, *Postwar*.

17 Pieter Lagrou, 'De l'histoire du temps présent à l'histoire des autres: Comment une discipline critique devint complaisante', *Vingtième Siècle. Revue d'histoire*, No. 118 (2013): 101–19.

18 Francis Fukuyama, *The End of History and the Last Man* (London: Hamish Hamilton, 1992).

1

Demobilizations

John Horne

It would be hard to deny that 1989 was a turning point in European history. It changed the balance of power on the continent. It dissolved the ideological conflict that had split Europe for nearly half a century and had divided each half of the continent internally, communism not being confined to the east or anti-communism to the west. It consigned communism as one contending economic model to history and promoted the other, a neo-liberal form of capitalism, to a position of hegemony. The year 1989 was also perhaps the last time that a European event – the fall of the Berlin Wall – was pivotal to the world. As communism collapsed and the Cold War ended, the importance of Europe, sustained since 1948 by its place at the heart of that conflict, dwindled. Europe became what it has remained – a significant region but only one of several in a world that has been redefined by the rise of China, a turbulent Middle East, the surge of militant Islam and an embattled United States trying to secure its own values and interests.

Yet, in this book, we argue that 1989 was more than a turning point. We contend that it began a postwar period of some duration, and that although this is now over, it helped create our contemporary history – the continuous present in which we live. We further propose that this being the case, the last of Europe's twentieth-century postwar periods ought to provide a powerful lens through which to look at the two previous ones, after 1945 and 1918, not only by way of comparisons that chart the distance travelled by the continent since the Great War but also in terms of the processes involved.[1] So what exactly was the period of change triggered by 1989? Does it provide new understandings of what went before, especially in the earlier postwar periods? These questions lie at the core of the book and, as explained in the Introduction, justify the regressive method we use.

Postwar periods and the process of demobilization

In addressing these issues, we assume that wars help shape postwar periods. But we also assume in turn that postwar periods play a key role in how wars are settled and how their effects are absorbed. Arguably, postwar periods are as important as the wars they resolve (or fail to resolve) precisely because they shape their legacy. In our case, this means that the postwar periods after the Cold War and the two world wars helped redefine twentieth-century European history. They had historical cogency.

Of course, other processes also changed the continent, interacting with the postwar periods while maintaining their own cogency. The economy is a case in point. The Cold War and the two world wars most clearly shaped politics, ideologies and collective experiences, while economic and social changes followed a different path and time-scale. It could be argued that the Second Industrial Revolution, which centred on a cluster of technical inventions in the 1880s (cheap steel, electricity, the internal combustion engine, etc.), drove 'Fordist' mass production and the related mass consumption that shaped European societies down to the 1980s.[2] A prolonged economic crisis from the 1970s signalled the shift to a third transformation based on information technology and electronics that reconfigured the international division of labour and, in the form of neo-liberal economics, influenced European integration.

Wars and postwar periods certainly affected these economic processes. In the west, they contributed to the welfare state with its redistribution of wealth, while in the east, the First World War and the Russian Revolution generated the communist command version of the Second Industrial Revolution. That version moulded the destinies of Soviet states during the Cold War but failed to make the transition to the Third Industrial Revolution. Yet the period from the 1880s to the 1980s had its own economic and social logic that represents a different time frame from those of the wars.

Europe had other wars, notably the Spanish Civil War. This foreshadowed the Second World War and was affected by it, as the victorious Nationalists gravitated to the Axis powers from 1939 but ended up after Axis defeat on the Allied side in the Cold War. Yet the Civil War was also part of a specifically Spanish trajectory that led from the final loss of the new world colonies in 1898 to war and dictatorship in the long mid-century and to liberal democracy from the late 1970s – well ahead of 1989.[3]

Caveats are important for the credibility of any thesis. Nothing explains everything. Far more important, however, is the explanatory power of what is proposed, which brings us to the subject of this chapter – demobilization. The Cold War and the two world wars were indeed global but they afflicted Europe more completely and with greater intensity than anywhere else on the planet. The zone from the Atlantic to the Urals and from Turkey to the Arctic constituted the principal killing ground of both world wars. It witnessed genocides in each of them – the attempted destruction of the Ottoman Armenians and Europe's Jews respectively. It also provided the laboratory for weapons of mass destruction that have haunted the world ever since (the exception being the atom bomb, developed in the United States and dropped on Japan). Once the USSR acquired nuclear capability in 1949, the spectre of mutual annihilation froze the dizzying escalation of warfare since 1914. In little more than thirty years, this had gone from infantry charges that Napoleon would have recognized to the obliteration of entire cities – along with the distinction between soldiers and civilians. 'Mutually assured destruction' (or MAD as it was known) kept the Cold War cold at its European and East Asian epicentres, which were the likely triggers of all-out war. The Korean War of 1950–53 and the Cuban Missile Crisis in 1962 were the exceptions that proved the rule since by hinting at the zero sum logic of a nuclear showdown, they avoided the ultimate military escalation.[4]

Because Europe was uniquely defined by war in the twentieth century, it experienced to the full the mobilization such wars required. First and foremost, this meant military and economic mobilization. Beginning with the French Revolution, Europe had invented the 'nation (or empire) in arms', which turned on the idea that all adult males owed the state short-term military service as the corollary of their status as citizens or subjects. Prussia in the mid-nineteenth century enhanced the practice by retaining conscripts as reservists into middle age. This meant that in wartime, the state could call up much of the adult male population into the armed forces, resulting by 1914 in armies of a size unknown a century earlier.[5] Great Britain, as a naval power, ignored conscription until the need for a continental-sized army in the First World War forced it to improvise 'national service', which it reintroduced for the Second World War and kept until the early 1960s. The United States followed a similar path.

However, it became apparent in the First World War that the industrialization of firepower (i.e. the application of the Second Industrial Revolution to armaments), in conjunction with a war of attrition, meant that the total resources of the economy were now vital to waging war. They included 'manpower' – the word dates from 1915.[6] Depriving the enemy of those same resources (including by starving and bombing its civilian manpower) was a strategy in its own right. Harnessing the economy to war thus produced a double mobilization, economic as well as military.

Ending war meant making peace. This entailed reversing the military and economic mobilizations. Unless men and women resumed civilian life and until the economy returned to normal production (from housing to consumer goods), peace could not be achieved. More than a moment, a year or even a 'turning-point', it was a process – demobilization. Yet demobilization in this material sense was also shaped by the hard politics of the war's outcome. It depended on whether a state was victor or vanquished, occupier or occupied and whether the defeated accepted their lot.[7] Military and economic demobilization was thus linked to a diplomatic settlement without which the war effort could not be wound down. For soldiers to go home and workers to resume normal production, war by definition had to be in the past tense.

However, Europe's twentieth-century wars were more than military and economic affairs. Many states felt that not only the balance of power but also sheer survival were at stake. Already in 1914, each camp saw its enemy as less than human. Germans rejected Western 'civilization' in favour of German 'culture', while the British and French dismissed the latter as a fig leaf for autocratic militarism.[8] The result was a mobilization of political and cultural values – and a sense of profound enmity – that gave meaning to the conflict. What was true of the First World War was truer still of its successor, whose ideological agenda originated in the antagonisms caused by political mobilization and breakdown during the Great War. This resulted in communism, fascism and fuller-blooded versions of liberal democracy than before. Combined with unprecedented death and suffering (and the accompanying language of 'sacrifice'), politics was transformed. Henceforth, it was hard to forge political legitimacy without invoking the *demos* (popular will), albeit in conflicting variants.

Yet, the 'dizzying escalation' of warfare from 1914 to 1945 meant that war itself as an arbiter of human affairs was called into question by both conflicts. By an irony of history, the Cold War avoided the human cost of the world wars (in Europe at least) precisely because unbridled military conflict threatened this time to make the planet uninhabitable. There were no combat deaths, no shattered cities and fewer refugees. But nowhere was there greater *fear* of such outcomes than in Europe, where a proxy war was waged by culture and politics in order to avoid them. Political and cultural mobilization became key features of the Cold War precisely because military mobilization remained an unrealized threat, a perpetual rehearsal.[9]

Ending war and making peace after all three conflicts thus meant political and cultural demobilization. Yet this was a different kind of process. If military and economic demobilization was a prerequisite for peace, this was not the case in the political and cultural spheres. Undoing the imaginary categories of wartime, dismantling the figure of the enemy and even reconciling past antagonisms were things that might happen, usually more slowly, but which equally might *not* happen.[10] Refusing cultural and political demobilization, or urging remobilization for a new war, was a possibility that would condition the kind of peace obtained. At the same time, the human cost of military conflict, whether actual as during the two world wars or virtual as during the Cold War in Europe, was intrinsic to such demobilization. Peace meant addressing not just the war that had ended but the nature of the war itself.

Of course, 'hot' and 'cold' wars are not the same. Commemoration suggests the difference. After the two world wars, monuments proliferated as a way of coming to terms with mass death and the cost of war. There are no such monuments to the Cold War although this is not to say that it went unmarked, especially in Eastern Europe. If death and destruction are intrinsic to war, then the Cold War in Europe was something else, and calling the years after 1989 postwar period is a misnomer – although they might still constitute a historical 'turning point'. But if a demobilization process did occur, albeit one in which the military aspect took second place to the economy, politics and culture, then the Cold War was a war, albeit of a novel kind, and Europe indeed experienced a third such period in the twentieth century.

After 1989

When on 9 November 1989, jubilant crowds demolished part of the Berlin Wall, it was rightly taken to mark the triumph of the Western Allies, liberal democracy and market forces over their Cold War opposites and antagonists. Like 11 November 1918 or 8/9 May 1945, it embodied a *Wende* (as the Germans call it), a turning point leading to a new era. As on those earlier occasions, other moments also marked the exit from war, including revolutions, attempted coups and the signing of peace treaties.[11] Across Eastern Europe, communist regimes succumbed in the 'velvet revolutions' of autumn 1989.[12] East and West Germany were reunified on 23 October 1990, 'Unity Day', after the four occupying powers (Britain, France, the United States and the USSR) signed the Treaty of Final Settlement. This resolved the unfinished business of 1945 and agreed the terms of reunification. On 25 December 1991, the Red Flag was lowered over the Kremlin as the USSR broke apart into Russia and other successor states following the failed putsch by communist hardliners against democratic reformers the previous August. Unlike in 1919 and 1945, there were no victory parades after 1989. Reflecting the nature of the Cold War and the way it ended, the military was less visible – except for a final march-past in June 1994 before the occupying powers left Berlin and the Russians quit Germany as a whole.

In the three years following 1989, a new diplomatic order confirmed the outcome of the Cold War by an unofficial calculus of victory and defeat. Germany was reunified but within the territory reduced by defeat in 1945 and on the basis of the border with postwar Poland established at Germany's expense and which West Germany had already accepted by the Treaty of Warsaw in 1970. Elsewhere, too, the change of regime in the former Soviet satellite states took place within the boundaries established in 1945 (apart from a split into separate Czech and Slovak states in 1993). Hence, what was defeated in 1989 in these countries was a regime, an ideology and a society with its own economy and way of life, all of which had been imposed from outside and which, but for the Cold War, would not have existed. Was this defeat or liberation – or self-liberation? Many embraced the last view, as the communist parties were swept from power in free elections. But it left the issue of what to do with the past and those who had held power during the communist years.

Russia was different. Even if those in power during the transition to the new states repudiated the Soviet past, Russia not only suffered the defeat of the regime that had made it a world power, but also lost people and territory (the Baltic states, Belarus, Ukraine and much of Central Asia) that had belonged to the Russian Empire for centuries and for which the weak Commonwealth of Independent States was no substitute. As European and global relations lost the bipolar axis of the Cold War, Russia retreated into relative impotence. Its weakness was compounded when, on 1 July 1991, its former satellites dissolved the Warsaw Pact, their alliance with the Soviet Union, which had been established in 1955 in response to West German entry into North Atlantic Treaty Organization (NATO). Any Russian return to Eastern Europe was definitively excluded when Poland, the Czech Republic and Hungary joined NATO in 1999, and the other ex-satellite states and the Baltic countries followed in 2004.

The political realignment of the continent paralleled this military reorganization when the members of the EEC, which had been set up in 1957, reconstituted that body as the European Union (EU) by the Maastricht Treaty in 1992 and opened it to Eastern European countries which met the criteria of liberal democracy, human rights and the rule of law. The bulk of the former satellite states and the three Baltic countries joined in 2004, followed by Bulgaria and Romania in 2007. The continent had thus been reorganized in military and political terms within three years of the fall of the Berlin Wall and had taken a new institutional shape on that basis within fifteen years.

The fact that the Cold War was concluded not by combat but by a mixture of diplomacy, a failed attempt to reform the USSR and internal pressure in Eastern Europe meant that military demobilization occurred in a minor key, mirroring the discretion of the armed forces in the transition from war to peace. Still, even if the scale was different from that of 1918–19 or 1945–46, there was a clear sense of standing the military down. As Dariusz Stola notes, nearly a million Soviet troops had left the former satellite states by 1994 while the Western Allies reduced their forces in Germany and redeployed their military capability on the basis that the Cold War was over. British forces in Germany in 1994 fell to 25,000 compared to 64,000 in the late 1950s, while the United States pulled a quarter of a million service personnel out of Europe.[13]

It was not just a question of conventional forces. The Cold War having been defined above all by the threat of nuclear annihilation, it was logical that military demobilization should centre on the reduction of nuclear arms. In two phases during the Cold War, nuclear weaponry had been 'frozen' precisely to limit the chances of a conflagration, although bipartite strategic arms limitation treaties between the United States and the USSR had not prevented a final round of brinkmanship with short-range nuclear missiles in Europe in the early 1980s.[14] Now, however, the nuclear arsenals could be substantially limited by negotiation and mutual inspection between partners rather than enemies. The bilateral Strategic Arms Reduction Treaty of 1991 (which came into force in 1994) significantly reduced stockpiles of nuclear warheads and delivery vehicles on the basis of parity between the United States and Russia, while Belarus, Ukraine and Kazakhstan renounced nuclear arms altogether.[15]

Economic enrolment in the Cold War having been less than that in the two world wars, economic demobilization also occurred in a minor key. Nonetheless, over fifteen years, as Table 1.1 shows, it yielded a 'peace dividend' as the defence burden of the major European powers, and of NATO's European membership overall, almost halved. Military spending in Russia declined even more dramatically compared to that of the USSR, and this would be so even if the low defence costs of Belarus and Ukraine were added. Peacetime spending benefited accordingly.

The nature of the Cold War, and the manner of its ending in Europe, meant that it left no ruined cities in urgent need of rebuilding as had happened to varying degrees after the two world wars. Yet 'reconstruction' after both those conflicts meant more than just battle damage. It extended to the infrastructure neglected during the war and to plans for social reconstruction generated by the war effort. Such plans, despite inevitable compromise, reshaped the domestic economic and social landscape after the Second World War within a reformed capitalism in Western Europe and (after a delay) through the changes attempted by Nikita Khrushchev after 1953 in the USSR.[17] If nothing comparable happened after 1989 in Western Europe, defeat in the east transformed the command economies of the communist countries (including Russia,

Table 1.1 Defence expenditure as per cent of GDP, 1980–2004: NATO and Russia[16]

Country	1980/84	1985/89	1990/94	1995/99	2000/04
UK	5.2	4.6	3.7	2.7	2.3
France	4.1	3.8	3.3	2.9	2.5
Germany	3.4	3.0	2.1	1.6	1.4
Italy	2.1	2.3	2.0	1.9	2.0
NATO Europe	3.6	3.3	2.5	2.1	1.9
The United States	5.8	6.3	4.6	3.3	3.4
USSR/Russia*	—	8.4/15.0	4.8	3.8	3.9

*Estimates for 1985/89 are for 1989 only. The figure for 1990–94 is in fact that for 1992–94.
GDP, gross domestic product; NATO, North Atlantic Treaty Organization.

Belarus and Ukraine) as collective assets were liquidated and the new states struggled to move from a failed version of the Second Industrial Revolution to the uncharted waters of the Third Industrial Revolution. As with 'reconstruction' in the south after the American Civil War, outside 'carpetbaggers', local entrepreneurs and members of the former political elites vied to take advantage of a forced but chaotic dismantling of the prior economic and social system.[18]

In the case of Germany, however, reconstruction acquired continental significance. Reunification meant the reintegration of the two German economies, with the additional handicap that the former German Democratic Republic (GDR) currency, the *Ostmark*, was absorbed at parity into the *Deutsche Mark*, thus removing a competitive exchange rate as one tool for modernizing the former east. On the contrary, the latter now became a charge on Germany at pre-1989 rates, entailing massive capital transfers. For over a decade, reconstruction of the east, with high unemployment and outmoded production, dogged the German economy as a whole. Yet, although the social shadow of the former GDR persists to this day, the basis was laid during that same period for the fiscal reform and expanded capacity that by the early 2000s had made Germany the powerhouse of Europe.[19] Without this economic and social reconstruction of the former GDR, reunified Germany could not have emerged as the pivotal state of the entire European project. In this sense, it stands as one of the most politically important instances of postwar reconstruction in the twentieth century – even if its scale was much less sweeping than that in the two Germanies and other shattered countries during the second postwar period, after 1945.

In these ways, therefore, Europe indeed underwent military and economic demobilization in short order after 1989, based on the hard politics resulting from Soviet defeat in the Cold War, even if 'reconstruction' in the former east played out over a longer time span. However, there was nothing automatic about cultural and political demobilization. As after the earlier wars, this turned on dismantling the mental categories of wartime. These might be imagined as a force field. At the positive end stood the two entities engaged in the conflict, each repelling the other ('liberal democracy', 'Soviet communism'), while at the negative end stood the imagined enemy that was part of their own self-construction – the 'evil empire' and 'capitalist imperialism'. A secondary polarity reciprocally opposed 'allies' (NATO, the Warsaw Pact) and also the 'enemy within' – domestic communists in the west, bourgeois and other 'dissidents' in the east, plus assorted spies and traitors in both.

The demise of the USSR switched off the force field of the Cold War (whose strength had declined during the Gorbachev years), abolishing as it did the ideological conflict and the great power contest that had divided Europe. China was no substitute, for it had no political stake in Europe beyond communist Albania, which fell in the final 'velvet revolution' in 1992. It embarked on its own transition to a form of state capitalism, ending 'Maoism' as a global force. Unlike in the 1920s, the former enemy no longer existed, and unlike after 1945, no new enemy replaced it.

Hence, the demobilization of Cold War culture and politics was a fairly easy process. A new field, defined by the Maastricht criteria, replaced the polarity of the Cold War. The EU and NATO resolved the antagonism of NATO and the Warsaw Pact. Dismantling the enemy within turned on dealing with the past – which meant the memory of communism as a minority opposition in the west and its role as the former regime in the east. Russia, however, which belonged to neither the EU nor NATO and which had not experienced communism as an external imposition but as part of its own national history, followed a different path of demobilization.

The postwar settlement already referred to was the principal agent of this process. The new security regime turned enemies into allies. The language of politics (east and west) quickly adjusted to a post-ideological world – or rather to a world with a single ideology that gave the impression of being post-ideological. Here, the 'internal enemy' had little relevance because interests and antagonisms were now mainly expressed within a consensus on liberal democratic values and market economics, both of which were enshrined in the European project and in the European human rights regime (the Council of Europe and European Convention on Human Rights). Significantly, there was no attempt as in 1945–46 to mount international judicial proceedings against former 'enemy' leaders.

This did not mean uniformity of views. In 2001, the EU decided to draft a constitution (comparable to that of the United States) that would enshrine its basic principles and consolidate integration. Despite divisions between secular and Christian versions of a 'European' identity, the Convention on the Future of Europe, chaired by former French president Valéry Giscard d'Estaing, completed its work in 2004. But when French and Dutch voters rejected the Constitutional Treaty that sought to give it effect in 2005, this marked the limit of the ability of the European project to express common political and ideological grounds for both camps after the Cold War.

The Cold War left a darker shadow in domestic politics. Of course, future-oriented ideologies vanished except on the margins so that politics in most countries (as in Europe as a whole) became more pragmatic. But even in the west, the shadow was palpable. It was sharpest in Italy where the implosion of Cold War politics helped destroy the political system of the First Republic, based on the hegemony of the Christian Democrats. The Communist Party, which had long embraced 'euro-communism' but was cast as the opponent of the system, became a conventional party and eventually the core of Italy's centre-left Democratic Party.[20] Politics was affected elsewhere, albeit less dramatically. Spanish communism, also euro-communist, declined precipitously, as did the French Communist Party, which had never repudiated the USSR. Part of its base has now transferred to the populist right.[21]

Yet, a far-left cultural and electoral space survived, approaching the size of the former communists' support in France. This suggests that a significant minority declined to reject the aspirations associated with the Bolshevik Revolution even if they were not prepared to defend Stalinist and other deformations of it. The way the Cold War ended (not with a bang but a whimper) and the continued appeal of Marxism as a critique of neo-liberal capitalism modified the rejection of communism as a 'totalitarian' ideology and thus as an equivalent to fascism. Many former communists were reluctant to engage in self-criticism – what the Italian intellectual, Vittorio Foa, dubbed their 'silence'. They saw communism as an idea that may have gone wrong but in whose name good had been done. Moreover, rejecting it would mean renouncing anti-fascism, a touchstone of the history of the left in the twentieth century.[22] And communists were not alone in judging the two ideologies differently.

In former Eastern Europe, by contrast, communist parties had supplied the regime not the opposition. While some ex-communists made a comeback in the 1990s in reaction to the dislocation provoked by free-market 'reconstruction', there could be no return to communism itself.[23] But dismantling the ideological animosities of the Cold War meant dealing with a past that was harder to sidestep than in the west. The archives revealed just how wide complicity with the security apparatus of the communist states had been. On a smaller scale and with more hesitation than after 1945, some members of the former regime were put on trial.[24] However since the communist era, unlike the Second World War, had lasted half a lifetime, judgements on the compromises with power that had been interwoven into ordinary life were delicate.

Consequently, in addition to a future predicated on recovered sovereignty within the EU, adjusting the past became the main way of addressing the Soviet occupation and the legacy of the communist era. Rather like the simplified myths of the Second World War supplied by resistance movements after 1945 in order to overcome the complexities of that conflict, the anti-communist resistance during the Cold War (1956 in Hungary, 1968 in Czechoslovakia, 1980–81 in Poland) served to distinguish the 'real' nation from Soviet occupiers and native 'collaborators'.[25] Yet, realigning the past to deal with the Cold War resurrected political demobilization after the Second World War, which had been frozen by the Soviet takeover, thus complicating the process.

How this 'double demobilization' was handled varied with the country in question. But to give just two examples, in Hungary (a pro-Axis state in the Second World War in which the fascist Arrow Cross came to power in 1944), the centre-right Fidesz Party forged a mythic national history in the 1990s that carefully distanced Hungary from both fascism and communism, each seen as imposed by external powers, thus eliminating the native versions of both. Rather differently, a Poland that was occupied by Nazi Germany and the USSR between 1939 and 1945, and whose civic sphere (through Solidarność) rejected communism more strongly than any other country, recovered its non-communist experience of the Second World War as it reconstructed national memory after 1989. A museum to the 1944 Warsaw Rising by the non-communist Home Army was only finally opened in 2004, for the subject had remained taboo in the Soviet era. The creation of the Museum of the Second World War in Gdansk in 2017 was however decried by the same politicians who supported the Warsaw Museum as antipatriotic and the scientific team was ousted, because it sought to enscribe the Polish experience in a European narrative and exposed some of the more somber faces of Poland's role in the war. Healing through history, however selective, was crucial to overcoming the legacies of the Cold War in Eastern Europe, a process that is still ongoing a quarter century after its end.

In Russia, revision of the past was more limited. After some disarray under Boris Yeltsin, who saw the whole Soviet era as a digression from Russian history, it proved impossible to discount the sacrifice of 27 million Soviet dead in the 'great patriotic war' of 1941–45 and to conduct a 'double demobilization'. Arguably, Russia experienced a 'culture of defeat' like that of Weimar Germany, which also suffered regime change, reduced borders and population loss, and which likewise found it hard to turn the page on the past. With lingering nostalgia for the Soviet era, which had lasted a lifetime, political and cultural demobilization remained problematic.[26] Vladimir Putin's presidency in 2000 marked the end of Russia's postwar period. His divergence from (and even opposition to) the EU, along with growing revanchist nationalism, showed that while Russia was still part of Europe, it was on its own, distinct terms. Equally part of this other Europe were Belarus and Ukraine. Both underwent a Russian-style 'reconstruction' under Soviet-style dictators but were subject to nationalist and democratic stirrings oriented towards the EU in the latter case.[27]

War itself constituted the final aspect of postwar demobilization. Oddly, the spectre of nuclear annihilation that had haunted Europeans for forty years seemed to evaporate along with the cultural force field of the Cold War. Of course, anti-war sentiment during the Cold War had been qualified by each camp's adoption of nuclear dissuasion and armed confrontation. This became clear in the crisis over short-range nuclear missiles in the early 1980s. Anti-cruise missile campaigners in Britain, Belgium, Italy and West Germany rejected the Cold War and dismissed American as much as Soviet 'imperialism' (if not more so); but they remained a minority. As for the Soviet peace movement, it had always been directed against Western imperialism rather than towards multilateral disarmament. However, peaceful liquidation of the Cold War, the reduction in nuclear arms and the enlargement of NATO diminished a specifically European preoccupation with the existential threat from war, even though the risk of nuclear catastrophe had by no means been removed from the planet.[28]

This made the brutal wars that accompanied the break-up of Yugoslavia from 1991 to 1995 all the more shocking, because the form in which war re-emerged was not nuclear but ethnic. Vicious struggles between Serbia and Croatia and within Bosnia-Herzegovina targeted national minorities – generating a new term, 'ethnic cleansing', for sadly familiar practices. Rape, massacre, internment and forced expulsions sought to simplify the fit between peoples and territories, with the worst excesses committed in Bosnia-Herzegovina mainly (but not solely) by Bosnian Serbs (backed by Serbia) against Muslim Bosniaks. What Norman Naimark has called the 'fires of (ethnic) hatred' reignited, and with them the nightmares of the mid-century.[29]

The phenomenon was indeed linked to those earlier episodes, rather than to any Balkan tradition of violence.[30] As a communist regime that lay beyond the zone liberated by the Red Army in 1945, Yugoslavia escaped the control of the USSR, which expelled it from the Soviet bloc in 1948, and pursued thereafter a careful balancing act between the two camps in the Cold War. A reformist socialism and diplomatic non-alignment supplied the politics of independence. Preserving that independence limited internal tensions in what remained one of the most mixed areas of Europe precisely because in spite of the intensity of ethnic violence, explusions and mass killings of the 1940s, Yugoslavia did not experience an 'unmixing' of populations to the extent Poland or Czechoslovakia did. In this case, the end of the Cold War and the fall of communism had the opposite effect to that elsewhere, leading to rapid remobilization for war along national and ethnic lines.[31]

Europe was thus unprepared for a crisis that disrupted its own trajectory of demobilization. In the end, the United States and NATO intervened to limit the partition of Bosnia by the Dayton Agreement of 1995. In principle, Dayton protected the rights of minorities, including their right of return. In practise, this proved impossible to enact, so Dayton, or rather the relations of force on which it was based, confirmed the 'ethnic cleansing' already carried out.[32] The outrage generated by the violence helped consolidate European commitment to international human rights and to the more vigorous implementation of international law that had been one result of the end of the Cold War. Most Europeans welcomed the International Criminal Tribunal for the former Yugoslavia, set up by the United Nations (UN) in 1993, and the International Criminal Court established in 1998.[33] This was some consolation. But the war (including the siege of Sarajevo, the Srebrenica massacre and the practical limits to Dayton) was an uncomfortable reminder, just when it seemed to be over, of Europe's violent century.

The postwar period after the Cold War lasted some fifteen years and its historical cogency derived, among other things, from a process of demobilization in the political and cultural as well as in the military and economic spheres. The process played out differently in the east and west of the continent, creating new divisions, both geographic and political, between Russia, whose historic borders were pushed eastward, and the two spheres of Cold War Europe, now united in the EU. But only Slovenia from former non-aligned Yugoslavia had joined the EU by the end of the period.[34] The ghosts of ideological and ethnic violence had not been fully exorcised. However, the defeat of the European constitution in 2005 and the grudging compromise of the Lisbon Treaty in 2007, followed by the banking crash of 2008 and the rise of anti-European parties in many states, all signalled a major change in the political and cultural landscape. The postwar period was over.

Broken continuities: after 1945 and after 1918

How did the demobilization that helped define Europe after the Cold War relate to the earlier periods after 1945 and 1918? If postwar periods formulated the major shifts in European history brought about by all three wars, we should expect the link between them to be discontinuous, a set of connected displacements. 'Broken continuities' may best sum up the relationship between them and thus the turning points that marked the history of the continent in the twentieth century as a whole.

At first sight, peace in 1945 was the opposite of that in 1989 as the Grand Alliance of Britain, the United States and the USSR imposed 'unconditional surrender' on Germany followed by military occupation. The defeat was both total and double – of Germany as a great power and of fascism as an ideology. In the following half-decade, Nazi leaders and high-ranking German officers were purged or put on trial (notably at the Allied War Crimes Tribunal at Nuremberg in 1945–46), while similar action was taken against 'collaborators' in former-occupied countries.

At the same time, the Allied powers decided at Yalta on the reorganization of Eastern Europe so as to revise the borders and minorities established after the First World War, when the region had been re-established on the basis of nation states, following the disintegration of the dynastic, multinational empires. To be sure, the Nazi project of racial destruction and mass murder and the Soviet policy of social engineering had achieved most of what amounted to a radical reorganization of peoples and territories in the course of the Second World War. But expulsions and revised borders were also part of the hard politics of peace in 1945–48. Among others, this concerned Germans ejected from Poland and Czechoslovakia and Poles expelled from the Soviet western Ukraine, which had been eastern Poland before the war. Hard on the heels of Nazi genocide, the Western democracies helped complete the un-weaving of minorities and frontiers that had marked much of Central and Eastern Europe (though less so the Balkans) in the decade from 1938 to 1948.[35]

Demobilization in Europe was destined to take place on the basis of these realities, with the added dimension that the war had been internal to most continental states, all of which had had their own fascists, communists, liberal democrats and other protagonists. Military and economic demobilization for most European countries involved herculean efforts to return to some kind of normality by reconstructing war damage and worn-out infrastructure, while in the Allied case also sustaining the burden of military occupation of the enemy. Penalizing the latter by expropriating industrial plants was one way to square the circle, pursued by the USSR for some time in East Germany. But it rapidly gave way in West Germany to the alternative of reviving the economy and so reducing the burden on the Allies.[36]

As the United States introduced Marshall Aid in 1948 and backed reconstruction of postwar economies more generally, there was a premium on identifying those elements and traditions, in Germany in particular, that were free of the taint of the enemy and which could provide a political foundation for reconstruction. This meant the veteran Social Democratic Party (under Kurt Schumacher) and the Christian Democratic Union, founded in 1945, with Konrad Adenauer emerging as the leader as well as first chancellor of the German Federal Republic in 1949. Achieving the equivalent goal in what became the Soviet occupation zone (not just in Germany but in Eastern Europe more broadly) meant repressing incompatible elements in favour of a one-party regime under Soviet control. In this way, the occupying powers created partners who mirrored their own needs and with whom wartime enmity could begin to be overcome in the business of reconstruction and restoring 'normal' life.

Efforts at continental-level reconciliation might have followed had general peace lasted. But it did not. For multiple reasons, the Cold War took hold from 1946 and reversed each element of the exit from the Second World War, investing them in the new conflict.[37] The balance of power envisaged at Yalta and Potsdam was turned into the division of Europe, beginning with the split of Germany into two states.[38] The ideological victory over fascism took *two* forms: communist and liberal democratic. The consolidation of nation states in Central and Eastern Europe had barely been completed when it was subordinated to Soviet hegemony as Stalin's grip tightened.

Thus, the postwar period for Europe as a whole after the Second World War ended very quickly. Cultural and political demobilization did indeed occur but it was caught up in a new mobilization for the Cold War and was profoundly marked by that fact. Yesterday's enemy became today's friend. Berlin passed in three years from being

Hitler's last redoubt to a symbol of liberty for the 'West' during the airlift of 1948–49. Denazification ended prematurely in both West and East Germany. The onset of the new conflict probably speeded up the process of reconciliation. But for the next forty years, this mainly took place *within* (not between) the Cold War camps.

In Western Europe, federation was initially held up as a political solution for overcoming past animosities. Proposed in the 1920s during the previous phase of Franco-German reconciliation, and renewed by the thinking of wartime resistance movements, it in fact stood little chance of success with states that had just won back sovereignty after Nazi occupation. It did, however, result in the Council of Europe (created in 1949), which supported a Europe based on law and human rights. More successful was the indirect path to integration via economic reconstruction, which as we have seen was a major concern of the postwar periods. It benefited all without too obviously restricting any, and offered fertile ground for practical collaboration between West European nations. It also supplied a discourse of postwar reconciliation. The European Coal and Steel Community of 1951 expressed both aspects, for it resolved the threat of a revived German heavy industry by internationalizing the latter and also pioneered the institutional framework of the European Economic Community (EEC), which was established by the Treaty of Rome in 1957.[39]

A parallel universe emerged in Eastern Europe that turned on the needs of communist command economies and also enabled former enemies to collaborate in the shape of fraternal 'people's democracies'. In reality, however, the Council for Mutual Economic Assistance (COMECON, founded in 1949) remained like the Warsaw Pact a vehicle of Soviet hegemony even when Moscow's grip loosened following Stalin's death in 1953 – as the suppression of the 'counter-revolutionary' revolts of 1956 in Hungary and 1968 in Czechoslovakia was to show.

Political and cultural demobilization after the Second World War of course played out within individual states as well as at the level of each Cold War camp. Divided Germany shows most clearly what was at stake. If 'total surrender' in 1945 meant anything, it was not only that the victors (to borrow Clausewitz's definition) would force the enemy to conform to their will but also that they would make the vanquished see the result of the war through the victor's eyes. In the long run, this is what happened, but in different versions, east and west.

Initially, most Germans shared neither side's view of the past. Although the Nuremberg Tribunal had been designed with the idea of morally re-educating Germans about the Nazi period, historians diverge in their evaluation of its impact.[40] The flaws are well known – retrospective justice and victors' justice. There was no question of letting the Germans charge the Allies with 'war crimes' for bombing German cities – an issue that only surfaced during the third postwar period in the 1990s.[41] Support for the new orthodoxy came initially from the domestic partners of the Allies, not from any general change of opinion. Yet given continued occupation, mobilization for the Cold War and the absence of any alternative, most Germans eventually rejected the Nazi past and accepted the former enemy as an ally – in the name of liberal democracy in West Germany and communism in East Germany.[42]

There was a clear distinction, however, regarding the Nazi genocide of Europe's Jews. For East Germany, anti-Semitism, like fascism, was an extreme deviation of imperialism that did not implicate the proletarian state. West Germany, on ...e other hand, took responsibility for the Nazi past and the genocide, symbolically and by reparation (*Wiedergutmachung*).[43] The postwar generation that came of age in the upheavals of the late 1960s internalized the creation of a new political culture based on the explicit rejection of Nazi anti-Semitism. The highly publicized trials in the 1960s and 1970s of those responsible for Auschwitz and Majdanek helped bring this about.[44] This political culture, which took defeat in May 1945 to be 'liberation from tyranny' (as West German president, Richard von Weizsäcker, officially put it in 1985), was founded on a revision of the past without which the reunification of Germany after 1989 would not have been possible.[45] Its diplomatic expression was *Ostpolitik*, or West German acceptance of the postwar frontier with Poland by the Treaty of Warsaw in 1970. Willy Brandt, social democrat chancellor and former anti-Nazi resister, sealed *Ostpolitik* when he knelt before the monument to the Warsaw Ghetto Rising. As a watching journalist remarked: 'He who does not need to kneel knelt, on behalf of all who do need to kneel, but do not.'[46] It was the single most important gesture of reconciliation in the second postwar period.

However, because Europe's ideological war divided individual states, and because so many of these had experienced the maelstrom of the Second World War, coming to terms with the resulting domestic divisions and their often devastating legacy was an issue for other countries too. Initially, liberated states created the myth histories based on the resistance already referred to. These served both to condemn and minimize native fascism and collaboration.[47] Such histories could not account for the real relations between occupied or allied countries and Nazi Germany, and so the postwar generation attacked them from the 1960s. In the French case, it produced what Henry Rousso called the 'Vichy syndrome', an 'ever-present past' that haunted the French until the turn of the century.[48] Here, too, the genocide of Europe's Jews became the key issue. For unlike the resistance, it had no redemptive possibility. Controversial trials of perpetrators in the 1990s helped opinion evolve to the point where, in 1995, President Jacques Chirac acknowledged the wartime French state's complicity in the genocide.

For Europe as a whole, the Holocaust (as it became known) only acquired its current status in the 1990s. During the Cold War, each side downplayed its rejection of fascism by reference to the current enemy (in the 1980s, Ronald Reagan's 'evil empire' was communism). Moreover, if addressing the Second World War and achieving a degree of internal reconciliation over a divided past was hard in the West, it was frozen by communist orthodoxy in the East. Only with the fall of communism and the reunification of the continent did the Holocaust become the overriding moral symbol of a violent century. A regime of universal human rights underpinned by international law was in fact the product of the second postwar period, immediately after the end of the Second World War, by reason not only of the Nuremberg Tribunal but also of the UN Conventions on Genocide (1948) and the Laws of War (1949), as well as the Council of Europe's introduction of a European Convention on Human Rights in 1950. But these achievements were also put on ice for most of the Cold War, with the partial exception of the Helsinki accords in 1975.[49] It was in 2005, at the end of the post–Cold

War era, that the EU and the UN both made 27 January (date of the Soviet liberation of Auschwitz in 1945) Holocaust Memorial Day and that Auschwitz itself became the first 'site of memory' for contemporary Europe as a whole.

Cultural and political demobilization was thus an extended process after 1945, lasting for the duration of the Cold War in each camp. It was also asymmetric. The culture and politics of liberal democracies better allowed former Nazis and fascists not only to rehabilitate themselves in the first half of the postwar period, but also enabled a painful and divisive past to be addressed in the second half. The latter phase was something the more coercive Soviet regimes of Eastern Europe could ill afford, owing to the constraints of communist orthodoxy and a more fragile legitimacy. As we have seen, the legacy of this bifurcated process was fundamental for the differences in post–Cold War demobilization in the two parts of Europe.

In view of what followed, it is an irony of history that many during the first postwar period, after 1918, believed in a political and cultural demobilization that would bring permanent peace after the 'war to end war'. The hard politics of the Paris peace conference in 1919 turned on the Allies' assumption that they had won outright victory over Germany, though most Germans viewed the Armistice (and hence the peace conference) as anything but unconditional – which is what led the Allies to insist on total surrender a quarter of a century later.[50] Likewise, the Allies wanted to try German military and political leaders for wartime 'atrocities' that were now covered by international law. In 1919, they sought to extradite nearly 2,000 of them for trial internationally, though in the face of resistance they allowed the Germans to try the charges. This resulted in 'justice of the vanquished' when in 1921 the Supreme Court in Leipzig exonerated most of the accused.[51] The fiasco made the Allies in the Second World War determined to hold international trials for unprecedented criminality on enemy territory at the war's end.[52]

Although the initial phase of the postwar period down to 1923 saw the imposition of a series of treaties by the Allied powers, notably that of Versailles, the judgement of the latter as to Imperial Germany's war guilt was not only rejected by most Germans but was also not unanimously supported by opinion in the Allied countries. When the American Senate refused to ratify the Versailles Treaty and the British became once more preoccupied with their empire, the postwar order rested on a fragile French hegemony over continental Europe. But it was on this basis that a measure of Franco-German reconciliation took place in the second half of the 1920s as Germany accepted its new western frontiers by the Treaties of Locarno in 1925 and entered the League of Nations the following year.

Real peacemaking between France and Germany thus occurred not at Paris in 1919 but after Locarno. The two foreign ministers, Aristide Briand and Gustav Stresemann, agreed that Germany would pay a reduced level of reparations and that in return the Allies would speed up withdrawal of their occupation troops from the Rhineland, which had been allowed for fifteen years so as to guarantee German fulfilment of the peace treaty. Crucially, however, both Briand and Stresemann agreed that the First World War had been a disaster for Europe. German entry into the League of Nations meant for both men that war would never again be used as a means to settle disagreements.[53]

Culturally, they demobilized. As Briand put it in welcoming the German delegation to Geneva:

> Peace for Germany and for France means that the series of painful and bloody encounters, which has stained every page of history, is over . . . No more wars, no more brutal and bloody solutions to our differences! . . . Away with rifles, machine-guns, cannon! Make way for conciliation, for arbitration, for peace.[54]

It was therefore logical that Stresemann should endorse Briand's plan in 1928 for a 'United States of Europe' under the League of Nations – the direct approach to European integration to which the indirect, economic path would be preferred after the Second World War. Indeed, the League itself was the first attempt at a supra-national form of governance. It not only provided for reconciliation of the major protagonists of the First World War but also sought to create the economic, social and political conditions for enduring peace, including collective security and world disarmament.[55]

In this perspective, war itself, not France or Germany, was the real enemy. 'Never again!', 'Ne jamais plus cela!', 'Nie wieder Krieg!' was a widespread feeling. It embodied a cultural demobilization of wartime mentalities in acts of mutual recognition and reconciliation not only between veterans but also by trade unionists, feminists, intellectuals and others from across the continent. Briand and Stresemann won the Nobel Peace Prize in 1926 and revulsion against industrialized warfare became embedded in the thinking of many Europeans. Reconciliation, however, could not overcome the corrosive effects of defeat on states that were determined to revise the peace treaties and which had the capacity ultimately to overturn them.[56] Both Italian fascists and the Nazis also continued to glorify war as a political and biological necessity, though Mussolini and Hitler (both of whom had fought in the Great War) were wary of another lengthy war of economic attrition. They wanted easy victories.

The 1920s also exposed the minorities' 'problem' in the new nation states, most of which were ethnically mixed. Like a nest of Russian dolls, one state's nationality turned out to be the minority in someone else's, especially in Central and Eastern Europe. While the League sought to make its members protect their minorities' rights, these were not vested in any supranational statute let alone protected by more than old-fashioned power diplomacy.[57] Hitler and Mussolini relentlessly exploited the League's language to 'protect' their own extraterritorial minorities (such as the Sudeten Germans), including by annexation. The minority 'problem' pointed to war. We shall never know whether the Nazis would have gained power without the 1929 crash and the Great Depression. But this first and fragile postwar period – further weakened by the isolation of the USSR – could not sustain economic meltdown and was over by 1933. Remobilization triumphed over demobilization.

More than a decade after the end of the last postwar period, what can we conclude about the broken continuities across all three periods and the process of demobilization? For the first time in centuries, the peace enjoyed by most of Europe is based not on an armed balance of power but on a set of common frameworks managed mutually by a majority of European nations. This fundamental change emerged indirectly from reconciliation in all three postwar periods. But its key incarnation came with the political demobilization and economic reconstruction of Western Europe in the 1950s. The price of enlargement of the EU in the third postwar period was borne by Russia, defeated in the Cold War, and now more isolated than at any time in modern history from most of the rest of the continent.

War has not been abolished as serious people thought it might be in the 1920s. However, the mass death in the First World War favoured reconciliation, especially in the West, and, reinforced by the catastrophe of its successor, has become a common reference. Few in Europe glorify war even if 'sacrifice' in the Second World War (including that of resistance movements) remains an important value in Britain, France, Italy, Russia and elsewhere. The spectre of a nuclear conflagration has receded. Reluctance to think in terms of war helps explain the shock of the Balkan conflict in the 1990s and also an unwillingness to conceive of the EU in military terms.

Of course, civilian deaths even more than military deaths lay at the heart of the Second World War and the ongoing fear of a nuclear conflict. The Cold War shaped but also limited the ways in which that reality could be addressed in the two parts of the continent. It is only since the end of the Cold War that Europeans have fully understood the Second World War as the central tragedy of the century, and so the basis of their efforts at reconciliation. While all of Europe was scarred by the violence, the genocide of the Jews – Europe's continental minority – emerged after 1989 as the supreme symbol of what humans are capable of doing to each other. The international human rights and new juridical regimes that came out of the Second World War enshrined that lesson in law. If by itself that is no guarantee, the economic and political framework of the European project seemed to many to provide the best practical security. This has made the challenges faced by the EU since the end of the post–Cold War period all the more significant.

The most persistent failure across all three postwar periods was the inability to guarantee minority rights. The main damage had been done by 1950, when the 'fires of hatred' seemed to have burned out, leaving a Europe emptied of a good deal of its religious and ethnic complexity – indeed, in some parts a continent of ghosts. It was also the issue least amenable to cultural and political demobilization, let alone reconciliation, precisely because the hard politics of the second and third postwar periods confirmed the simplified ethnic framework of nation states (compared to the first postwar period), which were the logical basis on which such reconciliation might be attempted. The hope that the new international human rights and legal regime framed after 1945 might prevent a recurrence of violence against minorities was tested and found severely wanting in the former Yugoslavia in the 1990s.

Nonetheless, evidence suggests that, cumulatively if indirectly, Europeans have been able to learn from their violent past in the last hundred years. It suggests, too, that demobilization in the three postwar periods has played a crucial role in that process. Yet historians know better than most that no gains are given and that without renewal, no understanding is permanent.

Notes

1 Carl Levy and Mark Roseman (eds.), *Three Postwar Eras in Comparison: Western Europe 1918–1945–1989* (Basingstoke: Palgrave, 2002). Apart from its exclusion of Eastern Europe and Russia, this is an interesting but heterogeneous collection, concerned above all by the notion of postwar 'stabilization'. For a brilliant exploration of the post-1945 period, albeit in a rather different sense to ours, see Tony Judt, *Postwar: A History of Europe since 1945* (London: Penguin, 2005).

2 David Landes, *The Unbound Prometheus: Technological Change and Industrial Development in Western Europe from 1750 to the Present* (New York: Cambridge University Press, 1969); Victoria de Grazia, *Irresistible Empire: America's Advance through Twentieth Century Europe* (Cambridge, MA: Belknap Press, 2006).

3 For the distinctive memory paths of twentieth-century Spain, see Michael Richards, *After the Civil War: Making Memory and Re-making Spain since 1936* (Cambridge: Cambridge University Press, 2013).

4 John Lewis Gaddis, *The Cold War* (London: Penguin, 2005); Melvyn P. Leffler and Odd Arne Westad (eds.), *The Cambridge History of the Cold War* (Cambridge: Cambridge University Press, 2010), 3 vols.

5 Daniel Moran and Arthur Waldron (eds.), *The People in Arms: Military Myth and National Mobilization since the French Revolution* (Cambridge: Cambridge University Press, 2003).

6 Keith Grieves, *The Politics of Manpower, 1914–18* (Manchester: Manchester University Press, 1990).

7 Paul Kennedy and William Hitchcock (eds.), *From War to Peace: Altered Strategic Landscapes in the Twentieth Century* (New Haven and London: Yale University Press, 2000).

8 Stéphane Audoin-Rouzeau and Annette Becker, *14–18: Understanding the Great War* (2000; translation from French, New York: Hill and Wang, 2002), 113–58.

9 Jessica Gienow-Hecht, 'Culture and the Cold War in Europe', in *Cambridge History of the Cold War*, ed. Leffler and Odd Arne, vol. 1, *Origins* (Cambridge: Cambridge University Press, 2010), 398–419.

10 For the idea of 'cultural demobilization', see John Horne, 'Guerres et réconciliations européennes au 20e siècle', in *Les 27 leçons d'histoire*, ed. Jean-Noël Jeanneney (Paris: Le Seuil, 2009), 137–45 (abridged version) and in *Vingtième siècle. Revue d'histoire* 104 (2009): 3–15 (full version). For its relevance to the First World War, see Horne, 'Kulturelle Demobilmachung 1919–1939. Ein sinnvoller historischer Begriff?', in *Politische Kulturgeschichte der Zwischenkriegszeit, 1918–1939*, ed. Wolfgang Hardtwig (Göttingen: Vandenhoeck & Ruprecht, 2005), 129–50, and 'Demobilizing the Mind: France and the Legacy of the Great War, 1919–1939', *French History and Civilization* 2 (2009): 101–19 (also on www.h-france.net).

11 Exiting war is a process more fully studied for the First World War than its successors. See Stéphane Audoin-Rouzeau and Christophe Prochasson (eds.), *Sortir de la Grande Guerre: le monde et l'après 1918* (Paris: Tallandier, 2008) and Robert Gerwarth and John Horne (eds.), *War in Peace: Paramilitary Violence in Europe after the Great War* (Oxford: Oxford University Press, 2012).

12 Timothy Garton Ash, *We the People: The Revolution of 89* (London: Granta, 1990; new ed., Penguin, 1999); Ralf Dahrendorf, *Reflections on the Revolution in Europe* (Piscataway, NJ: Transaction, 1990; new ed., 2004); Charles S. Maier, *Dissolution: The*

Crisis of Communism and the End of East Germany (Princeton: Princeton University Press, 1997).

13 Dariusz Stola, 'Moving Borders and Peoples', below, p.36; *BBC Newsonline* (20 July 2004), www.news.bbc.uk/2/hi/europe/3842031.stm, for the British army figures (accessed 18.1.2016). The British Army on the Rhine was wound up in 1994 and replaced by British Forces in Germany with 25,000 personnel.

14 Jeffrey Herf, *War by Other Means: Soviet Power, West German Resistance and the Battle of the Euromissiles* (New York: Free Press, 1991).

15 From a Cold War total of 70,000 warheads, the Strategic Arms Reduction Treaty limited the United States and Russia (by far the largest holders of nuclear weapons) to 6,000 strategic warheads and 1,600 delivery vehicles each. See Andrew Futter, *The Politics of Nuclear Weapons* (London: Sage, 2015), 3 and 137.

16 For the NATO figures, see 'Financial and Economic Data Relating to NATO Defence: Defence Expenditure of NATO Countries, 1970–1992' (NATO Press Service, 10 December 1992), 'Nato expenditure as percentage of GDP': 5; and 'Financial and economic data relating to NATO Defence: Defence expenditure of NATO countries, 1990–2010', 'Nato expenditure as percentage of GDP' (NATO Press Service, 10 March 2010): 6. The figures were accessed at www.nato. int on 25.2.2016. For Russian defence expenditure since 1992, see Stockholm International Peace Research Institute, database on 'Military Expenditure by country as a percentage of gross domestic product', at www.sipri.org (accessed 25.2.2016). For the controversy over Soviet defence expenditure and the best guess that in 1989 it ranged between 8.4 per cent and 15 per cent of the gross domestic product (GDP), see Mark Harrison, 'Secrets, Lies and Half-Truths: The Decision to Disclose Soviet Defence Outlays', working paper no. 55, *Political Economy Research in Soviet Archives* (PERSA) (26 September 2008), Department of Economics, University of Warwick.

17 Mark Mazower, Jessica Reinisch and David Feldman (eds.), *Post-War Reconstruction in Europe: International Perspectives, 1945–1949* (Oxford: Oxford University Press, 2011); Stephen Harris, *Communism on Tomorrow Street: Mass Housing and Everyday Life after Stalin* (Baltimore: Johns Hopkins Press, 2013).

18 Eric Foner, *A Short History of Reconstruction, 1863–1877* (New York: Harper and Row, 1990), 254–60.

19 Ulrich Herbert, *Geschichte Deutschlands im 20. Jahrhundert* (Munich: C. H. Beck, 2014), 1143–58.

20 Paul Ginsborg, *Italy and Its Discontents: Family, Civil Society, State, 1980–2001* (London: Allen Lane, 2001).

21 Marc Lazar, *Le Communisme: une passion française* (Paris: Perrin, 2002; new ed., 2005), 99–135.

22 Vittorio Foa, *Il Silenzio dei communisti* (Turin: Einaudi, 2002); Enzo Traverso, *Fire and Blood: The European Civil War, 1914–1945* (2007; translation from French, London: Verso, 2016), for a defence of Resistance political culture.

23 Paul G. Lewis, *Political Parties in Post-Communist Eastern Europe* (London: Routledge, 2001), 75–78.

24 Timothy Garton Ash, 'Trials, Purges and History Lessons: Treating a Difficult Past in Post-Communist Europe', in *Memory and Power in Post-War Europe. Studies in the Presence of the Past*, ed. Jan-Werner Müller (Cambridge: Cambridge University Press, 2002), 265–82.

25 Pieter Lagrou, *The Legacy of Nazi Occupation: Patriotic Memory and National Recovery in Western Europe, 1945–1965* (Cambridge: Cambridge University Press, 2000), 21–77.

26 For the idea of 'cultures of defeat', see Wolfgang Schivelbusch, *The Culture of Defeat: On National Trauma, Mourning and Recovery* (2003; translated from the German, London: Granta, 2003). For Soviet nostalgia, Svetlana Alexievitch, *La Fin de l'homme rouge* (2013; translation from Russian, Arles: Actes Sud, 2013).

27 Iver B. Neumann, *Russia and the Idea of Europe: A Study in Identity and International Relations* (London: Routledge, 1996), 158–93.

28 Lawrence Wittner, *Resisting the Bomb: A History of the World Nuclear Disarmament Movement, 1954–1970* (Stanford: Stanford University Press, 1997); Herf, *War by Other Means.*

29 Norman Naimark, *Fires of Hatred: Ethnic Cleansing in Twentieth Century Europe* (Cambridge, MA: Harvard University Press, 2001).

30 Maria Todorova, *Imagining the Balkans* (New York and Oxford: Oxford University Press, 1997), 184–89.

31 Misha Glenny, *The Balkans, 1804–1999: Nationalism, War and the Great Powers* (London: Granta, 1999), 622–62; Tim Judah, *The Serbs: History, Myth and the Destruction of Yugoslavia* (New Haven and London: Yale University Press, 1997), 113–310.

32 Glenny, *The Balkans*, 651–52.

33 Most EU countries were among the early signatories to the Rome Statute establishing the International Criminal Court (1998–99).

34 Slovenia entered the EU in 2004 and Croatia in 2013. Macedonia, Montenegro and Serbia are candidates and Bosnia-Herzegovina has potential candidate status.

35 Naimark, *Fires of Hatred*; Timothy Snyder, *The Reconstruction of Nations: Poland, Ukraine, Lithuania, Belarus* (New Haven and London: Yale University Press, 2004); Alfred-Maurice de Zayas, *A Terrible Revenge: The Ethnic Cleansing of East European Germans* (London: Palgrave Macmillan, 2006); Jessica Reinisch and Elizabeth White (eds.), *The Disentanglement of Populations: Migration, Expulsion and Displacement in Post-War Europe, 1944–49* (London: Palgrave Macmillan, 2011).

36 Alan Kramer, *The West German Economy, 1945–1955* (Oxford: Berg, 1990), 53–68; Alan Milward, *The Reconstruction of Western Europe, 1945–51* (London: Routledge, 1984).

37 For the historiography and debate on the origins of the conflict, see Martin McCauley, *The Origins of the Cold War: 1941–1949* (London: Pearson Education, 2008), 10–29.

38 Marc Trachtenberg, *A Constructed Peace. The Making of the European Settlement, 1945–1963* (Princeton: Princeton University Press, 1999), 3–91.

39 Derek Urwin, *The Community of Europe: A History of European Integration since 1945* (Harlow: Longman, 1991), 27–39; Alan Milward (with Federico Romero and George Brennan), *The European Rescue of the Nation-State* (London: Routledge, 1992), esp. 21–45.

40 Konrad Jarausch, *After Hitler: Re-civilizing the Germans, 1945–1995* (New York: Oxford University Press, 2006), p. 8. See also Donald Bloxham, *Genocide on Trial: War Crimes Trials and the Formation of Holocaust History and Memory* (Oxford: Oxford University Press, 2003), and Lawrence Douglas, *The Memory of Judgment: Making Law and History in the Trials of the Holocaust* (New Haven and London: Yale University Press, 2001). The first severely criticizes the motives and the

outcome of the trials, whereas the second defends the procedures adopted and notably their deliberately didactic function.

41 For the belated emergence of a public memory of the destruction of Germany by Allied bombing, see Robert G. Moeller, 'The Bombing War in Germany, 2005–1940: Back to the Future?' in *Bombing Civilians: A Twentieth Century History*, ed. Yuki Tanaka and Marilyn B. Young (New York: The New Press, 2009), 46–76.

42 Jeffrey Herf, *Divided Memory: The Nazi Past in the Two Germanys* (Cambridge, MA: Harvard University Press, 1997).

43 Ido de Haan, 'Paths of Normalization after the Persecution of the Jews: The Netherlands, France and West Germany in the 1950s', in *Life After Death: Approaches to a Cultural and Social History of Europe during the 1940s and 1950s*, ed. Richard Bessel and Dirk Schumann (Cambridge: Cambridge, University Press, 2003), 65–92; Herf, *Divided Memory*, 106–61.

44 Annette Weinke, 'Alliierter Angriff auf die nationale Souveränität? Die Strafverfolgung von Kriegs- und NS-Verbrechen in der Bundesrepublik, der DDR und Österreich', in *Transnationale Vergangenheitspolitik: Der Umgang mit deutschen Kriegsverbrechern in Europa nach dem Zweiten Weltkrieg*, ed. Norbert Frei (Göttingen: Wallstein Verlag, 2006), 37–93, esp. 73–93.

45 Richard von Weizsäcker, speech on the fortieth anniversary of the end of the Second World War, 8 May 1985, delivered to the Bundestag (www.bundespraesident.de, accessed 5.4.2016).

46 Willy Brandt, *My Life in Politics* (1989; translation from German, Harmondsworth: Penguin, 1993), 200.

47 Henry Rousso, *The Vichy Syndrome: History and Memory in France since 1944* (1987; translation from the French, Cambridge, MA: Harvard University Press, 1991); Lagrou, *Legacy of Nazi Occupation*.

48 Eric Conan and Henry Rousso, *Vichy: An Ever-Present Past* (1994; translation from French, Lebanon NH: University of New England Press, 1998).

49 Rosemary Foot, 'The Cold War and Human Rights', in *Cambridge History of the Cold War*, ed. Leffler and Arne Westad, vol. 3, *Endings* (Cambridge: Cambridge University Press, 2010), 445–65.

50 Harold Nicolson, *Peacemaking 1919* (London: Constable, 1933; new edition, 1943, Preface, xix–xx). Nicholson had been a junior diplomat in Paris in 1919. As a back-bench Member of Parliament during the Second World War, he insisted in the wartime edition of his memoir on the necessity of learning from the past and this time imposing on 'unconditional' surrender.

51 James F. Willis, *Prologue to Nuremberg: The Politics and Diplomacy of Punishing War Criminals of the First World War* (London and Westport, CT: Greenwood, 1982).

52 Michael R. Marrus, *The Nuremberg War Crimes Trials 1945–46: A Documentary History* (Boston and New York: Bedford, 1997), 18–38.

53 John Horne, 'Locarno et la politique de la démobilisation culturelle, 1925–30', in *14–18 Aujourd'hui-Heute-Today* (Paris) 5 (2002): 73–87.

54 Achille Elisa (ed.), *Aristide Briand Discours et écrits de politique étrangère* (Paris: Plon, 1965), 178.

55 Zara Steiner, *The Lights that Failed: European International History, 1919–1935* (Oxford: Oxford University Press, 2005), and for the economic dimension to the League, Patricia Clavin, *Securing the World Economy: The Reinvention of the League of Nations, 1920–1946* (Oxford: Oxford University Press, 2013).

56   Robert Gerwarth, *The Vanquished: Why the First World War Failed to End* (London: Penguin, 2016).

57   Carole Fink, *Defending the Rights of Others: The Great Powers, the Jews and International Minority Protection 1878–1938* (Cambridge: Cambridge University Press, 2004), 267–335 (esp. 276–79).

2

Borders

Dariusz Stola

Postwar periods are years of restabilization and demobilization, but also of change. This chapter presents two kinds of postwar political and social changes that profoundly transformed Europe in the twentieth century: the movement of state borders and the related movement of peoples.

Studies of state systems have pointed to a global tendency to replace large empires with smaller and more numerous nation states, resulting in reshaped political maps through the twentieth century. This transformation unfolded in a highly uneven way, with short periods of intensive state-remaking separated by decades of little or no change at all. Of the several such periods of intensive empire-into-nation-state-making, three in particular have significantly reshaped Europe.[1] These were exactly the three postwar periods that are the focus of this volume.

From the perspective of border and population movements, the third period, which is of primary interest here, lasted a few years into the 1990s. It ended gradually, with stabilization in the Balkans and the expansion of the North Atlantic Treaty Organization (NATO) and the European Union (EU) – two Western institutions established in the Cold War era – into the former Soviet bloc. Their eastward expansion, which had been very far from obvious in the early 1990s, was, to some extent, a consequence of the international instability, mass forced migrations and humanitarian catastrophes of the post–Cold War Balkan wars. When faced with the choice between exporting stability and importing instability, Western leaders chose wisely.[2] Indeed, Central and East Europeans had already opted for an occidentalist orientation.

The process of NATO enlargement, which began in the mid-1990s, and EU enlargement, which followed a few years later, provided an international framework for a new European order. This order has stabilized the borders and, to a large extent, conditioned international migrations. Despite being invented and developed in the other half of the continent, the project of European integration appears to have been made to respond well to the set of questions that have haunted Eastern Europe throughout the twentieth century. These questions are the focus of this chapter.

The EU is an organization sui generis, not a state. More specifically, it is neither a nation state nor an empire, the two solutions to the territory–population nexus that were tested in Eastern Europe throughout the twentieth century, sometimes with limited success, sometimes with catastrophic results. The project of European integration has offered a model that is supranational but not imperial, and in this sense, it appears to be the most recent in a series of responses to the disintegration of multi-ethnic, land-based empires that had ruled Eastern Europe before 1918. This order has made national government, and consequently national borders, less relevant and thus less controversial than they previously were. It has demanded high standards of liberal democratic governance, emphasizing respect for human and minority rights to a greater extent than the Versailles minority protection system did. It also has made EU internal borders more permeable for capital, people, goods, services and information, thereby fostering the development of transnational social spaces where labor migrants, businesspeople, policymakers, criminals, historians and other Europeans can increasingly interact. For other reasons, it has coincidentally made the intra-EU migration, and the choice of the place to live, more a private matter, a field to be governed by markets rather than by states. While this model poses various problems, it appears to provide avenues for resolving various other problems, the problems which this essay analyses.

An East European story

This essay in European history is largely about the eastern half of the continent.[3] In examining twentieth-century border changes and population movements, we see them strikingly concentrated in Eastern, Central and South-Eastern Europe. The dividing line between those European countries that experienced many such events during the century and those fortunate enough to see but few of them runs across the continent from Lübeck in the Baltic to Trieste in the Adriatic. I locate it west of the Stettin-Trieste line, which Churchill drew in his Iron Curtain speech, such that it includes East Germany. This now-defunct state was the key area for developments in the post-1989 and post-1945 periods (which Churchill could not have known about in February 1946). Neither, however, does this eastern half of the continent neatly correspond to the former Soviet bloc, as it includes Finland and Greece, as well as Yugoslavia, which, although communist, was not a Soviet satellite during the Cold War.[4]

Of the eight states that were established in Europe after the First World War, all but one emerged in the East.[5] After the Second World War, three states disappeared and one came into being, while ten others changed their borders. All but one of these (Italy) were east of the Lübeck-Trieste line. After the Cold War, sixteen new European states appeared on maps and four disappeared, none of which was in the West.

The Irish Free State was the only new state in Western Europe in the twentieth century. As for territorial shifts that did not involve state-making or unmaking, West Europeans did experience a few, namely, border changes at the expense of the losers, Germany and Austria, in Alsace-Lorraine, Eupen-Malmedy, Schleswig and Trentino. All of these occurred in the first of the three postwar periods. Later on, if we exclude the peculiar statehood of the French-occupied Saar in 1947–56 and Italy's territorial losses east of the line, only minor revisions of the West European borders took place, including two Italian villages (communes) ceded to France after the Second World War.

Similarly asymmetric is the history of postwar population movements. Western Europe was, of course, not free of forced migrations: In 1919 alone, the French government removed more than 150,000 Germans from Alsace-Lorraine, and thousands of involuntary migrants crossed other borders after the First World War.[6] In the second postwar period, British and Americans assisted in the compulsory repatriation of more than 2 million Soviet and Yugoslav displaced persons (DPs) from western zones of Germany, many of them against their will. Indeed, in all three postwar periods, Western Europe was the destination of thousands and millions of migrants, either from Eastern Europe or, in the 1990s, from outside the continent. Yet these flows were insignificant compared to their East European counterparts.

According to Ewa Morawska, who compiled data on various forms of forced migration in the twentieth century, expulsions, deportations, exiles and forcible repatriations, compulsory population transfers and panic-stricken flights may have affected as many as 80 million Eastern Europeans. Her estimate includes some 10 million refugees or expellees following the First World War, up to 25 million people displaced after the Second World War and around 4 million refugees and displaced persons of the post-communist period.[7] Most of those people were members of specific ethnic groups, targeted or affected by violence and discrimination.

What unites the vast and ethnically diverse space among the Baltic, Adriatic and Black seas, where the dramatic events described earlier took place, is their shared past of belonging to multi-ethnic, land-based empires before 1918, and a long search for an alternative stable state order afterwards. For several generations before the First World War, this territory had been divided among the Russian, German, Habsburg and Ottoman empires, each competing with the others for power and influence. Their borders might change, but the imperial order remained relatively stable. The spread of modern nationalism, combined with other aspects of European modernization, transformed the region's societies, economies and armies later but faster than they had in the West, and thereby undermined and eroded the order. The nationalizing of the region's peoples and lands, whether by a separatist movement for a new (or mythically restored) nation state or by its apparent opposite, state-sponsored Russification, Germanization or Magyarization, subverted both individual empires and their international system, and exposed the region to the dynamic of imperial collapse and nationalist struggle. It introduced a new way of conceiving of politics, focused on discrete populations and a state ideal founded on ethnonational homogeneity; this was so very different from the previous system of dynastic legitimacy and state sovereignty within clearly, but not ethnically defined, borders.[8]

The reordering of territory and the related mass, involuntary migrations had begun in the nineteenth century in the Balkans. The key factors of border and population movements that we discuss here had already been present and dramatically expressed in the two Balkan Wars of 1912–13: the legacies of the empire and looming domination of a neighboring power over vulnerable nations; ethnonationalist mobilization and a spiraling of violence; the search for congruence between the sociocultural space of ethnonation and the territory of the state; the zero-sum-game struggles for territory and people. The First World War, which began as a third Balkan war, helped spread these conditions northward. The war eventually eliminated two of the four regional empires. The two others were weakened considerably, but only temporarily. Thus, while Austria and Turkey did not play any significant role in later developments, Germany and Russia/Soviet Union did twofold.

Elsewhere in this volume, Pieter Lagrou claims that the 1918–1945–1989 triptych is 'the periodization of German history writ large'. It may look this way from a West European point of view. For the observers in the East, however, the triptych is as much Russo-centric as it is Germano-centric, especially if by 1918 we mean not only Compiègne but also Brest-Litovsk, and change 1989 for 1989–91. From a Central or Eastern European perspective, the three wars and their postwar periods were as much about the place and role of Russia/USSR in Europe (and consequently about the lands between them) as they were about that of Germany.

The 1990s as a postwar period

Histories of territorial settlements and forced migrations provide strong arguments for the claim that Europe after 1989 was in a postwar period. Both phenomena are correlates of war and the postwar consolidation of a new international order; the combination of the two elements even more clearly points to this. They have never occurred together and on such a scale without a preceding war, indeed, a major preceding war.[9] Similarly, the wave of many millions of European refugees, 'forced repatriates' and other displaced persons that marked the post-1989 period had no precedent unrelated to war.

Europe of the early 1990s was busy with state-making as never before. As a consequence of the collapse of Yugoslavia and dissolution of the Soviet Union and Czechoslovakia, sixteen new European states emerged: Belarus, Bosnia and Herzegovina, Croatia, Czech Republic, Estonia, Latvia, Lithuania, Macedonia, Moldova, Montenegro, Russia, Serbia, Slovakia, Slovenia, Ukraine and (later and still contested) Kosovo. This produced more than 11,000 km of new international borders. At the same time, German unification made the German Democratic Republic (GDR) disappear, together with 1,500 km of the intra-German border. All this increased the total length of European land borders by more than a third, to 36,000 km.[10]

This deeply altered the constellation of states in half of the continent. In particular, Ukraine, the second largest European state today, had led no sovereign existence in the modern era, except for a brief moment of contested independence in 1918–19. The third postwar period was also a turning point for the pre-existing states in Eastern Europe. Of Poland's three neighbors in 1989 none existed in 1993, having been replaced by five new states and the united Germany. Hungary, which had bordered all three erstwhile federations, now has five new nation states as its neighbors. Romania acquired three new neighbours and Bulgaria has gained two, while six other countries have one neighbouring state that did not exist in 1989.

Map 2.1 Europe, 1923.

Source: Duby (1997) and R. McNally and Co.'s (1924). © FNSP Sciences Po – Atelier de cartographie, 2018.

Russia has remained the largest state in Europe and the world, but the collapse of the Soviet bloc and Soviet state reversed nearly four centuries of Russia's westward expansion. The USSR was the heir and continuation of the Russian empire, albeit significantly transformed, and the Soviet satellites were Moscow's external empire.[11] The Soviet imperial space – its differential and hierarchical organization, structured by distinctive center–periphery relations, rapidly withered away or eroded in the 1990s. The patterns and dynamics of this process largely conditioned the European post–Cold War. Various relics of the empire still remain, and some clearly will continue to do so. The most important one, at least for this narrative, is the Kaliningrad exclave within the EU, NATO and Schengen zone: 15,000 km^2 of Russian territory (half the size of Belgium) and almost a million Russian citizens remain 400 km from the Russian mainland.

In contrast to the two previous postwar periods, the 1990s brought no territorial losses to Germany. On the contrary, a German state (the Federal Republic of Germany – FRG) was the only state to expand, which makes it seem the European victor of the Cold War. However, it did so within the overall framework of the territorial settlement of 1945, which meant the final approval of the losses it sustained in the Second World War. Similarly, the disappearance of the GDR-FRG border was unfinished business from the Second World War and Germany's occupation by the four powers.[12] For these reasons, 1990 for Germany constitutes both post–Cold War and a delayed end of the Second World War.

The population flow most typical for any postwar years is the relocation and reduction (i.e. dispersal) of military personnel. The high tide of such movements in the early 1990s is another argument for it being a postwar period. While these were much smaller than those that occurred after the two world wars, they were still on a massive scale. Moreover, because during the Cold War the presence of foreign troops was not a temporary incursion but a stable, decades-long part of the landscape, their exit was all the more important. The largest and longest-distance movements of this kind resulted from the disintegration of the Soviet empire and its military withdrawal, but the end of the Cold War enabled all its participants to reap a peace dividend by downscaling their armies. In the few years following 1988, the Soviet army decreased by some 2.5 million men, split into 15 national armies and withdrew from its bases in Central Europe. The latter change alone meant migration of a million people: servicemen, their family members and civilian personnel. Some 550,000 Soviets left East Germany while 400,000 left Czechoslovakia, Hungary and Poland. On a lesser but still substantial scale was the reduction of 700,000 US troops, including 250,000 in Europe.[13] Notably, soon after the Cold War's end, peace and the related troop reduction expanded globally. Between 1992 and 2005, the number of violent conflicts – primarily civil wars – declined by an astonishing 40 per cent, after four decades of prior increase.[14]

A regular postwar population movement, hardly noticeable in the Europe of the 1990s, was the return or resettlement of people displaced by wartime hostilities or occupation policies. Their absence in 1989 underlies the peculiar, combat-free character of the European Cold War. Of the violence that did occur, such as that in many countries in the late 1940s, in East Germany in 1953, in Poland and Hungary in 1956, in Czechoslovakia in 1968, in Greece in 1967–74, in Poland in 1970 and 1981–82 or in Romania in 1989, it was less intensive than in wars more generally and usually not directly related to the Cold War proper. Rather, these were domestic conflicts or conflicts within the blocs, as opposed to NATO-Warsaw Pact confrontations. In 1989, the people whom we could consider post–Cold War displaced persons were relatively few or they had been displaced several decades before; thus, by 1989, many had established roots in their new locations. The return of the Crimean Tartars, who had been deported to the Asian part of the USSR in the Stalin era, may be seen as a case in point. With a few exceptions, we can also include in this group some of the other

Soviet ex-deportees, mainly ethnic Germans, who, in the 1990s, emigrated to their 'external homeland' in the FRG (despite having never lived there before). Regardless, the numbers were much smaller than those of the two previous postwar periods: Post-1918 Europe saw millions, and post-1945 tens of millions of persons displaced by war.[15]

One wave of forced migration in the 1990s, with antecedents in the two previous periods, was the mass flight of refugees from the areas affected by local, mainly ethnic, violence. All three postwar periods were 'violent peacetimes', when state or paramilitary violence, unleashed by the collapse of the previous order and the struggle for a new one, made millions of civilians flee.[16] The wars in the former Yugoslavia uprooted half a million people in Croatia and 2.5 million in Bosnia (i.e. most of its population), of whom half sought refuge abroad and half were displaced internally. Another 850,000 people fled from the violence in Kosovo in 1999. The scale and intensity of these movements resulted largely from deliberate policies of ethnic cleansing, conducted mainly, but by no means exclusively, by various Serb forces against Bosnian Muslims.[17] In the former Soviet Union, the flow of refugees and other international migrants in need of protection exceeded 1.8 million, of whom two-thirds moved to Russia. There was a similar number of internally displaced persons within various post-Soviet republics, almost all of them outside the European part of the former USSR, in Tajikistan, Armenia and Azerbaijan. The tide of displaced persons peaked in the mid-1990s and then began to subside.[18]

Although dramatic and very intensive in some areas, the refugee flows of the 1990s were much smaller than those of their predecessors in post-1918 and post-1945. Their source areas were much more contained, and the fires of hatred that fueled them, while ominous, were lesser. Contrary to the two total wars, the Cold War in Europe did not leave a legacy of polarized national identities, mass suffering interpreted in ethnic terms or class hatred combined with revolutionary vision, as had been the case following the First World War. The world wars had also normalized mass violence and justified the expansion of the state's powers over its citizens, which the final years of the Cold War did not. Notably, the post-1989 period saw no population transfers or, for that matter, any other collective deportations at all. To this absence, which would have surprised observers in the two previous postwar periods, we will return later.

To be sure, the large involuntary migrations of the three periods under analysis did not result solely from ethnic diversity or the reordering of borders as such. Reordering, in and of itself, does not determine mass displacement, nor is ethnicity the ultimate, irreducible source of violent conflict. Ethnic violence is not just a higher degree of ethnic conflict but is also of a fundamentally different form, actively chosen by some; in other words, the violence that forced refugees to flee resulted from struggles for power framed in ethnic terms.[19]

Therefore, we have good reason to see the 1990s as a postwar period, despite the fact that its comparison to the post-1918 and post-1945 periods shows substantial differences . The differences result largely from the particular character of the European Cold War, combat-free and non-violent for many years before its end. The years of *detente*, with the Helsinki conference of 1975 at the apex, further distanced the 1990s from the more aggressive, early Cold War period. We could look at *detente* as a kind of postwar period after the 'first Cold War' of the 1950s and early 1960s, before the 'second Cold War' of the renewed East–West tensions and arms race of the 1980s. Notably, we can also see the Helsinki conference as a substitute for a Second World War peace conference, with its explicit aim to confirm the borders drawn in the second postwar period (which was the Soviet priority), and to protect human rights and cross-border personal connections (insisted upon by the West). Not incidentally, in the same year, Yugoslavia and Italy signed the Treaty of Osimo, which eventually confirmed their post–Second World War border in the region of Trieste.

From empires to nation states and back, and back again

In the post–Second World War period, the trends in state (re)making were opposite to what we have seen in the 1990s. As a consequence of the war, Moscow extended its rule further westward than ever before. The Soviet annexations made three Baltic States disappear from the map altogether, while four other countries – Finland, Poland, Czechoslovakia and Romania – lost large portions of their territories. Poland lost to the USSR almost half of its pre-war territory (46 per cent), but was compensated with German lands and the Free City of Danzig, making the Polish net loss 20 per cent, and Germany's 25 per cent, of what they had had in 1937. Together with the 'rationalization' of the new borders into straighter lines, these changes significantly decreased the total length of European borders. The emergence of two German states instead of one, and of the border between them in 1949, was an exception to the general decreasing tendency in the number of states and state border length, just as the disappearance of the GDR and its western border was an exception to the opposite trend in the 1990s.

In Eastern Europe, where the migratory and territorial changes were taking place, in terms of both border changes and population movements, post-1945 was quite similar to the war years and continued the wartime developments, while the post-1989 period differed strikingly from the last decades of the Cold War. In Western Europe, the pattern was the opposite: The late 1940s contrasted with the war years, while the 1990s continued the trends of the 1980s, with the stability of borders, unrestricted mobility within the EC and growing refugee inflows from other regions of Europe and the world. In the East, the emancipatory and diversifying logic of domestic and international transformations of the 1990s was opposite to the logic of Moscow's hegemony and the relative uniformity of communist regimes and policies in the pre-1990 period. The developments of the late 1940s – the border changes, the evolution of interstate relations and domestic regimes – followed a tendency that had dominated for several years.

The postwar period following the Second World War was part of a longer period of imperial *reconquista* of Central and Eastern Europe. Before Hitler's and Stalin's expansion projects clashed apocalyptically in 1941, they had jointly restored an imperial order, formal or informal, in almost all the European lands once ruled by the Romanovs, Habsburgs, Hohenzollerns and Ottomans. Twenty years after the dynasties had lost their domains, the empire struck back. It returned in a novel, more powerful form of a totalitarian state, armed with technological, organizational and (im)moral capacity for unprecedented social engineering and statecraft, to which border and

Map 2.2 Europe, 1955.

Source: Duby (1997) and Bartholomew (1959). © FNSP. Sciences Po – Atelier de cartographie, 2018.

population movements testify. Between 1938 and 1941, the Nazi and Soviet empires absorbed, destroyed or reduced eleven nation states of the region, beginning with Austria and Czechoslovakia, then Poland, Finland, Estonia, Latvia, Lithuania, Romania, Yugoslavia, Albania and Greece. The two new states that emerged as a consequence of this deconstruction, Slovakia and Croatia, were fully dependent on Germany. The two remaining ones, Hungary and Bulgaria, joined Germany in the spoils but became satellites, parts of Berlin's sphere of influence ('external empire') acting in an obvious center–periphery relation with their German patron. Over the course of these four years, independent nation states disappeared from the zone among the Baltic, Adriatic and Black seas.

Four years later, while the Thousand Year Reich had ended, there was no return to the pre-war *status quo ante*. The Soviet empire filled the void and imposed its own order. This imposition included substantial border changes and population transfers. Territorially, all but four of the above-listed states ended the 1940s either becoming smaller than they had been before 1938, or occupied, or fully annexed to the USSR.[20] The new, Moscow-designed parts of European borders followed rivers or straight lines, not unlike the colonial borders once charted by the European imperialists in Africa. Minorities were exchanged or unilaterally deported from or to all the states of the region except Bulgaria.

Moreover, the states were not independent in any meaningful way. To West European countries, the post–Second World War period meant restoration of independence, notwithstanding their war-induced exhaustion and the new influence exerted by the Americans. In the other half of the continent, the Soviet 'crushing of Eastern Europe' had begun before the war ended and continued throughout the next decade. While formally sovereign and United Nations (UN) members, the states of the emerging Soviet bloc were not half as independent as they had been before 1938, and decreasingly so.[21] This does not mean there was no distinction between the German and Soviet dominations, of course;[22] rather, it means that for a few years before, and for many years after 1945, the Wilsonian principle of national self-determination gave way to a supranational order, to imperial logic and practices originating from the USSR. In this sense, the Soviet bloc was another chapter in the long history of Eastern Europe's imperial orders. The Red Army brought to the region both a revolution and an old regime.

At the same time, it would be wrong to see the post-1945 Soviet domination as a simple return to the pre-1918 order, just under the sickle and hammer instead of the black eagles of the Russian, German and Habsburg empires. The Soviet Union annexed 600,000 km^2 of land and 25 million people, but even so, this represented but a minority of the land and people it took under its control as a consequence of the war. Stalin did not make Poland, Romania or Bulgaria new Soviet republics, which some of their communist leaders asked for. The communists would have made their populations welcome and democratically approve such a decision, just as they had done with populations of the lands annexed in 1939–40. To the contrary, Stalin helped consolidate them as nation states, more centralized, ethnically and culturally homogenous, militarized and economically autarkic than ever before.

Nothing demonstrated this consolidation better than the heavily guarded border infrastructure, with thousands of kilometers of barbed-wire fence and watch towers, which the communist governments erected in late 1940s, not only as the Iron Curtain isolating them from the West, but between themselves as well, in particular at the Soviet western border.[23] The new, post–Second World War imperial order in Eastern Europe was an innovative synthesis: Moscow-centred, socialist in content and national in form.

The expansion of the communist rule by the establishment of the Soviet bloc, instead of building socialism into one, growing country, as it had been up to 1941, was one of the most consequential of Stalin's (in)decisions after the Second World War. Its consequences were manifold, especially throughout the decades following 1956, when the satellites were allowed some diversity in their national paths to socialism, and dramatically so in the early post–Cold War period. The *Annus Mirabilis* 1989 and the peaceful disintegration of the Soviet bloc would have been very different, probably less miraculous and peaceful, had the satellite communist parties, armies, administrations and economies been incorporated into the USSR.

The establishment of the Soviet bloc in the post–Second World War period, composed of satellite but separate communist states, laid the foundation for the political dynamics forty years later. This was most apparent in the domino effect of 1989: the impact of the initial Polish events on Hungary, of Hungarian decisions on the GDR, of the developments in these three countries (and Soviet acquiescence to them) on Czechoslovakia, and finally the influence of the changes in the entire bloc on the Soviet Union itself. Notably, the disintegration of the Soviet Union began in the Baltic republics, the only pre–Second World War states fully incorporated into the USSR.[24]

Similarly, in migration history, the variety, intensity and directions of international flows in the 1990s contrasted with the earlier streams, or lack thereof, while the pre- and post-1945 movements have traditionally been depicted as belonging to a longer wave of forced migrations, stretching back at least through the 'black decade' of 1938–47.[25] The erection of fortified borders in late 1940s ended the black decade and marked the beginning of a period of probably the lowest international mobility in East European history. It also expressed the consolidation of the Soviet bloc as a Moscow-dominated system of territorially stable and closed (i.e. relatively isolated) communist states.

As much as it differs from the late 1940s, the post–Cold War period resembles that of post–First World War, when new states came into being, borders multiplied and Russia rolled back East. Post-1918 saw the first version of a Europe composed almost exclusively of nation states, the precedent for the Europe of today. The great reordering of the map after 1918 and 1989, respectively, followed a similar logic of nation state building out of larger multi-ethnic polities.

The First World War brought an end to the Romanov, Habsburg, Hohenzollern and Ottoman empires, and placed populations – not just borders or sovereign rulers – at the core of international politics. Participants in the Paris peace conference paid great attention to the state–population–territory nexus. Favoring the nation-state model, at least in Europe, they recognized the problems it had with inherited, postimperial diversity, and offered several solutions, ranging from experts looking into linguistic and ethnographic data and plebiscites to define optimal borders, to international protection of minority rights and population transfers. The latter two, as Eric Weitz points out, were two sides of the same coin. The most explicit approval for population transfer came in the Lausanne Treaty with Turkey, which provided international recognition of 'a compulsory exchange of Turkish nationals of the Greek Orthodox religion established in Turkish territory, and of Greek nationals of the Moslem religion established in Greek territory'. Proponents of similar solutions in the future will cite it as the legal precedent and proof of the effectiveness of transfer in discontinuing interethnic violence and stabilizing states.[26]

Map 2.3 Europe, 1993.

Source: Putzger (1995). © FNSP. Sciences Po – Atelier de cartographie, 2018.

The largest migration flows of the 1990s were also of a postimperial kind. These were the resettlement of the 'repatriates', that is, people moving to their alleged 'homelands' (which they often had left long ago, or to which they belonged only by virtue of their ethnic origin). The post-Soviet states tended towards an ethnonationalist principle that divided populations into the privileged titular nation and the rest. To the supporters of such policies, it appeared natural that ethnic Russians, Armenians or Estonians living outside of their titular republics should 'return to their historical homelands'. Not surprisingly, Russians and other Russophones, who had enjoyed a favorable position in the USSR, became the major group of such repatriates in the post-Soviet space.

In total, in the 1990s, about 4 million people resettled in the Russian Federation as repatriates, while more than half a million Russian speakers left the Caucasus and Central Asia for Ukraine and Belarus. The outflow was the largest from Kazakhstan, albeit in relative terms the erosion of Russophone population was greatest in the zones of violence such as the South Caucasus and Tajikistan. Russia also attracted many non-Russians, mostly Armenians and Ukrainians. Although Belarusians, Kazakhs or Turkmen were similarly moving to their 'historical homelands', the scale of these flows was much smaller. In general, repatriation was massive but far from ubiquitous, and ethnicity alone cannot explain it. Only a minority of the 25 million ethnic Russians and some 20 million other former Soviet citizens living outside their titular republics decided to resettle. In the Baltic states for example, despite the interethnic tensions, repatriation involved less than 10 per cent of ethnic Russians. More intensive was the outflow of the groups that enjoyed privileged immigration policies in countries outside the post-Soviet area, mainly ethnic Germans and Jews. For example, Kazakhstan has lost more than 80 per cent of its 1 million ethnic Germans. In total, 2.5 million German and Jewish emigrants left the post-Soviet space. Smaller but nonetheless substantial was the outflow of 150,000 ethnic Greeks to Greece.

To be sure, the disintegration of the USSR did not lead to an explosion of migrations but rather to a decline thereof. Between the last years of the USSR and the early 2000s, the migration flows between the (ex-)Soviet republics decreased from almost 2 million people annually to 700,000. This should not be a surprise, as the new international borders fragmented the once unified social, economic and legal space, making resettlement, and mobility in general, much more difficult. What did grow in the 1990s, and dramatically so, was migration into the Russian Federation: While in the 1980s it received a net immigration of 1.5 million people, in the following decade, it was 4.3 million.[27]

The patterns of post-Soviet resettlement flows resemble the 'unmixing of peoples' in the Balkans, as Lord Curzon had named the opposite flows of Muslim and Christian populations across the southward-moving Ottoman border in the long nineteenth century.[28] They were, and have been, the most recent of many postimperial migrations that since the nineteenth century have ensued in the vast belt of 'Rimlands', extending from the Baltic to the Near East and Transcaucasia. These migrations involved primarily the erstwhile ruling, or otherwise privileged, ethnic groups in a multinational empire that saw their status abruptly deteriorate into that of a minority in new nation states.

The imperial fragmentation included further remaking and unmaking of states – a process to which migration has all too often been central. While this process was repeatedly the key factor in mass population movements, the latter were by no means automatic or unavoidable, as evidenced by diverse migration propensities of ethnic Russians in the ex-Soviet republics or ethnic Germans in various Habsburg lands after the First World War. Except where whole communities were indiscriminately targeted for removal, the postimperial migrations were socially selective and, arguably, not always forced. Moreover, postimperial 'un-mixing' is not a short-term process that exhausts itself in the immediate aftermath of war or other political reconfiguration. It has been a protracted – if intermittent – process, spanning three-quarters of a century for Magyars and Germans, and more than a century for Turks. Russian gradual withdrawal from the peripheries of their vast empire, that is, the shift to a positive migration balance for the Russian Federation, began long before the Soviet collapse and certainly has the potential to continue on well into the future.[29]

From Brest to Belavezha

From the perspective of this essay, our first postwar period began not in Compiègne or Versailles, but in Brest-Litovsk, and in March rather than November 1918. On 3 March 1918, at the conference in Brest-Litovsk – once a fortress in the western borderlands of Russia, today a town at the Belorussian-Polish border – the delegations of Bolshevik Russia and the Central Powers signed the first peace treaty of the First World War. The conference became the key moment in the career of the principle of self-determination of nations. This idea not only dominated the Paris conference in the following year, but throughout most of twentieth-century statecraft *and* population transfers. Not incidentally, the three postwars under consideration have been recognized as the three key periods for the development of the principle.[30]

As Borislav Chernev points out, the diplomatic career of the principle began when the loud, Bolshevik support for this revolutionary, anti-imperialist idea came face-to-face in Brest-Litovsk with the self-interested, imperial plans for East-Central Europe held by the Central Powers.[31] The Powers' delegation welcomed the principle and used it effectively as a tool to legitimize their pushing Russia several hundred kilometers east. Austrian foreign affairs minister Ottokar Czernin put it explicitly in a letter to the German chancellor in November 1917: 'It would be our business to ensure that the desire for separation from Russia and for political and economic dependence on the Central Powers be voiced from within these [East European] nations.'[32] This strategy meant a transfer to Northeastern Europe of a process of ethnonational fragmentation, which, with a helping hand from European powers, had removed the Ottoman Empire from Southeastern Europe in the previous century. The Austrian and German imperial strategists decided for a controlled Balkanization of the Western Russian Empire, so as to establish a system of satellite nation states. It was a risky gamble, as it soon turned out. Several months later, Austro-Hungary followed the Balkan fate of the Ottoman empire, and Ottokar Czernin lost his family lands in what became Czechoslovakia.

The Central Powers forced Russia to abandon most of its European acquisitions gained since the time of Peter the Great, and allowed for the construction of new states between the Baltic and the Black Sea – in particular Ukraine. The first modern Ukrainian state was recognized at the Brest-Litovsk conference. Thus, despite the fact that the March 1918 treaties lasted not even a year, we can consider the conference as a stepping stone for the process of nation-state building in Eastern Europe. It was also the antecedent of another consequential conference, which took place close to Brest in the third postwar period: In December 1991, at a hunting estate in the Belavezha forest, 80 km north of Brest, the presidents of the Soviet republics of Russia, Ukraine and Belarus signed the agreement that dissolved the USSR.[33]

The road from Brest to Belavezha was neither direct nor straight. In between these two Wilsonian moments, the town of Brest was the scene of another event notable in our story: the joint Soviet–German military parade on 22 September 1939, which celebrated the successful partition of Poland. No event better illustrates the joint German–Soviet destruction of the Versailles order, and their division of the lands between the Baltic and the Black Sea into two imperial 'spheres of influence'. It also illustrates the argument that the narrative of the European twentieth century, structured by the three great wars and postwars, is as much Germano-centric as it is Russo-centric.[34]

The parade and the German–Soviet Boundary and Friendship Treaty, signed a week later, were to mark the end of war in Eastern Europe, not unlike the Brest treaty of 1918. They demonstrated Russia's return to the lands abandoned twenty years before, and Germany's acquiescence thereto. The Communist and Nazi revolutionaries who signed the treaty clearly shared a belief in radical methods of making international relations, states and societies. These methods took the solving of the state–territory–population nexus to another level. Notably, the secret protocol attached to the Boundary and Friendship Treaty outlined minority exchanges, sparking a long series of international agreements on population transfers in the following decade.[35]

If the Brest parade of 1939 marked a shift back from the national to the imperial solution of the nexus, how and when did the tide change again in favor of independent nation states, which we see in the 1990s? The internal, domestic factors in the nationalist victories in (post)communist states are considered in the following. Explaining their international conditions seems, however, more difficult. This would require determining why, at the moment of the communist regimes' implosion, there were no candidates for imperial domination of the region; indeed, this exceeds the scope of this essay. We can only go so far as to add that this absence was an important condition in the apparent lack of fear of establishing small, vulnerable states. The Croat, Slovene or Slovak leaders in the post–First World War period had had reasons to federate with their Czech or Serb neighbors, which their successors clearly did not see in the 1990s.

When inquiring as to what contributed to nationalist victory in the 1990s, we can point to two interesting shifts in the meaning, or application, of the principle of self-determination: During the Cold War era, the road from Brest to Belavezha went via places as distant as Bandung and Helsinki.

The principle of self-determination became so widely accepted in the course of the twentieth century not least because it was vague and allowed for diverse interpretations. In particular, despite being loudly proclaimed with respect to the territory of the vanquished following the First World War, this was done with no intention of undermining the colonial empires of the victors. Eventually, self-determination did contribute to decolonization after the Second World War, but in its travels across the decomposing overseas empires, the principle acquired a novel, territorial aspect, or definition.[36] This definition, first applied in international relations in the delineation of borders in postcolonial South America in the nineteenth century, and further developed for the postcolonial situations in Asia and Africa, took the name of *uti possidetis juris*. This meant recognition of pre-existing administrative boundaries as the borders between newly independent nations.[37] These distant developments, symbolized by the 1955 Bandung conference of Asian and African postcolonial states, contributed to post–Cold War European settlement. The *uti possidetis* became a basis of, and explicit reference for, the firm support by European Powers for maintaining pre-existing boundaries in the 1990s. The international recognition of the new states was, inter alia, based on their respect for these boundaries.[38] None of the new international borders in post–Cold War Europe was invented after 1989. They had all existed previously as internal borders within the federal states: They changed their status, but not their shape.[39]

The second detour on the Brest–Belavezha road was via Helsinki, the capital of the new territory of the human rights, which emerged during the Cold War era. The human rights doctrine, gradually enshrined in law during the Cold War, became a part of a legal mechanism to achieve a range of human rights *within* the territorial framework of states, rather than simply a tool to justify the dismantling of states. Many international statements on the territorial reconstruction of the 1990s stressed both the protection of human rights and the stability of borders, and referred specifically to the Helsinki Final Act.[40]

The predecessor of the human rights doctrine was the idea of international protection of minorities. The post-1918 period was the high moment of this idea, which had developed in response to the nation-state building in the European postimperial space, beginning, again, in the Balkans. At the Paris peace conference, all the new states of Eastern Europe had to sign treaties guaranteeing the rights of their respective minorities. The combination of minority protection and minority reduction (by 'exchanges of minorities' and 'national options') was the cornerstone of the post–First World War model of solving the national minority question, as it was understood at the moment. Its apparent failure, and the explosion of ethnic violence through the black decade 1938–47, led to the reframing of minority rights as universal human rights.[41]

The practical application of the rights doctrine had to wait some time, but in the third postwar period, it reached a point unimaginable in the 1920s or 1940s. A state's 'right to expel', which had been considered both rational and justifiable in the previous postwar periods, gave way to the 'responsibility to protect', including an obligation not only to prevent ethnic cleansing, but to reverse it. Howard Adelman and Elazar Barkan in their *No Return, No Refuge,* point at a striking shift in the moral evaluation and legal qualification of state-induced, forced migration of ethnic groups. That which, up until the late 1940s, was euphemistically called population transfer and perceived as a legal means to commendable goals of state consolidation and prevention of war, became condemned as a crime against humanity.[42]

It bears noting that the boundaries so stridently protected in the 1990s did not necessarily reflect the geographic distribution of ethnic groups, nor were they optimal in an economic or strategic sense. Sometimes they had been arbitrarily set and reset as internal administrative lines, as exemplified by the well-known case of Crimea, transferred by Khrushchev from Soviet Russia to Ukraine. The key reason to protect rather than redraw them as national borders was their pre-existence. Altering the borders (except by agreement) seemed likely to lead to a chain of violent fragmentations of states, producing instability and further ethnic conflicts, that is, Balkanization, as such a process became widely known in the first of our postwar periods. The recent Russian annexation of Crimea ignored this lesson of the past and opened a new, risky stage in the aforementioned process of East European (and Eurasian) territorial reordering.

In the 1990s, for most international organizations and Western leaders, annexation and partition had long been dirty words.[43] In the second half of the twentieth century, despite many political upheavals, the boundaries on the political map changed little. As any territorial gain by one state meant a loss for another one, which cannot but generate conflict, international law has strongly favored the status quo regarding borders. All states joining the United Nations solemnly renounce the use of war to expand their territory. The invention of the defensive state, which formally uses war only to deter or defeat threats to its territory, and made all ministries of war change their labels to ministries of defense, further stabilized the borders. In Europe, all the signatories of the Helsinki Act made no claims on others' territories – a previously unheard-of situation for this continent.[44] The 1990s were also a high point of European integration, and many saw the revival of ethnonationalist divisions in the East as backward and immature. Thus, having accepted the secession of Slovenia and Croatia as a consequence of the dissolution of federal Yugoslavia, Western powers denied the right to secession to the Serb-dominated areas of Croatia and Bosnia. Yet the Serb desire for the secession was fueled by a fear rooted in memories of the same bloody conflicts of the past that made other powers oppose the secession.

This controversy reflected an essential disagreement on what makes good statehood. The European leaders no longer believed that the ethnically homogeneous nation state was the most desirable model for a modern polity, or even a feasible one. Instead, their favored model was a liberal democratic state that respected human and minority rights. Such a state can allegedly function within almost any border, making the choice of pre-existing administrative borders as sensible as any other, with the added advantage of being less risky and costly than their change.[45] This contrasted with the position held by key powers in the previous periods under consideration. In post-1918, they had encouraged or approved borders drawn along ethnic lines and/or a process of ethnic homogenization through more or less compulsory minority transfers. Such apparent solutions were applied at the borders between Bulgaria and Greece, Greece and Turkey, Germany and Poland, France and Germany and Poland and Russia. In post-1945, the great powers had agreed that ethnic homogeneity in border areas was a prerequisite for stability in Central and Southeastern Europe. Local hatred and the desire of national leaders to get rid of some groups were in the background of the great resettlement programs of mid-1940s, but these programs were possible because of being part of the Soviet and British plans for a new order in Europe.[46]

There were, of course, also reasons other than political philosophy that made unlikely a Lord Curzon-esque charting of East European borders along ethnic lines in the 1990s. In post-1918 or post-1945, politicians could (inaccurately) claim that France or Germany was ethnically homogeneous. In the 1990s, this was evidently not the case. Millions of non-European guest workers, refugees and their Europe-born children had made many West European cities surprisingly similar in ethnic diversity to that of their

East European counterparts prior to the Second World War; meanwhile, many of the latter had lost this diversity. Some of the powers were also grappling with their own separatist movements, which they wisely did not want to bolster by endorsing separatism elsewhere. Through the 1990s and thereafter, it has been clear that the potential for state fragmentation in Europe has been by no means exhausted. In addition to the apparently effective secession of Kosovo, separatist tendencies have been visible not only in Bosnia but also in Belgium, France, Italy, Moldova, the Russian Federation, Spain, Ukraine and the United Kingdom, to list just the major controversies.

Similar factors protected the borders of the Soviet republics as these became nation states. Moreover, the dissolution of the USSR was relatively peaceful, cushioned as it was by the establishment of the Commonwealth of Independent States and carried out by the USSR's three core, founding republics: Russia, Ukraine and Belarus. We can hardly imagine such a peaceful end of the Soviet Union without the willingness of Russian leaders to abandon it. While Russia has supported Serbia in the post-Yugoslav conflicts, if we compare the Soviet and Yugoslav disintegrations, we see that Russia's role in the Soviet dissolution was more similar to that of Croatia than to that of Serbia in the Yugoslav case.

Yugoslavia requires us to refine

The aforementioned narratives of the 1990s as the third European postwar period of the twentieth century and as a return to the nation-state solution after a return of imperial order cannot explain the most dramatic chapter of the history of the 1990s. This is the chapter on the former Yugoslavia, a state which had been neither part of the Soviet empire nor a member of a Cold War alliance.

The end of the Cold War and the end of the Cold War division of Germany and Europe, symbolized by the fall of the Berlin Wall, seem to dominate popular images of 1989.[47] However, for many of the non-German participants in the events, the most important end in 1989 was the end of their communist regimes. The experience of the communist regime and its end unites all three dissolved states and offers a hint as to where to look for the causes of their fragmentation.

What seems the key to explaining the post-1989 border changes and the ensuing population movements is a particular, ethnonationalist way of dismantling, or leaving behind, the communist regimes, in particular the communist regimes of supranational polities. Among the decay and ruin of the regimes, ethnonational affiliation became the unifying characteristic, empowering the local national elites to use this to consolidate or expand their rule.[48]

Widespread and intensive ethnonationalisms had predated the communist regime, yet by the 1990s they were also a fruit of the evolution of the regime, its increasingly nationalist legitimization in particular.[49] In the societies of the 'advanced construction of socialism' (the 'really existing socialism') the ethnonational was pervasive, both in the communist nation states such as Poland or Hungary and in the communist federations: the USSR, Czechoslovakia and Yugoslavia. Rogers Brubaker has rightly stressed that Soviet institutions of territorial nationhood and personal nationality constituted a 'pervasive system of social classification, an organizing principle of vision and division of the social world, a standardized scheme of social accounting, an interpretative grid for public discussion, and a set of boundary-markers, a legitimate form for public and private identities'.[50] This seems to apply well also to Yugoslavia and Czechoslovakia. The federal governments of the three states were supranational in the same sense and to the same extent that their federated republics were ethnonational. In their demands for independence in the 1990s, the leaders of the Soviet and Yugoslav republics could call on the principles enshrined in their federal constitutions, which in turn had their origins in the principle of national self-determination.[51] As long as the communist parties maintained their monocentric regimes, these were slogans with limited practical consequences. Yet, when the regimes eroded at the Cold War's end, new ethnonationalist leaders (no matter if they had been communist party members or anti-communists) found in them a ready-made basis for their secessionist claims. The ethnonationalism was therefore both symbiotic with the late communist regime and sufficiently opposed to its ideology, to naturally become its successors. They offered ways to overcome or externalize the internal conflicts and desires for revenge resulting from decades of dictatorship and abuse.

The role of the ethnonationalist exit strategy seems obvious in case of the three federal states that disintegrated along ethnonational lines. It also appears, however, in the GDR, one of the two states of *ein Volk* that united in 1990. We may find it similarly in Poland and Hungary, where *national* unity above the political divisions and *national* compromise were the basis for the peaceful transition from communism, and in Romania, where the revolution of December 1989 defeated the Ceausescu regime under the national flag (with the Soviet-style coat of arms excised).

The post-communist ethnonationalism emerged from the communist one. The latter was not oxymoronic – because of the evolution of communist ideas and practices, from the initial revolutionary internationalism, deep suspicion of nationalism and struggle against it, into making it a pillar, and eventually the pillar of respective regimes. By accepting and then nurturing widespread nationalist emotions, which proved vital at the moments of the regimes' crises, the communist leaders laid the foundation for the disintegration of the Soviet bloc and their federal countries.

Notes

1   Andreas Wimmer and Yuval Feinstein, 'The Rise of the Nation-State across the World, 1816 to 2001', *American Sociological Review* 75, No. 5 (2010): 764–90. Andreas Wimmer and Brian Min, 'From Empire to Nation-State: Explaining Wars in the Modern World, 1816-2001', *American Sociological Review* 71, No. 6 (2006): 867–97.

2   Chris Patten, 'Speech at the Western Balkans Democracy Forum, Thessaloniki' http://ec.europa.eu/enlargement/archives/ear/publications/main/pub-speech_ thessaloniki_20020411.htm (accessed 22.6.2014).

3   This is not because its author comes from Central Europe and sees the world from an East European perspective. While these factors play a role, of course, they were among the many reasons he chose to write on the topic in this collective volume.

4   The same may be said about Albania, which left the Soviet bloc to join communist China in the 1960s.

5   These were Finland, Estonia, Latvia, Lithuania, Poland, Czechoslovakia, Yugoslavia and Ireland. We exclude the Free City of Danzig/Gdańsk and the Free State of Fiume, established in the first postwar period, and the Free Territory of Trieste, a product of the second one, whose sovereignty was limited.

6   Philipp Ther, *Ciemna strona państw narodowych: Czystki etniczne w nowoczesnej Europie* (Poznań: Wyd. Poznańskie, 2012), 137–40 (original German edition: Philipp Ther, *Die dunkle seite der Nationalstaaten: 'Ethnische Säuberungen' im modernen Europa* (Göttingen: Vandenhoeck & Ruprecht, 2011).

7   Ewa Morawska, 'Intended and Unintended Consequences of Forced Migrations: A Neglected Aspect of East Europe's Twentieth Century History', *International Migration Review* 34, No. 4 (2000): 1049–87. More accurately, these figures refer to displacements rather than persons displaced, as some individuals were relocated more than once. The degree of compulsion in these involuntary movements varied. See also Peter Gatrell, 'Introduction: World Wars and Population Displacement in Europe in the Twentieth Century', *Contemporary European History* 16, Special Issue 4 (2007): 415–26; Dariusz Stola, 'Forced Migrations in Central European History', *International Migration Review* 26, No. 2 (Summer 1992): 324–41.

8   The East European Borderlands, Rimlands, Warlands and Bloodlands, as they have been variously named, have recently attracted growing interest of contemporary historians; see Nick Baron and Peter Gatrell, *Homelands: War, Population and Statehood in Eastern Europe and Russia, 1918–1924* (London: Anthem Press, 2004); Peter Gatrell and Nick Baron, *Warlands: Population Resettlement and State Reconstruction in the Soviet-East European Borderlands, 1945–50* (Basingstoke: Palgrave Macmillan, 2009); Mark Levene, 'The Tragedy of Rimlands, Nation-State Formation and the Destruction of Imperial Peoples, 1912–1948', in *Refugees and the End of Empire: Imperial Collapse and Forced Migration in the Twentieth Century*, ed. Panikos Panayi and Pippa Virdee (New York: Palgrave Macmillan, 2011), 51–80; Alexander V. Prusin, *The Lands Between: Conflict in the East European Borderlands, 1870–1992* (Oxford: Oxford University Press, 2010); Alexander V. Prusin, *Nationalizing a Borderland: War, Ethnicity, and Anti-Jewish Violence in East Galicia, 1914–1920* (Tuscaloosa: University of Alabama Press, 2005); Timothy Snyder, *Bloodlands: Europe between Hitler and Stalin* (New York: Basic Books, 2010). For an analysis of a wider space in a longer period, see Alfred J. Rieber, *The Struggle for the Eurasian Borderlands* (Cambridge: Cambridge University Press, 2014).

9   As an expert in border history noted: 1989 'was followed by a revision of frontiers which had previously happened only after major wars'. See Malcolm Anderson, *Frontiers: Territory and State Formation in the Modern World* (Cambridge: Polity Press, 2004), 58.

10 The list of European states follows the catalogue of the UN Statistics Division. Data on border lengths are from the Central Intelligence Agency (CIA): 'The World Factbook' (https://www.cia.gov/library/publications/the-world-factbook/index.html, accessed 20.2.2012); for Russia, the calculation includes only its new European borders.

11 Maxim Waldstein and Sanna Turoma, 'Introduction: Empire and Space. Russian and the Soviet Union in Focus', in *Empire De/Centered: New Spatial Histories of Russia and the Soviet Union*, ed. Maxim Waldstein and Sanna Turoma (Burlington: Ashgate Publishing, 2013), 1–30; David Chioni Moore, 'Is the Post- in Postcolonial the Post- in

Post-Soviet? Toward a Global Postcolonial Critique', *Publications of the Modern Language Association of America* 116, No. 1 (2001): 111–28.

12 The GDR–FRG border did not disappear altogether. Restrictions imposed by the USSR in the German Treaty of 1990 have prevented the stationing of foreign troops and nuclear weapons in the territory of the former GDR, making the *Neuen Bundesländer* a special part of the FRG and NATO.

13 Ilko-Sascha Kowalczuk and Stefan Wolle, *Roter Stern über Deutschland: Sowjetische Truppen in der DDR* (Berlin: Links, 2001), 225. Mariusz Lesław Krogulski, *Okupacja w imię sojuszu: Armia Radziecka w Polsce, 1956–1993* (Warsaw: von Borowiecky, 2001); Robert E. Harkavy, *Bases Abroad: The Global Foreign Military Presence* (Oxford and Stockholm: Oxford University Press, 1989); US Department of Defense, 'Active Duty Military Personnel Strengths by Regional Area and by Country', 1987 and 1997, http://siadapp.dmdc.osd.mil/personnel/MILITARY/history/309hist.htm (accessed 10.4.2012). The exception in the Soviet/Russian withdrawal from Central Europe was the Kaliningrad exclave, a transit or destination place for many of the relocating troops, which in 1990 made it the place of highest concentration of military personnel in the continent.

14 Human Security Centre, *Human Security Report 2005* (Oxford: Oxford University Press, 2006), part V; Andrew Mack, 'Global Political Violence: Explaining the Post-Cold War Decline', in *Strategies for Peace: Contributions of International Organisations, States, and Non-State Actors*, ed. Volker Rittberger and Martina Fischer (Opladen and Farmington Hills: Budrich Verlag, 2008), 75–107.

15 Michael Marrus, *The Unwanted: European Refugees in the Twentieth Century* (New York: Oxford University Press, 1985), 296n.

16 Peter Gatrell and Nick Baron, 'Violent Peacetime: Reconceptualizing Displacement and Resettlement in the Soviet-East European Borderlands after the Second World War', in *Warlands: Population Resettlement and State Reconstruction in the Soviet-East European Borderlands, 1945–50*, ed. Peter Gatrell and Nick Baron (Basingstoke: Palgrave Macmillan, 2009), 255–68; Peter Gatrell, 'Trajectories of Population Displacement in the Aftermaths of Two World Wars', in *The Disentanglement of Populations: Migration, Expulsion and Displacement in Post-War Europe, 1944–49*, ed. Jessica Reinisch and Elizabeth White (Basingstoke: Palgrave Macmillan, 2011), 3–26.

17 Norman M. Naimark, *Fires of Hatred: Ethnic Cleansing in Twentieth-Century Europe* (Cambridge, MA: Harvard University Press, 2001), chapter 5; Ther, *Ciemna strona*; United Nations Economic Commission for Europe, *International Migration Bulletin No. 9* (1996); United Nations High Commissioner for Refugees, *The State of the World's Refugees, 2000* (Oxford: Oxford University Press, 2000), chapter 9.

18 Andrei V. Korobkov and Zhanna Zaionchkovskaia, 'The Changes in the Migration Patterns in the Post-Soviet States: The First Decade', *Communist and Post-Communist Studies* 37, No. 4 (2004): 481–508; Valery Tishkov, Zhanna Zayinchkovskaya and Galina Vitkovskaya, *Migration in the Countries of the Former Soviet Union* (Geneva: Global Commission on International Migration, 2005).

19 Rogers Brubaker and David D. Laitin, 'Ethnic and Nationalist Violence', *Annual Review of Sociology* 24, No. 2 (1998): 425; Katherine Verdery, 'Nationalism and National Sentiment in Post-Socialist Romania', *Slavic Review* 52, No. 2 (1993): 179–203; Panikos Panayi, 'Imperial Collapse and the Creation of Refugees in Twentieth-Century Europe', in *Refugees and the End of Empire: Imperial Collapse and Forced Migration in the Twentieth Century*, ed. Panikos Panayi and Pippa Virdee (Houndmills; New York: Palgrave Macmillan, 2011), 3–27.

20 The countries that were not reduced (or even did expand, at the expense of Italy) – Greece, Albania, Yugoslavia and Bulgaria – were incidentally those that had no border with the USSR.

21 Anne Applebaum, *Iron Curtain: The Crushing of Eastern Europe, 1944–1956* (New York: Doubleday, 2012). Yugoslavia, with its independent communist regime, was truly a land in-between East and West.

22 Hungarian writer Sandor Marai wrote that the Soviet soldier could not bring freedom because he himself had none, but he brought deliverance from the German terror (as quoted by Albina F. Noskova, 'Zwycięstwo i zniewolenie', in *Białe plamy – czarne plamy: Sprawy trudne w polsko-rosyjskich stosunkach, 1918–2008*, ed. Adam Daniel Rotfeld and Anatolij Vasil'evič Torkunov (Warsaw: PISM, 2010), 440). On the other hand, Hungarian or Bulgarian governments had had greater autonomy as German satellites before 1944, than they had as Soviet satellites four years later.

23 Sabine Dullin, 'L'invention d'une frontière de guerre froide à l'ouest de l'URSS (1945–1949)', *Vingtième siècle. Revue d'histoire* No. 102 (2009): 49–63; Dariusz Stola, *Kraj bez wyjścia? Migracje z Polski 1949–1989* (Warszawa: IPN, ISP PAN, 2010), chapter I.

24 Similarly, the dissolution of the USSR would have been much different, if possible, if the Soviet Union had not been an 'empire of nations' (even if the Russian one had a privileged position among them). See Francine Hirsch, *Empire of Nations: Ethnographic Knowledge and the Making of the Soviet Union* (Ithaca: Cornell University Press, 2005); Terry Martin, *The Affirmative Action Empire: Nations and Nationalism in the Soviet Union, 1923–1939* (Ithaca: Cornell University Press, 2001).

25 Stola, 'Forced Migrations'; Alfred J. Rieber *Forced Migration in Central and Eastern Europe, 1939–1950* (London: Frank Cass, 2000); E. M. Kulischer, *Europe on the Move: War and Population Changes, 1917–47* (New York: Columbia University Press, 1948).

26 Ther, *Ciemna strona*, 142–69; Eric D. Weitz, 'From the Vienna to the Paris System: International Politics and the Entangled Histories of Human Rights, Forced Deportations, and Civilizing Missions', *American Historical Review* 113, No. 5 (2008): 1313–43.

27 Andrei Korobkov and Zhanna Zaionchkovskaia, 'The Changes in the Migration Patterns'; International Organization for Migration, 'Migration Trends in Eastern Europe and Central Asia' (Geneva: International Organization for Migration, 2002); Eftihia Voutira, 'Ethnic Greeks from the Former Soviet Union as "Privileged Return Migrants"', *Espace populations sociétés/Space populations societies* No. 2004/3 (2004): 533–44. The figures refer to registered migrants only, excluding substantial illegal flows.

28 Marrus, *The Unwanted*, 41; Matthew Frank, 'Fantasies of Ethnic Unmixing: "Population Transfer" at the End of Empire in Europe', in *Refugees and the End of Empire*, ed. Panayi and Virdee, 81–101. The term 'unmixing' was not only misleading (as if pure, non-mixed populations were the natural state) but obscured how much mixture still remained.

29 Rogers Brubaker, 'Aftermaths of Empire and the Unmixing of Peoples: Historical and Comparative Perspectives', *Ethnic and Racial Studies* 18, No. 2 (1995): 191; Panayi, 'Imperial collapse'; Levene, 'The Tragedy of Rimlands'; Mark Mazower, 'Violence and the State in the Twentieth Century', *The American Historical Review* 107, No. 4 (2002): 1174.

30 Aviel Roshwald, *Ethnic Nationalism and the Fall of Empires: Central Europe, Russia, and the Middle East, 1914–1923* (London and New York: Routledge, 2001); Antonio

Cassese, *Self-Determination of Peoples: A Legal Reappraisal* (Cambridge: Cambridge University Press, 1995).

31 Borislav Chernev, 'The Brest-Litovsk Moment: Self-Determination Discourse in Eastern Europe before Wilsonianism', *Diplomacy and Statecraft* 22, No. 3 (2011): 369–87; Weitz, 'From the Vienna to the Paris System'. Lenin and Stalin had been outspoken on the principle for several years before the Brest conference; see for example Lenin's 'The Right of Nations to Self-Determination'. Lenin's article was first published in journal *Prosveshcheniye*, Nos. 4–6, 1914. Stalin's one was first published in the same journal *Prosveshcheniye*, Nos. 3–5, 1913.

32 Letter of Czernin to von Hertling of 10 November 1917, in: *Proceedings of the Brest-Litovsk Peace Conference: The Peace Negotiations between Russia and the Central Powers 21 November, 1917–3 March, 1918* (Washington, DC: U.S. Government Printing Office, 1918), 8, quoted by Chernev, 'The Brest-Litovsk Moment': 372.

33 The Baltic states regained their independence several months earlier: the European Communities' statement of August 1991 warmly welcomed 'the restoration of the sovereignty and independence of the Baltic states which they lost in 1940'. See Roland Rich, 'Recognition of States: The Collapse of Yugoslavia and the Soviet Union', *European Journal of International Law* 4, No. 1 (1993): 38.

34 Sławomir Dębski, *Między Berlinem a Moskwą: Stosunki niemiecko-sowieckie 1939–1941* (Warszawa: PISM, 2007). The town and fortress of Brest was first taken by German troops, who handed it over to the Soviets. A film footage of the parade and related Nazi-Soviet camaraderie is available online.

35 The Confidential Protocol to the German-Soviet Boundary and Friendship Treaty of 28 September 1939, http://avalon.law.yale.edu (accessed 20.1.2014).

36 Hurst Hannum, *Autonomy, Sovereignty, and Self-Determination: The Accommodation of Conflicting Rights* (Philadelphia: University of Pennsylvania Press, 1996), 27–28; Malcolm N. Shaw, 'Peoples, Territorialism and Boundaries', *European Journal of International Law* 8, No. 3 (1997): 481.

37 Steven R. Ratner, 'Drawing a Better Line: Uti Possidetis and the Borders of New States', *The American Journal of International Law* 90, No. 4 (1996): 590–624; Tomasz Srogosz, 'Geneza zasady "Uti Possidetis" w prawie międzynarodowym publicznym: kilka uwag o kształtowaniu granic państwowych w Ameryce Łacińskiej w XIX i XX wieku', *Czasopismo Prawno-Historyczne* 63, No. 2 (2011): 329–42.

38 Alain Pellet, 'The Opinions of the Badinter Arbitration Committee: A Second Breath for the Self-Determination of Peoples', *European Journal of International Law* 3, No. 1 (1992): 178–85. As per the USSR, the Belavezha agreement and the Charter of the Commonwealth of Independent States adopted in Minsk on 22 January 1993 included a clear 'recognition of existing frontiers'.

39 Fifteen new states had existed as (formally) autonomous republics within larger federal polities; the sixteenth (and most problematic) Kosovo had been an autonomous province of the republic of Serbia.

40 Shaw, 'Peoples, Territorialism and Boundaries': 482–96; Ana S. Trbovich, *A Legal Geography of Yugoslavia's Disintegration* (Oxford: Oxford University Press, 2009), 23–25. The statements include the Dayton Agreement, the EC Foreign Ministers' Declaration on the Guidelines on the Recognition of the New States, and their Declaration on Yugoslavia of December 1991.

41 Weitz, 'From the Vienna to the Paris System'; Mark Mazower, 'The Strange Triumph of Human Rights, 1933–1950', *The Historical Journal* 47, No. 2 (2004): 379–98.

42 Howard Adelman and Elazar Barkan, *No Return, No Refuge: Rites and Rights in Minority Repatriation* (New York: Columbia University Press, 2011); Stefan Troebst, 'The Discourse on Forced Migration and European Culture of Remembrance', *Hungarian Historical Review* No. 3–4 (2012): 397–414.

43 Chaim D. Kaufmann, 'When All Else Fails: Ethnic Population Transfers and Partitions in the Twentieth Century', *International Security* 23, No. 2 (1998): 120–56; Susan L. Woodward, *Balkan Tragedy: Chaos and Dissolution after the Cold War* (Washington, DC: Brookings Institution, 1995), 205.

44 Peter J. Taylor, 'The State as Container: Territoriality in the Modern World-System', *Progress in Human Geography* 18, No. 2 (1994): 153–54.

45 Ratner, 'Drawing a Better Line': 591.

46 Ther, *Ciemna strona*, chapter 3.1; Marina Cattaruzza, ' "Last Stop Expulsion" – the Minority Question and Forced Migration in East-Central Europe: 1918–49', *Nations and Nationalism* 16, No. 1 (2010): 121.

47 A very short (0.35 second) Google research on what is the 'Cold War symbol' leaves no doubt that it is the Berlin Wall and the divided Berlin in general.

48 For a sophisticated statistical analysis of nationalism's role in dismantling the Soviet Union, see Mark R. Beissinger, *Nationalist Mobilization and the Collapse of the Soviet State* (Cambridge: Cambridge University Press, 2002).

49 On nationalist legitimization of communist regimes see Amir Weiner, *Making Sense of War: The Second World War and the Fate of the Bolshevik Revolution* (Princeton: Princeton University Press, 2001). Marcin Zaremba, *Komunizm, legitymizacja, nacjonalizm. Nacjonalistyczna legitymizacja władzy komunistycznej w Polsce* (Warsaw: Trio, 2001).

50 Rogers Brubaker, 'Nationhood and the National Question in the Soviet Union and Post-Soviet Eurasia: An Institutionalist Account', *Theory and Society* 23, No. 1 (1994): 48.

51 See art. 4 of the Soviet constitution of 1924, art. 17 of the Soviet constitution of 1936, arts. 70 and 72 of the constitution of 1977.

3

Justice

Guillaume Mouralis and Annette Weinke

Does it make sense to use '1989' as the departure for a regressive analysis of European history? If we consider the versatility and malleability of 1919, 1945 and 1989 as symbols, it is clear that there is no simple and straightforward answer. A possible answer lies in the ways in which contemporaries drew analogies between these same turning points. Before and after the defeat of National Socialism, for example, members of the Western military coalition often compared the situation to that after the First World War and the failed attempts to convene an international tribunal to try crimes by the German leadership and soldiers. The fall of communism seems also to have evoked a sense of déjà vu. In unified Germany, advocates as well as opponents of lustration measures against communist elites pointed to the so-called lessons of allied de-Nazification. In some post-communist countries, redressing the communist past went hand in hand with retributive measures against former collaborators of the Nazi regime – a task which in some respects was considered as 'unfinished business' of the Cold War.

A comparison of the different conceptions of justice after 1989, 1945 and 1919 allows for a different argument, however. The new sub-discipline of 'transitional justice' (TJ), which emerged in the 1990s at the intersections of applied social science, diplomacy and political activism, has fostered a narrative of the 1989 events as the end of a longer historical trajectory that began with the ideas of the enlightenment and the revolutionary goals of '1789'. The fact that transnational human rights non-governmental organizations (NGOs) and international courts have become something of a worldwide growth industry during the past twenty-five years is embedded in a progressive storyline that celebrates the power of liberalism, individual rights to freedom and civil society.[1] In another version of this tale, the years from 1945 to 1948 are presented as a short interval in which liberal and socialist advocates of internationalism, human rights and humanitarianism sought to draw the right 'lessons' from the common struggle against Nazi barbarism.[2] According to Mark Mazower, this strand of literature uncritically presumes a 'commonly accepted late twentieth-century therapeutic model', in which 'public accounting of the past was good', while 'botched or failed purges were a sign of political ill-health or problems stored up for the future.'[3] The seductive and simplistic character of these teleological narratives calls not only for closer scrutiny by historians, but also makes a backward reading of twentieth-century history an intellectually fascinating and possibly heuristic endeavor. Moreover, it has been argued that historiography and social sciences may forfeit their emancipatory potential by uncritically adopting legal categories and tools.[4]

Critics of the normative TJ model often rightfully claim that during most of the twentieth century, 'justice' had a much broader meaning than is implied in current TJ and international criminal law (ICL) discourses. One of the main accomplishments of TJ as a political practice and academic research agenda can be discerned in how it managed to reframe the concept of justice by not only taking the liberal separation between political-institutional and economic spheres for granted, but also by making competing notions of justice almost invisible.[5] More than being *apolitical* or *unpolitical*, this discourse has a number of far-reaching *depoliticizing* effects: First, TJ ties regime change to a negotiated transition from authoritarian rule to representative democracy and liberal markets and second it narrows justice to the technocratic level of institution building and promoting the rule of law. This is technocratic in the sense that processes of socio-economic modernization, democratization and constitutional change, once considered the long-term projects of a pluralistic society, should now be implemented 'from above' by a handful of economic experts and policy advisors according to market criteria. Victim–perpetrator dichotomies provide a vivid example of the political implications of this discourse. Often these are based on the naive assumption that former victims of human rights violations, members of the 'silent' majority and the actual beneficiaries of the previous oppression share something like a moral consensus on assessments of 'just' or 'unjust'.

Critical TJ scholars and, more recently, a number of human rights historians, have argued that this narrow definition of justice is the product of what Nancy Fraser has called the 'justice interruptus' of the 'postsocialist condition'.[6] This strand of literature contends that the sudden emergence of human rights as a powerful transnational framework is actually connected to the parallel implementation of a global neo-liberal project, one that favors market deregulation, privatization and the opening of markets to foreign investments over inward-looking, state-interventionist strategies. Samuel Moyn, for instance, made the provocative observation that the birth of a new sense of justice, vested in the moral utopia of human rights, coincided with the death of political utopias.[7] Contrary to this, authors like Susan Marks and Mary Nolan interpret human rights and market fundamentalism as two crucial pillars of neo-liberalism. Rather than symbolizing the end of older political aspirations like equality and solidarity, they see the prescribed transformation of humans into self-interested, atomized individuals as the ultimate new goal and 'last utopia' left.[8]

The question is whether any of these interpretations adequately reflect the complicated entanglements between different conceptions of justice and the particular situation of a transitional setting – a constellation referred to herein as 'postwar justice moments'. At the same time, it has to be noted that the prefix 'post' is questionable, for it implies a simplistic succession from one sequence ('war') to the next one ('postwar'); this no longer reflects recent, more dynamic approaches that have shifted from a 'postwar period' *stricto sensu* to that of an 'exit from war'.[9] It is precisely the backward perspective that underscores the entanglement of processes and temporalities, since each postwar period is constructed and defined in relation to previous postwar periods.

This essay confronts the question of whether postwar situations have generated a particular notion of justice, and, if in the affirmative, whether this notion underwent any changes over time and how this has affected discourses and practices.

In each period under consideration, postwar justice has been shaped by at least three tensions: first, there is an ongoing tension between an individual conception of justice (that of criminal law or human and social rights), and a more collective approach to justice (the latter being either legalistic, like the post-1918 Wilsonian conception of international justice, or extralegal, traditional and archaic like the ethnic and/ or political purges seen after 1918, 1945 and 1989). A second tension can be observed throughout the century, that between a distributive conception of justice on one hand and a more rights-oriented notion on the other. The third and final tension juxtaposes a legal-institutional conception of justice with a more historical notion thereof, the latter being understood as achievement of justice through a 'lucid' examination of the past. As we shall see in this chapter, these tensions, although present in each postwar era, were more or less acute depending on the context. In other words, the relative weight of the divergent conceptions mentioned here experienced significant change over time.

In addition, the backward perspective of this volume invites us to reflect on the terms under which past experiences of justice are invoked in each postwar period: be it through the classical logic of legal precedent, the complex circulation and transformation of categories, savoir-faire and arguments over time and space[10] or the normative discourse on the (bad or good) 'lessons of the past', postwar justice is necessarily built on previous experiences. This contributes to the interweaving of conceptions and to the coexistence of seemingly contradictory practices.[11] Competing notions of the social, ethnic and religious characters of the future body politic led to different definitions of justice that could be applied to different majority and minority populations. As will be argued here, retributive policies with its quest for individual or collective accountability often directly or indirectly claimed to follow a path that had been laid out in other postwar periods or preceding conflicts, either by perpetuating or by reversing them. In the French case, for example, the purges and criminal trials mounted after the liberation from National Socialist occupation adapted and modified a set of (national) legal instruments that can be traced back to the Revolution and the nineteenth century. It was only in the 1960s that French domestic law began, in a twisted way, to integrate Nuremberg's (international) legacy. In Poland, Stalinist trials against Ukrainians, Belarussians and Lithuanians as well as pogroms against Jewish survivors of the Holocaust could be interpreted as belated reactions to the Soviet revolutionary civil war and the minority rights regime of the interwar period. In the twenty-five years since the end of communism, the release of new archival material has made it possible to historicize both conceptions of justice and effective practices thereof in at least a few of the postwar situations. Most of the studies that tackle the subject have taken a broad approach, generally including legal as well as political, social and cultural questions.

In the following essay, we will examine the three main postwar periods of the twentieth century *backwards*: Justice after 1989–90 is characterized by a certain contradiction in its conception as well as in its praxis. While most Eastern and Central European countries – except Germany – sought alternatives to criminal justice to deal with human rights violations under communist rule, the idea took hold that perpetrators from the Second World War – especially those involved in the genocide of European Jews – should be prosecuted according to a very extensive conception of judicial time. Immediately after the Second World War, retribution in the form of criminal sanctions against Axis criminals and collaborators became the central feature of postwar justice; however, unlike what can be observed in the 1980s and 1990s, this form of retribution was conceived as (basically) provisional. Finally, following the 'Great War', the inconclusive attempts to prosecute war criminals and the simultaneous development of public international law drew the contours of a postwar justice that sought to grant collective rather than individual rights.

After 1989–90

In the years following the breakdown of state socialism, most Eastern and Central European countries either renounced criminal justice or promoted alternatives such as commissions of enquiry and national agencies managing secret police files. Contrary to their predecessors in 1945 and 1918–19, the protagonists of post-'Cold War' justice could rely neither on general guidelines nor on a legal framework for addressing the state-sponsored injustices of communist regimes. With respect to the political crimes of communist dictatorships in East-Central Europe, however, a tradition of political and ethical ideas had emerged through the 'Helsinki process' and parallel domestic developments since the late 1970s.[12] The role of the so-called dissidents – in reality a heterogeneous group of intellectuals, academics, artists and workers' representatives – in bringing about the demise of state socialism and subsequent electoral turnovers should not be overstated, but their contribution before and after 1989 was also more than symbolic.[13] As Jiri Priban and Robert Brier have pointed out, the intellectual legacy of the opposition movements became crucial in the political and legal transformations of former communist countries. Their 'social imaginaire' profoundly shaped the processes of post-revolutionary constitution-making by providing a common normative understanding of life under the conditions of developed state socialism.[14]

In the late 1970s, when the regimes' need for legal legitimacy in internal politics and in the international level became more urgent, the inconsistencies between membership in international human rights conventions and domestic practices were increasingly exploited as a means of pointing to their inherent illegitimacy. Groups like 'Charta 77' embarked on a 'legalist' strategy and connected this to a specific concept of 'civil society' – paradoxically based on a romanticized and harmonious interpretation of liberal societies with a simultaneous rejection of Western individualism.[15] In addition to countering the ideological formula of 'socialist legality' with a universalistic human rights discourse, the dissidents also tried to reactivate certain virtues and values of (premodern) communal life – like individual freedom, solidarity, spontaneity and intellectual critique – considered to have been destroyed by 'immoralist totalitarianism'. The oppositional project of restoring a 'paradise lost', namely a divine order of reality, was potentially suited to blur or even to revoke traditional liberal distinctions between law and morality.[16] As the byproduct of a strategy termed as *antipolitics* or *non-political politics*, this naturalist or quasi-religious approach towards positive law and human rights formed an important part of the dissidents' legacy in the subsequent transformation processes in East-Central Europe. It had pervasive effects on the constitutional life and political culture of individual countries, and also accelerated their later accession into the so-called value community of the European Union.[17]

Another project that originated in the specific conceptions of the dissident groups was the demand for what we might call 'historical justice' meant, according to its proponents, as a pluralistic and 'honest' examination of the collective and individual past. As Michal Kopecek has recently argued, the 'politics of a non-violent historical compromise' was complementary to the invocation of human rights insofar as it advanced ideas like 'truth', 'authenticity' and self-critical introspection on national histories. The simple credo was that justice must begin at home. The marriage between a universalist rights language and the turn to a specific form of 'national-historical' introspection became a distinct feature of liberal and radical East-Central European dissident circles during the 1970s and early 1980s.[18]

In the early phase of the political transformation of 1989–90, the symbiosis of human rights activism and the call for historical justice turned into powerful tools of public mobilization. But contrary to the visions of the civic-republican dissidents, 1989 was not the hour for historical soul-searching and 'historical compromises' between old and new political forces. Instead, the communist past, symbolized by the contested issue of the security police files, became a political battleground that stood in stark contrast to the parallel roundtable talks, where the negotiating parties were striving for pragmatic and balanced agreements. In practically all East-Central European countries, the search for the personnel files of former Stasi informants and their confidential reports was driven by political actors.

The trope of 'historical lessons' was not only found in the dissident's discourses, but was also used in the debates about former East-German state employees.[19] In the last year of the German Democratic Republic GDR), the political struggles over Stasi files led to the adoption by the last People's Chamber of the first statute seeking to secure records and grant access to them. After the unification treaty went into effect, the law temporarily vanished into oblivion. This was by no means coincidental, since influential West German politicians and jurists considered the act dubious at the least. They saw several reasons why it fell short of Western legal standards. First, they argued that the files themselves were the product of politically motivated judicial proceedings and illegal intelligence activities, and therefore should be destroyed immediately. Second, it was pointed out that the GDR law violated the strict privacy and archival laws of the old Bundesrepublik. Shortly before the fall of the Honecker government in East Berlin, the West German Constitutional Court had expanded the concepts of the right to protection of privacy and the scope of the sphere of the intimate by including all kinds of 'person-related data providing information about the personal and factual circumstances of identified or identifiable individuals'.[20] Third, critics from West and East brought forward what they thought were 'lessons of history' that would undermine the implementation of the law. Given that in 1990–91 it was not politically expedient to publicly criticize the revolutionary character of the law on Stasi files, the critique resorted to a murky historical analogy: By trying to distinguish the 'compromised' from the less 'compromised', it was contended that the law would repeat mistakes the Western Allies had committed against nominal Nazi Party members. In other words, the envisioned vetting of former Stasi informers was equated with the presumably 'failed' de-Nazification experiment after 1945.[21]

Though we still know astonishingly little about the background of this particular legislation, we can nevertheless assume that such historical analogies struck a nerve with the ex-dissidents. Not only did they consider them to be historically inappropriate, many were also convinced that high-ranking representatives of the West German elite deliberately misinterpreted the purpose of the law because they were afraid of being exposed as well. They countered with the human rights argument, manifest in the principle of 'informational self-determination', already established in 1983 by the West German Constitutional Court in its famous 'census decision'.[22] They also turned the critics' historical narrative on its head: The modified adoption of the *Volkskammer*'s Stasi law was promoted as an act of belated repentance for a 'second guilt', stemming from West German ignorance about the Nazi past. To emphasize their point, the ex-dissidents staged a second occupation of the Stasi headquarters in September 1990, this time under the gaze of leading West German TV stations.[23] In the end, the former GDR opposition and their West German allies prevailed over their critics. On 20 December 1991, the Bundestag voted for the amended Stasi law and the establishment of a new federal agency under the leadership of the East German pastor Joachim Gauck.

With the exception of post-communist Poland, where it took politicians almost ten years to adopt administrative measures against former state functionaries,[24] most other centre-right and left-liberal governments decided sooner or later to confront the historical injustices of the communist period by vetting employees of the public service and by adjudicating cases against perpetrators of criminal offenses. In Hungary, for instance, the first democratic parliament passed a bill that intended to prosecute 'grave crimes' committed between 21 December 1944 – marking the formation of a Soviet-loyal provisional government and a security apparatus in Debrecen[25] – and May 1990, the date of the first free election.[26] The general assumption behind this legislation was that these crimes had remained unpunished due to 'political reasons'. In the early 1990s, this legislation was complemented by several rehabilitation and compensation laws designated for victims of political justice, illegal internment and displacement between 1945 and 1989, and a so-called Justitia plan that called for the complete 'screening' of the post-1956 political, economic and cultural elites. A novelty in the retributive legal framework was Act XC of 22 of 1993 and Act XXIII of 1994. While 1993 XC provided for the prosecution of war crimes and crimes against humanity committed against participants of the 1956 popular uprising, 1994 XXIII paved the way for investigations against members of parliament and high-ranking civil servants, who were offered discretion in return for a voluntary withdrawal from public life.[27]

Even before the separation of the Czech and Slovak republics in 1992, both parts of the country pursued different courses with respect to communist crimes. Due to their different historical experiences under state socialism, they represented two extreme positions in dealing with the legacies of the past. The Slovaks, who went from a 'velvet' to a 'national' revolution, saw the matter primarily as a means to finally detach themselves from Czech centralism. As such, the problems of unpunished crimes and forgotten victims were soon buried under a discourse of 'reconciliation' and 'national unity'. In 1996, the debate culminated in the abolition of the decommunization law and the passing of a law on the 'Immorality and Illegality of the Communist Regime'. The juridical politics of the past in the Czech Republic revealed the deep political and ideological cleavages that existed between the former dissidents surrounding president Václav Havel and the neo-liberal reformer Václav Klaus, leader of the Democratic Citizens Party and Prime Minister starting in 1992. Due to the rather erratic and uncontrolled publication of files from the former state security archive, the issue of secret collaboration with the communist regime became hotly disputed among the different political camps.[28]

Feelings of national continuity were to some extent strengthened in the 1990s by the unfolding of a parallel 'reopening' of post-1945 proceedings. This reopening started before 1989–90 but accelerated in the following decade. There were two main causes for this trend. First, the mobilization of survivors' and victims' heirs in connection with the shift in Jewish memory of the genocide played an important role. Second, and intimately related to the previous factor, the reception of international criminal norms within national law led to a distension of the traditional time constraints of domestic penal law: the extension and subsequent elimination of the statute of limitation for murder in the first degree (in West Germany) and the imprescriptibility of crimes against humanity and war crimes (in the countries – mostly from Eastern bloc – that had ratified the 1968 international convention on this issue[29]).

After the Cold War, proceedings against Nazi perpetrators and collaborators were (re)opened or pursued in various European countries: in (West) Germany, the judicial trend that was initiated at the end of the 1950s[30] continues to this day, albeit with ups and downs. Notably, a particular effort was made in the late 1980s and at the beginning of the following decade;[31] more recently, the Munich judgement in the Demjanjuk case (2011) paved the way for several investigations against former employees of the Auschwitz and Majdanek camps – all very old men.[32] In France, following the Lischka and Barbie trials (in Cologne in 1979–80 and in Lyon in 1987, respectively), the trials against the former militiaman Paul Touvier (1994) and the ex-regional prefect Maurice Papon (1997–98) for their complicity in crimes against humanity can be seen as a resumption of the post–Second World War *épuration* (purge).[33] If the call for justice (and especially criminal justice) for past human rights violations belongs nowadays to the repertoire of various intergovernmental and non-governmental organizations, its effective practice is in fact very selective: Mass crimes of the late colonial era (e.g. Sétif, Guelma and Kherrata in May 1945 in Algeria, or Madagascar in 1947)[34] and of decolonization (e.g. the Algerian War from 1954 to 1962) were not subjected to criminal justice. All complaints filed for crimes such as torture, summary execution or unexplained 'disappearance' committed by the French Army in Algeria (or by the ordinary police on metropolitan soil) during the Algerian War were consistently rejected by French courts, who were arguing that such acts were amnestied and did not meet the definition of 'crimes against humanity' as laid out in the Charter of the International Military Tribunal.[35] The situation was similar in Spain with regard to the civil war and Franco's dictatorship. In both countries, the aforementioned crimes are only indirectly evoked before courts in cases such as libel actions. More generally, the inflation of 'memory laws' (especially in France[36]) and the multiplication of legal qualifications of the past, at the national as well as the European level, led to growing litigation of historical matters before domestic and international courts.[37] This litigation pertains not only to criminal law, but also to civil law and other legal areas as well.[38]

This double tendency – selective judicialization of the older past versus avoidance of criminal justice for the recent past (except in Germany) – reflects, in part, internal tensions within the new field of TJ in the last decade of the twentieth century. The attempts to deal with the real-socialist past in Eastern and Central Europe are contemporary to the emergence of TJ as a mixture of knowledge and praxis at the beginning of the 1990s. Initially, the various actors – human rights activists, policymakers and legal experts – involved in the promotion of TJ thought that the specific context of what they called 'democratic transitions' required a new kind of justice, stressing the need for alternatives to criminal justice in the form of 'truth commissions'. More recently, criminal justice (especially in its international variant) was partly reappraised by proponents of TJ: This evolution is due to the growing involvement of legal professionals in many of the TJ programs supported by international organizations and NGOs such as the New York-based International Center for Transitional Justice. TJ emerged mainly outside Europe, but Europeans played a sizable role in its development, especially in the academic legitimization of the notion in the late 1990s.[39]

As early as November 1988, a group of social scientists, scholars of international law and human rights activists had begun to organize a gathering initiated by American philanthropic foundations. Under the auspices of the Aspen Foundation, at the famous ski resort in Aspen, Colorado, this group debated the limits of and opportunities for post-conflict justice. The main focus was on the new democracies in Latin America, but the East Central European countries were also considered as a potential case.[40] Subsequently, with the demise of state socialism, East-Central Europe quickly took centre stage in debates among international TJ experts. Leading dissidents like Adam Michnik and György Bence were invited to the meetings and provided important insights about their practical experiences in coping with the political, legal and ethical challenges of regime change. One factor which might have fostered the uneven and fragile coalition between Western TJ advocates – mostly activists and law professors from Anglo-American institutions – and members of the left East European opposition was the approach centred on human rights and self-reflexive historical justice. As noted earlier, it was this innovation which had been the main contribution of dissidents to the pre-1989 human rights discourse and which made them attractive new allies for the 'transitologists'.[41] Representatives from post-communist East-Central Europe and from unified Germany were considered key witnesses for the validity of the TJ approach because most of these countries had had to deal with the afterlife of two totalitarian dictatorships: Stalinism and National Socialism. According to TJ promoters, the liminal phase of democratic transition should be accompanied by a set of legal and educational measures, thereby balancing the interests of former perpetrators and victims in post-dictatorial societies. As a practical guideline, they envisaged the implementation of a set of legal or semi-legal tools, such as criminal proceedings, amnesties, lustrations, truth commissions and restitution laws.

In the 1990s, these ideas circulated among many people involved in international governmental organizations and NGOs.[42] Despite its vagueness and lack of clarity, the 'catch-all' concept (Frédéric Mégret) was adapted by supranational institutions such as the Human Rights Commission of the United Nations and the Council of Europe and was later also incorporated into the official guidelines of their human rights policy. From the perspectives of the individual states with a post-dictatorial past, this constellation created considerable tension both in the domestic and foreign policy spheres. On the one hand, these tensions arose from the fact that supranational institutions were sending mixed signals with regard to the constitutionality of certain retributive justice measures. For example, while the Governing Body of the International Labour Organization (ILO) called the Czech lustration law 'discriminatory', the Parliamentary Assembly of the Council of Europe defended it by arguing that the Czech state possessed the right to 'defend' itself against the ongoing presence of non-democratic elites in the public service.[43] On the other hand, international law partially superseded national (penal) codes.

Post-1945

The second global conflict was followed by multifarious purges in which criminal justice played a significant role. The powerful retributive – and especially penal – dimension of the whole process clearly distinguishes it not only from the subsequent postwar phase (the post–Cold War period discussed earlier), but also from the preceding one (the post-1918 period, which we will examine in the following). The Second World War was a conflict with many facets. First, it was a traditional military confrontation between various state actors. It exceeded previous wars not only because of its truly global dimensions, but also because it harnessed the maximum exploitation of natural, technological and human resources as well as mobilizing populations on all sides. For colonial powers like Great Britain, France, Belgium, the Netherlands and Italy, the war also had another effect. As in the First World War, their fighting power rested once again to some extent on the shoulders of the colonized people, which then had an impact on colonial relations after the war.[44] Second, the war morphed in character over the course of the fighting. What had started with the German invasion and occupation of Poland quickly turned into an actual megalomaniacal 'New Order' under Nazi rule.[45] 'By its end', writes the British-American historian Tony Judt, the war 'had mutated into a whole series of brutal local civil wars.'[46] Last but not least, it was a peculiarity of German warfare – later partially adopted by some of its allies – that it targeted not only enemy troops, but also included foreign populations and German and Austrian citizens. By choosing European Jewry as its main opponent, Hitler's Germany made sure to single out the most vulnerable minority group of all.

In retrospect, the multifaceted character of the war contributed to the emergence of different conceptions of postwar justice. One can discern three main discourses on justice, all of which emerged long before the fighting came to an end. The first was initiated by the exiled representatives of the occupied Central East European countries in late 1941. Led by the Polish prime minister Wladislaw Sikorski, who convened a conference in London in January 1942, the governments-in-exile issued the so-called St. James Declaration, which demanded 'organized justice' for the perpetrators of grave 'war crimes'.[47] Though hampered for diplomatic and military reasons, the declaration marked the beginning of a bigger international debate that gained momentum in the war's final phase. This debate revolved mainly around the question of whether it was politically expedient to create an international court to pass judgement on Nazi leaders, and whether to expand the definition of war crimes to encompass atrocities against Axis citizens and pre-war persecutions. While the British government did not want to risk repeating a debacle like the one they had experienced after the First World War, the Americans were quite determined not to repeat their 'failures' of 1919.

The second discourse had very distinctive features and was shaped by the specific sociopolitical context shortly before and after liberation. As national case studies have shown, this phase was often characterized by impassioned rhetoric and a collective desire for retribution and revenge.[48] 'Justice', as it was understood by national populations, had little to do with the subtleties of traditional criminal law or the weighing of individual guilt and accountability. Rather, it implied a larger public spectacle often conducted through raw and archaic public rituals (such as lynching or public humiliation of women), or mass proceedings against thousands of both major and minor 'Quislings'.

Finally, the third discourse on justice was basically concerned with the failure of the interwar minority rights system and the consequences of its disintegration for Eastern European Jews and other groups. Its spokespeople were mostly Jewish intellectuals, publicists and academics from East and East Central Europe who had managed to survive the Holocaust by emigrating to Great Britain, one of the few neutral European countries, or the United States. A common feature of all three of these discourses was that they were more or less built on a self-legitimizing pattern that implicitly or explicitly evoked the 'lessons of 1918–19' as a negative historical foil.

Although the scope and brutality of German crimes seemed to have induced greater awareness of human rights on an international scale, it is questionable whether a direct line can be drawn between a symbolic statement like the St. James Declaration and the Allied war crimes policy of 1945.[49] Despite the fundamental differences between the 'Big Three', a major common concern seemed to have been the question of 'just' versus 'unjust' wars. This reflected the evolution of international humanitarian law since the late nineteenth century and the way peace negotiations had unfolded after the First World War.[50] As Kirsten Sellars has emphasized, outlawing aggressive war was a particular priority for liberal US jurists like Robert H. Jackson, who first took the lead at the conference of legal specialists in London in the summer of 1945, and who later also dominated the indictment against the Nazi leadership in Nuremberg: 'Despite genuine disgust at Nazi atrocities, Washington believed that the regime's most heinous crime had been to draw the Allies into a ruinous global conflict.'[51] The fact that the London conference began on the same day as the adoption of the United Nations Charter in San Francisco symbolized the profound salience of the 'legalist paradigm' (Michael Walzer), which was conceived of as a central pillar of a global postwar 'justice' order. According to its inventors, it was to replace the old rights system of the League of Nations that even before the war had already been dismantled by the unilateral expansionism of the fascist aggressors Germany, Italy and Japan. Besides the development of revolutionary legal concepts, like the principle of individual accountability for crimes under international law, the Allies also promoted the innovative idea of historical and visual justice. Relying on the extensive use of written and film documents and an understanding of history focusing on grand narratives and empirical 'facts', the construction of overarching teleologic historical interpretations of the war was one of the primary goals of the whole trial program.

However, one of the major paradoxes at Nuremberg was that the approach was at once both backward- and forward-looking. The tensions between anti-colonial conceptions of justice and the traditional interests of Europe's colonial powers was an underlying theme not only at the International Military Tribunal (IMT) and the subsequent American trial program (Nuremberg Military Tribunals, NMT) at Nuremberg, but also in many smaller trials conducted before national military courts of the Allies.[52] Among prosecutors of the Office of the Chief of Counsel for War Crimes (OCWCC), a bench staffed mostly by conservative civilian judges and German defense lawyers, the most contentious issues included determining whether the protection of the 1929 Geneva Convention extended to 'irregular forces' and whether to recognize constraints of a proportionality principle in the execution of hostages.[53] The court's perception of German war crimes, both in the Soviet Union and in the Balkans, was that while these had been unusually harsh forms of retaliation that had transcended the limits of customary law, they had not been illegal per se. Accordingly, Pieter Lagrou has rightfully relativized the notion that the allied war crimes program was, in fact, a 'watershed' in international law.[54] With its conservative reading of international law, which reaffirmed established principles of state sovereignty and 'military necessity' at the expense of universalistic human rights, the Allied war crimes program foreshadowed the peculiarities of a state-centred judicial discourse that would later become a dominant feature of the European human rights regime during the early years of the Cold War.

While the punishment of Axis war criminals became a subject of international (in fact inter-allied) policy during the war, the sanction of collaborators was more a national matter, although a certain coordination of policy did exist in this area as well. The transnational policy towards Axis war criminals was elaborated in various arenas, primarily within the United Nations War Crimes Commission (UNWCC) and the main Allied governments, but also indirectly in academic forums, as well as in NGOs. Its most significant achievement was the trial of the twenty-four major war criminals and their organizations before the IMT in Nuremberg, from 10 November 1945 to 1 October 1946. It was an experiment that became essential to the entire process of postwar justice in Europe after 1945. Indeed, the IMT Charter defined several legal categories, some of which were new in international law, namely those of crimes against peace, crimes against humanity and the notion of conspiracy to commit any of these; it also introduced the concept of criminal organization. The Charter provided the legal framework for the prosecution of Nazi crimes in occupied Germany, encompassing not only the many trials before the military courts of the four Allied powers, but also those that the German judiciary had been authorized to organize up until the early 1950s.[55]

As the keystone of the Allied court program, the IMT made possible other trials: With the highest Nazi officials already convicted, middle- and lower-level perpetrators could not claim that they were being made to 'pay' for the actions of unpunished superiors. This was especially true given that IMT and most of all NMT jurisdiction allowed for scrutiny of the complex mechanics of the Nazi bureaucracy at the central level and clarified the highest level of criminal responsibility. These thousands of trials between 1946 and 1949, including the twelve 'successor' trials[56] organized by the Americans at Nuremberg and targeting doctors, lawyers and leaders of the SS Einsatzgruppen (SS special units), led to more than 4,400 convictions across the three Western zones and sentencing of nearly 700 criminals to death.[57]

If the judgement of Nazi criminals – part of the more general program of de-Nazification in Germany – was subject of an inter-allied and American policy, the purge of collaborators took on a more national character. 'Wild' purges, undertaken outside any legal framework in the months following the liberation of the occupied territories, took place mainly in Italy (about 15,000 deaths), France (nearly 10,000 deaths) and Yugoslavia (probably 60,000 deaths in Croatia).[58] In some cases, as in that of France, this violence targeted not only alleged collaborators but also women suspected of having had affairs with Germans were subjected to gender-based humiliation (public shearing in particular). In Central and Eastern Europe, these 'wild' purges took the form of collective punishment of minorities: So-called ethnic Germans, for example, were often expelled on suspicion of having supported the Nazi regime.[59] Paradoxically, these collective sanctions served to reinforce a national and ethnic homogenization that had begun in the aftermath of the Great War through the so-called population exchanges, and had been considerably amplified by the racial politics of the Nazis.

Quickly, however, the new authorities stemming from the Resistance sought to control these outbursts of violence and to replace them with legal purges carried out through judicial institutions. Such purges took two main forms: judicial and administrative or professional. Within these categories, there were significant variations from one country to the next. In general, criminal justice proved to be more severe against collaborators in the countries of Northern, Western and Southern Europe, where governments had been exiled: In Norway, for example, almost all members of the pro-Nazi party were tried (resulting in 17,000 prison sentences and 25 executions); per capita, severity was comparable in both the Netherlands (100,000 prison sentences; 40 executions) and Belgium (242 executions). Conversely, Italy experienced a superficial purge using criminal justice, which resulted in early amnesties (1946). In Greece, the approach was widely used as a pretext: The courts ultimately condemned more resistance members of the revolutionary left than actual collaborators.

Function and form of retribution have changed over time.[60] During the Second World War, retribution was conceived of within the framework of war: It was achieved through political executions ordered by partisans (e.g. Reinhard Heydrich in 1942 and Philippe Henriot in 1944) or had a preventive/dissuasive function (such as the Pucheu trial in Alger or the Krasnodar and Kharkov trials in the territories liberated by the Red Army). After the liberation, the function changed: Now the main aims were to punish those who had collaborated with the enemy, including by actively participating in their crimes, and to remove such collaborators from the key positions in public service.

While addressing collaboration was partly defined in inter-allied organizations, implementation remained within national purview. In September 1944, the UNWCC recommended the adoption of ad hoc legislation and the creation of national offices to centralize the prosecution of war criminals and their collaborators (so-called Quislings): Indeed, this was the origin of offices such as the Service de recherche sur les crimes de guerre ennemis (SRCGE) in France. Some of the members of this inter-allied organization played a significant role in their own country in designing and implementing the policies of retribution (i.e. the Czechoslovak Bohuslav Ecer or the Belgian Marcel de Baer). The UNWCC was responsible for coordination of national policies until its dissolution in 1948. This and other factors enabled the sharing and spread of categories, be they those articulated in the charter of the IMT or national categories such as the French *indignité nationale*. This new penal category (sanctioned by the 'dégradation nationale') can be traced back to the French Revolution and aimed to exclude from the national community those who had acted in an 'unworthy manner'. It inspired similar legislation in other European countries (e.g. the decree on 'épuration civique' in Belgium and the law on indignity in Greece).[61] Given the relative autonomy of legal systems within national boundaries, judicial retribution against collaborators and war criminals had also to be repositioned in the legal history of each country that had experienced German occupation. In the case of Belgium, which had been occupied during both world wars, the experiences of 1918 played a larger role than that in other countries, even though the post–First World War purge was very limited in comparison to what occurred after 1944–45.[62]

Ultimately, the penal tropism of justice in post–Second World War Europe was particularly strong. Some of the administrative and professional purges went through ad hoc courts built on the judicial-criminal model, leading to a certain 'judicialization' thereof. In particular, this was the case with the *Spruchkammer*, created in the American zone of occupation to scrutinize a wide range of Nazi supporters and to sanction the most compromised of them. Yet, this judicialization was not necessarily a guarantee of severity: This ambitious American program quickly became known as the (in)famous 'Mitläuferfabrik' (literally: Fellow-Travellers' Factory) analyzed by Lutz Niethammer.[63] In addition, this particular conception of retribution differed significantly from parallel contemporary ones. Retribution through legal means was primarily thought of as a *temporary* policy: From 1947–48 onwards, amnesty laws were adopted in all European countries, putting an (provisional) end to post–Second World War justice.

The experience of 1918 played a key role during and immediately after the Second World War, if only for a generational reason: Most actors involved in the development and implementation of postwar judicial policies had directly or indirectly experienced the Great War and its aftermath (unlike the significant generational gap between 1989 and 1945). After the Second World War, the previous postwar era was a political resource, providing both a legal precedent and, at the same time, a counter model. During the Second World War, in debates over the definition of Axis war crimes and the design of the appropriate judicial responses to these crimes, documents such as the report of the Commission on the Responsibility of the Authors of the War and on Enforcement of Penalties (presented on 19 March 1919 to the Preliminary Peace Conference) were widely quoted and commented on. Politically, the fight against Axis powers was a fight for a set of values and especially for justice. This was not only an abstract concept, but also – crucially – had a very concrete meaning: The perpetrators of war crimes and similar crimes would have to answer before the courts for their actions. Initially, this goal was expressed using vocabulary similar to that of the previous war, although using a more accurate legal language. A good example of this was the Moscow Declaration of October 1943, which called for criminal prosecution. Within the United Nations War Crimes Commission, established shortly after this declaration, the legal discussion built extensively on the post–First World War legal precedent, as evidenced by the debate over whether or not the 'list' of thirty-two war crimes, established in 1919, should be expanded. At the same time, the post-1918 precedent was seen primarily as a counter-model, an example to be avoided due to the fact that the Allies had failed, on the whole, to prosecute the authors of war crimes committed during the Great War. Indeed, the US representatives to the aforementioned Commission – Robert Lansing and James Brown Scott – were especially hostile to international tribunals.

Post–1918–19

One conundrum with which historians of the First World War grapple is to explain the astonishing persistence of legalistic internationalism. Despite the dramatic failure in preventing the outbreak of war, or in protecting soldiers and civilians from the destructiveness of total warfare once begun, in the years from 1914 to 1918, the commitment to international law and legal justice conceptions only surged.[64] During the last quarter of the nineteenth century, legalistic internationalism had become the prestige project of a small but well-organized elite of Euro-Atlantic experts in international law.[65] This transnational group of liberal *honoratiores* and cosmopolitans promoted the idea that in a world of growing interconnectedness, responsibility for world affairs should be put in the hands of lawyers rather than politicians. Their main accomplishments were the two Hague Conventions of 1899 and 1907, where for the first time the convening states agreed on the codification of the laws of war, the inception of a Permanent Court of Arbitration (1899) and the creation of an International Prize Court (1907).[66] Given that even an authoritarian and illiberal regime like the Wilhelminian Reich had become a member of the Hague system, the events of the summer of 1914 caused a deep shock for the adherents of legalistic internationalism. As Isabell Hull stated: 'The supreme test to arbitration came . . . when the British Foreign Minister, Edward Grey, belatedly proposed that Austria and Serbia used arbitration to settle their volatile dispute over Serbian responsibility for the Franz Ferdinand assassination.'[67] The end of this story is well known: Both Germany and Russia declined the offer, and the last chance for avoiding or delaying a military confrontation was lost.

With the beginning of the armed conflict, the community of international lawyers suffered a temporary identity crisis. Confidence in the law's potential as an instrument of interstate dispute was either severely harmed or completely lost. But not all of the legalists were willing to bury their idea just yet. While some of them turned away from law, others pleaded for a renewal and improvement of the Hague system, which, in their view, had left too many 'gaps through which states could evade the judicial or arbitral settlement of disputes'.[68] Before the war, the focal point of legalistic internationalism had been war prevention by judicial settlement and arbitration. During the war, other themes moved to the forefront. The direct violation of Belgian neutrality and other serious German and Austro-Hungarian war crimes aroused a great deal of public ire, not only in the Entente countries but also among neutrals. One consequence of the numerous high-profile crimes that were either sponsored or condoned by the German civilian leadership and general staff was that the Allies accelerated their propaganda war to a new limit, which meant that they sometimes also exaggerated or even fabricated atrocities. Another consequence was the emergence of a justice discourse that tied the call for legal justice with the demand for historical truth. Although this discourse overlapped, to some extent, with the official propaganda policy and the traditional 'colored books' campaigns of the European Foreign and War Ministries, it nevertheless introduced a new approach to mass violence. First of all, it departed from the notion that the Hague system had created a new spirit of obligation and submission to international law on which all 'civilized' nations had agreed. Second, it was argued that the 'new morality' would retain integrity and credibility only if it demanded the punishment of individual perpetrators.[69] Third, given new forms of state criminality, justice was seen as a task not only for national courts and the envisaged international tribunals, but also for historical scholarship and archival work.[70]

It was no coincidence that some of the men who had been ardent supporters of arbitration before the war later advocated criminal investigation and forensic historiography with respect to German war crimes. A prominent representative of this discourse was the London university professor Viscount James Bryce, a trained historian, jurist and retired diplomat who had spent several semesters at Heidelberg University. He headed a commission that investigated and published a controversial report on German atrocities committed in Belgium, and also produced – together with the renowned historian Arnold J. Toynbee – a comprehensive documentation of the Armenian genocide committed by the Ottoman Empire in 1915.[71] Publications by Bryce and Toynbee, the English lawyer John Hartman Morgan and the French literature professor Joseph Bédier differed in their academic standards, methodological approach and selection of sources, but they had a shared view on the underlying problem. By relying on eyewitness testimonies of soldiers and civilians, they produced instant narratives of the war that 'humanized' the legal abstractions and turned them into the tangible category of individual suffering.[72] This contributed to a considerable shift in the public perception of war-induced mass violence. The fact that humanitarian disasters were no longer considered a natural and inevitable byproduct of military confrontations between states, but instead as the consequence of moral choices made by individual actors, paved the way for a 'guilt' discourse that separated 'perpetrators' from innocent 'victims'. Another feature of this discourse was the individualization and personification of the war, as it became manifest in the symbolic issue of the German Kaiser and his unflattering reputation 'as the greatest criminal known'.[73] As soon as the actual fighting was over, this quickly culminated in an international debate about 'punishment, payment and prevention'.[74]

It is difficult to assess whether the activism of the legalists and their wartime debates over German atrocities actually worked to catalyze retributive justice concepts. While it is unlikely that the broader public had closely followed the expert debates on punishment and international norms, vengeful sentiment arose in reaction to national propaganda campaigns and a first wave of trials that had been cancelled due to German reprisals against Allied soldiers. Only in the last phase of the war did the question of criminal trials for German war crimes become an issue for domestic politics. Mark Lewis argues that in the fall of 1918, both the British and French governments deliberately rekindled public demands for punishment to mitigate domestic political cleavages and social unrest. He believes that mostly for tactical reasons, the dominant moderate forces supported nationalist demands for a 'Carthaginian Peace'. Their intent was 'to channel popular discontent, and [to] show that they were not going to capitulate to the domestic demands of the "forces of movement," which sought labor and welfare reform'.[75] In the long run, this approach not only turned out to be extremely inconsistent, but also became politically counterproductive, as the example of Lloyd George's notorious election campaign from December 1918 proves.[76] Moreover, it underlines the tension between competing conceptions of justice, since the project of the Triple Entente to prosecute war crimes was partly meant to stifle strong claims for social justice within the victorious countries.

During the Paris peace negotiations starting in January 1919, British and French politicians had to deal with two major problems. First, they had to take into consideration the expectations and demands of national constituencies that expected swift implementation of 'hang-the-Kaiser' slogans. Second, and serving to complicate the first, the ambitious plans for a comprehensive punishment program against state representatives of Germany, Bulgaria and the Ottoman Empire immediately became a major source of dispute between European and American delegates. As John Horne and Alan Kramer have argued, the US delegation was troubled 'by the lack of precedents for an international tribunal and the difficulty of trying cases on the basis of retrospective law'.[77] Confronted with American scepticism, Clemenceau tried to clarify the situation by convening two committees of legal experts. They were assigned the difficult task of renovating the Hague system to meet their current political needs. The debates of the Commission on the Responsibility of the Authors of the War and on Enforcement of Penalties and the Reparations Commission took several months and revolved around the question of 'war guilt', but also tackled the more practical issues of restitution and punishment.[78]

In the end, the recommendations of the legal advisors reflected the political fault lines between European and American partners concerning the creation of a postwar (legal) order. They were also an indicator that the incommensurable war experiences of the allies had elicited very different justice discourses that hampered the possibility of finding a consensual legal solution. While the European side pleaded for a modernized international law that should be based on a 'new sensibility' for legal justice in public opinion,[79] Woodrow Wilson and his foreign policy advisors did not want to see their vision of a 'just' postwar world order of peace and stability spoiled by the formalities and restraints of punitive justice. Lloyd George, who considered the issue of war crime trials as his personal project, countered with the argument that the new order would lack any moral credibility if it left perpetrators of atrocities unpunished. Referring to the famous pre-war conversation between the German chancellor Bethmann Hollweg and the British ambassador Goschen, the British premier declared: 'If the League of

Nations is to have some chance of success, it must not appear as just a word on a scrap of paper. It must have the power from this moment to punish crimes against international law. The violation of treaties is precisely the sort of crime to be of direct concern to the League of Nations.'[80]

In retrospect, it were most of all political divisions which prevented the enforcement of the penalty provisions in the treaties of Versailles, Neuilly-sur-Seine and Sèvres, despite contemporaries tending to blame this mainly on legal contestations. The League system as erected in 1920 was based on an understanding of justice that promoted ideas of consensual agreement, cooperation and mutual exchange on the account of international public law. According to this conception of justice, subjects of international law were mainly sovereign states and secondarily groups like national minorities. This became apparent once again in the extradition crisis of 1919–20, when the British cabinet wanted to make the Netherlands' entry to the League conditional on a willingness to extradite the Kaiser. Sir Eric Drummond, the League's first secretary general, begged the British to change their position. His argument was that, otherwise, German opponents of the League would be reaffirmed in their opinion that it was 'purely an Allied instrument to be directed against Germany, and not an organization for genuine cooperation between the nations'.[81] As we know today, the withdrawal of such a demand did not alter German and Turkish nationalists' convictions about the hegemonic character of international law and allied justice conceptions.

On the other hand, the institutional framework of the League represented less the triumph of 'internationalism over nationalism than of one kind of internationalism over others'.[82] Its distinctive, anti-formalistic architecture was the product of a tradition of American constitutionalism in combination with a specific perspective on the inherent problems of late-nineteenth-century European nationalism. In the view of President Wilson and his advisors, the main subjects of international relations were not individuals but national groups represented by nation states, according to a conception driven by a process of construction and naturalization of nationalities since the mid-nineteenth century.[83] In this light, the development of a system of international security and the creation of international jurisdictions were deemed to protect the rights of national groups, whether in the form of nation states or minorities recognized by law. This 'inter-national' or interstate conception of justice was based on collective rights and duties of 'peoples', reflecting the experiences with multinational empires and the rise of national liberation movements in the nineteenth century. It focused heavily on state sovereignty, homogeneous populations and a collective understanding of self-determination in the form of minority protection as articulated in Wilson's Fourteen Points as well as in the Paris Peace Conference. As has been demonstrated by Eric D. Weitz, this national-liberal tradition crystallized in two inseparable aspects of the peace treaties (1919–23): the 'language (and practice) of majorities and minorities'[84] on the one hand and the mass deportation of individuals believed to belong to minority groups (as in the case of the Lausanne Treaty of 1923 endorsing the massive 'population exchange' between Greece and Turkey) on the other.[85]

In diametrical opposition to what happened during and immediately after the Second World War, the American 'third party' opposed an international criminal jurisdiction, generally arguing for moderate peace conditions instead. James Brown Scott, who opposed his French and British counterparts in the Commission on the Responsibility of the Authors of the War and on Enforcement of Penalties (see earlier mention), was – interestingly – at the same time a strong proponent of the Permanent Court of International Justice (PCIJ). As advisor to the American representative Elihu Root at the Consultative Committee of Jurists (responsible for drafting the PCIJ statute), he campaigned for the so-called obligatory competence of the court, a proposal ultimately defeated by the Committee in favor of optional competence.[86] Brown's position clearly indicated the kind of international justice envisioned by the Americans during the peace conference. The strong trend to grant rights to ill-defined national groups according to an 'inter-national' conception of justice was also accompanied by the development of other forms of justice. According to the preamble of Part XIII of the Versailles peace treaty, 'the League of Nations has for its object the establishment of universal peace, and such a peace can be established only if it is based upon social justice.'[87] In keeping with this aim, the Treaty created the International Labor Office (ILO) to promote international social norms.[88]

The unprecedented growth of intergovernmental organizations dedicated to various forms of international justice (adjudication, arbitration, promotion of social norms) favored the emergence of a new group of experts, especially in the European cities where these institutions had their seat (e.g. Geneva and the Hague). Sharing new beliefs such as the 'outlawry of war', while being torn between their national and international allegiances, they contributed to the production of an international legal capital made up of a number of converging political, legal and diplomatic resources.[89] The *jurisconsults*, or law experts, who first debated national-socialist war crimes in London during the Second World War (i.e. in the UNWCC and predecessor organizations) were partly socialized and professionalized in this international group of experts during the inter-war period. During the First World War, however, in the United Kingdom as well in France, plans were developed to sanction violations of the rules of warfare through criminal justice. Ultimately, however, this occurred in the national courts of the vanquished countries (Germany and Turkey) rather than in an international court as had been hoped by prominent officials. Furthermore, the initial Franco-British aim of prosecuting heads of state (especially Wilhelm II) for waging an aggressive war and violating the neutrality of Belgium and Luxemburg eventually failed.[90]

In 1919 and 1920, around 200 Turkish officials responsible for the mass killing of Armenians during the war were prosecuted in court martial in Istanbul (called Constantinople until 1930).[91] These thirty-five trials resulted in the condemnation of seventeen men to death, mainly in absentia; in the end, only three of these were executed. These trials took place due to the pressure of the Great Powers, especially Great Britain, and in a context of quasi–civil war between European Turkey, whose capital was occupied by the Allies, and Anatolia, controlled by a nationalist government based in Ankara. In this situation, imperial and inner-political considerations interfered significantly with the proceedings. The Ottoman courts in Istanbul, for example, prosecuted not only those accused of perpetrating the Armenian massacres, but also some of the nationalist leaders in Ankara, including Mustapha Kemal. While the Treaty of Sèvres that had been signed by the Ottoman government on 10 August

1920 foresaw the extradition 'of those responsible for the massacres for trial by an international tribunal yet to be constituted',[92] the signatories to the Treaty of Lausanne two years later agreed upon a general amnesty.

Another set of seventeen war crime trials took place before the German Supreme Court in Leipzig (*Reichsgericht*) between 1921 and 1927. Initially, the Allies wanted 'at least 1,590 Germans to be extradited on war crimes charges' (i.e. mainly killings of civilians during the invasion of Belgium and France, crimes against prisoners of war and deportations of civilians).[93] After tough negotiations, wherein the British played a conciliating role, the Allies 'acceded to the request of the German government to prosecute the accused' before a domestic court. Furthermore, they reduced the original list to 862 alleged war criminals. The first wave of trials (1921–22) saw light sentences handed out, in cases primarily chosen by the British. In most other cases regarding the German land war, selected by the Belgian and French, the Leipzig trials turned into an exercise aimed at exonerating the defendants. This occurred in about 1,700 cases, including those comprising the original extradition list as well as those condemned in absentia by Belgian and French courts.

Beyond their failure, keenly felt by contemporaries and serving to shape the experience of allied officials and jurists during the Second World War, the Istanbul and Leipzig trials and their prolegomena contributed to a renewal of the international reflection on war crimes. New concepts, such as crimes against humanity, emerged during the conflict;[94] meanwhile, while members of armed forces were effectively prosecuted for war crimes, the possibility of trying heads of state for waging an aggressive war entered the realm of serious discussion.

Conclusion

The regressive or backward overview of the twentieth century's three main postwar periods sketched in this chapter highlights the circulation – in various forms – of conceptions, experiences and practical knowledge related to justice in these contexts. This transmission of knowledge occurred not only across geographical and social spaces, but equally (indeed, by definition) across time. As we have seen, the conception and praxis of postwar justice after 1989, 1945 and 1918 underwent profound changes; these changes, however, were not necessarily successive given the usual overlapping of historical processes. After the Cold War, most Central and Eastern European countries were reluctant, for various reasons (including practical constraints and real political considerations), to address human rights violations of the communist era with criminal justice. While retribution was sought – except in unified Germany – the transgressions of the 'recent' past were low on the list of policy priorities. Conversely, the last decade of the century was marked in Western Europe – especially in France – by the j(re)opening of prosecutions against the Second World War perpetrators, particularly those involved in the genocide of European Jews. After 1945, retribution in the form of criminal trials became, if not the only, at least the central feature of postwar purges. But unlike our contemporary notion of justice as almost timeless, the retributive process in the immediate aftermath of 1945 was conceived of as provisional. From 1947–48 onwards, a wave of amnesty laws in occupied Germany as well as in most European countries put a temporary end to post–Second World War purges. After the Great War, the inconclusive attempt to bring war criminals of the Central Powers to justice and the simultaneous development of a public international justice – embodied by the Permanent Court of International Justice – delineated a specific form of postwar justice, one aimed at guaranteeing collective rights of nation states and national minorities rather than securing individual rights of all human beings.

What, then, is to be gained from the experiment of a backwards reading of judicial discourse and practice in twentieth-century European history? First, it seems to confirm the assumption that conceptions of justice evolved with larger strategies to cope with the political and social turmoil of war, civil war and revolution. In this respect, the conception and application of legal and semi-legal instruments comprised disparate aspects. National and international law fostered specific understandings of mass violence and (state) collaboration that became crucial in setting the agendas in the different postwar judicial moments. In all three 'post' situations, the idea of legal justice was tied closely to the notion of historical 'truth' about specific forms of violence in the past. Justice was a contested issue not only between states, but even more so among non-governmental actors. If we compare the situations after 1989, 1945 and 1918, the latter often saw attempts to challenge the official conceptions of justice and appropriate postwar policies of the past. In particular, legalistic internationalism and human rights served as a kind of way in for groups and individuals who had not previously been part of the (foreign) policy establishment of their countries. At the same time, the development of postwar justice was accompanied by professionalization of the corresponding activities (i.e. the emergence of a generation of *jurisconsults* familiar with intergovernmental organizations and international justice in the interwar period; the birth and growth of expertise on ICL in the context of the Nuremberg trials; and significant professionalization of TJ from the end of the 1990s).[95] Indeed, while it is often hazardous to evaluate the impact of justice policies on post-authoritarian societies, it is easier to analyze the social and professional effects on those who conceived and implemented these policies. As we have seen, postwar justice after 1989 and 1945 built, to some extent, on the professional experience of the previous generations of experts (those of the post-1945 and post-1918 periods, respectively).

A second point is that justice discourses generally departed from the notion of an imagined precedent. As argued here, the recurrent discourse on 'historical lessons' was not only connected to specific war experiences, but also to legal coping strategies that were used as reference points by different actors. Analogous to representations of 'Versailles' in historiography and public memory, it has become common to claim that the failed attempt to punish German, Bulgarian and Turkish war crimes after 1918 served mainly as a negative *topos* in later postwar moments. However, in reality, the situation was more complicated. Some of the legal frameworks of 1918 were reactivated in 1945 for the purpose of punishing acts of 'unpatriotic' behavior, while after 1989, the post–Second World War experience played a significant role in the way real socialism was dealt with (especially in the German case).

Third, it should be noted that debates over justice in the twentieth century have been utterly Eurocentric. To some extent, this was an effect of Germany's repeated role as the model for state-sponsored aggression and violation of international rules. From early on, the German case functioned as a kind of yardstick of European (and American) justice discourses. In addition, communism also originated as a European phenomenon, although Western Cold War discourses tended to 'Sovietize' it. A further factor was in the legal framework, which generally reflected the categories and concepts of nineteenth-century nationalism and imperialism. Although the hegemonic character and related selectivity of European justice debates are more or less indisputable, it would be wrong to claim that there were uniform reasons for this. It is important instead to acknowledge the paradigmatic limits in reflecting the scope and depth of postcolonial justice discourses in an age of late-colonial violence and neo-colonial rights regimes. On the other hand, postwar justice in Europe never unfolded autonomously from the wider world. As we have seen, the American 'third party' played a diametrically opposite role after 1918 and 1945, respectively. While in the first case the United States opposed war crime trials, they went on to accept retribution through judicial means during and after the Second World War. After 1989/90, postwar justice in Europe took place in an international context where similar experiences, previously in South America and simultaneously in South Africa, could not be overseen.

If we now consider the story in chronological order, we are ultimately bound to note the rise of the 'trial' throughout the twentieth century, although this trend has been discontinuous. This can be explained by the potential of this form, whose functions are multiple and can be promoted by various actors for different purposes. Postwar trials were assigned not only for retributive functions, but also to serve the needs of pedagogy, history and memory. Furthermore, public trials such as the Eichmann case would produce, according to some authors, a form of 'discursive solidarity', encouraging a public deliberation on the past.[96] In addition, this kind of trial has roused the interest of researchers as the producer of historical sources on the war itself. This is obvious not only in the case of trials against Nazi perpetrators, but also in that of the Leipzig trials after the Great War.[97]

Notes

1 Paradigmatic for this particular perspective: Ruti G. Teitel, *Humanity's Law* (Oxford and New York: Oxford University Press, 2011).

2 Paul G. Lauren, *The Evolution of International Human Rights: Visions Seen* (Philadelphia: University of Pennsylvania Press, 2011 [1998]).

3 Mark Mazower, 'Reconstruction: The Historiographical Issues', *Past & Present* 210, No. 6 (2011): 21.

4 Pieter Lagrou, 'De l'histoire du temps présent à l'histoire des autres. Comment une discipline critique devint complaisante', *Vingtième Siècle. Revue d'histoire* No. 118 (2013): 101–19, here 113–114.

5 According to Hannah Franzki and Carolina Olarte, this marks a fundamental difference from the German-speaking discourse on the concept 'politics of the past', which emphasizes the dimension of political and socio-economic struggle in the context of regime changes; Hannah Franzki and Carolina Olarte, 'The Political

Economy of Transitional Justice. A Critical Theory Perspective', in *Transitional Justice Theories*, ed. Susanne Buckley-Zistel et al. (London: Routledge, 2013), 201–21.

6 Nancy Fraser, *Justice Interruptus: Critical Reflections on the 'Postsocialist' Condition* (London and New York: Routledge, 1997).

7 Samuel Moyn, *The Last Utopia: Human Rights in History* (Cambridge, MA: Belknap Press of Harvard University Press, 2010), 214. See also Nicolas Guilhot, *The Democracy Makers: Human Rights and International Order* (New York: Columbia University Press, 2005).

8 Susan Marks, 'Four Human Rights Myths', *LSE Law, Society, and Economy Working Papers* No. 2 (2012), available online: https://www.lse.ac.uk/collections/law/wps/WPS2012-10_Marks.pdf (accessed 7.11.2016); Samuel Moyn, 'A Powerless Companion: Human Rights in the Age of Neoliberalism', *Law and Contemporary Problems* 77, No. 4 (2014): 147–69. On this debate see also Mary Nolan, 'Human Rights and Market Fundamentalism in the long 1970s', in *Toward a New Moral World Order? Menschenrechtspolitik und Völkerrecht seit 1945*, ed. Norbert Frei and Annette Weinke (Göttingen: Wallstein Verlag, 2013), 172–81.

9 Bruno Cabanes and Guillaume Piketty, 'Sortir de la guerre: jalons pour une histoire en chantier', *Histoire@Politique* No. 3 (2007): 1.

10 Liora Israël and Guillaume Mouralis, 'Introduction', in *Dealing with Wars and Dictatorships: Legal Categories and Concepts in Action*, ed. Liora Israël and Guillaume Mouralis (The Hague: Asser Press & Springer, 2014), 1–20.

11 Legalistic procedures and at the same time ethnic purges; criminal justice and at the same time settings conceived as an alternative to a penal approach.

12 A critical view on the implications of the so-called Helsinki effect is provided by Robert Brier: 'From Civil Society to Neoliberalism and Armed Intervention? Human Rights and the Legacies of "1989"', *Remembrance and Solidarity Studies* No. 3 (June 2014): 157–88, 173; see also Jiri Priban, 'Political Dissent, Human Rights, and Legal Transformations: Communist and Post-Communist Experiences', *East European Politics and Societies* 19, No. 4 (2005): 553–72, here 556–58.

13 On the debate between Timothy Garton Ash and Stephen Kotkin, see Timothy Garton Ash, '1989!', *New York Review of Books*, 5 November 2009; Philipp Ther, '1989 – eine verhandelte Revolution', *Docupedia-Zeitgeschichte*, 11 February 2010, available online: http://docupedia.de/zg/1989?oldid=108803 (accessed 18.3.2016).

14 Brier, *Civil Society*, 173; Priban, *Dissent*, 556–58.

15 Brier, *Civil Society*, 170.

16 Jiri Priban, 'Reconstituting Paradise Lost: Temporality, Civility, and Ethnicity in Post-Communist Constitution-Making', *Law and Society Review* 38, No. 3 (2004): 407–32, here 412.

17 Milan Horáček, 'Die Aufarbeitung der kommunistischen Diktatur in Tschechien – Eintrittskarte in die' europäische Wertegemeinschaft'?', in *Aufarbeitung der Diktatur – Diktat der Aufarbeitung? Normierungsprozesse beim Umgang mit diktatorischer Vergangenheit*, ed. Katrin Hammerstein et al. (Göttingen: Wallstein, 2009), 215–22.

18 Milan Kopecek, 'Human Rights Facing a National Past. Dissident "Civic Patriotism" and the Return of History in East Central Europe, 1968–1989', *Geschichte und Gesellschaft* 38, No. 4 (2012): 573–602, 576.

19 Guillaume Mouralis, *Une épuration allemande: La RDA en procès, 1949–2004* (Paris: Fayard, 2008), 284 sq.

20 Bundesdatenschutzgesetz 1977, quoted from Inga Markovits, 'Selective Memory: How Law Affects What We Remember and Forget about the Past: The Case of East Germany', *Law and Society Review* 35, No. 3 (2001): 513–63, 523.

21 Annette Weinke, 'Der Umgang mit der Stasi und ihren Mitarbeitern', in *Vergange nheitsbewältigung am Ende des zwanzigsten Jahrhunderts*, ed. Helmut König et al. (Opladen: Springer Verlag, 1998), 167–91, 178.

22 Markovits, 'Selective Memory', 523.

23 Weinke, 'Der Umgang', 179.

24 Klaus Bachmann, 'The Polish Paradox: Transition from and to Democracy', in *Transitional Justice and Memory in Europe (1945–2013)*, ed. Nico Wouters (Antwerp and Cambridge: Intersentia, 2014), 327–50, 345.

25 Anne Applebaum, *Der Eiserne Vorhang: Die Unterdrückung Europas 1944–1956* (München: Siedler Verlag, 2013), 110.

26 Renáta Uitz, 'The Incomplete Transition in Hungary', in *Transitional Justice*, ed. Nico Wouters, 289–326, 297. On the making of the bill, see Gábor Halmai and Kim Lane Scheppelle, 'Living Well is the Best Revenge: The Hungarian Approach to Judging the Past', in *Transitional Justice and the Rule of Law in New Democracies*, ed. James A. McAdams (Notre Dame: University of Notre Dame Press, 1997), 155–84.

27 Ignác Romsics, 'Regime Change in Hungary', *Remembrance and Solidarity Studies* No. 3 (June 2014): 111–40, 136.

28 Jan Pauer, 'Die Aufarbeitung der Diktaturen in Tschechien und der Slowakei', *Aus Politik und Zeitgeschichte* 56, No. 42 (2006): 5–32.

29 Convention on the Non-Applicability of Statutory Limitations to War Crimes and Crimes against Humanity, 26 November 1968, available online: https://www.icrc. org (accessed January 2016). France is not part of this Convention but 'stated' the imprescriptibility only for the 'crimes against humanity' through a 1964 law.

30 Annette Weinke, *Eine Gesellschaft ermittelt gegen sich selbst: die Geschichte der Zentralen Stelle Ludwigsburg 1958–2008* (Darmstadt: Wissenschaftliche Buchgesellschaft, 2009).

31 Andreas Eichmüller, 'Die Strafverfolgung von NS-Verbrechen durch westdeutsche Justizbehörden seit 1945. Eine Zahlenbilanz', *Vierteljahrshefte für Zeitgeschichte* No. 56 (2008): 626–27.

32 In January 2015, about ten of them were still subject to criminal proceedings. In 2013 and 2014, the central judicial office in Ludwigsburg has investigated about eighty former Auschwitz and Majdanek employees. Because of the age of the individuals involved and the lack of evidence, only a small part of these investigations was declared admissible by the prosecutor's offices; *Tageszeitung* 27 (2015). "Derzeit zwölf Schergen auf der Spur", *Die Tageszeitung*, 9/4/2015, https://www.taz.de/Archiv-Suche/!5013444&s=majdanek/.

33 Henry Rousso, 'Introduction', in Henry Rousso, *Vichy, l'événement, la mémoire, l'histoire* (Paris: Gallimard, 2001) ; see also Jean-Paul Jean and Denis Salas (eds.), *Barbie, Touvier, Papon…: des procès pour la mémoire* (Paris: Autrement, 2002).

34 For an overview, see Yves Benot, *Massacres coloniaux: 1944–1950: la IVe République et la mise au pas des colonies françaises* (Paris: La Découverte, 2013); Raphaëlle Branche, *La Guerre d'Algérie: une histoire apaisée?* (Paris: Editions du Seuil, 2014 [2005]), chapter 3.

35 Arrêt de la Cour de Cassation dans l'affaire Aussaresse, 17 June 2003. FIDH, 'communiqué du 18 juin 2003', available online: https://www.fidh.org/fr (accessed January 2016).

36 Marc-Olivier Baruch, *Des lois indignes? Les historiens, la politique et le droit* (Paris: Tallandier, 2013).

37 Katrin Hammerstein et al. (eds.), *Aufarbeitung der Diktatur – Diktat der Aufarbeitung? Normierungsprozesse beim Umgang mit diktatorischer Vergangenheit* (Göttingen: Wallstein, 2009); Georges Mink and Laure Neumayer (eds.), *History, Memory and Politics in Central and Eastern Europe. Memory Games* (Basingstoke: Palgrave Macmillan, 2013).

38 Antoine Garapon, *Peut-on réparer l'histoire? Colonisation, esclavage, Shoah* (Paris: Odile Jacob, 2008).

39 Guillaume Mouralis, 'The Invention of "Transitional Justice" in the 1990s', in *Dealing with Wars and Dictatorships. Political and Legal Categories in Action*, ed. Liora Israël and Guillaume Mouralis (The Hague: Asser Press & Springer, 2014), 83–100.

40 Paige Arthur, 'How "Transitions" Reshaped Human Rights: A Conceptual History of Transitional Justice', *Human Rights Quarterly* 31, No. 2 (2009): 321–67, 325.

41 Annette Weinke, *Gewalt, Geschichte, Gerechtigkeit. Transnationale Debatten über deutsche Staatsverbrechen im 20. Jahrhundert* (Göttingen: Wallstein, 2016); an English version of the book is scheduled for 2018 and will be published by Berghahn Books, Oxford/New York.

42 Sandrine Lefranc, 'La professionnalisation d'un militantisme réformateur du droit. L'invention de la justice transitionnelle', *Droit et société* 73, No. 3 (2009): 561–89.

43 Jiri Priban, 'Oppressors and Their Victims: The Czech Lustration Law and the Rule of Law', in *Justice as Prevention. Vetting Public Employees in Transitional Societies*, ed. Alexander Mayer-Rieckh and Pablo de Greiff (New York: Social Science Research Council, 2007), 308–46, 328.

44 By the war's end, British debts to India amounted to 1.3 million pounds; Nicholas Doumanis, 'Europe and the Wider World', in *Twisted Paths: Europe 1915–1945*, ed. Robert Gerwath (Oxford: Oxford University Press, 2007), 355–80, 377.

45 Arnold J. Toynbee and Veronica M. B. Toynbee (ed.), *Hitler's Europe* (London: Oxford University Press, 1954).

46 Tony Judt, 'The Past Is Another Country: Myth and Memory in Postwar Europe', in *The Politics of Retribution in Europe*, ed. István Deák, Jan T. Gross and Tony Judt (Princeton NJ: Princeton University Press, 2000), 293–323, 295.

47 Quoted from Mark Lewis, *The Birth of the New Justice: The Internationalization of Crime and Punishment* (Oxford: Oxford University Press, 2014), 154.

48 See the case studies in Deák, Gross and Judt (eds.), *Politics of Retribution*, and in Norbert Frei (ed.), *Transnationale Vergangenheitspolitik: Der Umgang mit deutschen Kriegsverbrechern in Europa nach dem Zweiten Weltkrieg* (Göttingen: Wallstein, 2006).

49 This is the underlying thesis of Elizabeth Borgwardt, *A New Deal for the World: America's Vision for Human Rights* (Cambridge MA: Belknap Press of Harvard University Press, 2005).

50 Daniel Segesser, *Recht statt Rache oder Rache durch Recht? Die Ahndung von Kriegsverbrechen in der internationalen wissenschaftlichen Debatte 1872–1945* (Paderborn: Schöningh, 2010).

51 Kirsten Sellars, *The Rise and Rise of Human Rights* (Stroud: Sutton, 2002), 27.

52 See Kim C. Priemel, *The Betrayal. The Nuremberg Trials and German Divergence* (Oxford and New York: Oxford University Press, 2016).

53 Florian Dierl and Alexa Stiller, 'Von Generälen und Partisanen. Die Verbrechen der Wehrmacht in Südosteuropa und der "Geiselmord-Prozess" im Kontext des Kalten Krieges', in *NMT. Die Nürnberger Militärtribunale zwischen Geschichte, Gerechtigkeit und Rechtschöpfung*, ed. Kim C. Priemel and Alexa Stiller (Hamburg: Hamburger Edition, 2013), 230–54.

54 Pieter Lagrou, '1945–1955: The Age of Total War', in *Histories of the Aftermath*, ed. Frank Biess and Robert Moeller (New York and Oxford: Berghahn Books, 2010), 287–96, 294.

55 In cases of war crimes, crimes against peace and crimes against humanity committed by Germans against Germans or stateless persons.

56 Kim C. Priemel and Alexa Stiller (eds.), *Reassessing the Nuremberg Military Tribunals: Transitional Justice, Trial Narratives, and Historiography* (New York and Oxford: Berghahn Books, 2012).

57 Norbert Frei, 'Nach der Tat. Die Ahndung deutscher Kriegs- und NS-Verbrechen in Europa – eine Bilanz', in *Transnationale Vergangenheitspolitik*, ed. Norbert Frei, 7–36; Marie-Bénédicte Vincent, 'Punir et rééduquer: le processus de dénazification (1945–1949)', in *La dénazification*, ed. Marie-Bénédicte Vincent (Paris: Perrin, 2008), 9–88.

58 Klaus-Dietmar Henke and Hans Woller (eds.), *Politische Säuberung in Europa: die Abrechnung mit Faschismus und Kollaboration nach dem Zweiten Weltkrieg* (Munich: DTV, 1991).

59 István Deák, 'Introduction', in *Politics of Retribution in Europe*, Deák, Gross and Judt (eds), 4.

60 Olivier Wieviorka, 'Les mécanismes de l'épuration', *L'Histoire* No. 179 (1994): 44.

61 Anne Simonin *Le déshonneur dans la République: une histoire de l'indignité 1791–1958* (Paris: Grasset, 2008).

62 Pieter Lagrou, 'Poor Little Belgium? Belgian Trials of German War Criminals, 1944–1951', in *Dealing with Wars and Dictatorships*, ed. Israël and Mouralis, 123–143; Dirk Luyten, 'Dealing with Collaboration in Belgium after the Second World War: From Activism to Collaboration and Incivism', in *Dealing with Wars and Dictatorships*, ed. Israël and Mouralis, 59–76.

63 Lutz Niethammer, *Die Mitläuferfabrik. Die Entnazifizierung am Beispiel Bayerns* (Berlin: Dietz, 1982).

64 Glenda Sluga, *Internationalism in the Age of Nationalism* (Philadelphia: University of Pennsylvania Press, 2013), 32–44.

65 Martti Koskenniemi, *The Gentle Civilizer of Nations: The Rise and Fall of International Law, 1870–1960* (Cambridge and New York: Cambridge University Press, 2002).

66 Isabel V. Hull, *A Scrap of Paper: Making and Breaking International Law during the Great War* (Ithaca: Cornell University Press, 2014), 2.

67 Hull, *A Scrap of Paper*, 33–41; Lewis, *The Birth of the New Justice*, 20.

68 Stephen Wertheim, 'The League of Nations: A Retreat from International Law', *Journal of Global History* 7, No. 2 (2012), 210–32, 212.

69 Lewis, *New Justice*, 30.

70 Weinke, *Gewalt, Geschichte, Gerechtigkeit*.

71 Trevor Wilson, 'Lord Bryce's Investigation into Alleged German Atrocities in Belgium, 1914–1915', *Journal of Contemporary History* 14, No. 3 (1979), 369–83; John Horne and Alan Kramer, *German Atrocities, 1914: A History of Denial* (New Haven & London: Yale University Press, 2002).

72 Weinke, *Gewalt, Geschichte, Gerechtigkeit*.

73 Quoted from Margaret Macmillan, *Peacemakers: The Paris Conference of 1919 and Its Attempt to End War* (London: John Murray, 2001), 173.

74 MacMillan, *Peacemakers*, 171.

75 Lewis, *The Birth of the New Justice*, 33.

76 Walter Schwengler, *Völkerrecht, Versailler Vertrag und Auslieferungsfrage: Die Strafverfolgung wegen Kriegsverbrechen als Problem des Friedensschlusses 1919/20* (Stuttgart: DVA, 1982), 88.

77 Horne and Kramer, *German Atrocities*, 331.

78 Weinke, *Gewalt, Geschichte, Gerechtigkeit*.

79 Lewis, *New Justice*, 46.

80 Quoted from James F. Willis, *Prologue to Nuremberg: The Politics and Diplomacy of Punishing War Criminals of the First World War* (Westport, CT: Greenwood Press, 1982), 78.

81 Quoted from Lewis, *New Justice*, 56.

82 Wertheim, 'The League of Nation', 211.

83 Eric J. Hobsbawm, *Nations and Nationalism since 1780: Programme, Myth, Reality* (Cambridge and New York: Cambridge University Press, 1990).

84 Eric D. Weitz, 'From the Vienna to the Paris System: International Politics and the Entangled Histories of Human Rights, Forced Deportations, and Civilizing Missions', *The American Historical Review* 113, No. 5 (2008): 1313–43, 1331.

85 Weitz, 'From the Vienna to the Paris System', 1334.

86 Pierre-Yves Condé, 'Causes de la justice internationale, causes judiciaires internationales', *Actes de la recherche en sciences sociales* 174, No. 4 (2008) : 24–33.

87 The Versailles Treaty, June 28, 1919: Part XIII, Section I: Organisation of Labour, available online: http://avalon.law.yale.edu (accessed 7.11.2016).

88 Sandrine Kott, 'Une "communauté épistémique" du social? Experts de l'OIT et internationalisation des politiques sociales dans l'entre-deux-guerres', *Genèses*, No. 71 (2008): 26–48.

89 Guillaume Sacriste and Antoine Vauchez, 'Les "bons offices" du droit international: la constitution d'une autorité non politique dans le concert diplomatique des années 1920', *Critique internationale* 26, No. 1 (2005): 101–17.

90 On war crimes during the First World War, see Alan Kramer, 'Combatants and Noncombatants: Atrocities, Massacres, and War Crimes', in *A Companion to World War I*, ed. John Horne (Chichester: Wiley-Blackwell, 2010), 188–201.

91 Taner Akçam and Vahakn N. Dadrian, *Judgment at Istanbul: The Armenian Genocide Trials* (Oxford and New York: Berghahn Books, 2011); Alan Kramer, 'The First Wave of International War Crimes Trials: Istanbul and Leipzig', *European Review* 14, No. 4 (2006): 441–55.

92 Kramer, 'The First Wave', 445.

93 Kramer, 'The First Wave', 446–51; Gerd Hankel, *Die Leipziger Prozesse. Deutsche Kriegsverbrechen und ihre strafrechtliche Verfolgung nach dem Ersten Weltkrieg* (Hamburg: Hamburger Edition, 2003).

94 Lewis, *The Birth of the New Justice*, 64–77.

95 Guillaume Mouralis, 'Lawyers versus Jurisconsults. Sociography of the Main Nuremberg Trial', in *Justice in Wartime and Revolutions: Europe, 1795–1950*, ed. Margo de Koster et al. (Brussels: Archives Générales du Royaume, 2012), 325–36.

96 Mark Osiel, *Mass Atrocity, Collective Memory, and the Law* (New Brunswick, NJ: Transaction Publishers, 1997), 43–44.

97 Alan Kramer, 'The First Wave', 450.

4

Futures

Péter Apor

The end of the Cold War brought a liberating moment of creative fantasy into the imagining and planning of possible futures. Various visions of what would possibly occur as well as plans of what should have desirably occurred emerged during the first few years following 1989. The efforts made on planning future processes demonstrate that elites in Europe, educated middle classes, professionals, wage earners and students in many ways all considered 1989 as an opportunity to overcome the conditions of the Cold War, which then was seen as the hindrance for improving the future. Elites, intellectuals and large proportions of European societies found it very likely that the future was possible to anticipate, that it was possible to foresee large and decisive trends of social developments, and therefore it was possible to plan even large systematic changes. However, the multiplication of ideas about and attempts to plan the future also suggests that crucial components of prognosis about further development had been shaken and the future of Europe itself had become uncertain.

Twentieth-century Europe was particularly rich in various political and cultural projects for the future that – all differences notwithstanding – shared deeply engrained modernist presumptions. In fact, the world of modernity is a world that constructs its present in the backyard of a projected tomorrow. Hence, the future represents both a challenge and an opportunity for the governance of modern societies. The question of how societies' futures could be steered and controlled became the central issue of political, intellectual and cultural life in nineteenth- and twentieth-century Western modernity.

Clearly, the mechanisms of tackling the uncertainty of future around 1989 were based on these broader modernist political and cultural programmes of governing the future and were particularly shaped by the emerging expertise of 'future studies' of the 1960s and 1970s, the legacy of which was still very vivid during the 1980s and 1990s.[1] Nonetheless, the hopes and fears concerning the future as well as the ways to cope with them show striking similarities with the two other postwar periods of twentieth-century Europe, roughly the years between 1918–22 and 1945–49. This chapter tries to make sense of these discontinuities and seeks to link these commensurable aspects of the postwar periods together. It also asks if these interlinked discontinuities reveal a specific set of techniques for managing the future in the postwar periods, if in effect there was a specific postwar 'regime of the future'.[2] Such an analysis requires the extension of the scope of investigation beyond considering the politics of the future as the asset of nation states or international affairs.[3] Visions and plans of the future concerned more than the political body of communities. They incorporated, in fact, crucial aspects of the human environment and the deepest layers of individual identity.

Shaping the future: 1989

The multiplicity of plans concerning the future of Europe in the years following 1989 is striking even at first sight. Visions about the future and theories of ideal states and societies that will or should emerge in the future are certainly not the unique property of the early 1990s. Utopian thinking translated into political programmes and activity is a strong legacy of European political and social theory and was arguably a powerful element of twentieth-century politics.[4] Nonetheless, the striking feature of post-1989 plans about the future is their general reluctance to formulate visionary ideologies and abstract ideals for the salvation of mankind. Apparently, these programmes were happy to translate their values and ideals into forms of very concrete practical action, including the definition of responsible institutions and political bodies or the listing of economic measures and institutional reorganization to be carried out.

Both German governments elaborated action plans to realize the unification of the two states. Between 1989 and 1991, government economists developed four plans for transforming the command economy of the Soviet Union and Russia. Similarly, a scheduled plan for withdrawing troops from Germany was accepted by the USSR and West Germany in 1990. The 1991 report of the Club of Rome formulated possible programmes to balance the rapid consumption of resources and to fight economic and welfare decline.[5] In 1992, the successive steps for making the European Union were codified at Maastricht.

The number of these action plans that were so obviously formulated immediately after the end of the Cold War is an evidence that significant groups of Europeans – political and cultural elites, professionals, managers of economy and also urban lower classes and village dwellers – were convinced of the necessity to influence, prescribe and pre-format the future. In the quest for mastering the future, a few areas were given priority, particularly the use of political foresight and economic forecasting. Experts and politicians typically intervened in the management of political communities with the aim of shaping future developments. These areas typically included the national and international systems of states and statehood; demographic, welfare and health programmes and economic restructuring.

The future of Germany was central to these planning processes. West German chancellor Helmut Kohl presented a plan of German unification on 28 November 1989 in the Federal Parliament in Bonn. His proposal of ten measures did not simply concern the fields, which politics was called to address in order to foster the unity of West and East Germany. Rather, the document contained a diachronic series of interventions that gradually expanded the areas of cooperation between the two governments, economic systems and communication and transport infrastructure. These steps that Kohl proposed were successively based on each other, and the document itself suggested, therefore, that if the logic of the temporal order was followed, it would conclude in a unified Germany.[6] His East German colleague, Prime Minister Hans Modrow also formulated a plan of gradual unification on 1 February 1990, which suggested a confederal state structure of West and East Germany.

In a similar manner, the programme of the economic transformation of the Soviet Union in 1989 and then of independent Russia in 1991 followed the logic of temporally successive interventions. The first of these plans was elaborated by Leonid Abalkin in late 1989, which defined a set of successive stages that the Soviet economy should have passed before a real market economy would have been born. All of the alternative plans of economic transformation such as that of Nikolai Petrakov or of Stanislav Shatalin and Grigory Yavlinsky worked with the same components, particularly with the liberalization of prices, privatization and demonopolization. The difference among them was the exact order of the economic measures and the deadline which they set as the end of a successful transformation.[7]

Remarkably, the recasting of the international system of Europe occurred also following the logic of detailed planning. Military security was to be achieved according to a schedule that prescribed various measures for years ahead as between 16 and 20 July 1990, German chancellor Helmut Kohl and Soviet president Mikhail Gorbachev agreed to reduce forces in the territory of the two German states by 1994. The Maastricht Treaty of 7 February 1992, which is the founding document of the European Union, set the frames for a scheduled plan of the forthcoming integration including the date (1999) for introducing the common currency.

Political foresight and economic forecasting were applied in combination in two areas – ecology and demography – where governments and international bodies actively intervened in order to influence future developments. Around 1989, European politicians and intellectuals participated actively in global programmes that centred on sustainable development. The idea of sustainable development has increasingly influenced programmes of combined economic and environmental planning and also impacted the processes of European integration since the 1992 Earth Summit in Rio de Janeiro. The Rio de Janeiro conference of the United Nations endorsed a 'global sustainable development action plan' (Agenda 21), which set sustainability not only as an abstract wish of the future, but rather as a goal to be achieved. Documents and conventions that resulted from the congress set guidelines for concrete measures such as the efficient use of mineral resources, the growing use of recycling or the decrease in the emission of polluting materials. The Rio summit was preceded by an intensive preparatory phase, when national governments and expert bodies prepared national action plans. The conference was crucial also in generating new areas of expertise in 'sustainability science'.[8]

During the early 1990s, national governments and European Union organs tried to intervene in demographic processes and to influence future population developments both in terms of quantity and quality. Typically, such programmes combined family policy measures, child-care allowance systems and ways of managing motherhood and female employment. Interestingly, the impact of such policies was regularly assessed during these years: both at the European level by the Population Policy Acceptance Survey and at the national level by studies on the impact of family policies. These surveys were all concerned with answering the question of how it was possible to influence demographic processes in the future, and, hence, should be seen as evidence of the general acceptance of the need to intervene into future population developments. These ideas and plans after 1989 did not represent a very radical change; in fact, they continued trends in 1980s. However, these programmes reflected several new post–Cold War concerns stemming from accelerating and partly also new forms of migration, notably the increasing movement of extra-European citizens towards Eastern Europe and the similarly rising number of Eastern European migrants towards Western Europe. These new waves of migration also contributed to the sharpening of already existing debates about fertility decline. Following 1989, data concerning population growth or decline were not interpreted in the context of the rivalry between capitalist and communist systems, but rather they were framed as questions relevant to define Europe's new role in a globalizing world. Demographic statistics now forecast the declining share of European population in the world and raised concerns about the generally ageing inactive population in both halves of the continent, particularly, its impact on social welfare and pension systems. Action programmes and impact assessment queries reveal the belief in the possibility of impacting childbearing rationally, either by influencing the cost–benefit analysis that was allegedly attached to marriage and children or by shaping those moral and cultural frames, which were believed to define demographic patterns.[9]

The concerns with demographic prediction developed in close relationship with the latent re-emergence of ethnonationalist understandings of political communities. In the early 1990s, discussions about how to establish and preserve genetic heritage and whether it belonged to ethnic-national groups or larger human population groups became integral parts of debates about sustaining cultural and national identities and, thus, of debates about how it was possible to secure the future of political bodies. Research on genetic diversity was also fed into discussions about the temporal trajectories of political communities: their development in the past and possible roads to take in the future, such as the global Human Genome Diversity Project that was launched in 1990.[10]

Apart from elites, who were concerned with securing the future of the Earth, Europe or their nations, managers running companies and individuals forecasting their life prospects were also convinced that they had to intervene in their own futures. Strategic forecast and planning have long been an integral part of business management. Nonetheless, around 1989, experts, companies and agencies started to offer expertise based on the methods of economic forecasting or even on the discipline of 'future studies' to help managers in long-range thinking. Business-related individuals were taught that the assessment of the future, like sales forecasting, was important since it made one able to intervene in the future by careful financial planning, investment plans and methods of forecasting such as surveys and expert analyses.[11] In fact, agencies such as the Visions Centre for Futures Creation in Sweden that was founded in 1992 offered its services also to individuals to orientate them better in strategic thinking and long-range planning.[12]

It is clear, that around 1989, leaders of political communities, managers of companies and individuals looking forward strategically were not only confident that they had to try to master the future, but also that such measures were entirely possible. Varieties of long-range planning that defined practical steps to be taken few years ahead in temporal order and contained somewhat more flexible, but still clearly formulated, ideas for longer time spans were broadly used. Methods of forecasting that objectified and standardized possible developments of the future in statistical series of numbers counting demographic growth or decrease, ratio of economic investment and produce or expected duration and relevant costs of life were similarly part of making politics, economics or everyday life in Europe. Science, innovation and technology were believed to free human life from the unpredictable consequences of changes in nature. The confidence in intervention into the future was based on a particular understanding of society and social developments. Society seemed to be composed of a manageable number of components – like political interests, economic efficiency, international contexts, demographic changes or changes of the natural environment – the relationships among these aspects also seemed to be detectable, and, lastly, these factors seemed to determine temporal processes.

The range of action plans, which were designed to achieve strategic goals, generated forms and opportunities of exercising power for a set of institutions and sociocultural groups. Governments and politicians gained areas of legitimate intervention, independent intellectuals gained opportunities to shape social and moral reforms, professional expert groups increased their relevance in designing policies and the importance of businessmen grew in creating long-range economic strategies. Through the intensified debates about opportunities in the future, even individuals realized that their subjective insurance strategies or modes of constructing physical identities endowed them with greater control over their bodies and souls.

Attempts to intervene into the future and techniques of influencing it had long-vested expertise with significant powers. During the nineteenth century, it had, indeed, become possible to intervene into and to influence the future in many ways. Modern European societies have developed various tools and mechanisms for constructing and governing their futures, including powerful tools of science, technology and humanities developed in symbiosis with the model of the world in which they were situated.

By means of technological innovation, the development of new machinery and the growth of rationalized and standardized scientific knowledge, it became possible to generate social and economic processes, which made their impact on production, sales, living conditions and social structure in a longer than immediate time frame. Novel institutions, such as insurance, emerged which made it possible to influence income, financial conditions, material and cultural consumption and, hence, social status in the future. At the same time, new numerically objectified methods of analysing and predicting temporal changes such as by means of statistics were developed.[13] Even if the liberal individual as the subject of planning was replaced by governments and state bodies during the twentieth century, 'cultures of planning' remained crucial in giving orientation and order to the future and in rendering rational attitudes towards prediction conceivable.[14] In the effort to strive for the goals of tomorrow – whether or not they were explicitly formulated – the modern sciences and ideologies constructed a world and its individual societies as subjects of administration and rational governance.

The post-1989 confidence in the possibility to master the future and the expertise in the uses of its means were the direct legacy of the emergence of 'future studies' from the 1960s. Governmental programmes, teams of experts and institutions were established in the United States and in the USSR, and also in many countries of Western and Eastern Europe to reach a number of 230 of such units in 1979. Rooted in the Cold War competition for global domination, these initiatives, nonetheless, developed various procedures to forecast probable tendencies of future economic, political and social development in various areas of the Earth. They also elaborated proposals to develop programmes that could influence such developments, particularly in the economic and political processes of the Third World and military competition. Based on standardized scientific procedures and objectified series of data, these institutions claimed a shift in the management of future: Experts believed that statements about the future now transgressed the borders of mere prediction, which was conceived as a generally abstract irrational attitude towards the future, and was transformed into grounded forecasting, which was seen as a practical and rational way to learn about the future.[15]

Shaping the future: 1918 and 1945

The number of concrete action programmes that intervened into the future as well as the areas and methods they focused on relate the post-1989 years to the post–First World War and Second World War periods. In the two previous postwar periods, a multiplicity of projects emerged that not only imagined, but rather designed the future in the shape of action plans that aimed at achieving clearly defined preset goals. Planning the future created a similarly broad range of modes of exercising powers for a similarly rich set of institutions and individuals. The two postwar periods and the post–Cold War years differed from peacetime interventions into the future in their use of a comprehensive set of action plans that addressed all important aspects of societies simultaneously.

The temporal logic of consecutive political interventions to shape a future state was already apparent in the principles of 17 July 1945 Allied conference at Potsdam. The plan of measures agreed set the goal of re-establishing independent regional and municipal administration in Germany and defined the steps to be taken (demilitarization, de-Nazification and decentralization). Arguably, the most grandiose purposeful intervention into the European system of states in the post-1945 period was the Marshall Plan, and subsequently the European Recovery Program, initiated by the Truman administration in 1947. The programme was clearly an investment into the future: The United States transported preset amounts of free goods to participating countries, which those were expected to request in advance. (Western) European governments, thus, had to precalculate their needs and plan ahead their future investments. Although the programme massively impacted the re-structuring of European economies, it also contained the political goal of shaping the future: to generate a set of democratic, free-market, pro-US and anti-Soviet states next to the emerging Soviet sphere of influence in Eastern Europe.[16]

The idea of planning for the future was instrumental in the recasting of European states and international system after 1918, as well. The creation of a system of independent nation states replacing former composite empires was informed by the belief that empires represented an irrational and contingent, thus, unpredictable form of governance, which was seen by influential politicians, particularly by Georges Clemenceau, as the main cause of the war. Consequently, to prevent future conflicts and to secure the desirable future, a 'rationalized' system of predictable states had to be actively created. International institutions, particularly the League of Nations, or the control over Germany became similarly means to actively influence the future: to prevent wars in Europe.[17]

European interventions into state systems with the purpose of influencing the future were not confined to the continent. Particularly after 1945, elites in Western Europe were sensitive also to the possibility that the future of Europe might be decided in the Third World. It seemed that the newly independent and colonial nations represented the terrain where the ideological battle between communism and the 'Free World' would be resolved. It was in these areas that the challenge of communism was felt tangibly, but it still seemed possible to contain its threat. Success in hindering its progress was seen largely in terms of developing attractive ideas about the future for these societies. It was argued that if the Third World could be 'Westernized', if it could be made similar to Europe, then the future of Europe would be saved from the spread of communism. The development of such visions was firmly linked to active interventions into the future: fostering 'modernization', the transition towards industrial societies by means of shaping political and cultural values and disseminating technology.[18] The rationalized, planned nature of decolonization is eloquently illustrated by the birth of the independent government in India. On 20 February 1947, in the House of Commons, Clement Attlee, the British prime minister scheduled the establishment of independent governments in British India to take place before June 1948. Indeed, a new royal commissioner, Lord Mountbatten, was appointed to oversee the systematic execution of the pre-planned timetable of decolonization.

Similar to the post-1989 period, postwar European economies were the subject of several planning programmes, as well. The intervention of the central authorities and the definition of certain production targets and necessary investment by the governments were the typical measures of post-1945 reconstruction, at least up to 1947, the launching of the Marshall Aid programme. In 1946, public services, such as major transport infrastructure, telecommunication networks and energy sector, were either newly taken into state control as in Britain or governments completed similar previous processes as in France, where the state already possessed large proportions of these branches before the war. The state, nonetheless, was certainly reluctant to take everything into its own control, especially to nationalize all means of production and to establish direct state control over enterprises and trade unions. Nonetheless, interventions into national economies were clearly directed at future targets and were based on standardized methods of forecasting. Planning in Western Europe meant the systematic coordinating activity of governments to maximize the productive potential of the whole economy and to predict and establish as precise as possible long-term growth rates. Markets were expected to operate more predictably in order to make the planning of future economic goals possible.[19]

Although, after 1918, the general wish was rather to return to pre-war normalcy and less to experiment with radical new economic and social innovations,[20] several European governments, intellectuals and social reformers designed plans to re-organize the allegedly not-fully effective economies, and social and political structures. All these programmes shared the intention to impact upon economic productivity, working conditions and the management of household and families in the foreseeable future. Influential ideas concerning how to use technology and scientific methods to optimize efficiency throughout society were developed in the United Kingdom, France and Germany, but had an impact on most countries of the continent. 'Scientific management' in Britain, the 'scientific organization of labour' in France and the 'rationalization' programmes in Germany, where even a special governmental body, the Reichskuratorium für Wirtschaftlichkeit, was set up in 1921 to coordinate such efforts, shaped important intellectual and professional interventions in the post-1918 years. 'Rationalization', thus making things effective by scientific methods, became measures that social reformers and governmental organizations applied to shape in a systematic way the outlook of families, housework, sexuality and reproduction, the social body and health-care systems in the future.[21]

Planning, however, meant a more subtle and rigid means to influence the future in post-1945 Eastern Europe already before the communist takeover. The plan symbolized for Communist parties the envisaged deep social and cultural transformation of the nation. The plan acquired mythical character for postwar Eastern European communists and was much more than an effective programme of Postwar reconstruction: It was rather seen as a long-awaited means of bringing about a profound moral reconstruction and social transformation. This linking together of the planning of economic reconstruction and certain moral concerns was not exclusively the privilege of communist leaders or leftist intellectuals. On the contrary, such tenets were shared by several Catholic and Protestant intellectuals, as well.[22]

Planning as a means to influence the future stretched beyond the areas of economy in contemporary Western Europe, as well. Following 1945, a radical turn towards understanding the future as the constant growth of material abundance through technological innovation occurred.[23] The experience of the war, the collapse of nation states throughout the continent, on the one hand, and the demise of democratic structures and the rise of aggressive oppressive states, on the other, convinced the majority of European political leaders and concerned intellectuals that their societies needed a more equal distribution of consumer goods and income, which was seen as vital for better social integration and more stable state structures. Postwar economic programmes typically aimed at not simply restoring economic capacities to pre-war levels, but had the manifest goal to expand such capacities, to increase production spectacularly in order to create larger economies and richer societies. Interventions into the future by setting objectives in advance about the levelling of incomes, particularly through the integration of agricultural labourers and the increase of wages in the industry, or government subsidized housing and the commitment to full employment were inherent parts of postwar government programmes.[24]

The comprehensive nature of planning the future in the postwar years was linked to the objectives of regeneration and national renewal. Beyond the area of the economy, planning was used in programmes for regenerating national communities both in terms of population numbers and healthy bodies. Various governments elaborated various programmes to tackle the issue, which ranged from extensive child-care benefits to anti-abortion campaigns. The United Nations' Population Commission already made predictions on possible future demographic trends in 1946. To balance the forecasted demographic decline, most European governments expanded family allowance programmes in the course of the postwar years. National health insurance schemes, pension programmes and unemployment benefits were developed in a variety of European countries.[25] The systematic intervention to improve health and hygiene expanded beyond communities and reached down to the level of individual lives. The years following the Second World War were the period of the rise of plastic surgery and the increasing use of medicine, which were applied to influence the future of individual bodies by prolonging either its youthful outlook or healthy composition. Although, such interventions were the outcome of military initiatives, during the post-1945 period, they were increasingly appropriated by civilians and, thus, became the means of shaping the future of individual physical identities.[26]

Just as was the case after 1945 or 1989, interventions into demographic processes became an important area of influencing the future in a systematic way after 1918. Governments realized the importance of population statistics in social planning and also encouraged the improvement of demography as a useful means to forecast. After the end of the First World War, population forecasting had vital, even though somewhat absurd implications, particularly in the Franco-German and East-Central European contexts. French political elites were terrified by the prospects of having a future Germany with 70 million inhabitants facing 38 million French in a future conflict.[27] Similarly, Hungarian and Romanian authorities tended to calculate and also actively influence the numbers of ethnic Magyars or Romanians, most importantly in the contested Transylvanian region. The concerns about low postwar birth rates, which projected forward the decline of fertility and population growth, largely shaped population policies in Europe following 1918. In this period, most governments pursued actively pronatalist policies supported by several demographic experts and concerned intellectuals.[28] The French programmes for reconstructing East-Central Europe typically contained elements of the welfare state, health policies, improving medical systems as well as promoting pronatalist measures. Pronatalism was not the only measure undertaken to influence foreseen demographic developments, however. Various social health programmes to combat alcoholism and tuberculosis and to develop effective birth control emerged in many European states during the early 1920s.[29]

In Central, Eastern and Southeastern Europe, the concepts of social hygiene, however, were firmly linked to the idea of securing the future of the nation state. Since most of the newly established nation states defined themselves as the states of their ethnic majority, their future was indissolubly connected to the continuity of their ethnic identities. Thus, the cultural, but increasingly, the biological heritage of such ethnonations appeared as vital to be detected, stored and cultivated. If the modern state wanted to become the guardian of the future, as the argument went, it had to become the protector of biological capital. Eugenics, hence, emerged as a proper science of the future: It offered a rational, predictable and controllable process of constant renewal. Through establishing the 'objective' components of degeneracy and decline, it seemed possible to select elements of rejuvenation that would establish humanity's future on truly healthy foundations.[30] Although, such ideas emerged throughout Europe, the most influential and extensive network of experts for planning the future by means of biomedicine emerged in Weimar Germany in the early 1920s.[31]

The focus of government and expert intervention in the field of social hygiene was the individual. Individuals themselves, however, were also concerned with shaping their own futures. The number of insurance contracts and private health insurers quickly grew in the 1920s, particularly in Germany, which contributed to the spectacular increase of joint-stock insurance companies in the period. Following the First World War, private health insurance was a concern well beyond its traditional consumers, the low-earning working classes: The insurance companies in Germany or Switzerland, for example, expanded their clientele into wealthier middle classes.[32] Plastic surgery, a means to actively intervene into one's life expectations in the future, was invented after the First World War.[33] In the post-1918 period, the most important subject of interventions into individual identities, however, was the gendered body. Typically left-wing socialists such as the Austrian Marxist Max Adler or Leonhard Frank developed plans with the intention to produce techniques for shaping the future of male bodies.[34] These programmes of regeneration generated the multifarious cohorts of experts and expertise of influencing the future, creating space for a complex set of interventions and a complex range of expertise.

Remarkably, most of the important enquiries into the direction of the future, namely considerations regarding the meaning of history and philosophies of history of the twentieth century, were published in the three postwar periods. These were, however, not only gloomy visions of decline or celebrations of the glory of Western civilization in the future but also suggested programmes of how to avoid the fall or how to sustain the triumph. In short, these philosophies of history were attempts to provide theoretically founded techniques of mastering the future. Oswald Spengler's *Der Untergang des Abendlandes* from 1918 suggested the plan of 'Prussian socialism' not only to stop the decline of civilization at the German borders, but also to establish a state that would fit adequately to the conditions of the future and, thus, would be able to rule it.[35]

R. G. Collingwood, Karl Jaspers and Jacob Taubes, who in the post-1945 period realized the secularization of theological eschatology in the form of modern beliefs in historical progress, all established the moral and actual responsibility of individuals for the future. Societies and individuals, as they in general claimed, would be able to rule the future if they recognized the essential historically conditioned nature of human life. If societies understood that the past inherently shaped the life of the present, they would act in the present in a more conscious and reflected way with the constant perspective of shaping the future.[36] This is true also for Löwith's excessive criticism on eschatological thinking. If the European quest for identifying the meaning of history was based on false principles of conceiving the future as purpose-built, then only the unconditional realization of the senseless nature of the future could prepare societies for adequately tackling the real challenges of future eras.[37]

That the goal of philosophy of history in postwar eras is to provide theoretical means for mastering the future is sharply clear in the case of Francis Fukuyama. Fukuyama's statement made first in 1989, then subsequently in 1992 about the final victory of liberal democracy (since this political, social and cultural system represents the end of history in terms of eschatology) represents an attempt to predict in exact terms what sort of political, social and cultural development it was possible to expect in a period when in reality the future role and weight of alternative models in a global setting were still elusive and unclear. To make liberal democracy theoretically the outcome of future processes was an attempt to prevent theoretically the unfolding of alternative scenarios.[38]

The multiplication of possibilities

The development of alternative possibilities of the future that Fukuyama himself wanted to obstruct was typically shared in the Europe of the postwar eras. The multiplication of action plans for systematic intervention into state systems, demography, economy or individual identities is important, but it is not the only aspect that relates the post-1989 years to the postwar periods of the twentieth century. The multiplication of plans reflected the common experience that the future was open with many possibilities, which were, however, not simply visions, abstract ideal states or pressing worries, but were actually possible, realistic scenarios that were all conceivable in very concrete terms.

First of all, in both of the postwar periods that followed the First and Second World Wars, the emergence of supranational integrations and the reconstruction of independent nation states as roads towards the future seemed equally possible.[39] On the one hand, the fact that the pre-war empires of Austria-Hungary, Russia and Ottoman Turkey collapsed and fell into new republics convinced many Europeans that the nation state marked the tendency of future development. Between 1945 and 1949, such beliefs were echoed throughout Europe, as nation states were reconstructed after years of German occupation throughout Europe.[40]

On the other hand, the success of supranational and imperial projects seemed also very probable during the postwar years. Several European intellectuals, particularly in France, Germany and Austria, developed plans of a future united Europe around 1922 and believed in the birth of the new European elite of minds and the overcoming of national rivalry in a future supranational community. In 1948, such views were echoed, among many others, by Julien Benda who saw the shift from nationalism to internationalism and the resurrection of the European spirit which would shape the future of the continent.[41] The acquisition of former German colonies by the British and the French after 1918 convinced many that imperial expansion would continue. However, the unexpected success of the Bolsheviks in Russia turned the forthcoming world revolution and global socialist federation into a tangible future for many others. Although these expectations were not realized after 1918, the military victory of the Red Army in 1945 brought the idea of communist Europe once again palpably close.[42]

Second, both after 1918 and after 1945, it was a commonly held belief that Europe's global role was challenged by the United States and Asia. It seemed very likely that the United States would take over Europe's place in global hegemony, but it seemed similarly possible that Japan or China could step forward and claim such roles. Intellectuals such as Hermann Hesse, D. H. Lawrence or Bronislaw Malinowski in the early 1920s rediscovered the appeal of the extra-European world and believed that the cultures of Africa and Asia would provide models for the revitalization of Europe.[43] For most Europeans in both postwar periods, however, the United States was an image of the future, an image that summed up the expectations towards progress and modernization. The United States had the capacity to imagine and formulate what most Europeans hoped for from the postwar world both in 1918 and 1945: the promise of a just, efficient and good life. However, such images concerned more than material growth and technological innovation. The United States was seen by many as the stimulator of activities and programmes to move Europe towards the future; to mobilize new energies in exhausted, disappointed and decrepit Europe; to rejuvenate societies; to regenerate communities and to protect them against the temptations of cultural atavism. As Raymond Aron commented on the impact of the Marshall Plan, the United States returned the hope and energy for the future to Europe. The Italian communist theoretician, Antonio Gramsci, tended to view the American combination of Fordism and scientific management as a possible model for the socialist future. In the early phase of post-1945 occupation, the spectacle of jolly, well-fed and well-dressed US soldiers and their well-polished technological equipment created suddenly the images of the United States as the land of plenty and modernity palpable.[44]

Nonetheless, after both the First and Second World Wars, there was sufficient evidence to imagine equally the harmful outcome of these processes. Following the two Great Wars, many feared the repercussions of American impact on the European future. In 1919, Paul Valéry, for instance, saw in the United States the ultimate achievements of industrial civilization, where efficiency was developed to its highest degree, but which, at the same time, eliminated humanism, the individual and instinctual.[45] For many, it was exactly the US influence on Europe that would endanger national recovery and the future of a just society. For some political theorists, American cultural influence would threaten the essence of Western civilization, while allegedly replacing its essential plurality with a forced uniformity. For a variety of intellectuals and cultural critiques, the American future was seen to threaten spiritual corruption and the decline of humanity. Particularly, in postwar West Germany, the American offer for future modernity was associated with sheer, inhuman technology and a barbaric insensitivity to high cultures.[46] The Pope also condemned American consumption as undermining spiritual values and European high culture in 1948. In many instances, Americans physically threatened the regeneration of the nation. Male citizens of countries where American soldiers were stationed observed with indignation and discontent that local women were open to socialize with US private soldiers (GIs), which often ended up in marriages.[47]

The disorientation concerning individual physical identities was a more general experience of the two postwar periods. Intellectuals, politicians and ordinary former combatants drew very different conclusions from the radical experience of the war between 1914 and 1918. Humanist intellectuals were convinced that the future of men would be healthier masculine bodies rejecting bellicose brutality, but endorsing personal freedom and solidarity with humankind. Several former frontline combatants, however, like the German Ernst Jünger or Benito Mussolini believed that from the trenches a new type of male body emerged, which would master wartime brutality, integrate advanced technology into its new self and turn them into creative energies instead of rejecting them.[48] New female bodies, in contrast, appeared possibly to threaten personal identities in the future. As urban spaces began to be saturated by the spectacular figure of new short-haired manly looking female bodies, cultural critiques started to fear that such corporeal novelties would destroy first the female, then subsequently also the male sex.[49]

Similarly, the post-1945 years challenged conventional ideas concerning the healthy bodies of men and women. On the one hand, the relative absence of men in domestic societies encouraged women to endow their bodies with traditional male qualities of physical strength and endurance. On the other hand, the brutal experience of wartime male violence made European societies more open to accept more 'feminine' tender and sensual male bodies. Nonetheless, the typical idea that war-torn societies needed rapid regeneration soon reproduced conventional bodily stereotypes free of experiments. If women represented the future, they did so because of their role as mothers, as creatures to create and nurture the new world.[50]

Post-1989 debates about the future in Europe were shaped by strikingly similar sets of possibilities. At the end of the Cold War, the plans of European integration, regional cooperations like the Visegrad 4 group, projects of the Eastern expansion of the European Union and the North Atlantic Treaty Organization (NATO) and intensification of partnership programmes with Russia suggested that 1989 would turn the dream of European federation into reality. Nonetheless, the break-up of federal states in Eastern Europe, the birth of a number of independent national states (including Russia itself) replacing the Soviet Union in 1991, the violent clash among ex-Yugoslav republics in 1991–93 and the peaceful division of Czechoslovakia in 1993 hinted at the possibility that ways of integration may not be the only possible future. From a certain perspective and from a certain period following the end of the Cold War, it seemed that the future of European political communities would make a new era of the nation state, this time defined sharply in ethnic terms. This was particularly true in post-communist Eastern Europe, where the dismantling of the quasi-Soviet empire contributed to various efforts at redefining national identities and a renewed fascination with the nation state.[51] Observing the various regional secessionist movements in Western Europe, however, such as the Lega Nord in Italy,[52] Catalan and Basque separatism in Spain, Breton ethnic revival in France and Scottish nationalism in the United Kingdom, many observers concluded that in the near future European elites would have to live together with the institutionalization of national particularism.

In the post–Cold War years, debates about the rearrangement of the relationships among the alternative models for global modernity and particularly about the place of Europe in them produced many possible transcripts of the future. Japan provided powerful imagery of a possible future of modern capitalist societies with its over-technologized, computerized, automatized daily life and with its striking urban landscape of high-rise buildings and fully artificial street views without any natural vegetation.[53] The accelerated economic growth of South-East Asian 'small tigers', which several analysts saw around 1989 as an explicit model for the economic transformation of post-communist Eastern Europe and others considered as the possible road also for making Western European economies more efficient, created the impression that the future of Europe lay somewhere outside the continent, in somewhat alien non-European cultures. The rising popularity of oriental cultures and the attraction of various mixtures of religious, lifestyle and mystical elements partly taken from extra-European cultures together with New Age movements was a clear sign that many Europeans sought for the resources of social and individual rejuvenation in Asia, Africa or Latin America.[54]

The expectation that the United States would unavoidably shape the outlook of post–Cold War Europe seemed plausible. It was US president Bush and his diplomacy which played an unquestionable role in the negotiations with the moribund Soviet Union and especially on the future of its former satellite states in Eastern Europe. The United States played a crucial role in fostering the reunification of the two German states, even taking sides against official French worries. The United States played a significant role in encouraging European governments to speed up the integration process and was an important partner in shaping the political systems and economies of the emerging democracies in Eastern Europe. Besides, US military and political administration was crucial in containing the war among the successor states of former Yugoslavia.[55] Influential cultural critiques and several political figures expressed their conviction that post-1989 Europe would be an American-type mass society. The American cult of the free market, individualism and consumer cultures was imagined as a model of modernity that seemed very likely to make a beneficial impact on European societies in the near future. American technological innovation was felt by economic and political elites to improve future business and policymaking in Europe. Beyond elites, ordinary Europeans endorsed rather similar innovation in their everyday lives, including household utilities, shopping and eating out.[56]

However, it was also possible to think about the likely repercussions of the forthcoming Asian and American influence on Europe. Accelerating immigration, which spectacularly transformed Western European metropolises into multicultural and multi-ethnic places which was a striking new experience in the countries of the former Soviet bloc, was often perceived with discontent and fear by more indigenous white populations and generated popular movements against it. Similarly, many intellectuals conceived the expected 'Americanization' of Europe with fears and worried about the impacts of materialism, egoism, alienation and cultural deterioration. During the early 1990s, in many European countries, fierce debates occurred concerning the harmful effects of the 'Americanization' of visual cultures, particularly television series and Hollywood movies. US investments in mass amusement became the icons of future moral corruption and cultural decay, as the spectacular condemnation of Euro Disney in France illustrated.[57]

The early 1990s was a period of the emergence of various alternative models concerning the future of individual identities. The accelerating establishment of new sexual sub-cultures, gay, lesbian or trans-sexual movements, supported claims about the diversification of the future individual body. Images of contemporary pop culture and the visual outlook of fashion, which increasingly produced androgynous male figures, were conceived as evidence of the future blurring of the bodily appearance of the sexes. Typically liberal critiques hailed such developments as a progress of individual freedom that made sexual identity a matter of personal choice. More conservative commentators saw them as the evidence of moral decay that threatens humanity in the future. In any case, the growing debates about proper sexual types transformed the future of the male and female bodies into a matter of speculation.[58]

Containing uncertainty

The opening up of the future and the multiplication of possible scenarios certainly had a destabilizing effect. In the postwar periods, the typical experience of the future was the growing uncertainty concerning forthcoming developments. However, the problem concerned more than the difficulty to see clearly what sort of events would possibly occur. What became uncertain concerned the components that normally were conceived to give a direction to the temporal process: states, international systems, economic and social structures and cultural canons. The absence of their clear understanding, in turn, made the direction of history unsure, constituting, in short, a critical challenge to the 'regime of the future' of modernity. The ability to intervene into the future, first of all, presumed a 'future': the possibility to conceive new events, which would bring qualitative changes in social structures, in cultures, in the modes of making politics and in economic production, the opening up of 'horizons of expectations'.[59]

At the same time, however, the confidence in influencing the future is based on a certain level of unchanged constant elements of the temporal process. The ability to plan and calculate responsibly presumes the continuity of components that frame the perception of temporality and the idea that time, in fact, progresses to somewhere. As Zygmunt Bauman put it, such a design-driven rationality creates an image of a continuous world, which also presupposes a specific understanding of time that is cumulative, linear and final, since only such temporal order enables projections into the future and the gradual physical-technological constructions of a grand social-political project.[60] The great wars of the twentieth century and the collapse of the Cold War order shattered these fundamental principles of modernity: They, in many ways, suspended modern temporal order. Projects of the future in the postwar periods were developed against the disturbed order of temporality, the 'crises' of 'postwars'.[61] Securing regeneration, the policies of mastering the future emerged in the context of postwar crises, saturated by the perception of disorientation, decline, but also hope.

The arguably most typical intervention into the future after 1989, which was the combination of political, legal and economic transformations in the countries of post-communist Eastern Europe, reveals what exactly programmes of future regeneration aimed at. The 'transition', in fact, was a set of prescribed measures, which all post-communist governments were expected to follow in a strikingly similar fashion: dismantling state-run economies, privatization and Euro-Atlantic integration and introducing multiparty parliamentary systems. The 'transition process' eventually prescribed a 'normative future'. Post-communist societies were expected to reach a rather uniform state at the end of this process: political and economic structures like the 'West'.

Understanding the mechanisms of shaping the future in such normative terms rendered it the subject of simple technical expertise. Government officials and diplomats of Western European and North American states in concert with international organizations like the International Monetary Fund (IMF) and the World Bank advised the states to follow such a course of steps. Beyond the level of governments, a whole range of expert cultures emerged: Western European and North American economists, consultants and managers flooded Eastern European government offices and economies.[62] In turn, many Eastern European experts travelled and studied in the West the ways of managing market economies, welfare policies and transition processes. Although the 'transition' is normally used to interpret the transformations of post-communist Eastern Europe, the end of the Cold War encouraged the normative shaping of the future in similar terms for Western European societies, too. The 1992 Maastricht Treaty prescribed the process of the political, economic and cultural integration of Europe and facilitated the harmonization of legal systems, market and employment regulations as well as fields such as research and education. Western European societies were also expected to go through a 'transition', which prescribed very similar final results at the end of the process.

Although planning the respect of human rights, democratic representation, effective economies and the broad access to education and welfare benefits is very different from enforcing the establishment of communist dictatorships, the idea of limiting the possible scenarios in the future and, thus, creating a normative future certainly featured the transition of Eastern Europe after 1945, as well. Communist party leaders normally envisaged 'socialist societies' as the future and even understood various temporal phases of the road leading to this final goal. However, up until late 1947, a variety of ways seemed possible to reach the goal. Party leaders and ideologists debated if this transition had to be interpreted as a proto-socialist state of workers and peasants pursuing the tasks of democratic transformation, a means of slow and peaceful development to socialism or simply a not-yet-socialist transitory phase, the form of various 'national roads' to socialism. The meeting of East-Central European Communist parties in Poland on 22 September 1947, when they decided to found the Cominform, had, in fact, the aim to limit the number of possible scenarios and to master the uncertainty of the future these implied. During the meeting, the Soviet leadership prescribed a uniform set of measures to pursue unanimously by its allies and severely criticized those who kept the future open for alternative scenarios.[63]

The methods of mastering the future in the postwar periods were not particularly new, but their use was certainly different from that in periods of peace. It is the component of containment that makes the mechanisms of influencing the future in the postwar eras different from similar practices of other periods. In these circumstances, the interventions into the future aimed at limiting the number of possible scenarios and, hence, containing the uncertainty of the temporal process: in short, restoring the predictability of historical development in order to reconstruct the ability of shaping the future by the conventional techniques of modernity – planning, foresight and forecast. The regeneration of societies, economies, political systems and cultural creativity in the postwar periods was also a regeneration of modern temporality, an intervention to 'normalize' time.

Notes

1   Jenny Andersson, 'The Great Future Debate and the Struggle for the World', *American Historical Review* 117 (2012): 1411–30.
2   This history of the future differs from the program of David J. Staley, in which he argues for the competence of historians to imagine possible future scenarios by imitating historical methodology proper. David J. Staley, 'A History of the Future', *History and Theory* 41 (2002): 72–89. An example from 1989: W. Warren Wagar, *A Short History of the Future* (Chicago: University of Chicago Press, 1989).
3   The state is the subject of David C. Engerman's program for writing histories of the future. Engerman, 'Introduction: Histories of the Future and the Futures of History', *American Historical Review* 117 (2012): 1402–10. Cold War international relations is the arena of the uses of prediction and forecast in the work of Matthew Connelly and others: Matthew Connelly, Matt Fay, Guilia Ferrini, Micki Kaufman, Will Leonard, Harrison Monsky, Ryan Musto, Taunton Paine, Nicholas Standish and Lydia Walker, ' "General, I Have Fought Just as Many Nuclear Wars as You Have": Forecasts, Future Scenarios, and the Politics of Armageddon', *American Historical Review* 5 (2012): 1431–60.
4   Frank E. Manuel and Fritzie P. Manuel (eds.), *Utopian Thought in the Western World* (Cambridge, MA: Belknap Press of Harvard University Press, 1979); Russell Jacoby, *The End of Utopia: Politics and Culture in an Age of Apathy* (New York: Basic Books, 1999).
5   Alexander King and Bertrand Schneider, *The First Global Revolution: A Report by the Council of the Club of Rome* (New York: Pantheon Books, 1991); Donella. H. Meadows, Dennis L. Meadows and Jorgen Randers, *Beyond the Limits: Confronting Global Collapse, Envisioning a Sustainable Future* (Post Mills, VT: Chelsea Green Publishers, 1992); Peter Moll, 'The Discreet Charm of the Club of Rome', *Futures* 25 (1993): 801–5, and Moll, *From Scarcity to Sustainability – Future Studies and the Environment: The Role of the Club of Rome* (Frankfurt – Bern: Peter Lang, 1991).
6   *Frankfurter Rundschau* (29 November 1989), 6.
7   Shatalin and Yavlinsky counted with an exact number of 500 days. Péter Kenéz, *A History of the Soviet Union from the Beginning to the End* (Cambridge: Cambridge University Press, 2006), 268–69.
8   Desta Mebratu, 'Sustainability and Sustainable Development: Historical and Conceptual Review', *Environmental Impact Assessment Review* 18 (1998): 502–3. *Sustainability and the U.S. EPA* (Washington: The National Academies Press, 2014), 21–23.

9   European Commission, *European Public Opinion on the Family and the Desire for Children*. Eurobarometer 32 (Brussels: Commission of the European Communities, 1990); Didier Blanchet and Olivia Ekert-Jaffe, 'The Demographic Impact of Fertility Benefits: Evidence from a Micro-Model and from Macro-Data', in *The Family, the Market and the State in Ageing Societies*, ed. John Ermisch and Naohiro Ogawa (Oxford: Clarendon Press, 1994), 79–104. Ferenc Kamaras, Jiřina Kocourkova and Hein Moors, 'The Impact of Social Policies on Reproductive Behaviour', in *Population, Family and Welfare: A Comparative Survey of European Attitudes*, vol. 2, ed. Rossella Palomba and Hein Moors (Oxford: Clarendon Press, 1998), 242–61; Jacqueline Hecht and Henri Leridon, 'Fertility Policies: A Limited Influence?', in *The Changing Population of Europe*, ed. Daniel Noin and Robert Woods (Cambridge, MA, and Oxford: Blackwell, 1993), 62–75; Anne Hélène Gauthier, *The State and the Family: A Comparative Analysis of Family Policies in Industrialized Countries* (Oxford: Oxford University Press, 1996); Béla Tomka, *A Social History of Twentieth-Century Europe* (London and New York: Routledge, 2013), 9.

10   Human Genome Diversity Committee 1993 Summary Document, Incorporating the HGD Project Outline and Development, Proposed Guidelines, and Report of the International Planning Workshop held in Porto Conte, Sardinia (Italy) 9–12 September 1993, vol. 2002. Available online: http://www.stanford.edu/group/morrinst/hgdp/summary93.html (accessed 20.8.2002).

11   Ken Holden, David A. Peel and John L. Thompson, *Economic Forecasting: An Introduction* (Cambridge: Cambridge University Press, 1990), 3.

12   http://www.framtidsbygget.se/E (accessed 23.9.2014).

13   Michael Adas, *Machines as the Measure of Men: Science, Technology, and Ideologies of Western Dominance* (Ithaca: Cornell University Press, 1989); Geoffrey Clark, Gregory Anderson, Christian Thomann and J.-Matthias Graf von der Schulenburg (eds.), *The Appeal of Insurance* (Toronto: University of Toronto Press, 2010); Viviana A. Rotman Zelizer, *Morals and Markets: The Development of Life Insurance in the United States* (New York: Columbia University Press, 1979); Roy Kreitner, *Calculating Promises: The Emergence of Modern American Contract Doctrine* (Stanford: Stanford University Press, 2007); Greg Eghigian, *Making Security Social: Disability, Insurance, and the Birth of the Social Entitlement State in Germany* (Ann Arbor: University of Michigan Press, 2000); Theodore M. Porter, *Trust in Numbers: The Pursuit of Objectivity in Science and Public Life* (Princeton: Princeton University Press, 1996).

14   Dirk van Laak, 'Planung. Geschichte und Gegenwart des Vorgriffs auf die Zukunft', *Geschichte und Gesellschaft* 34 (2008): 305–7, 323; Dieter Gosewinkel, 'Zwischen Diktatur und Demokratie. Wirtschaftliches Planungsdenken in Deutschland und Frankreich: Vom Ersten Weltkrieg bis zur Mitte der 1970er Jahre', *Geschichte und Gesellschaft* 34 (2008): 332; Anselm Doering-Manteuffel, 'Ordnung jenseits der politischen Systeme: Planung im 20. Jahrhundert. Ein Kommentar', *Geschichte und Gesellschaft* 34 (2008): 388–401; Robert Heilbroner, *Visions of the Future: The Distant Past, Yesterday, Today, Tomorrow* (New York: New York Public Library, 1995), 49, 65–66.

15   Wendell Bell, *Foundations of Futures Studies: Human Science for a New Era* (New Brunswick, NJ: Transaction Publishers, 1997), 47–65.

16   Tony Judt, *Postwar: A History of Europe since 1945* (London: William Heinemann, 2005), 41–99.

17   François Fejtö, *Histoire de la destruction de l'Autriche-Hongrie: requiem pour un empire défunt* (Paris: EDIMA/Lieu Commun, 1993).

18 Odd Arne Westad, *The Global Cold War: Third World Interventions and the Making of Our Times* (Cambridge: Cambridge University Press, 2005), 33–34.

19 Robert Millward, *Private and Public Enterprise in Europe: Energy, Telecommunications and Transport, 1830–1990* (Cambridge: Cambridge University Press, 2005), 171–93; Andrew Shennan, *Rethinking France: Plans for Renewal 1940–1946* (Oxford: Oxford University Press, 1989), 224–86.

20 Alan S. Milward (with Federico Romero and George Brennan), *The European Rescue of the Nation-State* (London and New York: Routledge, 2002), 37.

21 Carole Sachse, 'Rationalizing Family Life – Stabilizing German Society: The "Golden Twenties" and the "Economic Miracle" in Comparison', in *Three Postwar Eras in Comparison: Western Europe 1918–1945–1989*, ed. Carl Levy and Mark Roseman (Basingstoke: Palgrave, 2002), 175, 178. Atina Grossmann, *Reforming Sex: The German Movement for Birth Control and Abortion Reform, 1920–1950* (New York: Oxford University Press, 1995), chapters 4 and 5.

22 Bradley F. Abrams, *The Struggle for the Soul of the Nation: Czech Culture and the Rise of Communism* (Lanham, Boulder, Toronto, New York and Oxford: Rowman and Littlefield, 2004), 187.

23 Mark Roseman, 'Defeat and Stability: 1918, 1945, and 1989 in Germany', in *Three Postwar Eras in Comparison: Western Europe 1918–1945–1989*, ed. Carl Levy and Mark Roseman (Basingstoke: Palgrave, 2002), 263–64.

24 Milward, *The European Rescue of the Nation-State*, 25–37.

25 Martin Lengwiler, 'The Rise of Mixed Welfare Economies in Europe, 1850–1945', *The Appeal of Insurance*, ed. Geoffrey Clark, Gregory Anderson, Christian Thomann and J.-Matthias Graf von der Schulenburg (Toronto: University of Toronto Press, 2010), 190. Gauthier, *The State and the Family*, 60, 65; Margaret S. Gordon, *Social Security Policies in Industrial Countries: A Comparative Analysis* (Cambridge: Cambridge University Press, 1988), 5–8, 45, 145, 293.

26 David Serlin, *Replaceable You: Engineering the Body in Postwar America* (Chicago: University of Chicago Press, 2004), 3–4.

27 Douglas Johnson, 'France's German Question, 1918–1945–1989', *Three Postwar Eras in Comparison*, 238.

28 Erika Kuhlman, *Of Little Comfort: War Widows, Fallen Soldiers, and the Remaking of the Nation after the Great War* (New York: New York University Press, 2012), 126; Susan Pedersen, *Family, Dependence, and the Origins of the Welfare State: Britain and France, 1914–1945* (Cambridge: Cambridge University Press, 1993); Gauthier, *The State and the Family*, 36–58.

29 Marius Turda and Paul J. Weindling, 'Eugenics, Race and Nation in Central and Southeast Europe, 1900–1940: A Historiographic Overview', in *Blood and Homeland: Eugenics and Racial Nationalism in Central and Southeast Europe, 1900–1940*, ed. Marius Turda and Paul J. Weindling (Budapest and New York: Central European University Press, 2006), 2–12.

30 Roger Griffin, 'Tunnel Visions and Mysterious Trees: Modernist Projects of National and Racial Regeneration, 1880–1939', in *Blood and Homeland: Eugenics and Racial Nationalism in Central and Southeast Europe, 1900–1940*, ed. Marius Turda and Paul J. Weindling (Budapest and New York: Central European University Press, 2006), 418–45.

31 Aristotle A. Kallis, 'Racial Politics and Biomedical Totalitarianism in Interwar Europe', *Blood and Homeland*, 391.

32 Lengwiler, 'The Rise of Mixed Welfare Economies', 184, 192.

33 Serlin, *Replaceable You*, 3–4.

34 Max Adler, *Neue Menschen: Gedanken über sozialistische Erziehung* (Berlin, 1924),
    69. Leonhard Frank, *Der Mensch ist Gut* (Zurich: Europäische Bücher, 1918); George
    L. Mosse, *The Image of Man: The Creation of Modern Masculinity* (New York and
    Oxford: Oxford University Press, 1996), 119–21.

35 Oswald Spengler, *Der Untergang des Abendlandes*. Vol. 1: *Gestalt und Wirklichkeit*
    (Vienna: Braumüller, 1918); Vol. 2: *Welthistorische Perspektiven* (Munich: C. H. Beck,
    1922).

36 Robin G. Collingwood, *The Idea of History* (Oxford: Clarendon Press, 1946) ; Jacob
    Taubes, *Abendländische Eschatologie* (Berne: A. Francke Verlag, 1947); Karl Jaspers,
    Vom Ursprung und Sinn der Geschichte (Munich: R. Piper, 1949).

37 Karl Löwith, *The Meaning of History* (Chicago: University of Chicago Press, 1949).

38 Francis Fukuyama, 'The End of History?', *National Interest* 16 (Summer 1989): 3–18
    and *The End of History and the Last Man* (London: Hamish Hamilton, 1992).

39 Charles Maier, 'Empires or Nations? 1918, 1945, 1989…', *Three Postwar Eras in
    Comparison*, 41–66.

40 Christopher Seton-Watson, 'The Nationalist Challenge to Stability in Eastern and
    Central Europe: 1918–1945–1989', *Three Postwar Eras in Comparison*, 86–96; Joachim
    von Puttkamer, *Ostmitteleuropa im 19. und 20. Jahrhundert* (Munich: Oldenbourg,
    2010); Eric Hobsbawm, *The Age of Extremes: The Short Twentieth Century, 1914–1991*
    (London: Michael Joseph, 1994).

41 Jessica Wardhaugh, Ruth Leiserowitz and Christian Bailey, 'Intellectual Dissidents
    and the Construction of European Spaces, 1918–1988', *Europeanization in the
    Twentieth Century: Historical Approaches*, ed. Martin Conway and Kiran Klaus Patel
    (New York: Palgrave Macmillan, 2010), 21, 30–32.

42 Kenéz, *A History of the Soviet Union*, 27–33.

43 Adas, *Machines as the Measure of Men*, 389–90.

44 David W. Ellwood, *The Shock of America: Europe and the Challenge of the Century*
    (Oxford: Oxford University Press, 2012), 275, 286–87, 293–94, 304, 309–10, 355.

45 Stephen Gundle, 'Visions of Prosperity: Consumerism and Popular Culture in Italy
    from the 1920s to the 1950s', *Three Postwar Eras in Comparison*, 154, 157; Ellwood,
    The Shock of America, 72–77, 84–85, 98, 108.

46 Wolfgang Lepenies, *The Seduction of Culture in German History* (Princeton: Princeton
    University Press, 2006), 9, 146.

47 Ellwood, *The Shock of America*, 290, 302, 313–14, 324, 329–30, 334, 336, 341–42, 365.

48 Ernst Jünger, *Der Kampf als inneres Erlebnis* (Berlin: E. S. Mittler & Sohn, 1922),
    32; Mosse, *The Image of Man*, 110, 112–13, 115; Adas, *Machines as Measure of Men*,
    382–83.

49 Ute Frevert, *Women in German History: From Bourgeois Emancipation to Sexual
    Liberation* (Oxford: Berg, 1993), 178; Mary Louise Roberts, *Civilization without
    Sexes: Reconstructing Gender in Postwar France, 1917–1927* (Chicago: University of
    Chicago Press, 1994), 53; Mosse, *The Image of Man*, 9, 147.

50 Claire Duchen and Irene Bandhauer-Schöffmann, 'Introduction', in *When the War
    Was Over: Women, War and Peace in Europe, 1940–1956*, ed. Claire Duchen and Irene
    Bandhauer-Schöffmann (London and New York: Leicester University Press, 2000),
    2–3; Mosse, *The Image of Man*, 181; Sachse, 'Rationalizing Family Life', 188–89.

51 Judt, *Postwar*, 637–700; John R. Lampe, *Yugoslavia as History: Twice There was a
    Country* (Cambridge: Cambridge University Press, 1996).

52 Robert Lumley, '1968/1989: Social Movements in Italy Reconsidered', *Three Postwar Eras in Comparison*, 208–10.

53 Ellwood, *The Shock of America*, 443.

54 Carl Levy, '1918–1945–1989: The Making and Unmaking of Stable Societies in Western Europe', *Three Postwar Eras in Comparison*, 12.

55 Judt, *Postwar*, 637–57.

56 Ellwood, *The Shock of America*, 447–48.

57 Ellwood, *The Shock of America*, 465, 470.

58 Mosse, *The Image of Man*, 186–87, 189, 191, 194; Carol Lee, *Talking Tough: The Fight for Masculinity* (London: Arrow Books, 1993), 152; Gertrude Himmelfarb, *The Demoralization of Society: From Victorian Virtues to Modern Values* (New York: Knopf, 1995), 11.

59 Reinhart Koselleck, *Futures Past: On the Semantics of Historical Time* (Cambridge, MA: MIT Press, 1985); Lucian Hölscher, *Die Entdeckung der Zukunft* (Frankfurt a/M: Fischer Taschenbuch Verlag, 1999).

60 Zygmunt Bauman, *Liquid Modernity* (Cambridge: Polity Press, 2000).

61 Ivan T. Berend, *Decades of Crisis: Central and Eastern Europe before World War II* (Berkeley: University of California Press, 1998).

62 Tony Judt, *Postwar*, 685–90.

63 Vladislav M. Zubok and Constantine Pleshakov, *Inside the Kremlin's Cold War: From Stalin to Khrushchev* (Cambridge, MA, London: Harvard University Press, 1996), 125–37; Joseph Rothschild, *Return to Diversity: A Political History of East Central Europe since World War II* (New York: Oxford University Press, 1989), 125–32; Richard J. Crampton, *Eastern Europe in the Twentieth Century* (London: Routledge, 1994), 255–60; George Schöpflin, *Politics in Eastern Europe, 1945–1992* (Oxford: Blackwell, 1993), 57–74.

5

States

Pieter Lagrou

No single event shaped our European present in a more profound and continent-wide way as much as 1989. Still, contemporaries and historians struggle to qualify the nature of events that happened that year. The Velvet Revolution was, in many ways, not really a revolution. Indeed, the Cold War that came to an end was, in many ways, not really a war, and the New Europe that emerged was in many ways not really new, but rather an extension of the Old Europe. Real change only came to the East, while the West was allowed to continue to think that nothing of fundamental importance had really happened on the domestic scene. Placing 1989 firmly on the map of our historical conscience is a fundamental challenge to political and historiographical debates alike. It stands at the heart of controversies over the shape and very nature of the European Union and its place in the world. It defines the watershed between past and present, and thereby the range of action for historians. The status of 1989 as a chronological boundary is also undefined – both, as it is generally admitted but rarely interpreted, the end of a Short Twentieth Century that is rapidly receding into the past and the beginning of a still unarticulated present.[1] Inevitably, the nebulous nature of 1989 throws us back to 1918 and 1945, those other obvious caesura of the twentieth century that moulded the present of their own aftermaths. Capturing 1989 using the tools and concepts – complete with implied expectations and language – developed by historians to understand the twentieth century comes down to adding this as a sequel to the two previous ones, in order to apprehend both the differences and the similarities.

1989, 1945 and 1918 were moments of rupture with the past, moments of destruction for an ancient order and the states that incarnated that order. Four empires that still shaped the major part of European territory – only one of which we could consider a nation state – and a bourgeois order cemented by the predominance of census suffrage collapsed in the conflagration of the First World War. Fascism, one of the recipes for reconfiguring a New European Order of strong states, was defeated in the second moment of rupture, and the physical, moral and ideological wreckage inflicted by Europe upon itself at this time placed the continent under the guardianship of two predominantly non-European powers during the second postwar period, which lasted half a century. Communism, that other recipe for building a strong state and formulated at the start of the century when the bourgeois and imperial order fell, disappeared in 1989. Yet, 1989 does not seem equal to 1918 and 1945 as a defining negative moment of *Nie Wieder*, a violent rupture with the past that engenders a utopian vision for a new future. Communism disappeared in 1989, but it had been defeated as a political model long before. Its discredit had preceded collapse. It was the cause, not the consequence of defeat. This is in keeping with the undefined nature of the post-1989 period, singularly lacking in both utopian thought and a need to collectively combat phenomena such as war, imperialism, bourgeois hegemony, fascism and policies of mass murder on an unprecedented scale.

The triptych 1989–1945–1918 is an unabashedly Eurocentric way of conceiving history, or, rather, it is the periodization of German history writ large. First and foremost, it was German borders, German statehood and German political regimes that were fundamentally transformed three times over. Indeed, 1918 only affected the Netherlands, Switzerland and the Scandinavian and Iberian countries domestically because of the fallout of events abroad. Switzerland, Sweden, Ireland, Turkey, Spain and Portugal likewise observed 1945 from the relative comfort of non-involvement in the conflict, and none of the Western countries underwent border change or massive and enduring population displacement. Many Europeans west of the Rhine witnessed 1989 as a strange spectacle in far-away places that did not affect their daily lives in any noticeable way. While 1989 was the year of regime change in most European Soviet satellite states, paving the road for German unification, it was the collapse of the Soviet Union in 1991 that brought a much more profound transformation on a global geographical scale as well as in terms of the chronology of the twentieth century. If 1989 was about the geopolitical retreat of the Soviet Union from the sphere of influence acquired in 1945, 1991 was the end of a regime and an ideology that had dominated or inspired roughly half of the globe in search of alternative solutions to capitalism and liberal democracy since 1917. Even if 1989 acquired currency as a shorthand for the implacable chain of events linking the fall of the Wall to the storming of the parliament building in Moscow, symbolically Berlin still totally eclipses Moscow, much in the way 1918 eclipses 1912, 1917 or 1923, and 1945 eclipses 1938, 1943 or 1947. The 1989–91 sequel is understood through the prism of Vaclav Havel rather than Michael Gorbachev, let alone Boris Yeltsin. Our Eurocentrism leads us to confound cause and effect. Throughout this chapter, we will try to avoid this conceptual trap, even if we continue to use the shorthand of 1989 to refer to a larger chain of events initiated by crucial change in the Soviet Union.

Certainly, 1989 allows us to insert the European experience into a global context. For example, 1989 is also the year of the Tiananmen Square massacre, the repression of a student revolt triggered by Michael Gorbachev's visit to Beijing and the consequent expectations that China might follow the path of democratic change then underway in Europe. The Chinese regime was resistant to geopolitical changes in ways that Europe's political regimes were not, not even those steering a course independent from Moscow, such as Yugoslavia, Albania and, to a lesser extent, Romania. The period 1989–1991–1994 also comprised momentous change in South Africa, with the previously inconceivable peaceful end of the Apartheid regime that had been founded in 1945. Elsewhere, the democratic impetus was either halted, such as in the failure of the Oslo talks in 1993 and the perpetuation of colonial violence in Palestine, or derailed by ethnic violence, such as in Rwanda and (once again) Yugoslavia. As such, in many ways, the end of the Cold War had a more genuinely global impact than that of both world wars, insofar as the latter, while destroying a European order, had not instantly also destroyed the colonial order.

In writing the history of the twentieth century in a triple jump, setting foot in 1918, 1945 and 1989 implies, much as in the Olympic discipline, three steps covering two intervals of very unequal length. If the unity of action linking both world wars has an incontrovertible character, 1989 is a very much belated end to the epoch inaugurated in 1945, occurring long after other, no less profound transformations that had changed the European continent beyond recognition. The seismograph of social history certainly puts 1989 a few scales below 1918 and 1945. Apart from plunging birth rates in the East, the demographic impact of 1989 is hardly perceptible. Far fewer people died from political, let alone military, violence Europe-wide in 1989 than those who died from traffic accidents in even a single of some of its smallest nations. Even though freedom of movement had been the central and urgent demand of the mass demonstrations during the autumn of 1989, the dismantling of the Iron Curtain precipitated only minor migrations: In the case of Hungary, for example, these were far less significant than those of 1956. If, by the end of the twentieth century, European societies had become new societies in many regards due to aging, new family models, extra-European immigration and industrial decline, none of these transformations resulted from the events of 1989. By the early 1980s, the combined forces of decolonization, the emergence of a consumer society, the sexual revolution, the full-scale assault on the Welfare State initiated by neoconservatives in the late 1970s and the electoral breakthrough of the extreme right left little intact of the political order that had rebuilt Western Europe after 1945. Crucially, though, these experiences are what made Western Europe such a peculiar place, especially when compared to Eastern Europe. The year 1989, therefore, is neither more important nor more fundamental than 1962, 1968, 1979 or 1981. However, if the issue at stake is the making and un-making of states, measuring the impact of geopolitical change on Europe as a whole and conceptualizing the crucial link between domestic and geopolitical change, 1989 alone can be seen to equal 1945 and 1918.

Framing 1989 as the sequel of 1918 and 1945 does, then, constitute a challenging research agenda. The first challenge is geographical: These three moments are European moments, not in a limitative way, but in terms of the intellectual imperative to transcend the national or regional level. The years 1989, 1945 and 1918 are moments of domestic change in national societies, polities, states and regimes that cannot be understood outside of their geopolitical context. They force us to think together and to embrace in an integrated attempt to conceptualize East and West, the Balkans and the Baltics, Sicily and Ireland and Warsaw and Athens.[2] The second challenge is chronological: Instead of offering a teleological or genealogical narrative, whereby what precedes is reduced to the cause of what follows, we will assume the challenge of articulating how our questions about how the present results from 1989 force us, in fact, to revisit the two previous sequels. This implies to question the validity of historians' instinctive reflexes to apply previously developed tools, concepts, vocabulary and methods from one sequel to the next, and to consider these as the only prism for understanding subsequent events. As such, this regressive method is also an exercise in emancipation from our own frameworks of thought and our tendency to reduce the new to ever more of the old. Historians, politicians and commentators have incessantly been reducing 1989 to a sequel of 1945 or the simple closure of a parenthesis. Now is the time to question, as systematically as possible, to what extent this is a valid intellectual operation versus merely a lens that distorts our perception of our present and prevents us from understanding it on its own terms.

Embracing in a single sweep three historical moments and an entire continent can allow us to challenge crucial notions on which we have built our historical understanding. What is a revolution, compared to the implosion of a regime hollowed out by long-standing erosion of its legitimacy? Why did the collapse of the Tsarist regime trigger so much more violence than the collapse of the Soviet regime? What is it we are talking about when referring to the Cold War as a war? Is the end of the Cold War followed by a postwar period in any way that makes sense in the light of how historians have dealt with the previous two postwar periods? Does cultural demobilization always follow the end of a war, or can it also precede it, if that war is a Cold War? Are the social and political changes that occur after a war necessarily the result of the war experience, or is the destruction brought by war first and foremost an opportunity to implement various changes projected, hoped and campaigned for during the periods of geopolitical stalemate that prevented them before the outbreak of the said war? The year 1918 allowed for the general implementation of universal suffrage and forms of national self-determination, which had constituted the horizon of political expectations since the late nineteenth century; similarly, 1945 allowed for the creation of comprehensive welfare states rooted in the experience of the 1930s no less than the 1940s. What projects did the 1970s and 1980s have in store that the geopolitical window of opportunity at the end of the Cold War made possible?

The twentieth century that bridges these three moments does not stand out as the century of democracy, when compared with the nineteenth and with the incipient twenty-first century; similarly, neither does the twentieth century stand out as that of nationalism. It was, however, unquestionably the century of the nation state: No other chronological sequence witnessed the creation of more modern states, nor an even remotely comparable expansion of state power in terms of the increases in the share of the gross domestic product (GDP) spent by governments, in the number of civil servants and in areas of human activity regulated and supervised by the state in both the public and private spheres. The fact that the state took the centre stage of history in this period had everything to do with the introduction of universal suffrage, which vastly increased both the expectations of the population vis-à-vis the state and the legitimacy of the state vis-à-vis its individual citizens. During the nineteenth century, universal suffrage was characterized by its rarity; during the twenty-first century, it seems characterized by disaffection.

It might therefore be rewarding to question the impact of our three moments of change from the perspective of the state. War was the ultimate test of the superiority or inferiority of state structures: War greatly increased the powers wielded by the state over its citizens, and postwar politics were first and foremost about reinventing the state – a state capable of overcoming and preventing once and forever the woes of war. Debates about what citizens could legitimately expect from their state were inevitably grounded in an analysis of what had caused war; about what had gone wrong and about the causes of weakness, defeat and destruction. The study of postwar moments shows that the development of modern states has not been characterized by linear, incremental growth, but by growth spurts linked to the window of opportunity offered by the challenges of reconstruction and the inflation of expectations caused by the re-establishment of peace.[3] Beyond Max Weber's definition of the state as a 'compulsory organisation with a territorial basis' exercising the monopoly of force, wars and their postwar periods revolutionize the role and the reach of the state.[4] This in turn sparked debates on the need for a return to the self-imposed limits and the ideological neutrality of the liberal state in peace time, after the unchecked extensions under the exceptional conditions of military mobilization for total war and ideological mobilization by totalitarian regimes, by thinkers as opposed as Karl Dietrich Bracher, Raymond Aron, Hannah Arendt, Franz Neumann and Theodor Adorno.[5]

In the first section of this chapter, we will therefore try to show how, in debates on the shape and nature of postwar states, not only historians, but contemporaries of 1989, 1945 and 1918 have consistently read twentieth history backwards, that is, tried to understand the present with the concepts, tools and ideologies of the previous time sequel. This quite often meant that they misunderstood history as it unfolded in most unexpected ways. In the second section, we will try to show how 1989, 1945 and 1918 were genuinely European moments, and to some extent shared experiences that defined a new European present. We will thus attempt to challenge the Iron Curtain that is still very much dividing the ways in which contemporaries and historians conceive the European past and present.

How contemporaries of 1989, 1945 and 1918 have read the twentieth century backwards

As previously noted, 1989 was not a year of military defeat or victory in an armed – if cold – conflict. One of the belligerents forfeited, thereby depriving the opposite side of the satisfaction of triumph. Nor was 1989 a year of revolution in any classical sense, due to the absence of wide-scale violence, utopian thought and *tabula rasa*. It was first and foremost a moment of implosion of failed state structures. As such, it very much contradicted the very core of the theory of the totalitarian state, premised upon the precedent of Nazi Germany. The totalitarian state was deemed to be different from its predecessors because of the degree of control it wielded over its population, through propaganda, surveillance and repression. Imperial Germany had to some extent – and not only in the resentful and apologetic retrospection of German nationalists of the 1920s – been defeated on the home front, in 1917.[6] No such popular disaffection occurred in the summer of 1944, when the von Stauffenberg conspirators painfully discovered how lonely they were, or in the following months during which the German society seemed committed to collective suicide rather than rebellion or desertion. The lesson learned by totalitarianism theory was thus that only total defeat and unconditional surrender could bring such a regime to an end. Negotiating with moderate elements in the power elite or encouraging popular dissent were a waste of time and proof of a total lack of understanding of the real functioning of a totalitarian state. The Munich Syndrome thus became the ultimate, if historically unconvincing, argument for hardliners and warmongers for decades to come: negotiate with a totalitarian regime to avoid military conflict and you will be sure to get a full-fledged world war instead.

This line of reasoning justified the dropping of the atomic bombs on Hiroshima and Nagasaki in August 1945. If imperial Japan was indeed a totalitarian state, the only alternative to the bomb would have been an allied landing in mainland Japan, facing fanaticized enemies bent on kamikaze rather than diplomacy. Tsuyohsi Hasegawa has since demonstrated that negotiating with the partisans of surrender within the Japanese war council had been a real option, had the ultimatum only been phrased in such a way as to allow the Japanese to salvage the emperor.[7] In the end, the Americans insisted on unconditional surrender, dropped the bomb and left Hirohito on his throne. Apparently, Nazi Germany and imperial Japan each belonged to a different class of political regimes, after all. The nuclear build-up launched by Ronald Reagan in the 1980s subscribed to the same belief: Only force could bring a totalitarian enemy to his knees, since it was vain to count on internal dissent – which, by definition, was impossible. Spied upon, infiltrated and terrorised, any form of opposition would be nipped in the bud by an all-efficient and omniscient state before it could begin to wield any influence whatsoever. While Reagan perhaps should have known better, he can be excused by the fact that none of the intelligence agencies, Kremlin watchers, sovietologists, historians, social scientists or even exiles and militants had correctly diagnosed the frailty and imminent collapse of the communist states. It remains a delectable irony of history that no one overrated the efficiency of state-led economies more than American neoconservatives.

In the framework of this book, it seems particularly significant to underline that it was the lessons learned from 1945 that prevented contemporaries of the late 1980s from understanding the events they were witnessing on their own terms, from reading the signs of the present, rather than bygone, times. In 1945, it would indeed have been difficult to pretend that the regime collapsed from internal weakness. Nazism did not fall prey to its unpopularity with the German population, but rather to its military hubris. In the process, it had involved German soldiers and citizens to such an extent in massive crimes against neighbouring populations, especially to the East, that Nazi propaganda had some credibility in warning Germans to expect nothing short of full retaliation, a fate that made the alternative of fighting to the death an attractive option. The German *Widerstand* was exceptional in its social and military insignificance, only gaining symbolic significance retroactively. Likewise, Italian fascism found more support in the Italian society between 1926 and 1938 than the liberal state had ever achieved between 1861 and 1922. The *Antifascismo*, the opposition to domestic dictatorship before 1943, unlike the *Resistenza*, the insurgency against German occupation afterwards, never was a mass movement. Had Mussolini abstained from initiating the invasion of the Balkans and participating in the invasion of France and the Soviet Union on Hitler's side, like his fellow fascist Franco wisely did, the prospects for political survival of Italian fascism well beyond 1945 seemed much better than those of Francoism, facing as the latter did the divisive legacy of the civil war.[8] Nazi and fascist propaganda had turned military superiority into the ultimate proof of political superiority, thereby paving the road for the general acceptance of the superiority of the Soviet and capitalist liberal systems from 1943 onwards. The arbiters of the European civil war that had been raging for three decades ultimately came from beyond the Urals (for 80 per cent of the German military deployment) and beyond the Channel and the Atlantic Ocean (for the remaining 20 per cent). In the years leading up to the conflagration of September 1939, it was not fascism, but rather liberal democracy and parliamentarism that had been emphatically diagnosed with a terminal condition. To most continental Europeans, the Summer of 1940 appeared as the start of a new postwar period and a New Order of indefinite fascist superiority, built on the ruins of the unsuccessful experiment with the democratic order that had been conducted after 1918. It is only after Stalingrad that projections of a postwar of another order started to creep into European private opinions. Looked at from the perspective of the decade 1933–43, parliamentary democracy, not fascism, seemed doomed. We will return to this analysis and its impact on conceptions of the state a little later in this chapter.

June 1940, but in some ways May 1945 no less, served to undermine what many had taken to be the lesson learned in 1918: the superiority of democratic nation states over authoritarian empires. Democracy had suffered defeat in 1940; the *Volksgemeinschaft* in 1945. Back in 1918, British parliamentary democracy and the French Third Republic had triumphed over an ill-assorted alliance of multinational empires and authoritarian emperors. France in particular embodied the triumphant model of a modern nation state that had implemented universal suffrage and turned its 'peasants into Frenchmen'[9] since the 1870s. The constitution of the Third Republic became the model copied in the dozen of new states of the Europe born in 1918.[10] The peoples' prisons had not withstood the test of total war and simply dissolved under its extreme pressure. Soldier-citizens had put up a braver fight than soldier-subjects, including and even particularly in the allied camp, evidenced by the total meltdown of the Russian front. It came as no surprise that the sick men of Europe – in Constantinople, Vienna and Petersburg – could not stand up to modern nation states. Nationalists in the Habsburg, Ottoman and Tsarist empires had claimed so for decades, with the active encouragement of French and British diplomats and *agents provocateurs*. The empires themselves had tried to adopt some elements of the nation state in their projects of modernization: the Tsarist empire by reinforcing its policies of russification, the Habsburg empire by becoming a double monarchy in 1867 and the Ottoman empire first by promoting some form of cross-national identity under Ottomanism and then increasingly ceding to the Young Turk nationalist ideology. Ultimately, their unsuccessful attempts further enfeebled their multinational statehood. National self-determination seemed the only viable path towards the formation of a modern state, allowing for popular legitimacy, economic efficiency and thus military might. Popular sovereignty also involved universal suffrage. Wilhelmine Germany had failed on this account, since the nominal universal suffrage adopted in the Imperial constitution served merely to obfuscate the lack of democratic accountability of the Kaiser. The fact that universal suffrage also implied the promise/threat that ethnic majorities could dispose of ethnic minorities in the future Europe contributed to its popularity among those who could legitimately expect to be on the side of the majority within the borders of a given independent-state-to-be. In short, 1918 seemed to confirm all the hopes and expectations of liberty, equality and fraternity cherished by national revolutionaries since 1789 and 1848. It marked the turning of the page, once and for all, on the *Ancien Régime* on the European continent.

How unforetold were 1989, 1945 and 1918? Did they fulfil historical expectations, confirm forebodings or take their contemporaries aback? On this account, 1989 stands out as an utter surprise, the lead up to which had completely eluded contemporaries. This also helps to explain the subsequent eagerness to provide retrospective accounts, quite unrivalled by prospection. In the event, no one could really claim, 'I told you so.' This amounts to quite an astounding failure of the social sciences, precisely in the decades of their greatest boom (the 1960s to 1980s). Never before had so many historians, political scientists, sociologists and so forth been paid by governments to apply the tools of their disciplines to the contemporary world, and never had they been more confident in their capacity to produce adequate prognoses. In the end, not only did they fail to grasp the significance of the events unfolding before their very eyes, but the concepts they had developed since 1945 very much prevented them from understanding what they saw. Rarely have facts offered such a brutal rebuke to theory. These same social scientists reacted with instant and astounding inventiveness: The very certainties that had blinded them to the process of collapse of communist systems were now guiding the new discipline of transitology and its warehouse of normative and unquestioned knowledge about how to become successful free markets and democracies.

With respect to 1945, this too was the source of some embarrassment. Since parliamentary democracy had been declared clinically dead on the continent in 1940, only two contenders for political supremacy were left standing: fascism and communism. With the lion's share of the fighting conducted by the Soviet Union, 1945 seemed to vindicate the Marxist anti-fascist interpretation of the 1930s. If fascism was the ultimate stage of capitalist development, the need for the resurrection of bourgeois capitalist liberal democracy was an improbable conclusion. In this light, the political order of East and Central Europe seemed more compatible with pre-war and wartime expectations than that of Western Europe. Overall, therefore, only 1918 seemed to many to confirm predictions of both doom and wishful thinking about the imminent collapse of the ancient order, of the peoples' prisons, of the bourgeois hegemony and of many a tyrant. But then again, the satisfaction gained through hopes fulfilled proved very short-lived indeed in interwar Europe.

The invention of otherness: bridging incommensurable experiences, East and West

The weakness of Soviet satellite states in Central and Eastern Europe has since 1989 been explained in various ways.[11] A first set of explanations is obviously economic: The planned economy outperformed its capitalist rivals during the phase of forced industrialization in the 1950s and 1960s. Unhindered by voters' expectations and the contingencies of the electoral process, the targets of the five-year plan – rather than consumer demand – commanded the economy, carrying with them the promise that soviet-style economies would, in a foreseeable future, overtake West European economies in output, GDP and pro-capita income.[12] Sputnik and Yuri Gagarin had been merely a foretaste of the scientific, technological and economic superiority of the system. Although it is true that the oil shock of 1974 hit Eastern European economies particularly hard, it cannot be disputed that the communist state struggled disproportionately to manage an increasingly complex economy, losing the technological edge it seemed to have in the 1950s and failing to satisfy consumer demands, especially in cases in which consumers of the worker paradises compared their standard of living with those of workers in Western Europe.[13] By the early 1980s, European communist states had embarked on a reckless policy of contracting massive debts on international financial markets to satisfy consumer demands, all the while being increasingly incapable of earning back foreign currency through their ever-less-competitive exports. The state-led economy had thus effectively inserted itself into the instabilities of the capitalist system.

The singularity of these developments as pertaining exclusively to Eastern and Central Europe, and thereby explaining the collapse of communist states and the resilience of Western European liberal-democratic states can be easily overstated. After all, Western European societies saw comparable challenges after the oil shocks of the early 1970s: industrial decline, a spiralling public debt burden, challenges to the sustainability of the Welfare State and brutal social conflicts. Seen from Potsdammer Platz, Warsaw or Bucharest, Western standards of living seemed to boom. In Kreutzberg, Glasgow and Charleroi, as well as more generally in West European self-perceptions, the 1970s and 1980s were experienced as years of chronic economic crisis and austerity, symptoms of a dysfunctional growth model, or, in the words of an influential Belgian economic historian at the time a 'broken circle of prosperity'.[14] The spectacular U-turn of François Mitterrand's economic policies, eighteen months after his election victory in 1981, in an alliance with the Communist party and as part of a programme of extending state control over the economy, shows a striking contemporaneity of economic dilemmas, east and west of the Iron Curtain. What set François Mitterrand (born in 1916) apart from Janos Kadar (born in 1912) and Wojciech Jaruzelski (born in 1923) was not so much ideology or economic analysis, since all three advocated some mix of private enterprise and state intervention in the economy, and had massive recourse to foreign loans on international capital markets, but rather the constraints of economic cooperation. While the Hungarian and Polish economies traded only marginally with their Comecon partners, by 1981, the French economy had become interdependent with the European economies participating in the then-European Communities, an interdependence that ruled out an economic experiment on the scale of Mitterrand's electoral promises. While Soviet satellite states thus disposed of a greater autonomy in designing their economic policy than their West European counterparts, they ultimately succumbed to the unhealthy combination of economic autarchy and foreign debt.

A second set of explanations for the weakness of Soviet satellite states in Central and Eastern Europe since 1989 is political. From the 1970s onward, the Communist parties were increasingly unable to monopolize the public space and socialize the younger generations. Part of the intelligentsia, a class more effectively cherished by the regime than even the working class, engaged itself in various, often informal forms of activism in favour of peace and disarmament, the environment and human rights, especially after the signing by their own governments of the Helsinki Final Act in 1977.[15] Their activism was symbolically, rather than sociologically, important. Likewise, the Catholic Church in Poland and protestant churches, especially in East Germany, despite having cozied up to the regime in the 1950s and 1960s (following an initial brutal confrontation in the 1940s), went on to – and were permitted to – channel alternative loyalties to mass audiences, steering a more independent course, especially after Karol Wojtylla's papal election in 1978. The mass appeal of Solidarność after 1981, a trade union uncontrolled by the party, was a much-underestimated portent that the days of the one-party state and of totalitarian control were over, even behind the Iron Curtain.

Totalitarianism theory suggests that the totalitarian states are characterized by the absence of separation between party and state. Any formal distinction that may have survived forty years in power were pure masquerade for what was, in fact, a one-party dictatorship. Once again, however, 1989 seems to challenge this received wisdom. What effectively collapsed in 1989 was the legitimacy of the party. The party – not the state – was washed away by popular protest. Here again, a simple opposition between East and West seems a gross simplification. First of all, 1989 did not hit all European Soviet satellite states in the same pervasive and instant way. The breakaway from one-party rule and a state-led economy was relatively clean in the so-called Visegrad countries, named after the Hungarian border town on the Danube, where the leaders of Hungary, Poland and Czechoslovakia – after 1993 Czech Republic and Slovakia – have met since 1989. In the Balkans, the transition was much slower and quite a bit murkier. The pre-1989 political elites remained firmly in control of the state and the economy for another decade, both through revamped social-democratic parties and new populist formations. Romania and Bulgaria remained relatively authoritarian regimes plagued by corruption and ethnic tensions with their Hungarian and Turkish minorities, respectively, until the late 1990s and beyond. Albania descended into chaos and anarchy by the mid-1990s, with a massive exodus, a collapsing banking system due to pyramid schemes and soaring criminality. Enver Hoxha's successors proved equally unable to maintain either the control and isolation established over forty years of paranoid dictatorship or to negotiate a gradual opening up of the political process and the economy. Yugoslav politicians like Slobodan Milosevic and Franco Tudjman had anticipated the demise of the communist ideology by adopting an increasingly violent nationalist discourse in the mid-1980s. Slovenia managed to extract itself early on from the Yugoslav civil war, followed five years later by Croatia. Conversely, some form of political stabilization only came to Serbia a full two decades after 1989. A quarter century later, Macedonia, Bosnia-Herzegovina and Kosovo are still, to different degrees, international protectorates rather than sovereign states.

The enduring power of communist elites in the Balkan countries and the surprising return to power – following entirely legitimate electoral victories – of post-communist socio-democratic parties in the Visegrad countries in 1992–93 (yet another unintended consequence of the economic shock therapy prescribed by Western economists) show the resilience and stubborn popularity of the Communist parties as organizational structures. In addition to being the tools of totalitarian dictatorship, Communist parties developed into sprawling service industries for their membership and beyond, through youth and trade union branches, job procurement and cultural and sports activities. The continuing existence of small National Front parties after 1948 – Christian-democrat, peasant, liberal or national-democratic parties – is also most often too easily dismissed as a simple alibi for the monopoly of power exercised by the Communist party; were this the case, the role they played in and after 1989 would be incomprehensible.

The diversification of political parties into purveyors of social services as a way to gain a popular allegiance that politics alone could not mobilize characterizes the multiparty systems in Western Europe no less than the one-party rule of popular democracies. Political pluralism during the Cold War years in Western Europe is a less straightforward concept than it seems. The unmitigated majority rule in Great Britain was structurally more in common with the political system of the United States than with most West European democracies. Despite elements of proportional representation, strong conservative and social-democratic parties also dominated electoral politics in West Germany, Austria, the Scandinavian countries and, after 1958, in France. Political alternation was an exception, rather than the rule. The Swedish Social Democratic Party was in power from 1932 through 1976, the West German Christian-Democrats of the CDU-CSU from 1949 through 1966, the Gaullists in France from 1958 through 1981 and the Austrian Social Democrats from 1970 through 1983. Alternating coalitions with small liberal parties and longer spells of grand coalitions in Germany and Austria moved politics to a consensual middle ground. Coalition governments ruled all through the Cold War period in Italy, Belgium and the Netherlands, as well as in France until 1958. Most of these governments were short-lived, but their composition remained almost unchanged. In the case of Italy and the French Fourth Republic, this was because the exclusion of the largest party – the communists – left no alternative combinations. The most remarkable characteristic of the political landscape of Western Europe during the Cold War, as compared to the interwar years, was voter loyalty. Basically, all the players present at the start in 1945 were still in the game in 1989, while few new players had entered the field. While the scores may have fluctuated from one election to another, landslide victories or electoral collapse never matched pre-1940 or post-1989 levels. Parties entered into power-sharing arrangements that extended far beyond governmental decisions, known as *Proporz* in Austria, *lottizzazione* in Italy and *verzuiling* in the Netherlands and Belgium. These arrangements involved the organizational sprawl of political parties through youth movements, trade unions, health insurance companies, cooperative banks, football teams and theatre clubs. They also coincided with the build-up of comprehensive Welfare States, whereby the political parties and their affiliated organizations became the primary ticket window of public funding for healthcare, social housing, subsidized vacations and public jobs.

Interestingly, the Cold War–style mass parties and the political landscape they had built experienced their first serious challenges in the 1980s, with the electoral successes of regional parties, environmental parties and, most spectacularly, parties from the extreme right in France, Flanders and Austria. Total collapse of the political landscape closely followed 1989 in Italy. By 1993, a major corruption inquiry – exposing the hidden side of *lottizzazione* – caused the dissolution of all the major political parties, a change in the electoral law and the rise to power of Silvio Berlusconi, whose political party was merely a branch of his commercial media empire (the dependency had usually been the other way around during the Cold War years). It is fair to say that the renewal of political elites was more profound in Italy by 1995 than in any of the former communist states, including the Visegrad countries. The landslide victory of a political novice and populist like Pim Fortuyn in Rotterdam in 2002 or the second round of the presidential election in France the same year, pitting far right leader Jean-Marie Le Pen against the incumbent right-wing candidate Jacques Chirac, showed that the age of the traditional mass party as Europe had known it throughout the Cold War years was over.

European states – East, North, South and West – all faced fundamental challenges to their postwar organization, challenges which had been gathering pace over the course of the 1970s but accelerated considerably during the 1980s: industrial decline and soaring public debt on the one hand and a breakdown in the capacity to produce political legitimacy of traditional mass parties and their political personnel, on the other. The monism of the communist states – economic autarchy and single-party rule – prevented them from responding adequately, while the built-in flexibility of Western European states – economic interdependency and the emergence of new, even if highly instable, party formations – allowed for their survival. Quite obviously, the events of 1989 also contributed crucially to the survival of the political model of West European states. In 1983, France had had to bow in a quite humiliating way before the economic might of West Germany. In 1990, Germany accepted to share its monetary sovereignty with its European partners in exchange for their support for German unification. Had 1989 not happened, it seems the future of European integration would have been compromised, and with it the very essence of the postwar process of West-European stabilization. The impact of 1989 was to deepen European integration long before it started to broaden it. Similarly, the dissolution of most West European Communist parties in the wake of 1989 contributed considerably to the flexibility of party politics in Western Europe, by injecting a previously immobilized mass of voters into the political game, which, incidentally, served in part to fuel a tide of right-wing populism. The counterfactual speculation of what would have happened to Western European political regimes had they not been forced to reinvent themselves following the events of 1989 is not altogether irrelevant when discussing the place of 1989 in the 1945–18 sequel.

The double crisis of the new mass party and of some form of interventionist Welfare State in the 1980s challenged the two central lessons learned in 1945: that universal suffrage had to be channelled through efficient mass organizations (a lesson taught by interwar labour parties, Communist parties and, of course, most successfully of all, by fascist parties) and that the capitalist economy could not be left to its own devices. Adam Smith's theory of the invisible hand maintaining the equilibrium of the free market was incompatible with universal suffrage, which enfranchised the working classes to demand that their governments intervene in the economic cycle, rather than patiently bear out the hardships until the end of a given downturn.[16] The consensus on which the second postwar states were built and that emerged between 1943 and 1946 – from Belfast to Bialystock – thus shared some central elements: no dismantlement of the warfare state, but rather its expansion into the Welfare State and economic planning. The slogan that national liberation was an empty measure without social liberation clearly echoed in the debates over what had been left unfinished at the end of the first postwar period. As a result, core industries were nationalized – in Britain and France well before Czechoslovakia and Romania. Health insurance, old-age pension and unemployment benefits were introduced under state schemes and land reform created legitimacy for Communist parties in rural societies that had little to gain from the dictatorship of the proletariat.

As Alan Milward has convincingly argued, state sovereignty had acquired a whole new meaning after 1945.[17] This time around, the state would not be seen as weak and ineffectual, as had been the case in the interwar years. The first postwar period, in the wake of 1918, had already shown that planned economic recovery for France was dependent on some form of sovereignty over German economic resources, but the experiment of military occupation of the *Ruhrland* had been inconclusive. The trajectory of Jean Monnet, from the *Commissariat du Plan* to the European Coal and Steel Community, is thus not an accident; rather, this was representative of the evolution of European public opinion at large. The economies of scale needed to save the new postwar state in Western Europe and to prove the viability of parliamentary democracy in the twentieth century required states to move beyond national boundaries. So, while the people would have strong states, they would at the same time have even less control over their own affairs. By 1960, the Common Agricultural Policy would come to regulate even those economic and geographic reaches traditionally most impervious to state control throughout European history. The recipes chosen by East and West of the Iron Curtain may have been different – European technocracy versus national autarchy of state planning – but the aims were convergent, rooted in shared lessons drawn from history.

As far as ideas about the role of the state are concerned, it would be problematic to present the consensus of 1943–45 as a democratic catharsis. The unpredictable course of the war had changed horizons of expectations and switched political allegiances. The most authoritarian overtones had been dropped, but the new consensus regarding the kind of state needed in the postwar era differed little in its analysis from that of the preceding period. Indeed, 1940 had also been perceived as the start of a new postwar era and, just as in 1945 and 1989, it had created a rather short-lived European consensus, based both on the idea that military superiority was the expression of political superiority and on an analysis of the deeper causes of weakness in the pre-war years. The military collapse in 1940 only confirmed what many had come to accept as the innate weakness and inferiority of the liberal state. It was not until the end of 1941 that it became clear that the war was far from over, and only in early 1943 did the argument of military superiority as a litmus test of political superiority start to turn against fascism. The ingredients of the consensus of 1940–41 were antiparliamentarianism, corporatism and various indigenous versions of national socialism as well as, above all, the need for an efficient state headed by a strong executive. The trajectory of Henri De Man from his *Plan du Travail* in 1933 to his manifesto of June 1940, affirming the 'collapse of a decrepit world' and the 'failure of the parliamentary regime and capitalist plutocracy', is in that regard as illustrative of a transformation of European opinion as Monnet's was a decade later.[18]

De Man and his contemporaries read 1940 backwards in terms of their analysis of the decade that started with the financial crisis of 1929. The Soviet economy had quite obviously been immune to the instabilities of stock markets. Mussolini's policies of economic autarchy had helped to spare Italy from the worst fallout. Adolf Hitler's social and economic policies after 1933 had been spectacularly successful, absorbing mass unemployment after less than two years in power. In the United States, Roosevelt seemed to deliver the proof that only a presidential regime, with a strong executive, was capable of implementing the ideas of state intervention which its main architect, the Londoner Keynes, had failed to sell to his own government, paralysed as it was by the rules of the parliamentary system. The welfare state and parliamentary democracy seemed, more than ever, incompatible. The calls for regime change in the 1930s in Europe's old parliamentary democracies were, first and foremost, calls for a stronger state.

The younger democracies created during Europe's democratic spring of 1918 did not live to witness either the crisis of 1929 or the Nazis' onslaught of 1939–40 (with the exception of Czechoslovakia). The year 1918, like 1940, 1945 and 1989, had created a fleeting European consensus, based on the proclaimed superiority of a victorious political model, and also on the debates in the preceding decades on the deeper causes of the turmoil. During the late nineteenth and early twentieth centuries, both the campaign for universal suffrage and the militancy of nationalist movements had done much to inflate the expectations of what a fully legitimate state was capable of doing. For the former, the liberal state was weak and ineffectual, because unfair electoral laws allowed a minority to hijack the political agenda, defend the sacrosanctity of private property and turn the defence of the status quo into an economic doctrine. Universal suffrage would ensure that the state got its priorities right and extirpate poverty, poor housing, tuberculosis, alcoholism and war. For the latter campaign, the denial of the right of people to direct their own affairs produced alienated imperial states, living anachronisms of illegitimacy and ineffectualness. The national state, wherein *Volk* and *Staat* would coincide, language, a sense of national belonging and solidarity, would bring about economic development, political stability and social justice instead of imperial discrimination.

Measured against these expectations, the new states that emerged from the rubble of Europe's old order in 1918 could only disappoint. Universal suffrage was now a universal European reality (for male adults) and about a dozen nations were set free from the people's prisons in which they had been trapped until the end of the war. The new states were, however, burdened with debt, struggling with devastated economies and mass unemployment. The constitutional model that most had copied from the French Third Republic gave full powers to the newly legitimized parliaments, but electoral fragmentation led to weak and, on average, short-lived governments, and to states unable to deliver what was most expected from them: land reform, full employment, stable wages and ambitious social programmes. National self-determination had shattered economic networks and reversed economies of scale. Far from solving the national question, Wilson's Europe was riddled with explosive minority conflicts. Liberal democracy was not the shortest route to an efficient state in the eyes of many, not least Bolsheviks, fascists and especially those old-fashioned statists who had rapidly ended Europe's democratic spring in the early 1920s: Hungary's Horty, Spain's Primo de Rivera, Portugal's Carmona, Poland's Pilsudski, Albania's Zog and Yugoslavia's Alexander.

Conclusion

The legitimacy of political regimes crucially depends on their ability to produce an efficient state, a state capable of facing the challenges of the day. The apparent inability of politics to rein in the forces of financial speculation and to regulate, rather than refinance, the international banking system, has recently done considerable harm to the standing of Barack Obama as a political leader and the European Union as a political institution. The calls for a stronger state are relatively recent, however. In light of the history of the last few decades, who would have expected the Welfare State to monopolize the debates in the American Congress for over a decade, or to see international bankers vilified and the nationalization of their banks hailed as a solution? If we widen the chronological scope of our perspective, however, the call for a strong state emerges as a rare example of an invariant in European history.

Only twenty-five years ago, 1989 created a European consensus, based on the proclaimed superiority of a victorious political model. The model that was triumphantly exported was not the model of a strong state, but rather that of a weak one. The remedy for post-socialist societies was to follow the cure that Western European nations had theretofore too cautiously applied to themselves – with the probable exception of Margaret Thatcher's Great Britain: simply less state, less Welfare State and rapid privatization as a shock therapy. Negotiations with trade unions were something to fight for in Gdansk in 1981, but certainly to fight against in Yorkshire in 1984 and anywhere else after 1989. Sovereignty reclaimed from Soviet control did not extend to popular sovereignty over economic resources.

The consensus of 1989 was not only an instance of victorious hubris, but it also reflected debates that had taken place in the preceding decade over the deeper causes of social, economic and political weakness, both in the Eastern and the Western parts of the continent. The states of the second postwar period, both popular and parliamentary democracies, had been successful in reducing poverty and income inequality; democratizing education and providing housing and healthcare, economic growth, jobs, rising standards of living and political stability. By the mid-1970s, the boom of state-led economic reconstruction had lost its momentum and the credo of the ever-expanding state some of its aura. The trauma of economic collapse, social and political polarization and, ultimately, war, slowly became a distant memory and the price to pay for social cohesion in terms of fiscal transfers less obviously accepted. For the socialist states, where the state and the regime were synonymous, this could only lead to a terminal regime crisis. For the Western parliamentary democracies, the retreat of the state into its nineteenth-century laissez faire model was an ideological option for self-styled neo-liberals and their de facto neo-conservative creed.

The Europe of 1918 was overwhelmingly a continent of peasants. It was only in Britain that less than 10 per cent of the population made a living from agriculture. For most of Southern and Eastern Europe, the figures varied from 60 to over 80 per cent and places like France, Denmark and Austria were in the 40 to 50 per cent range. This was a most unpromising setting for the working-class revolutions predicted by Karl Marx, but admittedly even less promising for the durable success of bourgeois democracy. If workers were a small minority in most of the new countries, the bourgeoisie was tiny and sometimes even completely absent. What the vast majority of newly enfranchised citizens expected from universal suffrage in 1918 was thus, logically, first and foremost land reform. The failure of liberal democracy to implement land reform, or, more often, the fear of the landowning gentry that it actually might, are the essential context pieces for understanding the collapse of parliamentarism in Italy, Poland, Albania, Bulgaria and Spain. Land reform, not proletarian insurrection, can explain the success of endogenous communist revolutions in Russia, Yugoslavia and Albania. Cooperative farms and collectivization in the East, and the Common Agricultural Policy in the West would be belated responses to the formidable challenge of the rural crisis in mid-century Europe – a challenge that probably goes much further to explain the success of interwar fascism than any other. Anti-fascist welfare policies, involving fixed prices for food and thus agricultural produce, public investment in industrial development and job creation, urban planning and massive construction of social housing, show the extent to which European states were the central agents in the transformation of European societies into post-agricultural and partly post-industrial societies by the end of the twentieth century. Even if social inequalities have been increasing very rapidly since the 1980s, they are still smaller than what they were in 1918. Mass, extreme poverty, linked to subsistence farming, has been almost eliminated everywhere on the continent. From the vantage point of 1918, European societies have in effect become middle-class societies; this can be said of all European countries, with the possible exception of Albania, and this regardless of the political ideology driving those states. The central role of the state in regulating social and economical processes is what makes Europe such a peculiar place, compared, for instance, with Latin America, where the incapacity of the state to address the rural crisis has caused chronic rural guerrilla warfare, uncontrolled urban proletarianization in shanty towns, military dictatorships and economic instability. The emergence of a middle-class society is, in Latin America, characteristic of the incipient twenty-first century and definitely not of the twentieth century. If European societies face today shared challenges and share societal structures that, while diverging, have more in common with each other than with any other geographical unit, it is, in spite of divergent ideologies and political regimes, and in spite of contrasting outcomes of 1989, 1945 and 1918, because of the effective convergence of what powerful states made them into.

The impetus for a democratic state in 1918, for an authoritarian state in 1940, for a social state in 1945 and finally for as little state as possible in 1989 has systematically lacked stamina. Yet, concepts of state during these postwar periods were at each of these turning points not just dictated by the victors of the latest military, economic or ideological contest, but rooted in debates about what had gone wrong in the pre-war decade. The state has its own inertia, like a giant ocean steamer. Those who sink after a collision with an iceberg are, after all, exceptions. States are solid vessels, hard to steer off course. The legitimacy of political regimes, on the contrary, which crucially depend on their own efficiency, is ethereal. Therefore, while all through the twentieth century, the state never stopped expanding its role in society, quite a number of political regimes have nonetheless evaporated.

Notes

1 Eric Hobsbawm, *Age of Extremes: The Short Twentieth Century, 1914–1991* (London: Michael Joseph, 1994).
2 See Pieter Lagrou, 'Between Europe and the Nation: The Inward Turn of Contemporary Historical Writing', in *Conflicted Memories. Europeanizing Contemporary Histories*, ed. Konrad Jarausch and Thomas Lindenberger (New York and Oxford: Berghahn Books, 2007), 69–80.
3 See John E. Hall, ed., *States in History* (Oxford: Blackwell, 1987).
4 Weber, *Economy and Society: An Outline of Interpretive Sociology*, ed. Guenther Roth and Claus Wittich (New York: Bedminster Press, 1968) 1, 56, quoted in Marc Allen Eisner, *From Warfare State to Welfare State. World War I, Compensatory State Building and the Limits of the Modern Order* (University Park: Pennsylvania State University Press, 2000), p. 28.
5 See Mark Hewitson, 'Inventing Europe and Reinventing the Nation-State in a New World Order', in *Europe in Crisis. Intellectuals and the European Idea, 1917–1957*, ed. Mark Hewitson and Matthew D'Auria (New York and Oxford: Berghahn, 2012), 63–81.
6 For a balanced assessment from the perspective of social history, see the introduction to Jay Winter and Jean-Louis Robert, *Capital Cities at War: Paris, London, Berlin, 1914–1919* (Cambridge and New York: Cambridge University Press, 1997).
7 Tsuyoshi Hasegawa, *Racing the Enemy. Stalin, Truman and the Surrender of Japan* (Cambridge, MA: Harvard University Press, 2005).
8 James Kurth and James Petras, *Mediterranean Paradoxes. Politics and Social Structures in Southern Europe* (Oxford: Berg, 1993).
9 After Eugen Weber, *Peasants into Frenchmen: The Modernization of Rural France, 1870–1914* (Stanford: Stanford University Press, 1976).
10 See Mark Mazower, *Dark Continent: Europe's Twentieth Century* (London: Allen Lane, 1998).
11 See the excellent comprehensive analysis offered by Robin Okey in *The Demise of Communist East Europe: 1989 in Context* (London: Arnold, 2004).
12 See André Steiner, *The Plans That Failed: An Economic History of the GDR* (New York and Oxford: Berghahn, 2010).
13 For a challenging deconstruction of the oil shock as an ideological but enduring construction of self-understanding of the 1970s and 1980s, see Rüdiger Graff and Kim Christian Priemel, 'Zeitgschichte in der Welt der Sozialwissenschaften. Legitimität und Originalität einer Diziplin', *Vierteljahresheft für Zeitgschichte* 594 (2011): 479–508 and Rüdiger Graff, *Öl und Souveränität: Petroknowledge und Energiepolitik in den USA und Westeuropa in den 1970er Jahren* (Berlin: De Gruyter Oldenbourg, 2014).
14 Herman van der Wee, *Prosperity and Upheaval: The World Economy, 1945–1980* (Berkeley: University of California Press, 1986) [1983 for the original Dutch edition].

15 See Padraic Kenney, *A Carnival of Revolution – Central Europe 1989* (Princeton, NJ: Princeton University Press, 2002). On the impact of Helsinki, see also Samuel Moyn, *The Last Utopia: Human Rights in History* (Cambridge, MA: Belknap Press of Harvard University Press, 2010).

16 See Ronald Findlay and Kevin H. O'Rourke, *Power and Plenty: Trade, War, and the World Economy in the Second Millennium* (Princeton, NJ, and Woodstock: Princeton University Press, 2007).

17 Alan S. Milward (with Federico Romero and George Brennan), *The European Rescue of the Nation-State* (London: Routledge, 1992).

18 See Mario Telo, *Le new deal européen: la pensée et la politique sociales-democrates face à la crise des années trente* (Brussels: Editions de l'Université Libre de Bruxelles, 1988) and Kiran Patel, *The New Deal: A Global History* (Princeton and Oxford: Princeton University Press, 2017).

6

Democracies

Martin Conway

Democracy, it seems, is a story that only makes sense when told forwards. The narrative of the progressive unfolding of a democratic model of society forms an integral element of how Europeans understand the emergence of their contemporary society. In particular, the five grand discourses of contemporary European democracy – the expansion of the suffrage, the deepening of structures of social welfare, the effacing of the structural inequalities experienced by women, the transition to a multiracial and culturally pluralist society and the overcoming of national antagonisms in a united Europe – all imply an understanding of democracy as an ever-swelling river that has flowed steadily towards the present day. This current has certainly encountered obstacles of self-interest, as well as in the middle decades of the twentieth century some determined efforts to deflect its course; but in the end, the strength of the almost unconscious momentum towards democracy has carried it through a series of political and social enlargements towards the embedding of its current inclusive form as the default setting of European society. Seen from the vantage point of the present day, the history of twentieth-century democracy thus becomes quite literally a progressive parade. Proceeding forward through the resonant dates of 1919, 1944–45, 1968 and 1989 – as well as other dates with more specific national resonances – it becomes the story of the victory of democracy over both its opponents and its own former limitations.[1]

That any such teleological discourse occludes the shortcomings of the present-day political order is perhaps self-evident: its Eurocentric script and the message it carries of the values of Europe serving as a template by which other societies should be judged, and held to account, are at odds with the realities of a world (and a European continent) which is now emphatically global. Moreover, the identification of Europe with a particular democratic model constrains the politics of a continent beset by structural problems of economics and of governance, and reinforces the gulf between Europe's democratic rulers and the disempowered ruled. Democracy, it seems, might have ceased to be the solution to contemporary Europe, and risks becoming part of the problem.[2]

These, however, are present-day concerns; more relevant to our purpose in this chapter is to ask whether the pervasive understanding of democracy as a forward-moving process makes for good history. This is not an easy question to answer. There are, of course, some relatively simple games of virtual history which can be invoked in order to throw into question the democratic momentum of Europe's twentieth century. What if the German empire had emerged triumphant from the battles of 1917–18, thereby imposing its hybrid model of authoritarian rule and parliamentary politics on an expanded central Europe? Or what if, as seemed likely in 1940–41, the Nazi empire had forced its remaining military enemies into submission, thereby dousing the embers of the Second World War and establishing an emphatically non-democratic New Order from Ukraine to the Atlantic? Or, indeed, what if a more ambitious and simply revolutionary USSR had pursued its expansion westwards after 1945, mobilizing its communist allies to bring about a series of communist-oriented regimes across Central and Western Europe? All such scenarios suffer of course from the fundamental weakness that they did not happen; but none can be dismissed as inherently implausible. Moreover, the purpose in invoking them is not somehow to assert the accidental character of historical events – Cleopatra's nose replaced by Churchill's premature death, as it were – but to emphasize the degree to which the ascendancy of democracy was dependent on a particular hierarchy of forces which could have been – and at particular moments was – rather significantly different. Seen in this way, the history of Europe's twentieth century appears less as a succession of democratic successes, and rather more as a series of awkward and contested transitions – what David Runciman has recently termed a 'haphazard and episodic' history of democracy – in which the winners and the losers were not defined in advance.[3]

A more intellectually serious way of approaching this same question, however, is to question the assumptions of continuity that underpin the contemporary narrative of democracy. Why, in brief, do we assume that the various models of European modern democracy, stretching from 1789 to the changes of regime that occurred with pleasing symmetry 200 years later, had some essential common core? Histories of democracy, of which there are in truth surprisingly few, tend towards the long term.[4] Unlike, say, histories of fascism which rightly emphasize the specific, the material and the contextual in order to demonstrate why particular circumstances – military defeat, economic chaos or the impotence of parliamentary regimes – gave rise to regimes of the extreme right such as Nazi Germany, Italy or Vichy France,[5] histories of democracy tend to privilege the more gradual accumulation of institutions, mentalities and social experiences. Thus, to take the most striking example, the ascendancy of democratic regimes in Europe west of the Iron Curtain that occurred in the years immediately following the Second World War tends to be regarded not as the product of a particular material and diplomatic context but as the expression of the tendency of Europeans to come home to democracy whenever they are presented with the opportunity to do so.[6]

This vision of the history of democracy as a long-term and incremental process of accretion has, however, many shortcomings, of which perhaps the most obvious, as Geoff Eley has rightly identified, is that it tends to neglect the extent to which democracy was a product of conflict, and of the efforts of those who sought to bring it about.[7] In addition, however, it tends to empty particular democratic experiences of their historical specificity. Thus, if we want to understand the nascent democratic cultures of the Weimar Republic in the 1920s, of Spain after the death of Franco or of East-Central Europe after the events of 1989, we should do better to explore their particular circumstances, much as we would, say, the reasons for Nazi victory in 1933 or for the communist consolidation of power in Poland or Czechoslovakia after 1945. Democracy, too, has its specific causes, and no two democratic regimes in twentieth-century Europe were the product of a common causality.

This specificity of particular democracies was also evident in the way that democracies often defined themselves against other democratic regimes. One of the most strongly felt tasks in West Germany after 1945 was to forge a democratic regime that would not be Weimar; just as in Czechoslovakia, France or Italy at the same time, there was a wish to create new democratic regimes which would not replicate the perceived errors or short-comings of their national predecessors.[8] Democracy therefore, if it does progress, tends to do so less by emulation than by a more dialectical process of rejection and innovation. The democracies created in Germany after the First World War or in East-Central Europe after 1989 derived their energy from the wish to reject what they regarded as the false democratic principles of their immediate political predecessors, nor were such antipathies simply focused on the past. Those democratic regimes that were established in Western Europe after 1945 defined themselves against the People's Democracy – the Volksdemokratie – of the communist east, but more subtly against what was perceived as the alien democratic order of the United States with its overmighty presidency and populist municipal and congressional politics.[9] To make a European democracy in the 1950s was therefore consciously to make a new democracy in opposition to other models, both those existing elsewhere and those of the recent past.

Indeed, not all democracies within Europe were the same. The sense that each nation of Europe possesses its own understanding of democracy, rooted in specific national experiences, language and social structures, has of course been a prominent theme of Europe's modern history, and one which has been invoked at different points in recent decades to justify opposition either to the encroachment of American diplomatic or commercial imperialism during the Cold War or to the more recent pretentions of European institutions to impinge on national sovereignty.[10] 'Our' democracy has rarely been perceived as universal but instead as a particular heritage circumscribed by a shared history, by borders, language or indeed race. Such national and historical understandings of democracy do of course often serve evidently political purposes, drawing in western Scandinavia on the celebration of a long-standing popular heritage, or in Britain on a particular reading of a national past to provide a historical foundation for the Westminster model of the United Kingdom, while delegitimizing its alternatives.[11] Yet, such national heritages are not merely self-serving narratives. The shape of democracy – notably the roles of parliaments, monarchs, presidents and federal institutions – has quite obviously been markedly different in, say, France, Germany and Britain across the twentieth century. Moreover, the narratives within which particular historical understandings of democracy are expressed have possessed their own power, creating river beds from which democratic structures have only diverged at particular moments of social crisis or state collapse, such as in Germany in 1918–19 or in France in 1940 and 1958.

The need to understand democracies as specific, discontinuous and particular phenomena therefore raises questions about the validity of reading democracy forwards. Not only has its progress been less than remorseless, but the emphasis placed on its forward momentum tends to prevent us from asking the harder questions about why democracy has taken distinct shapes at different times. But are those problems necessarily resolved by reading democracy backwards? To seek the origins of the present in the past risks merely replicating the present-mindedness that characterizes much writing about democracy. Thus, rather than a quest for origins, a backward history of democracy needs to be based on an assumption of the differentness of the successive forms of democracy that have developed in twentieth-century Europe. Rather than going in search of the democratic source of the Rhine, a regressive history of democracy needs to emphasize discontinuities and jump-cuts; or, to put it more directly, it simply needs to make less sense.

This chapter will therefore explore the different shapes of democracy that emerged in Europe during the three postwar moments of 1989–90, 1945 and 1918–19. In each case, democracy was not the author of its own success. It emerged in part because of the demise of alternative models of state rule and political organization, and also because at each of these points of transition in European history, democracy provided the most flexible means of delivering the three foremost characteristics of regime durability in the contemporary era: effective state governance, the successful negotiation of conflicts of class and economic inequality and the construction of a stable framework for relations between rulers and ruled. But that underlying continuity of purpose should not occlude the more substantial differences that existed between the three democratic eras. On each occasion, democracy emerged not because of its past heritage or essential qualities, but because it appeared to offer the most viable vehicle for negotiating the present and the immediate future.

Democratic consolidation after 1989

The starting point of such an exercise must therefore be to examine the democratic order that emerged in Europe, in both former east and former west, after 1989. What Jurgen Habermas famously termed these 'rectifying revolutions' have of course been accompanied by much celebration both of the 'return' of East-Central Europe to a (non-Russian) European mainstream and of the completion of the victory of democracy over its ideological opponents.[12] What of course is most interesting about such narratives is not that they fail to provide a full account of the reasons for the regime changes of that year and its immediate aftermath, but that they appeared to be proved true by what happened over the course of the subsequent two decades. The European unification implemented through the twin frameworks of the European Union and of the North Atlantic Treaty Organization (NATO) integrated the states of the east within Western European and Atlanticist models of cooperation, established a model of democratic rule which became the new norm for conducting politics across a large swathe of East-Central Europe from the Baltic to the Balkans. The manifold shortcomings of this norm, at least when judged according to universal yardsticks of genuine pluralism, participation, honesty and transparency, are of course well known, providing ample opportunity for the populations and leaders of 'Old Europe' to question – albeit with a remarkable blindness to the shortcomings of their own regimes – the democratic credentials of the new states of the east. But, seen in a longer historical perspective, it is not their shortcomings that are as important as the way in which the regime changes of 1989 led to the establishment of a new era of European democracy which lasted for roughly twenty years from the demise of the state-socialist regimes to the economic crisis and consequent erosion of democratic governance that began in 2008.

What one might term, with considerable over-simplification, this Third Democratic Era of Europe's twentieth century was based around four principles: the ascendancy of a neo-liberal and international (even global) capitalism; the integration of nation states within wider European structures of governance and legal authority; the election (however imperfect in practice this proved to be) of rulers by the ruled; and the subordination of the rule of the state authorities to a panoply of legal and constitutional principles intended to defend and assert rights, be they economic, cultural, confessional or simply human.[13] Democracy was, according to this model, neither simple nor direct. It rested on a complex and somewhat unstable compromise based on the rules of the market (or more concretely of the economically powerful), of technocratic bureaucrats (notably those based in European institutions), of elected political leaders and of judges. Its record was unsurprisingly mixed, of which the failure to prevent or resolve promptly the wars that occurred in the former Yugoslavia during the 1990s was only the most flagrant example. More pervasive, however, was the way in which this model of democracy struggled to respond to many of the aspirations and grievances of large sections of the population, giving rise to a wider sense after the turning of the new millennium of a 'crisis of democracy'.[14] This was evident in the east in transitions to more or less explicit forms of authoritarian presidential rule, and also in the west in the surges in support for new regional political forces, populist movements and parties of the extremes of right and left which defined themselves as more authentic and democratic than the established parties of the centre-left and centre-right.

The fault line that gradually emerged after 2000 between the democratic politics of Silvio Berlusconi and Viktor Orbán, on the one hand, and those of Angela Merkel and of the institutions of the European Union (EU), on the other, owed something to the complex heritages of Europe's twentieth-century past; but, more immediately, it was the consequence of a perceived crisis of representation and indeed of democracy. The highly personalized politics of individual leaders, based on short-term coalitions of interest and of grievance, which characterized the political rhetoric of Berlusconi, Marine Le Pen and many others in both east and west, was very different from the bureaucratized continuities of European institutions and the dense structures of socio-economic negotiation which had long characterized the democratic politics of much of Western Europe. In place of a language of structures and of rights, the language of the new populism called for the primacy of the national, the will of the majority and a defensive protection of those who were defined as the 'true' people.[15]

There was little that was particularly new in such rhetoric, which recalled strongly the critiques already voiced regarding parliamentary regimes in the interwar years.[16] But the very fact of the substantial audience that these criticisms gained after the economic crash of 2008 serves to emphasize the need to explain the ascendancy of democratic politics over the previous 20-year period. There were, after all, many alternative paths which could have been taken after the revolutions of 1989; and the fact that they were not demonstrates the unremarkable but necessary truth that democracy requires explanation, rather than celebration.

The particular coexistence among capitalist, bureaucratic, elected and legal forms of democracy that took shape in Europe, east and west, after 1989 owed something to circumstance, and more particularly to the temporarily extreme imbalance between the respective influence exercised within Europe by the United States and (Soviet) Russia; but it also rested on the sinews of power which had emerged within late twentieth-century Europe. The ascendancy, from the end of the 1970s onwards, of a neo-liberal model of global and finance-driven capitalism within Europe profoundly reshaped the possible contours of democracy, specifically marginalizing alternative economic policies and more generally limiting the capacity of rulers to assert significant control over the most powerful economic decision makers.[17] In addition, the Great Leap Forward that took place in the powers of the EU in the era of Delors, Kohl and Mitterrand destabilized the historic compromise between national and multinational forms of power that had characterized post-1945 Europe, establishing a new domain of European decision-making, in which democracy derived not from the rule of the people but from the respect for democratic norms and the limited participation (via the European Council and the European Parliament) of democratically elected representatives. The erosion of nation state and political power by these international economic forces and the EU was however limited. Much of the emotional and symbolic force of democracy remained rooted in the rituals of national elections, the patterns of parliamentary rule and the primacy that national democratic politics retained in popular perception. If the exercise of power became consistently more opaque and transnational in the final decades of the twentieth century, it was still on the national political stage that the drama of democracy was primarily played out. Indeed, this became all the more so, after 1989, as the demise of the state-socialist regimes led to the recreation, and celebration, of the institutions of the national democratic traditions of East-Central Europe.

Thus, the model of democratic politics which developed across the expanded European space after 1989 was one that operated at a series of different but interdependent levels. Free-trade agreements, legal frameworks, conventions (European and universal) of human rights, European institutions, national parliaments and the pretentions of increasingly assertive regional governments and administrations created a complex democratic culture which no longer possessed the hierarchical clarity of the post-1945 era. That was not, however, a weakness. At its heart, the network of democratic institutions – as well as the broader influence of concepts of a free society – created a situation in which any radical alternative to democracy was difficult to imagine, and still less to bring into existence. There remained of course nuances on the margins, especially in terms of the languages of democracy articulated by the new social movements that emerged in the 1970s,[18] but the most tangible demonstration of the strength of the European democratic order in the two decades following 1989 was the way in which it largely drew the oppositional parties of the new right into a democratic mainstream. The re-emergence of a radical-right politics in Europe from the mid-1980s onwards, most notably in France, Belgium and Austria, was indicative of the latent disaffection of significant sections of the population with the political and social order. Yet, the political trajectory of Haider's Freedom Party in Austria, the Front National in France and the Vlaams Blok/Belang in Flanders was largely towards collaboration in the institutions of the existing democracy, rather than their overthrow. They became outsiders within the democratic institutions, denouncing the established elite while taking on positions of responsibility at the local, regional and on occasions national levels.

The self-definition of fin de siècle Europe as a fundamentally democratic society, characterized by freedoms of expression, of individual and collective rights and of a legally protected tolerance, gained considerable reinforcement by wider global trends. The emergence of a radicalized Islam which defined itself against Western societies encouraged a defensive mentality, especially after the Al-Qaida attacks on 11 September 2001 and their European re-enactment in the transport bombings in Madrid in 2004 and in London in 2005, which took as its starting point the perceived need to defend democratic freedoms against those, both without and within, who rejected such freedoms. At the state level, this defence of democratic freedom provided justifications for both the reinforcement of measures of internal policing and external engagement in military campaigns in Afghanistan, Iraq and Libya, which in turn provoked large-scale campaigns of opposition within a number of European societies. However, more profoundly, the perception that Europe was once again at war with those in or from the global South who did not share a distinctly European understanding of a democratic society encouraged a latter-day popular-front mentality of democratic defence. Much as previous generations of Europeans had mobilized against fascism, or against a Stalinist communism, Europeans saw in their engagement against a militant model of Islam their role as the custodians of a particular basket of democratic freedoms. Europe was different because it was democratic.

The unexpected victory of democracy after 1945

Perhaps the most obvious, but also necessary, point to make about the Second Democratic Era that established itself in Europe, west of the Soviet sphere of military and diplomatic influence, after 1945 was that its origins, character and underpinnings were different in almost all respects from those of the post-1989 era. There were of course evident similarities, which, when reading history forwards, can provide threads of continuity. The establishment of European structures of multinational governance in the 1950s and the gradual maturation of a discourse of human rights in the aftermath of the mass killings of the 1940s were two such important bridges between the two eras. But, read backwards, such continuities seem much less important. Few of the factors that characterized the success and limitations of democracy in Europe after 1989 were present in the same way after 1945, and consequently the democracy that emerged after the Second World War had different origins and a different shape, even when it was constructed in many of the same places and buildings.

The democracy of this second postwar era was above all a solution to a perceived crisis of governance. The military, ethnic and ideological conflicts that swept across

Europe from 1936 to 1948–49 had in most respects destroyed, either temporarily or more permanently, the structures and sinews of the state rule. The anarchy, or liberation, of the mid-1940s was mitigated by various forms of improvised military or executive government, but the most urgent self-appointed task of Europe's postwar rulers was to bring the territories and populations of a fragmented continent back under the rule of an effective government.[19] This was reflected in the character of the reintroduction of democracy: There was no sudden restoration of popular sovereignty. Instead, the new political order took the form of the carefully managed rolling out of a structure of constitutions, elections and referenda which, together with projects of social and economic reform, were intended to reconcile the ruled to their rulers, as well as to undercut the more local structures of informal democratic power – of resistance groups and of local committees – that had flourished in Europe during the latter war years.[20]

The democracy of the post-1945 era was therefore from the outset a democracy of the relatively powerful, which reflected the changed social relations of power in the postwar order. Tied indissolubly to the resources of a much-expanded state, the new democracy tended to favour the interests and values of the middle class and of rural populations at the expense of those of the working class who had been the principal victims of the economic depression of the 1930s and of the chaos of the war years. As a consequence, the equality of the postwar era was more civic than social in character. Enhanced rights – including, finally, female suffrage – were granted to all, or at least to all those who had access to national citizenship.[21] But the social benefits of the structures of welfare and personal taxation were less evenly distributed. Women, families and the disabled were all the particular beneficiaries of a welfare system that focused on what were perceived to be the most blatant social problems generated by the war years,[22] but which also, as a pervasive culture of affluence established itself, tended to fail to address (or even to see) the more profound forms of social inequality – of income, of education and of housing – which remained.[23] Not surprisingly, therefore, the principal political beneficiaries of the new democratic order were the parties of the centre-right. It was above all the new Christian Democrat parties, built on the coherence of the Catholic social milieu but also on the wider material interests of provincial, female and middle-class voters, who set the tone of the new democracy, emerging as the durable fulcrum of government in West Germany, Austria, the Low Countries and Italy, as well as more briefly in France.[24] Democracy, it seemed, had tilted to the (centre) right, winning the majority of elections at the expense of an increasingly embattled socialism, while integrating the truncated territories of Western Europe into the military and security alliances of the Cold War, and expelling the communists within West European states from all but certain bastions of municipal and trade-union power.

This was, however, also a democracy that worked. Refloated by the rapid economic growth of the postwar decades, and buttressed by the financial, technical and bureaucratic resources of a state that was much better able to buy and retain the loyalty of its citizens,[25] democracy became above all a system of rule. Parties and parliaments were in many respects the most visible symbols of this new democracy, but it was supplemented by what became a dense undergrowth of parastatal and associational institutions which collaborated with the state in the business of democratic government.[26] Welfare programmes, infrastructural projects, economic planning and education were the *grands projets* of this new democracy, which for the first time spilled substantially beyond the frontiers of the nation state to create a plethora of institutions of multinational governance that culminated at the end of the 1950s in the Treaty of Rome and the establishment of the European Economic Community (EEC).[27] Europe (as these institutions misleadingly came to label their more limited frontiers) provided the new defining framework of democracy from the later 1950s, reshaping, as it did so, the internal balance of the European continent towards its western territories. Within this limited geographical space, democracy became more pervasive but also somewhat tamer, as it expanded from periodic elections into the daily ethos of municipal and national governance, the provision of welfare and the rather deliberate civic education of its citizens.

More so than the two other periods of postwar democracy, the democratic regimes of the post-1945 era constituted a framework with defined edges: a template of effective governance which defined itself against the communist east, as well as against what were widely perceived to be the failed democratic regimes of the interwar years. This was therefore a democracy which privileged its present efficiency over its past: a democracy which was self-consciously peaceful, confining the tensions of socio-economic conflicts within corporatist structures of negotiation, and seeking, through the use of more effective structures of policing, to keep the disruptive dynamics of crowds off the streets. Not all problems, however, were able to be confined in such a way. The unpredictable violence of decolonization and insurgency, spilling across the Mediterranean from Algeria into the politics of metropolitan France, destroyed the Fourth Republic while ensuring that its Gaullist successor adopted in its early years a distinctly more authoritarian model of rule.[28] More widely too, democracy in its post-1945 variant found itself increasingly on the defensive from the early 1960s onwards, as new generations of postwar citizens chafed against the limitations of managed bureaucratic rule and a constrained freedom of expression. Citizens were again pushing against the frontiers of democracy, importing into West European politics more radical democratic languages learnt (or rather gauchely imitated) from the decolonized South and from the social struggles in the United States as well as from Maoist China and Vietnam.[29]

The institutions of democracy, whatever their alarmed guardians such as Raymond Aron might have feared,[30] were not fundamentally challenged by the social and cultural upheavals of the later 1960s, but their rule was visibly more contested. The waves of industrial strikes which occurred in France, Britain and Italy, and the violent movements of self-determination which developed in most notably Northern Ireland, and the Basque Country as well as the movements of new-left mobilization across West European states, were all indications that democracy could no longer be constrained within a single template.[31] Instead, West European politics had a new volatility. Social movements such as a newly radicalized trade unionism, feminism and anti-nuclear campaigns each developed new forms of participatory politics and brought crowds emphatically back onto the European political stage, while the demise of the authoritarian regimes in the Iberian peninsula – most strikingly the sudden fall of the Salazar-Caetano regime in Portugal in April 1974 – created a new sense of the possibilities of radical democratic politics. Less visible, but equally significant, was the fact that the air of renewed social and political conflict encouraged the emergence of neo-liberal discourses of democracy which, though often initially counter-revolutionary in their purposes, developed a more thoroughgoing critique of the state-directed character of postwar democracy in the name of economic enterprise and a newly individual freedom. Expanded in this way to both left and right, the democratic spectrum of the postwar years had lost its centre ground, and increasingly its self-definition.

The democratic moment in 1918

The democracies that emerged in Europe in 1918–19 were, like their successors after 1945, the products of war, and more particularly of the outcome of wars. But there, one is tempted to say, the similarities ended. Part of the explanation of course was that they were very different wars. If the Second World War acquired, at least in its final years, the sense of an ineluctable struggle between different sides, each possessed of its own distinctive ideological character, the First World War never acquired such a defined shape. It remained an agglomeration of distinctive regional wars fought within and outside Europe by dynasties, by regimes, by armies and by peoples. This diversity was evident too in its diverse legacies for democratic politics. The war had no neat conclusion. Though the Central Powers surrendered in November 1918, warfare continued for a number of years afterwards: across the undefined frontiers of the new Soviet state; between the new states competing to succeed the collapsed empires of Central and Eastern Europe and most powerfully within states, as social, ethnic and political conflicts overcame the authority of state authorities from Ireland, to Germany, Hungary and Italy.[32]

Most obviously, the war, and the prolonged period of institutional weakness that occurred in its aftermath, created a broad demand for more democracy. The most immediate victor of the war was the enfranchised citizen. This was Europe's twentieth-century republican moment, the generalization of the principles of 1789 to the majority of the continent, including in some cases (but not in the spiritual home of those principles in France) the enfranchisement of women alongside men. The regimes that emerged from the wreckage of the First World War, west of the Soviet Union, were equipped with a whole new box of democratic instruments: elected presidents (alongside a few largely ceremonial monarchs), parliaments as the embodiment of popular sovereignty, referenda to decide contested frontiers and legal codes and constitutions to protect individual and collective rights. Not all of this new apparatus worked entirely effectively. Soldiers were often reluctant to follow the orders of civilian officials, and civil servants and judges often placed their loyalty to the higher authority of the state above the legislation of parliaments. But, as the public diplomacy of the postwar peace conferences eloquently expressed, these changes had shifted the primary locus of power away from royal courts and councils of state, and into the debating chambers of parliaments and conferences, which acted under the scrutiny of press and people.

This, however, represented only the democratic headline. The victory of the principle of responsible government marked the culmination of the century-long struggle between representative government and its various ancien régime, monarchical and imperial alternatives. But, even as it came about, that model of democratic rule was challenged by new and more horizontal forms of democratic community, which flourished in the violent political cultures generated by war, defeat and the collapse of state authority.[33] Violence was endemic almost everywhere in 1918–19. The Bolshevik Revolution of 1917, followed by that of Bela Kun in Hungary in 1919, and the quasi-revolutionary upheavals that occurred elsewhere across Central Europe from Helsinki to Munich, Berlin and northern Italy asserted much more direct models of democracy which, though they built on the heritage of the Paris Commune of 1870–71, were driven by the immediate desires of populations for social justice and self-government.[34] These myriad soviets, communes and neighbourhood and factory committees which proliferated in Europe from 1917 to the early 1920s were gradually repressed by state authorities, and also by a new genus of nationalist and counter-revolutionary movements – often markedly paramilitary in character – which sought to use the weapons of violence to restore order and authority. The Freikorps of former German and Habsburg soldiers who ranged widely across Central Europe and the various units of the White forces in Hungary as well as subsequently the squadristi of the Fascist movement in northern Italy were opposed not only to the radical democracy of their red opponents, but also to the liberal democracy of new parliamentary regimes, most notably that of the Weimar Republic. But they too possessed a language of democracy. Their vision (in its different linguistic formulations) of a popular or national community, a Volksgemeinschaft, was of a community purged of its alien elements and restored to some form of essential unity, in which old hierarchies of social status would be replaced by an egalitarian ethos of camaraderie and ethnic solidarity. It was a vision born of the violence of the First World War, and often based on the fraternity of battle, but which was sustained and developed throughout the subsequent decades, providing the energy behind not only the gradual federation of the Nazi movement out of its diverse precursors, but also the wide range of paramilitary and extreme-right movements which, notably in France, were such a prominent feature of interwar politics.[35]

As a consequence, democracy never acquired an uncontested institutional or ideological definition in the interwar years. What was in many respects the First Democratic Era remained in effect a struggle between different definitions of democracy. Popular community-based definitions of democracy – the democracy of communes and of communities – competed alongside the more disciplined people's democracy of international communism and the democracy of the movement – of the people and of the Volk – for ascendancy over the parliamentary republican systems which had appeared triumphant in the immediate aftermath of the First World War. Indeed, what had appeared so new at the moment of Allied victory in 1918 soon came to seem an outmoded and ineffective model of government, weakened by the division and alleged self-interest of parliamentary parties and its inattention to the 'true' grievances of the people. Parliamentary regimes of democracy survived in North-Western Europe and in Scandinavia and Czechoslovakia, but elsewhere, such regimes had been overturned or transformed by the end of the 1930s into structures of single-party, presidential or authoritarian rule.[36]

More so than at other points in the twentieth century, democracy proved to mean different things to different people in Europe after the First World War. What had in the decades prior to 1914 appeared to be a mainstream vision of a liberal parliamentary order of representative government, which gradually expanded to incorporate both larger numbers of voters and a wider range of forms of social welfare, was displaced in the years following 1918 by a much more contested world of divergent democracies. In the various forms of political violence which occurred on the streets of German cities during the 1920s and early 1930s or in Austria in 1934, in the communities, both rural and urban, of Spain during the mid- and late 1930s and in the myriad Resistance movements that emerged in Western and Southern Europe from 1942 to 1944, democracy was a slogan, a vision and a cause, but rarely a model.[37] Democratic aspirations were not coterminous with democratic institutions, and even within supposedly monolithic regimes such as the Third Reich or Stalin's Russia, the aspiration to hold rulers to account and to voice popular demands could emerge in often unexpected ways. Borrowing (and misusing) Zeev Sternhell's description of the New Order movements of the 1930s in France, democracy was neither right nor left.[38] It had become a contested public space in which Europe's increasingly articulate and politically literate citizens sought to advance different definitions of the popular sovereignty of the nation, of the people or simply of the neighbourhood.

Conclusion

There are therefore virtues in writing democracy backwards. Rather than flowing forwards ineluctably, democracy emerges as a properly historical phenomenon, invested at each moment with distinctive political, economic and ideological characteristics. Approached, as has been the case in this article, from the top down, it also provides (as this book as a whole is intended) new ways of thinking about the shape of Europe's twentieth century, in which long-term processes of change seem less important than the particular moments of transition – the hinges upon which Europe's twentieth-century history have swung. Rather than a narrative of democratic evolution, we are presented with an archipelago of loosely interconnected democratic regimes, each of which may have been influenced somewhat selectively by the lessons of the past, but each of which was very much formed by its present.

However, it is also necessary to remember that democracy is not merely a system of rule but also a collective and individual phenomenon, experienced by communities and by individuals. Seen from the bottom up, this consumption of democracy also changed considerably. This is especially so, when one considers those populations of Central Europe who experienced most directly the successive regime transformations of the twentieth century. For the inhabitants of, say, Budapest, Prague or Berlin, or any number of smaller communities in the same region of Europe, the experience of democracy across the three postwar moments of 1989, 1945 and 1918–19 had few significant similarities. On each occasion, there was a sense of liberation: from alien rule, and from ethnic or class oppression, or simply from the burdens and hardships of war. But the political languages of democracy were on each occasion very different. Collective ethnic or linguistic emancipation from imperial rule (in 1918), the destruction of social privilege and the construction of a more egalitarian community (in 1945) and the exercise of personal intellectual and economic freedom (in 1989) were all aspirations which could be encapsulated under the catch-all term of democracy, but their practical and emotional content was very different. Therefore, just as it is easy to exaggerate the continuity of democratic regimes, so too would it be mistaken to assume a continuity of democratic aspirations. What made people want to live in a democracy in 1989 was rather markedly different from the motivations which had led previous generations to espouse democracy seventy years earlier.

This malleability of democracy, and of the aspirations which it can embody, might of course point to one of the principal reasons for its durability: Each society was democratic, but each in its own way. Therefore, just as there was no single template of democratic political structures across the twentieth century in Europe, so there was no single way of consuming democracy. Instead, democracy was invested with different meanings, partly because of different material circumstances, and party also because of evolutions in the nature of citizenship. If Europeans of 1918–19 understandably perceived democracy principally as a means of collective empowerment, of taking power for themselves, this was much less evident in 1945 and 1989. Instead, these subsequent democratic moments were much more concerned with the nature of the democratic society they were seeking to create and the exercise of collective and individual rights.

It is not therefore only the languages of democracy which vary over time, but also their content. Reading history backwards, it becomes easier to see not only how democracy meant different things at different times, and indeed in different places, but also how regimes and movements which the conventional political lexicon places outside of democracy could also contain democracy. The populations of the Stalinist Soviet Union or the Third Reich of the 1930s were very conscious of the democratic rights they were denied by their rulers, but this did not exclude a certain sense of democracy, expressed for example in the empowerment of Soviet workers over their managers, or the collective identity of the Nazi Volksgemeinschaft. To make such comparisons is not somehow to efface the essential differences between regimes of democracy and other forms of political regime, but to remind us that the history of democracy in twentieth-century Europe has been much wider than a selective canon of regimes.

Notes

1 See the cautionary comments of Jan-Werner Müller in his *Contesting Democracy: Political Ideas in Twentieth-Century Europe* (New Haven and London: Yale University Press, 2011), 2–6.

2 Habermas is an eloquent exponent of such latter-day pessimism, in which the project of Europe and of democracy become fused as elements of a contemporary crisis.

See notably the texts republished in Jürgen Habermas, *The Lure of Technocracy* (Cambridge and Malden: Polity, 2015).

3 David Runciman, *The Confidence Trap* (Princeton and Oxford: Princeton University Press, 2013), xi.

4 See *Ibid.* and Barbara Wejnert, *Diffusion of Democracy: The Past and Future of Global Democracy* (Cambridge: Cambridge University Press, 2014).

5 See, for example, the specific local studies of fascism provided in Paul Corner, *Fascism in Ferrara, 1915–1925* (London: Oxford University Press, 1975); Peter Fritzsche, *Rehearsals for Fascism: Populism and Political Mobilization in Weimar Germany* (New York and Oxford: Oxford University Press, 1990); Kevin Passmore, *From Liberalism to Fascism: The Right in a French Province, 1928–1939* (Cambridge: Cambridge University Press, 1997); Robert Paxton, *French Peasant Fascism: Henri Dorgères' Greenshirts and the Crises of French Agriculture, 1929–1939* (New York and Oxford: Oxford University Press, 1997).

6 I have discussed these issues in Martin Conway, 'The Rise and Fall of Western Europe's Democratic Age, 1945–1973', *Contemporary European History* 13 (2004): 67–88.

7 Geoff Eley, *Forging Democracy: The History of the Left in Europe, 1850–2000* (New York and Oxford: Oxford University Press, 2002), 24–32.

8 Sebastian Ullrich, *Der Weimar-Komplex: Das Scheitern der ersten deutschen Demokratie und die politische Kultur der frühen Bundesrepublik 1945–1959* (Göttingen: Wallstein, 2009).

9 Giuseppe Saragat, *Socialismo democratico e socialismo totalitario: Per l'autonomia del Partito Socialista* (Milan: Critica sociale, 1946), 20–25; Alessandro Brogi, *Confronting America: The Cold War between the United States and the Communists in France and Italy* (Chapel Hill: University of North Carolina Press, 2011), 191–93.

10 Richard Kuisel, *Seducing the French: The Dilemma of Americanization* (Berkeley: University of California Press, 1993); David Ellwood, *The Shock of America: Europe and the Challenge of the Century* (Oxford: Oxford University Press, 2012).

11 Joseph A. Lauwerys, ed., *Scandinavian Democracy: Development of Democratic Thought and Institutions in Denmark, Norway and Sweden* (Copenhagen: Danske selskab, 1958); Jussi Kurunmäki and Johan Strang, ed., *Rhetorics of Nordic Democracy* (Helsinki: Finnish Literature Society, 2010).

12 See notably Jeffrey C. Isaac, '1989 and the Future of Democracy', in *Between Past and Future: The Revolutions of 1989 and Their Aftermath*, ed. Sorin Antohi and Vladimir Tismaneanu (Budapest and New York: Central European University Press, 2000), 39–40. See also the influential thesis of Francis Fukuyama: Francis Fukuyama, *The End of History and the Last Man* (London: Hamish Hamilton, 1992).

13 Vladimir Tismaneanu and Bogdan Jacob, *The End and the Beginning: The Revolutions of 1989 and the Resurgence of History* (Budapest and New York: Central European University Press, 2012).

14 The literature on the contemporary crises of democracy has become enormous in recent years. For characteristic examples, see Wolfgang Streeck, *Buying Time: The Delayed Crisis of Democratic Capitalism* (London, 2014); Anthony Grayling, *Democracy and Its Crisis* (London: Oneworld, 2017). See also Colin Crouch, *Post-Democracy* (Cambridge: Polity, 2004).

15 The term populism has become something of a catch-all means of characterizing the emergence of new political movements: see notably Jan-Werner Müller, *What is Populism?* (Philadelphia: University of Pennsylvania Press, 2016).

16 Similarities between the politics of the interwar years and those of contemporary Europe have been a feature of much recent commentary: see the critical observations in James McDougall, 'No, This Isn't the 1930s – But Yes, This Is Fascism', *The Conversation* (16 November 2016): http://theconversation.com/no-this-isnt-the-1930s-but-yes-this-is-fascism-68867.

17 Müller, *Contesting Democracy*, 220–27; Philip Mirowski and Dieter Plehwe, ed., *The Road from Mont Pèlerin. The Making of the Neoliberal Thought Collective* (Cambridge, MA, and London: Harvard University Press, 2009).

18 Andrew Tompkins, *Better Active than Radioactive: Antinuclear Protest in France and West Germany* (Oxford: Oxford University Press, 2016); Stephen Milder, *Greening Democracy. The Anti-Nuclear Movement and Political Democracy in West Germany and Beyond, 1968–1983* (Cambridge: Cambridge University Press, 2017).

19 See, for example, Geoffrey Warner, 'Allies, Government and Resistance: The Belgian Political Crisis of November 1944', *Transactions of the Royal Historical Society*, Fifth Series, 28 (1978): 45–60; Martin Conway, *The Sorrows of Belgium: Liberation and Political Reconstruction, 1944–1947* (Oxford: Oxford University Press, 2012), 13–124.

20 See, for example, Megan Koreman, *The Expectation of Justice: France, 1944–1946* (Durham and London: Duke University Press, 1999); Rebecca Boehling, *A Question of Priorities. Democratic Reform and Recovery in Postwar Germany* (New York and Oxford: Berghahn, 1996); Tom Behan, *The Long-Awaited Moment. The Working Class and the Italian Communist Party in Milan, 1943–1948* (New York: Peter Lang, 1997).

21 For example, Molly Tambor, ' "An Essential Way of Life": Women's Citizenship and the Renewal of Politics in Italy', in *After Fascism: European Case-Studies in Politics, Society and Identity since 1945*, ed. Matthew Berg and Maria Mesner (Vienna and Berlin: Lit, 2009), 209–14.

22 Tara Zahra, *The Lost Children. Reconstructing Europe's Families after World War II* (Cambridge, MA, and London: Harvard University Press, 2011); Robert Moeller, *Protecting Motherhood: Women and the Family in the Politics of Postwar West Germany* (Berkeley, Los Angeles and London: University of California Press, 1993).

23 Stuart Middleton, ' "Affluence" and the Left in Britain, c. 1958–1974', *The English Historical Review* 129 (2014): 107–38; Christiane Reinecke, 'Localising the Social: The Rediscovery of Urban Poverty in Western European "Affluent" Societies', *Contemporary European History* 24 (2015): 555–76; Winfried Süss, 'A "New Social Question"? Politics, Social Sciences and the Rediscovery of Poverty in Post-Boom Western Germany', in *Poverty and Welfare in Modern German History*, ed. Lutz Raphael (New York: Berghahn, 2016), 200–3.

24 Martin Conway, 'The Age of Christian Democracy. The Frontiers of Success and Failure', in *European Christian Democracy: Historical Legacies and Comparative Perspectives*, ed. Tom Kselman and Joseph Buttigieg (Notre Dame: Notre Dame University Press, 2003), 43–67; Maria Mitchell, *The Origins of Christian Democracy: Politics and Confession in Modern Germany* (Ann Arbor: University of Michigan Press, 2012); Richard Vinen, *Bourgeois Politics in France* (Cambridge and New York: Cambridge University Press, 2010).

25 On the refashioning of the state in postwar Europe, see particularly Philip Nord, *France's New Deal: From the Thirties to the Postwar Era* (Princeton: Princeton University Press, 2010). On the gradual maturation of ideas of planning, see also Jackie Clarke, *France in the Age of Organization: Factory, Home and Nation from the 1920s to Vichy* (New York and Oxford: Berghahn, 2011), 164–69.

26 Richard Kuisel, *Capitalism and the State in Modern France* (Cambridge: Cambridge University Press, 1981), 187–247; Anthony J. Nicholls, *Freedom with Responsibility. The Social Market Economy in Germany 1918–1963* (Oxford: Oxford University Press, 1994).

27 Alan Milward (with Federico Romero and George Brennan), *The European Rescue of the Nation-State* (London: Routledge, 1992).

28 Jim House and Neil MacMaster, *Paris 1961: Algerians, State Terror and Memory* (Oxford: Oxford University Press, 2006). See also Todd Shepard, *The Invention of Decolonization: The Algerian War and the Remaking of France* (Ithaca and London: Cornell University Press, 2006).

29 Michael Seidman, *The Imaginary Revolution: Parisian Students and Workers in 1968* (New York, Berghahn, 2004); Jan-Werner Müller, 'What Did They Think They Were Doing? The Political Thought of (the West European) 1968 Revisited', in *Promises of 1968. Crisis, Illusion and Utopia*, ed. Vladimir Tismaneanu (Budapest and New York: Central European University Press, 2011), 73–102.

30 Raymond Aron, *La révolution introuvable: réflexions sur la révolution de mai* (Paris: Fayard, 1968); Aurelian Craiutu, 'Raymond Aron and the Tradition of Political Moderation in France', in *French Liberalism from Montesquieu to the Present Day*, ed. Raf Geenens and Helena Rosenblatt (Cambridge: Cambridge University Press, 2012), 277–82.

31 Gerd-Rainer Horn, *The Spirit of '68: Rebellion in Western Europe and North America, 1956–1976* (Oxford and New York: Oxford University Press, 2007).

32 This is the principal thesis of Robert Gerwarth, *The Vanquished. Why the First World War Failed to End* (London: Allen Lane, 2016).

33 Mark Jones, *Founding Weimar: Violence and the German Revolution of 1918–1919* (Cambridge: Cambridge University Press, 2016).

34 Francis L. Carsten, *Revolution in Central Europe, 1918–1919* (London: Maurice Temple Smith, 1972) ; Stephen Smith, *Red Petrograd: Revolution in the Factories, 1917–18* (Cambridge: Cambridge University Press, 1983), esp. 200–8.

35 Robert Gerwarth, 'The Central European Counter-Revolution: Paramilitary Violence in Germany, Austria and Hungary after the Great War', *Past and Present* No. 200 (2008): 175–209; Matteo Millan, 'The Institutionalisaton of *Squadrismo*: Disciplining Paramilitary Violence in the Italian Fascist Dictatorship', *Contemporary European History* 22 (2013): 551–73; Robert Soucy, *French Fascism: the First Wave, 1924–1933* (New Haven and London: Yale University Press, 1986).

36 Michael Mann, *Fascists* (Cambridge and New York: Cambridge University Press, 2004).

37 Dirk Schumann, *Political Violence in the Weimar Republic, 1918–1933. Fight for the Streets and Fear of Civil War* (New York and Oxford: Berghahn, 2009), esp. p. xiv; Tom Buchanan, 'Anti-fascism and Democracy in the 1930s', *European History Quarterly* 32 (2002): 39–57.

38 Zeev Sternhell, *Neither Right nor Left: Fascist Ideology in France* (Berkeley: University of California Press, 1986).

7

Empires

Malika Rahal

In the spirit of this book, examining three postwar periods from the vantage point of colonial empires, or of former colonies, is a useful way to test the framework of a European-focused chronology. This alternative perspective reveals that intense violence or outright war took place outside of Europe during what we may have considered until now times of peace, or interwars. In other words, the rhythm of peace and wartime, or violence and peace, differs significantly when seen from the former empire.

Is it then possible to juxtapose European and non-European chronologies so that they might be analysed together? And can the notions of postwar periods and aftermaths of war create a common canvas for exploring the history of Europe along with that of its (former) possessions, or should they be seen as mutually exclusive histories? In order to address these questions, this chapter will explore 1989, 1945 and 1918 by focusing on non-European regions that were, or came to be, under European colonial rule during the first postwar period that we are concerned with, that following the First World War. These territories are mainly located in Africa, the Arab World and Asia, and by 1989 had become independent. This chapter will examine the nature of each event – 1989, 1945 and 1918 – from the perspective of the (former) colonial empires, and discuss whether or not each of them is indeed a postwar period. This exploration is a first step towards a connected history of the postwar periods, as it sheds light on the nature of the relations between Europe and the rest of the world from colonial to postcolonial times, and also on the relation – whether causal or not – between European and non-European events by following the movement of violence, arms and troops from European-centred world wars to colonial and postcolonial world wars.

Year 1989, the other world war?

The premise of this book, which is to consider 1989 as a postwar period in its own right (in particular in Europe where the war was cold), raises in turn the question of the nature of the event in the Global South where it was *all but* cold, and in particular in the recently decolonized countries. Can 1989 be considered the end of a war, and the beginning of a postwar period?

In Europe and the USSR, '1989' was a major event, and was indeed reminiscent of other endings to wars, in part due to the dramatic succession of events, and the theatrical unity of time and place. In the transition from war to peace and the rearranging of the world, new opportunities opened up, pushing individuals and groups to struggle for a place within the new society in the making. Hope for the future grew alongside both a sense of bereavement for the world that was being pushed back into the past and anxiety that the change may not be for the best, or even for the better. The collective fervour, the sense of liberation, the immediate gain in terms of freedom to move across what used to be impermeable borders and the lifting of the pressure of police apparatus were equally evocative of an ending of war. Was there a similar phenomenon – either in the shape of single event or a wave of comparable events – in the Global South?

The main region in which the collapse of the Iron Curtain might have had an equivalent is Eastern Asia, where the divide between the blocs was sometimes described as a 'bamboo curtain'. In communist China, students had been involved in demands for political reform and their movement, followed by intellectuals and workers, led to large demonstrations and hunger strikes having a revolutionary feel comparable to what was taking place in Europe. Indeed, these were followed by the Tiananmen Square demonstration that began on 15 April 1989. The martial law implemented on 20 May and on 4 June and the army's intervention and killing of demonstrators blocked the process of political reform. In South-East Asia, Vietnam and Laos remained politically communist, despite dramatic liberalization of their economy: To this day, together with China, they represent three of the handful of countries in the world that remain single-party socialist states claiming attachment to communism. In this context, and despite the dramatic economic reforms experienced in Vietnam or China, there was no event comparable to what was taking place in Europe.

Things are different when examining Africa in 1989. Let us begin with Benin, which for several years was considered the pioneer of the democratic movement in Africa, and a model of transition.

In January 1989, students demonstrated in Cotonou and Porto Novo, demanding payment of their scholarships. But under the regime of military-installed president Mathieu Kérékou, the government was bankrupt. The president made political concessions, but demands developed to include better treatment of political detainees. By December 1989, the president announced that the People's Revolutionary Party of Benin would no longer be committed to Marxism-Leninism, and that the country would move to multipartism.[1] A new constitution was adopted by referendum, general elections were planned for February 1991 and presidential elections for March, during which Mathieu Kérékou was trounced by Nicéphore Soglo, a former World Bank official.

The end of Kérékou's Marxist-Leninist regime is of course reminiscent of events in Europe, both in timing and nature. Moreover, there were direct influences, as the end of communist regimes in Europe increased pressure on Kérékou to give in to popular demands. However, some ingredients in the Beninese transition were specific to the Third World, the most important being the issues of national debt, rescheduling of debt and increased foreign pressure via two Bretton Woods institutions that came into their own in the 1980s: the World Bank and the IMF, whose structural adjustment plans

Benin signed in June 1989. In the 1980s, the question of debt was becoming central, to the point where Nigerian writer (and 1986 Nobel Laureate for literature) Wole Soyinka argued in favour of cancelling the debt of African states as both reparation for the slave trade and a necessary step to allow them any chance at economic development. Such adjustment plans forced states to drastically cut social spending, thereby upsetting state-led economies and fuelling discontent.

By December 1994, thirty-five sub-Saharan countries had undergone some form of regime change. Not one state still formally claimed to be a single-party regime,[2] and competitive elections and leadership turnover had taken place in many countries. The most famous regime transition was the unlocking of the stalemate in South Africa, though the South African situation had its own peculiarities due to the nature of the regime and the high level of violence in the preceding years: In 1990, the ban was lifted on the African National Congress, and the first democratic elections were organized in 1994. Not only can the South African case be considered the end of a civil conflict in its own right due to the level of violence in the prior years, but also, influenced as it was by transitional situations elsewhere and with its Truth and Reconciliation Commission, it developed as a model of transition from civil war to peace. In most other African cases, transitions were democratic, and electoral competitions had sometimes taken place as early as 1985–89 (in Botswana, Gambia, Mauritius, Senegal and Zimbabwe). Throughout the continent there was a revolutionary dimension to the political ferment that brought about reforms; in turn, rapid reforms fuelled a revolutionary atmosphere.

The economic crisis, with the added pressures of the international 'adjustment plans', weakened the states' social support; the emergence of new forms of mobilization and new demands now extended to encompass culture, language and minority groups, and even to religion. The creation of new parties, organizations and new spaces for public debate fuelled the atmosphere of ebullience and effervescence that had begun earlier in the 1980s, even before the end of the Cold War. In several countries, popular discontent and demands, as well as the possibilities created by political reform, engendered both a climate of uncertainty and fear – particularly of the threat of military coup, violence or war, and one of enthusiasm for the creation of new organizations, parties or associations, new forms of expression and popular involvement in the public sphere. In the recently independent nation states, the compromises born from independence seemed stymied and no longer able to sustain regimes without some measure of democratic transformation.

In the Middle East and North Africa, Algeria was the only country to be chronologically in sync with sub-Saharan African countries: Throughout the 1980s, it experienced a series of popular protests contesting the single-party regime, while facing economic and financial difficulties worsened by the collapse in the price of oil in 1985. International pressure and economic reform drove discontent and political demands, until the youth riots of October 1988 forced the government to end the single-party regime in 1989. In a revolutionary atmosphere, the rise of political Islam in the form of the Islamic Salvation Front (FIS) was dramatic.

It was exacerbated by the international context of the Second Gulf War led against Saddam Hussein's Iraq in January and February 1991, the first being the Iran–Iraq war of 1980–88. The war followed the occupation of Kuwait on 2 August 1990 by the Iraqi army. One factor contributing to this was Iraq's rising debt – reminiscent of the rising debt which was strangling African countries – a debt chiefly owed to Saudi Arabia and Kuwait. The US decision to intervene militarily in Iraq, approved by the United Nations (UN) Security Council, was to a large extent explained by concerns over Saddam Hussein's threats to Saudi Arabia. However, the very possibility of intervention was created by the new balance of powers that followed the end of the Cold War. Iraq had long been an ally of the USSR, and – along with the other similar Arab regimes such as Syria – an irritant for American foreign policy. This new military intervention by a Western power in the Middle East caused significant outrage in the region and was a watershed moment for many political movements. Osama Bin Laden's career is in that respect revelatory: He was born to a respected family of Saudi Arabia and raised with the Sa'ud princes. After the Red Army took over Kabul in 1979, he settled in Peshawar where he developed training camps for Arab combatants. In 1990, he first offered his services to the Sa'ud ruler, before breaking with the regime after it had requested US military intervention. The fact that Afghanistan-based combatants thus turned against Saudi Arabia as well as against the United States (who had supported them in the struggle against the Soviets) had vast consequences, as Bin Laden continued to train Jihadists and export Jihad, most successfully to Bosnia, Egypt and Algeria.[3] In Algeria, the FIS gained significant momentum during the Second Gulf War, as it managed to revamp the figure of formerly secular, Ba'athist foe Saddam Hussein as a champion of Islam, and a victim of neo-imperialist intervention in the Middle East. In so doing, it reclaimed part of the Ba'athist, Arab-nationalist legacy, which had until then been the prerogative of the left.

After the FIS victory in local elections in the summer of 1990, the party was prevented from assuming power through general elections by a military coup in January 1991. The country began its descent into a decade-long civil war between armed jihadi groups and the national army. While other countries in the Middle East and North Africa (MENA) region experienced some level of internal pressure for political change, Islamist contestation and even jihadi violence, as well as economic turmoil and international pressure, they nonetheless resisted change until twenty years later and the 'Arab Revolts' of 2011.

Algeria's version of 1989 calls into question the chronology and nature of the event in several ways. With the Iranian revolution of 1979 serving as a model for the FIS, and combatants trained in Afghanistan spreading both ideological content and military experience to the armed jihadi groups, the aftermath of 1989 was connected to 1979 in a way that was not obvious in sub-Saharan Africa.

On the African continent, Algeria was hardly the only country to face violence in the wake of political change. The transition away from autocratic single-party regimes did not always go smoothly: Elections and political competition were at times linked to (and often considered the cause of) new forms of violence, in which culture, language and ethnic lines of divide played an essential role. Upsurges of violence during competitive elections became a common feature of African politics. In Burundi, after twenty-seven years of military dictatorship, elections were organized in 1993: The assassination of newly elected Hutu president Melchior Ndadaye in October 1993 by Tutsi soldiers led to several years of civil war. And in Rwanda, narratives of the Tutsi survivors of the genocide identify the multiparty system put in place by the constitution of 1991 as the starting point of yet another episode in the recurring anti-Tutsi violence that had begun as early as 1959, an episode which ultimately led to the 1994 genocide.[4] Turmoil in both countries was one of the causes for the largest conflict of all: Rwanda and Burundi became involved, along with Uganda, Angola, Zimbabwe and Namibia and non-African economic interests, in a five-year war in the Democratic Republic of Congo, a war sometimes dubbed 'the Great African War' or 'the African World War' (1998–2003). This conflict developed in the wake of the first Congolese war, during which Laurent-Désirée Kabila had overthrown Mobutu and seized power. That war had caused between 3.9 million and 5.4 million casualties, whether through combat, disease or famine, making it the deadliest conflict since the Second World War. For many, the two events form but one war.[5]

One of the main arguments for labelling the Great African War a world war is the scale of foreign intervention. The timing and form of foreign intervention (or lack thereof) – notably French 'Opération turquoise' – in Rwanda was obviously critical. By the same token, intervention in the Congo involved a number of Western players, namely the United States, and also France and Great Britain, who were both involved in enhancing the European Union (EU) military power in Africa, as well as non-European economic interests.[6] However, making the Great African War a direct consequence of the collapse of the bipolar system would ignore the interconnection of regional dynamics, neo-imperialist forms of intervention and attempts by former colonial powers such as Britain, France or even Belgium to protect or regain their influence on the continent. While all of these must be understood in the context of the post–Cold War period, the end of the Cold War alone cannot adequately explain them.

In many African countries, there was indeed a hope for democratization and political transition, though this was not the case for MENA countries nor for East and South-East Asia once the political transition in China had been thwarted by repression. In turn, the relationship between this (mostly African) process and the European 1989 must be considered. While the European 1989 fuelled the transition in several countries, there were specific Third World, African and postcolonial – not to mention neo-imperialist – dynamics at play. Focusing on 1989 from outside of Europe therefore has the effect of 'provincializing Europe' and places the fall of the Iron Curtain as one of a series of world events leading to the transition of a number of political regimes. Moreover, the notion of 1989 as an end of war is strangely reversed in the non-European context: Rather than an end of war, it appears to have been the beginning of a period of violence and wars. Seen from outside Europe, and more specifically from Africa, 1989 was not the end of a war but the start of a period of war that culminated in the war in the Congo, a war comparable in scale to the European world wars of the twentieth century.

Year 1945: end of war or beginning of war?

Before jumping backwards to the previous postwar period under scrutiny in this volume, a precautionary question needs to be posed. Identifying 1989 as the end of *something*, for instance, as the breakdown of the postcolonial compromise that sustained the new parties that had achieved independence and the strong regimes born from independence begs us to identify the beginning of the cycle which ended in 1989. Is it possible that 1945 is the beginning of that which ended in 1989? And if not, then what is the founding event, of similar or greater magnitude that we may be missing by following a European-centred framework? But, let us begin with our opening question: Is 1945 an end of war in the colonial empires in the same way that it is in Europe? Or – as was the case with 1989 – is it the start of the period of violence and war outside of Europe?

Because of the simultaneity of the end-of-war celebrations and the reactivation of colonial violence by imperial powers aiming to reassert their domination over their colonies, the most emblematic date and place to launch this discussion is 8 May 1945 in the French empire, where two simultaneous events took place.

In Algeria, a series of demonstrations throughout the country had begun on 1 May, and culminated with the celebrations of the end of the war, on 8 May. In the east, in Sétif and Guelma, demonstrations turned into anti-European violence after demonstrators were shot by French troops. Repression of the colonized population lasted for several weeks, involving army, police and European militias. Cities were bombarded from warships at sea. The toll is unknown, but was in the tens of thousands.

This event obliterates other episodes that are nevertheless essential to understanding its meaning. In the French protectorate of Syria and Lebanon, where treaties of independence had been signed in 1936 that were never enforced, frustration increased during the war, as the Free French occupied the territories but refused to grant independence despite General Catroux's June 1941 promises.[7] Warships were sent to Beirut in May 1945, sparking violence against the French troops and a wave of strikes in the main cities of Damascus, Homs, Hama and Aleppo. To regain control, General Oliva-Roget ordered bombardments; the bombing of Damascus was particularly devastating. It was only in April 1946 that French troops left the region, and that both countries finally achieved independence.

The chronology of 8 May 1945 for the French in Algeria and Syria is striking due to simultaneity and symbolism. While in other countries the chronology is less neat and more complex, it nonetheless also reveals how the Second World War fuelled nationalist movements and shaped their demands precisely at the time when colonial powers aimed to regain control: in Madagascar for instance, the uprising only began in March 1947, following campaigns for self-determination based on explicit reference to the Atlantic Charter of 1941 and the Brazzaville Conference of 1944. Significantly, its leaders expected Americans and British to pressure France into granting the country its independence. It was only in 1960, however, that Madagascar finally became independent.

As was the case in Africa and the Middle East, the colonial powers' desire to reassert their imperial domination during the final moments of the Second World War was obvious in East Asia, where Japan had expanded to occupy large parts of the pre-war colonial empires, including the Indochina peninsula, Burma, Thailand, Indonesia and the Philippines.

The Second World War had galvanized nationalist movements; circulated new ideas, such as those contained in the Atlantic Charter of 1941; led the imperial powers to promise more and raised demands of the dominated peoples. Not only had Japanese occupation undercut the influence of the former imperial powers – both effectively and symbolically – but the Japanese had also developed a powerful anti-colonial rhetoric, and based their authority on mobilization of the masses. In Indonesia, during their three-and-a-half-year occupation, the Japanese government had promised independence, even allowing nationalist leader Sukarno to travel the country and give nationalist speeches aiming to mobilize for the war effort.[8]

The end of the Second World War was the time to reassert the threatened authority of the imperial powers: Allied troops set to the task of reinstating civilian administrations in the Japanese-occupied territories. The US-led Southwest Pacific Command reoccupied the Philippines in 1945. Hopes stirred by the end of the war, and uncertainties around transition – which are characteristic of immediate postwar periods – created in Indonesia as elsewhere, interstices that encouraged nationalist movements to undertake bold moves. On 17 August 1945 – when news of the Hiroshima and Nagasaki bombings were still only a rumour – Indonesian nationalist leaders Sukarno and Hatta declared independence and announced the creation of a government. At the head of the South East Asia Command (SEAC), Lord Mountbatten had set out with both British and British Indian troops to reoccupy the country, leading to the bloody Battle of Surabaya of November 1945, during which the city was heavily shelled. The conflict, which began in 1945, lasted until the agreements reached in August 1949 in The Hague.

Individual careers, such as Lord Mountbatten's, reveal the continuities between Second World War and wars of independence. Appointed Supreme Allied Commander of SEAC by Churchill, the British officer had overseen the reconquest of Burma concluded just before the end of the war, and later that of Indonesia that continued beyond the end of the war.[9] Faced with the changed attitude of the civilian populations and the new dynamics of the nationalist movement, officers such as Mountbatten transformed aims of operations from winning the war against Japan to recolonization. But this transfer from Second World War to colonial war violence is not uniquely military in character. In Algeria, one of the key players of the May 1945 repression was sous-préfet André Achiary. Raised in Algeria, he joined the Resistance during the war, supporting the landing of 8 November 1942 (in November 1943, he received the 'médaille de la Résistance' from the hands of General de Gaulle). After the May 8 demonstrations in Guelma, he organized a European militia and an illegal Tribunal de Salut public, perpetrating extrajudicial executions of hundreds of men.[10]

The transition from Second World War to colonial wars raises many questions. For countries such as France or Great Britain, involving their armies in such theatres of conflict de facto delayed the return to civilian life for men who had become ill adapted to peacetime. Just as empires had in the past provided a destination for those seeking economic opportunity or adventure, for the brutalized metropolitan societies at the end of the Second World War, they offered an opportunity to continue to wage war. For civilians involved in resistance movements, or simply unable to cope with life in peacetime after the intensity of war years, empires allowed them to pursue war and violence at a safe distance from the metropolis. The pattern of French wars is a striking example of continuous warfare from the World War of 1939–45, through the war in

Indochina (1946–54), to the Algerian war (1954–62). The return of many Second World War veterans was thus delayed until 1962, with each war inheriting the army and men left by the previous, and adding its own specific experiences. It is therefore necessary to rethink the correlation between wars in Europe (and more generally the Global North) and wars in the empires.

In recent years, research has emphasized the way imperial violence was imported into Europe, with its techniques, know-hows and levels of cruelty 'from colonial genocide to holocaust'.[11] For instance, the 1904–5 massacres of the Herero and Nama population of what is now Namibia by the German colonial troops were 'rediscovered' in 1985 and classified as a genocide, leading academics to discuss continuities between colonial violence and violence of the Second World War.[12] Many of the practices of war, artefacts and tools of violence were suddenly seen to have been invented, tested or perfected, in the laboratory of the colonial possessions. Yet, examining 1945 from the colonies reverses this perspective, and the directionality of the flow of violence, with levels of violence, war and brutalization also moving from the Europe-centred World War to the empire. The way in which the conduct of colonial conflict was conceived and accepted by European societies was unmistakably branded by the intensity of the experiences of the Second World War that was just ending; empires offered outlets to the brutalized societies, their armies and weaponry, and played an essential role in the way the European postwar period was managed.

This leaves us with two questions. The first is how to qualify the new period that starts in 1945 in order to understand the nature of 1945 itself.

Seen from the colonial empires, is 1945 solely or mostly understandable as the beginning of the Cold War? In the empire, the Cold War was not so cold, as the superpowers waged proxy wars that contributed to the state of atomized, asymmetrical wars. The French war in Indochina that began in 1946 and for which the United States came to bear most of the financial brunt in the context of the Cold War, or the Korean War in 1950, both of which can be read in the context of the advent of Communist China in 1949, show how the Cold War interfered and intertwined with wars of independence. Moreover, the possibility of playing one superpower against another offered nationalist movements a historic window of opportunity for success in their struggle against imperial powers.

Nevertheless, as writes Mark Philip Bradley, decolonization should by no means be reduced to the Cold War: 'the global move toward decolonization was rooted in local particularities that long preceded, ran parallel with, and ultimately persisted beyond the Cold War'.[13] The Non-Aligned Movement, which began to organize in Bandung in 1955, aimed to avoid entering a not-so-Cold war, as well as maintaining the possibility of benefitting from the conflict between superpowers, both of which had pledged anti-colonialism – in the case of the United States, after its own colony of the Philippines was granted independence in 1946 – or claimed to support peoples' emancipation – as did the Zhdanov doctrine. In the two decades following 1945, during which over forty states where born, such conflicts also have everything to do with independence.[14]

The question stemming from this re-evaluation of 1945 as the beginning of a new period of war, rather than a postwar period, is that raised in the introduction to this section: Can another postwar period be identified between 1989 and 1945, while a majority of countries from the Global South were achieving independence, many of them through wars, episodes of war or violence?

The relationship between independence and war in turn raises a number of queries. For one thing, respective attainments of independence were hardly synchronized in one single event: From the independence of the Philippines in 1946, through that of India in 1947, of most African countries in the 1960s, and as late as the independence of the Portuguese colonies in Africa in the 1970s and even of Namibia in 1990, there is no meaningful or definitive date that encapsulates these events in the collective.

Moreover, independence was not always synchronized with wars and uprisings. In Kenya, independence was achieved in 1963, four years after the end of the Mau Mau uprising (1952–1959), and therefore technically, it was not achieved through war. In other cases, the chronology is even more confusing: In Indonesia, while the Dutch only granted independence in 1949 after several years of conflict, they now officially recognize the 1945 Declaration of Independence, thus blurring the distinction between pre- and post-independence war even further. Moreover, not all independence was achieved through war, and in several cases, where there was a war, it happened following actual independence. Palestine was the object of a partition plan, voted by the United Nations on 30 November 1947 to end British colonial domination over the territory. The various names given to the 1948 war that followed this plan and Ben Gurion's declaration of independence are revealing of what is at stake: In Hebrew, it is the war of liberation (*Milkhemet HaShikhrur*), or the war of independence (*Milkhemet Ha'Atzma'ut*), whereas in Arabic, it is the catastrophe (*Nakba*). While the war sanctioned the end of British colonial rule over Palestine, it forged the new nation state of Israel on the demise of the still-born state of Palestine. As happened elsewhere, the creation of one state implied the abortion of other possibilities: In Palestine, it was the potential of one state for two peoples, or of two states for two peoples; in India and Pakistan, the partition precluded the possibility of a single state; in the Arabic-speaking countries, it was the dream for a unified Arab nation that disintegrated once and for all in the aftermath of the Second World War. In other words, peri-independence wars were not always war *for* independence, but rather wars that forged states.

Rarely did countries experience no violence at all in the period between 1945 and their independence, no war-after-the-war and therefore no after-war. In a complex period, with a multiplicity of conflicts that had to do with the struggle for independence as well as with the Cold War, what we have in fact are multiple events that carry considerable symbolic power.

Even in countries in which independence was not achieved through war, narratives of independence – one is tempted to say myths of independence – follow a pattern. The main model of such a narrative is the Algerian war for independence, considered in the Third World as the mother of all independence events, as is revealed by the (Third-) worldwide popularity of Egyptian filmmaker Youssef Chahine's film *Gamila al-Gaza'iriyya* (1958),[15] which turned war hero Djamila Bouhired into a Third World and revolutionary icon in Latin America, Africa, Asia and the Arab World, where she is still immensely popular to this day. The Algerian war for independence, led by the National Liberation Front (FLN), contributed symbolically as well as materially both to simultaneous struggles for independence and to those that came later. Rendered into words (most strikingly by Frantz Fanon), photographs and film, it also provided previous independence events with a narrative model influencing the way violence, armed struggle and revolution were emphasized, and gave independence a collective date: 1962. Along with the Indochina war against France, and the Vietnam War against the United States, it contributed to a highly militarized aesthetic of liberation struggles, visible in William Klein's 1969 film on the Panafrican festival of Algiers,[16] and in revolutionary art of South American guerrilla movements, as well as North American radical political movements such as the Black Panther Party.[17]

Taking independence as an end of war therefore risks falling afoul of the myth, considering all countries to have followed the same model and glossing over the diversity of the pathways to independence. Indeed, recent works have underscored in several cases the distance between the myth and the actual process of independence and state building.[18] But taking the myth seriously is also necessary for understanding its historical reality, and the potency of the militarized cultures that developed in the Global South from the 1950s to the 1970s. It is also essential to understanding how the periods that begins with independence are periods of transition, opportunity and utopia equivalent to other postwar periods under scrutiny in this volume, bearing in mind that the resonance of independence is an event beyond the newly independent countries themselves. The left-wing movements of Central and South America, the radical and revolutionary movements of North America and even the youth movements that crystallized in 1968 in Europe demonstrate how independence constitutes world history events.

To the question of 'when does the cycle that ends in 1989 begin?' we now have another possible answer. In the African countries, where 1989 appeared to be the collapse of the compromise that sustained the strong regimes born from independence, the beginning of the cycle is not 1945, but rather may indeed be independence itself. This chronologically complex event of independence, for which '1962' could be used only as imperfect shorthand, is arguably (in the sense that it is *worth arguing*) an end of war, followed in each individual situation by a postwar period enmeshed in the processes of state- and nation-building.

However, 1989 is yet another imperfect date to signify the collapse of the post-independence consensus. For one thing, we have seen it to be effective mainly in the sub-Saharan African context. Secondly, 1989 crystallized the energy and contestation that had been developing throughout the 1980s. Finally, when examined from the former imperial territories as a time of crisis of the independent states born after the Second World War, 1989 must be integrated in a more complex chronology, or series of events of which it is neither the first nor the last. The last wave of African independence events (the Portuguese colonies of Mozambique, Angola and Cape Verde obtained their independence in 1975 and Zimbabwe obtained its independence from Great Britain in 1980) brought to a close the 'age of independence' and weakened the third-worldist dynamics of the existing states. The tipping point between the age of independence and their progressive weakening is more clearly marked in North Africa, the Middle East and Southwest Asia: While the revolution had previously been considered necessarily socialist and third-worldist, the Iranian revolution of 1979 provided the new revolutionary model of a successful Islamist revolution, thus bolstering Islamist movements throughout Muslim majority countries; the Soviet occupation of Afghanistan provided them with a training field and an experience of combat that would strengthen them for decades to come. The occupation of the Grand Mosque of Mecca by an armed group contesting the regime of the Sa'ud family in November and December 1979 or the much less dramatic occupation of the Institute of Law in Algiers by Islamist students the same year are only examples of the emergence of Islamist movements, and were part of much broader, multifarious state contestations that developed in the 1980s. In other words, it is not unreasonable to consider 1989 as the apex (or perhaps an apex) of the process that began with the end of the age of revolution and independence in 1979.

Year 1918: demobilization, circulation of violence and the manufacturing of dominated states

In travelling backwards towards the previous postwar period – that of the First World War beginning in 1918 – we come to the time when European domination was reaching its peak, and Europe and its non-European possessions were the most synchronized. Here again, widening the scope beyond Europe is revelatory of the nature of the event worldwide, and raises the question of whether what was in Europe the end of a war was for colonial empires the beginning of the period of conflict that would bring these empires to a close.

By pitching colonial powers against each other, the First World War opened up new territorial opportunities for European powers and offered the chance for a last-minute scramble for territory, reshuffling the cards between winners and losers of the war. The fact that only days after the declaration of war (even before landing in France), British forces attacked German Togoland is illustrative of the strategic importance of imperial territories during the conflict.[19]

Early on in the war, the Ottoman Empire had been an object of competing Franco-British aspirations. The better-known attempt to divide up the Ottoman Empire between the Entente powers was the Sykes–Picot agreement, signed as early as May 1916 between British and French representatives. However, the Ottoman Empire proved a more difficult enemy to defeat after its success in the Dardanelles, leading the British to encouraged the notorious 'Arab revolt' in order to divide Arabs and Turks. They supported Sharif Hussein of Mecca and his sons, Faisal and Abdallah, in their political and territorial claims. During the war, imperial powers – and in particular those nations that had acquired their colonial territories in more recent times – were confronted with uprisings. This was the case in Libya, where the Italian conquest had only taken place in 1911–12: During the war, the region of Misrata revolted and managed to maintain a semi-autonomous status for several years. By the same token, the Portuguese were faced with revolts in Angola and Mozambique, which they suppressed. Nevertheless, despite such significant episodes and the changing of hands of many territories, European domination over the empire was never threatened: British and French key possessions of Algeria, Egypt, India and Indochina remained firmly in hand.

The long postwar period and the numerous treaties that aimed at resolving the conflict and organizing peace sanctioned new positions, reflecting a new balance of powers on the ground. The process of settling the war was not only the opportunity to redistribute pre-existing colonial territories, but also to assert European hegemony over new non-European territories. This involved drawing new borders, creating new (dominated) states, inventing legal forms of domination and waging new wars of conquest.

In the colonial empires, the Great War had been a time of mobilization, circulation of men, ideas and political practices. Intense labour and combatant mobilization led to increased movement. The British Raj, for example, provided 1.4 million men organized into the British Indian Army, composed of British and Indian soldiers, which fought mainly in the Middle East.[20] Throughout the conflict, Morocco under French protectorate provided the French army with 45,000 infantrymen and auxiliaries, many of whom had enlisted for economic reasons. The postwar demobilization meant that they would either return to their countries or go on to wage the colonial conflicts that riddled the interwar period. The British Indian Army, which had been heavily committed in Mesopotamia, Egypt and Palestine during the war, stayed on in Palestine until the end of the British Mandate in 1948; it had also been deployed to the Third Anglo-Afghan War of 1919.

Many French colonial troops fought in Syria during the repression of the Great Revolt of 1925–27. Some of them also fought with the French army in the Rif War in Morocco, wherein the Moroccan combatants of Abd al-Karim al-Khattabi opposed Spanish troops (from 1921 to 1926), and later French troops as well (from 1925 to 1926). The careers of those generals who led Europeans armies in Morocco emphasize the role of the Riffian conflict as a precursor of the Second World War, in connection with the development of authoritarian regimes in Europe: On the Spanish side, the army was led by Miguel Primo de Rivera and Franscisco Franco, and on the French side by Philippe Pétain, all of whom would play crucial roles in the future of both Spain and France. But as we did when examining 1945, we can here again reverse the directionality of violence and brutalization to consider Rif as the sequel to the First World War, during which the weaponry that had been developed in Europe was perfected, notably by the use of Yperite (mustard gas) bombs as well as other chemical weapons. Aerial bombings – the first of which is considered to have taken place in 1911 in Libya during the Turkish–Italian war – developed during the Great War and were one of the weapons of choice during these 'wars after the war'. This was the case during the Riffian war, and also in Afghanistan: Aerial bombings had been used heavily to quash an uprising on the Afghan–Indian border in 1917, and the third Anglo-Afghan war of 1919 is known for the heavy bombings of Dacca, Jalalabad and Kabul.[21] During the Iraq revolt of 1920, the British forces used aerial bombings as a form of 'aerial policing' to repress populations using fewer of the (Indian) troops on the ground, causing upward of 6,000 Iraqi casualties as opposed to 500 British and Indian combatants. Both public opinion and British politicians saw this method of warfare as unpleasant, but it was made more acceptable by distance from the metropolis and by the racial representations of the targeted populations.

All in all, 1918 functioned similarly to 1945 in terms of the relationship between the postwar period and the empires. Violence and combat continued despite the end of the war, with World War morphing into colonial conquest (rather than reconquest as was the case in 1945), and colonial territories serving as lands of opportunity for the military professional to pursue their careers. They also allowed European armies to absorb all of those whose rapid demobilization might cause political unrest, in particular the numerous colonial troops.

The resolution of the war took place over a period of five years through peace treaties, several of which dealt specifically with the colonial territories or former Ottoman Empire territories now under European domination: the Versailles Treaty of June 1919, the Sèvres treaty of August 1920 (following the San Remo conference of April 1920) and the Lausanne Treaty in July 1923. This postwar period was a period of transition, change and instability as well as a period branded by attempts at imposing a new order. Instability extended well beyond the war and was apparent through the number of ongoing conflicts. These were either directly or more loosely connected to the First World War, not only because imposing order and peace took time, but also because of aspirations to prolong the state of war, and to gain more ground before borders solidified.

In the postwar period, international relations came to be organized around a new player: the League of Nations, which was created in 1920 as a result of the Versailles Peace Conference. Territorial reorganization and imposition of a new postwar order took place in an atmosphere imbued by the ideas of the Wilsonian era.

During the war, empires had provided a labour force that travelled to the metropole, filling in the places left vacant by mobilized Europeans. Both in the army and in civilian jobs, the experiences of suffering institutionalized forms or racism, as well as being exposed to metropolitan European cultures, had lasting effects on the development of new ideas and political practices. Circulation within the empires developed anti-colonial consciousness and deepened nationalist ideas, and many of those who had travelled became agents of the spreading of new subversive ideas. A case in point of such political and social ferment is that of Nguyên Tat Thanh, the future Hô Chi Minh, who, having lived in London during the time of the war, moved to Paris in 1919, in order to be close to the growing Vietnamese community. In the postwar period, he developed his political writings, joined the French socialist party, and made contact with the Communist International. It was from Paris that he created the communist network in Vietnam itself.[22] Several of the political parties that would later be instrumental in achieving independence in their respective countries were created in the 1920s by emigrant workers, as is the case of the Étoile Nord-africaine, created in Paris in 1926. Many of them referred directly to the new concepts that framed international relations. The Destour party, for example, was created in Tunisia in 1920 by men who explicitly referred to Woodrow Wilson's Fourteen Points and the notion of self-determination. Forms of political practice revealed the belief in a new spirit of international relations: petitions, letters sent to Europeans parties (or to Woodrow Wilson in person) and delegations to Paris or London. The very act of negotiating and treaty signing created new opportunities for international contact, when representatives of various territories, generally carefully chaperoned by 'their' imperial power, met in Paris with the (mistaken) expectation that they could determine their own future. The image of Faisal bin Hussein's delegation to Paris, which included T. E. Lawrence, is well known. But the Egyptian Wafd delegation was also present, despite opposition of their British handlers, with its leader Saad Zaghlul. The group's arrest upon their return to Egypt and subsequent deportation to Malta was one of the causes of the 1919 revolution. The Wafd, which had developed during the war as an informal organization, was to become one of the most influential parties in the history of the country.

Under the auspices of the new League of Nations, the postwar period was characterized by the invention of a new legal territorial entity, the mandate, that was to be applied to the peoples defined in article 22 of the Covenant of the League of Nations firstly as people living in territories having lost sovereignty in the past war ('those colonies and territories which as a consequence of the late war have ceased to be under the sovereignty of the States which formerly governed them'), and secondly by their inability to govern themselves ('peoples not yet able to stand by themselves under the strenuous conditions of the modern world') ('The Covenant of the League of Nations', signed 28 June 1919).

According to the Treaty of Versailles, German territories were to be entrusted to victorious powers. Germany's western African empire, consisting of the Cameroons and Togoland, was therefore divided between France and Britain. German East Africa was shared between Britain (Tanganyika) and Belgium (Ruanda-Urundi). Finally, German South-West Africa was mandated by the League of Nations to South Africa, until the independence of Namibia in 1990. The Pacific also saw similar reallocation of formerly German territories, as German New Guinea became a League of Nations mandate under the administration of Australia (it remained so until 1949), while the Pacific territories north of the equator were mandated to Japan (until the Second World War).[23]

This system allowed the carving up of Ottoman territories into smaller territorial units of state-like dimension (Palestine, Syria, Iraq, Jordan). These territorial entities were in fact much smaller than the Hashemite dream of an Arab kingdom. Their very creation, along with the British support for Zionism following the Balfour Declaration of 1917, was a sign that Hashemi Arab nationalism was defeated and must now adapt to these new, multiple and small territories, subject to European domination under the mandate system. The careers of the Hashemi brothers are significant for their attempt to adapt to the new order that was emerging: Faisal, former leader of the 'Arab Revolt', was proclaimed king of the Arab Kingdom of Syria in March 1920 by the Syrian National Congress government. However, the San Remo conference of April 1920 granted France the League of Nations mandate over Syria, and following the Franco-Syrian war (and the Syrian defeat at the Battle of Maysalun, on 24 July 1920), Faisal was ousted from power. Following the Cairo Conference of March 1921, he was made king of Iraq, under British domination, and his continued attempts to reunite Iraq and Syria were repeatedly thwarted by the mandate system and the existence of new borders and states. Even at that time, academics working in politics and international relations questioned the discrepancy between the principles of the mandate system and the imperial powers' behaviour in the territories mandated to them. One of them was Philip Quincy Wright, whose work reflects his interest in the issue of maintaining peace, but questions the mandate system and the way its spirit and legality are distorted to wage war.[24]

While there were a few new, Middle East States that were created outside of the mandate system, these were also under close European supervision, as in the case of the emergence of the Sa'ud dynasty. Prior to the war, Abd al-Aziz Ibn Sa'ud had been recognized by the Ottoman Wali of Nedj. However, when, after his 1922 trip to the region, Amin Rihani published *The Arab Kings*, he gave equal importance to Husayn of Mecca, Imam Yahia of Yemen and Abd al-Aziz Ibn Sa'ud. By the time the book was published in 1925, the balance had shifted, as Ibn Sa'ud asserted his authority. He conquered Hijaz and took Mecca, and signed an agreement with the British to delineate the borders of his kingdom; in 1927, the Jeddah agreement prevented the Sa'uds from claiming territories of other British-protected kingdoms. The kingdom of Saudi Arabia was officially proclaimed in 1932 and was one of the poorer states in the world until the discovery of oil reserves in 1938. By that time, oil companies were ready to insure hegemony of the North over the kingdom.

The most surprising feature of these postwar states is how durable they have proven themselves to be. Since the Arab Spring of 2011, and even more so since the creation of ISIS (the Islamic State in Iraq and Sham organization, *aka* Daesh) in June 2014, considerable attention has been given to the carving up of the Ottoman Empire by European powers in the wake of the First World War. It has been written that the Middle East countries were artificially – and badly – forged by Europeans, with the logical conclusion that powers foreign to the region should suppress the 'children of England and France' as one author called Syria, Jordan, Iraq as well as Israel and the permanent non-state of Palestine and redesign, hopefully better, new territorial entities.[25] However, while imperial powers were at work fashioning borders and states in the postwar period, more recent historiography has shown that local dynamics should not be written out of this process.

These depict the postwar period not merely as European powers inventing and applying new forms of domination, but also show populations at a very local level seizing the possibilities offered to them by the new lexicon of international relations (and notions such as 'self-determination', 'nation-state', 'minority' or 'nationality') to develop their own strategies, forward demands and transform their own identities which were discussed in the process of defining their nationalities.[26] The end-of-war treaties, and the mandate system opened up questions of nationalities, which each new dominated state had to manage during the interwar period. After the Lausanne treaty of 1923 officially ended the dependency of Syrians and Lebanese on the Ottoman state, nationality codes were adopted in both countries in 1925 to manage the transition from Ottoman nationality, previously defined in 1869, to state nationality. Even in older states, this was the time to create nationalities. In Tunisia in 1914, against the better judgement of the French authorities, they had to create a definition of Tunisian nationality in order to prevent Muslim immigrants from Algeria or Libya claiming French or Italian nationality; this would have blurred the racial divide between

'European' and 'native'.[27] Tunisian nationality would later become a powerful tool in the hands of the nationalist movement.

With the mandate system as the favoured instrument of hegemony during this period (as the protectorate had been at the end of the nineteenth century), the postwar period saw the birth of a latticework of new and dominated states that proved surprisingly durable, because – despite their contradiction with local aspirations – they framed the anti-imperialist struggles within the perimeters of states, which would rapidly transform into national frameworks.

Conclusion

This regressive exploration of three postwar periods as seen from the (former) imperial possessions reveals a finer chronology where postwar periods are never ends of war, but rather the start of new periods of wars: In 1945 and 1918, these are wars of conquest, reconquest or for the preservation of the colonial order. Likewise, 1989 signals the beginning of a new era in which the risk of war (civil wars, wars waged by the sole superpower and even World War) is increased. But this examination also inscribes 1989 as part of a longer timeline: In the Arab world and Africa, 1989 appears to be both the child of 1979 as well as the anticlimax of 1962. Viewing 1989 as simply the end of the Cold War now appears as only one of the possible interpretations of both the date and the events.

What this exploration has also revealed is the alternation of wars waged by the Global North at home and those waged in their empires or in countries born from an independence movement. The journey backwards, and more particularly the milestones of 1945 and 1918, bring to light that, when it comes to waging war, colonial possessions have been used by the North in two ways. Firstly, they have served as training and experimentation grounds for weaponry and tactics that were later put to use in Europe-centred conflicts. Secondly, these territories have also been used to manage transitions back to peace after major wars, allowing imperial powers to handle their demobilization processes (by selectively committing their troops to new conflicts and thus delaying their return home and the troubles that would ensue), and to put to use in faraway lands the equipment and ammunition amassed during the World War.

This in turn brings us back to our understanding of 1989, by raising the question of the involvement of countries from the global North in conflicts in the South since 1989. How much of the involvement of European forces in the African Great War had to do with the necessity to put to use the men, equipment and know-how that would otherwise have been made redundant by the end of the Cold War? And how much of the United States' decision to attack Iraq in 1991 can be explained by the need to find outputs for the war industry, now that the Cold War was over?

Such hegemony over the Global South has outlasted political independence events and assumed new shapes and forms. As made abundantly clear by the 2003 war in Iraq, as well as the 2011 intervention in Libya, it now seems to involve the possibility of dismantling states born of independence, and thereby contributing to the increased level of world insecurity.

Notes

1 Michael Bratton and Nicholas van de Walle, *Democratic Experiments in Africa: Regime Transitions in Comparative Perspective* (Cambridge, UK, and New York, NY: Cambridge University Press, 1997), 1–2.

2 Bratton and van de Walle, *Democratic Experiments in Africa*, 8.

3 Gilles Kepel, *Jihad: The Trail of Political Islam* (London: I. B. Tauris, 2006, revised edition), 299–323.

4 Jean Hatzfeld, *Dans le nu de la vie* (Paris: Seuil, 2005).

5 Gérard Prunier, *Africa's World War: Congo, the Rwandan Genocide, and the Making of a Continental Catastrophe* (Oxford: Oxford University Press, 2009); Filip Reyntjens, *The Great African War: Congo and Regional Geopolitics, 1996–2006* (Cambridge: Cambridge University Press, 2009).

6 Catherine Gegout, 'The West, Realism and Intervention in the Democratic Republic of Congo (1996–2006)', *International Peacekeeping* (27 April 2009).

7 Anne Bruchez, 'La fin de la présence française en Syrie: de la crise de mai 1945 au départ des dernières troupes étrangères', *Relations internationales* 122, No. 2 (2005), 17.

8 Adrian Vickers, *A History of Modern Indonesia* (Cambridge: Cambridge University Press, 2012, second edition), 96.

9 T. A. Heathcote, *British Admirals of the Fleet: 1734–1995* (London: Pen and Sword, 2002), 183–190.

10 Jean-Pierre Peyroulou, *Guelma, 1945: Une subversion française dans l'Algérie coloniale* (Paris: La Découverte, 2009), 94–98.

11 See, for example, Olivier Le Cour Grandmaison, *Coloniser, Exterminer: Sur La Guerre et l'État Colonial* (Paris: Fayard, 2005); and Henning Melber, 'How to Come to Terms with the Past: Re-Visiting the German Colonial Genocide in Namibia', *Africa Spectrum* 40, No. 1 (2005): 139–48.

12 Casper W. Erichsen and David Olusoga, *The Kaiser's Holocaust: Germany's Forgotten Genocide and the Colonial Roots of Nazism* (London: Faber, 2011).

13 Mark Philip Bradley, 'Decolonization, the Global South, and the Cold War, 1919–1962', in *The Cambridge History of the Cold War*, vol. 1, ed. Melvyn P. Leffler and Odd Arne Westad (Cambridge: Cambridge University Press, 2010), 464–85.

14 Robert J. McMahon, ed., *The Cold War in the Third World* (Oxford: Oxford University Press, 2013), 1.

15 Youssef Chahine, 'Gamila al-Gaza'iriyya', fiction film,1958, 123 min, starring Magda, Ahmed Mazhar and Salah Zulfakar.

16 William Klein, 'Festival panafricain d'Alger', documentary film, 1969, 102 min.

17 Sam Durant, ed., *Black Panther: The Revolutionary Art of Emory Douglas* (New York: Rizzoli, 2007).

18 For a recent example, see Frederick Cooper, *Citizenship between Empire and Nation: Remaking France and French Africa, 1945–1960* (Princeton, NJ: Princeton University Press, 2014).

19 Alexander Sydney Kanya-Forstner, 'The War, Imperialism, and Decolonization', in *The Great War and the Twentieth Century*, ed. J. M. Winter and Geoffrey Parker (New Haven and London: Yale University Press, 2000), 231–62.

20 Partha Sarathi Gupta and Anirudh Deshpande (eds.), *The British Raj and Its Indian Armed Forces, 1857–1939* (New Delhi and Oxford: Oxford University Press, 2002).

21 Sven Lindqvist and Linda Haverty Rugg, 'Bombing the Savages', *Transition* No. 87 (2001): 48–64.

22 Pierre Brocheux, *Ho Chi Minh: A Biography* (Cambridge University Press, 2007).
23 William Roger Louis, *Great Britain and Germany's Lost Colonies, 1914–1919* (Oxford, Clarendon Press, 1967).
24 Quincy Wright, *Mandates under the League of Nations* (Chicago: University of Chicago Press, 1930); Quincy Wright, 'The Bombardment of Damascus', *The American Journal of International Law* 20 (1926): 263–80.
25 David Fromkin, *A Peace to End All Peace: The Fall of the Ottoman Empire and the Creation of the Modern Middle East* (New York: Owl Books, 2001).
26 Benjamin Thomas White, *The Emergence of Minorities in the Middle East: The Politics of Community in French Mandate Syria* (Edinburgh: Edinburgh University Press, 2011).
27 Mary Dewhurst Lewis, *Divided Rule: Sovereignty and Empire in French Tunisia, 1881– 1938* (Berkeley: University of California Press, 2013).

8

Markets

Paolo Capuzzo

One could look at the three postwar periods of the European twentieth century as a triumphal march of the affirmation of the market economy and of the American model of a mass consumer society, albeit with some European peculiarities such as the higher share of gross domestic product (GDP) assigned to the welfare state. Moreover, the success of this pattern of market economy and mass consumption was accompanied by an increasing integration of the European market, which itself was forged by the three postwar periods.

After the end of the First World War, the reorganization of European markets did not succeed in laying the basis of a stable economic cooperation. Revanchism inspired the economic settlements enacted by the Peace Treaties, with the consequence that it became difficult to pursue any policy of cooperation among European economies that was capable of overcoming short-sighted national interests, and which could easily degenerate into nationalistic conflicts.[1] After the Second World War, the hegemony of the United States and USSR on either side of a divided Europe deeply influenced or even forced fundamental changes in the economic systems on which the recovery of European societies were based. Western Europe embraced the American pattern of a society based on mass consumption, in which private welfare was deemed to be the major guarantee against communism and a fundamental factor of political stabilization and legitimization. This process occurred with some resistances because it implied a deep cultural change. Consumer cultures had been defined within stronger social hierarchies in Europe than was the case in the United States,[2] and the development of the mass market as a fundamental economic engine implied the erosion of these symbolic boundaries, as they acted as a force of market fragmentation. This external American influence was accompanied by an internal process of market integration within Europe, the aim of which was both to avoid a new devastating European war and to create the optimal conditions for developing competition and efficiency. Market integration and mass consumption became related goals to be pursued in order to guarantee prosperity to the population and stability and legitimization to the political regime. In contrast, in Eastern Europe, the Soviet pattern of an authoritarian political regime – which was the dominant force organizing social life and the economy – was extended from the USSR to the satellite states surrounding it. In the Soviet system, there was no market mediation among social life, private choices and production.

Material production was determined by the state and this contributed to reinforce the control on lifestyle and social behavior, which was actively pursued by the repressive apparatus of the totalitarian state. By choosing what to produce and fixing the prices, the state was necessarily highly influential in determining the lifestyle and daily life of its citizens.

In both Western and Eastern Europe, the experience of the first postwar period and its tragic consequences was crucial in determining a fundamental shift in the history of European societies. This shift was heavily influenced by forces which were probably perceived as external by the majority of the European population, namely Asian bolshevism and American consumerism – but they were reinforced by the military outcomes of the Second World War.

These two competing economic and social models became a fundamental issue of confrontation during the Cold War, and in 1989 one seemed to have definitely prevailed over the other. In the aftermath of the fall of the Berlin Wall, the liberal market economy seemed to stand out as the best means to organize economy and society. This happened after a conflict – which had lasted throughout the so-called short twentieth century – but finally it seemed that the market economy could deploy its beneficial effects throughout Europe. Thus, the political economy promoted after 1989 in the former Eastern bloc aimed at setting up the basis of a market economy, albeit sometimes imposed in a forcible way. These policies were seen as a premise for the eastward enlargement of the European Union, which would finally result in the achievement of a huge common European market.

Taken together, there are therefore good reasons underlying the narrative of the triumphal affirmation of the capitalist market economy in Europe, accompanied by the progressive overcoming of the old political barriers erected by those anti-liberal regimes which opposed it: nationalists, fascists and communists. Nevertheless, the deep crisis which in recent years has affected the European project and the economic difficulties with which most European countries are faced, do not suggest taking this narrative for granted, without scrutinizing it in greater detail. In particular, it is necessary to look at the three postwar periods more closely, analyzing the actors and forces which interacted pursuing specific goals and obtaining specific results, be they those which were expected or not. By doing this, the narrative of a superior system based on intrinsic forces which had simply to overcome resistances over the course of a long war, in order to spread its beneficial effects, will appear at least to be dubious. Rather than an ineluctable affirmation of the principles of the market economy and of the mass consumer society, the realization of a common European market seems to have been the result of specific continental and global historical conjunctures, in which specific historical factors played an important role.

The end of the second postwar settlements: the crisis of the 1970s

Looking at the three postwar periods from the point of view of markets and consumption requires us also to pay particular attention to the crisis of the 1970s as the turning point when the post-1945 settlements came to an end and a new paradigm – which would heavily influence the post-1989 transition – came into being.

Especially during the 1980s, the international affirmation of neo-liberal policies as the best means to overcome the crisis of the 1970s had a profound impact on an initially reluctant Western Europe. The free market, the privatization of state-owned industries and the withdrawal of state economic intervention promised to be the fundamental tools necessary to revive the declining European economy. Thanks to the mediating function of the free market, it appeared that individual freedom and economic efficiency could be happily reconciled. In fact, many European countries in the late 1970s had been promoting a sort of renationalization of their markets in a surreptitious way. This seemed to be the easiest way, in the short term, to face the global crisis, in a similar way to the prevalent reaction to the crisis of the 1930s. But this policy was cut short by the decisions of the European Court, which acted to censure all measures which could serve as obstacles to the liberalization of the European Economic Community (EEC) internal market. In the following years, the political initiative aimed at reinforcing the European market was relaunched and had as its main promoter the European Commission presided over by Jacques Delors.

In the 1980s, the successful neo-liberal philosophy emphasized the role of the open global market as the main engine of economic development and advocated the removal of trade barriers in order to reawaken the so-called animal instincts of capitalism. Western European economic policies were influenced by the neo-liberal global reconfiguration of the driving forces of capitalism, which forged a new economic geography in which transnational financial and industrial networks further weakened the capacity of the nation states to control their own economic space. Some key instruments and aims which had been at the core of the Western European recovery after the Second World War – and which had nurtured the economic miracle in the 1950s and 1960s (notably full employment, a public economy and a welfare state) – were marginalized, or even considered as the causes of the economic crisis of the 1970s that had to be removed. Moreover, the European states had to face a real and present difficulty in the form of the fiscal crisis that put severe limits on public expenditure and required a cut in public-sector functions, social spending and economic subsidies.

Since any single national reaction within the globalized dimension of capitalism in the 1980s would have been too weak, European reformers promoted a stronger integration of Europe in order to create a space in which a wide market and a powerful industrial structure could be regulated internally according to the principles of a new welfare system, and could act powerfully at the global level. Already in the late 1970s a firm basis had been established for a currency system which linked all countries within a narrow band of fluctuations, but it was during the term of presidency of Jacques Delors at the European Commission (from 1985 onwards) that an ambitious plan aimed at further integration of the European market was developed. The Plan Delors can be seen as an attempt to react – according to European political traditions and values – to the neo-liberal international hegemony, by trying to develop a European path within the wider process of globalization. Its aim was the full integration of labour, services and financial markets in Europe, an ambitious goal which had to confront significant differences among the European countries, concerning matters such as taxation, licences, state regulatory devices and commercial legislation. The principal European states realized that the new competitive conditions of global capitalism could be confronted more effectively with a strong unified continental market within which it would be possible to develop opportunities and competitiveness. Delors presented a White Paper which planned the removal of all obstacles to the free circulation of goods and people throughout Europe and pointed to the ambitious aim of creating a unified market not only of industry but also of services. This was a crucial point because in the late 1980s the European and global economies were reviving, thanks to the dramatic expansion of services provided both by the old sectors – banks and insurance companies – as well as by emergent sectors, notably information technology, media and marketing. An effective policy of unification was therefore needed to balance the different fiscal systems throughout Europe, particularly indirect taxes which could influence substantially the functioning of the market. This was a huge task which implied strong political backing in all countries, as well as a change in the pattern of governance of the EEC which abandoned the requirement of unanimity for taking decisions. As a consequence, in the late 1980s, the Commission was able to rapidly achieve the liberalization of the circulation of capital; the unification of the road-haulage and transportation markets, as well as of insurance and public contracts and the mutual recognition of high-school diplomas and secondary-school certificates among the European countries.

At the end of the 1980s, Delors also achieved the restructuring of the European budget by bringing about an increase in the share of European state taxes devoted to the European Union. Moreover, the Commission obtained the reduction of the agriculture subsidies, which till then had accounted for most of the common European expenditure. This enabled a substantial increase in structural and cohesion funds, which were particularly important for those peripheral countries which entered the EEC in the 1980s, after more or less long-lasting dictatorships: Greece, Portugal and Spain. For those countries, the structural funds represented a sort of Marshall Plan, which could help to accelerate processes of modernization.

The end of the Cold War and the European market

If Western Europe was rapidly moving towards a unified market, in which backward countries were also catching up with the richer ones – as was the case of Ireland, Spain and Portugal, the per capita gross domestic product (GDP) of which grew by more than 25 per cent in the 1980s – the situation was entirely different in the Eastern bloc. The gap between Eastern and Western Europe increased in the 1980s in contrast to the trend during the 1970s when the Eastern European economies had not been affected to a significant extent by the wider economic crisis. The richest country in the Eastern bloc, Czechoslovakia, had 59 per cent of Britain's per capita GDP in 1973, 62 per cent in 1980 and 53 per cent in 1989. In other countries, the situation was even worse: In the 1980s, Hungary moved from 49 per cent to 42 per cent of Britain, Poland from 44 per cent to 35 per cent and Romania from 32 per cent to 24 per cent. These figures revealed a complete breakdown of the Eastern European economies in the 1980s, after the previous decade when the ghost of the final crisis of capitalism had fleetingly awakened the political fantasy of the Soviet ruling class.[3] The stagnation in the 1980s, in face of the relaunching of the Western capitalist market economy and the consequent renewed expansion of an individualist consumer society, accelerated the delegitimization of the socialist countries. The policy of Perestroika adopted in the USSR, which returned to the market as a basic principle of the economy – although in a system of competition between state-owned companies – was an official recognition of the historical success of the market economy over the socialist state-driven organization of economy and society. Moreover, this reform process aimed at opening closer commercial relationships with Western Europe and the United States. Thus, one can say that in 1987 the long competition between the two patterns – socialist and capitalist – had already come to an end.

The end of the Cold War did not really change the roadmap as drafted by Delors and his Commission for bringing about the unification of the European Market. In 1992, the Maastricht Treaty fixed the conditions for the economic convergence between the partner states which would be necessary in order to create a single European currency. Meanwhile, a program of industrial and research policy was developed, as well as the creation of new European infrastructures and the promotion of technological innovations. This was certainly not intended to be a form of Keynesian public spending, but instead it aimed at making the European market more efficient in an attempt to respond to the fierce challenge presented by American and Japanese competition. The collapse of socialism in 1989 – after the understandable enthusiasm of the first months – left a difficult situation for Eastern European countries except for the former German Democratic Republic (GDR), which could count on the support of West Germany that promoted the rapid reunification of the two countries. Commercial treaties were established with Czechoslovakia, Poland and Hungary which were considered as the most reliable future partners of the European union (EU), but the recovery of the Eastern European economy was largely left to private Western European investors.

Eastern European countries were encouraged to transform themselves according to neo-liberal principles. This was deemed to be a necessary requirement in order to create a future possibility for them to join the European Union. The social differences between East and West were enormous, and were doomed to intensify following the implementation of neo-liberal economies. The ten countries which strove for entry into the EU accounted for about 20 per cent of the European population but only 5 per cent of the GDP. Moreover, they had a significant share of their working population employed in low-productivity agriculture (between one-quarter to one-fifth depending on the countries concerned). Neo-liberalism, which encountered some difficulties in establishing itself in Western Europe – because of the resistance of a corporatist organization of society – could be easily and radically implemented in Eastern Europe, since the previous political and social institutions were rapidly dismantled. This resulted in the clash of traditional economic sectors, unemployment and inflation, causing a deep economic crisis. Some countries were able to recover in the second half of the 1990s as they reached the same GDP as they had possessed in 1989 (Albania, Czech Republic, Hungary, Poland, Slovakia and Slovenia), while for other countries the crisis still persisted at the beginning of the twenty-first century.

Western European private investments were decisive for the economic revitalization of Eastern Europe. In particular, they focussed on the service economy, notably banks, telecommunications and retailing. But the industrial sector was also able to develop thanks to a process of restructuring by Western European companies which sought to profit from the lower labour costs of Eastern Europe by delocalizing labour-intensive forms of production. This was very important for the European middle-rank technology industries in which their global competitors such as India or China could profit from a huge cheap labour reserve. But these industrial investments were not directed to the countries where labour was cheapest, but rather towards those which could offer a well-qualified labour force cheaper than that of Western Europe. Moreover, the increase in employment and salaries helped to open new markets for European multinational companies in Eastern Europe and to develop new economies of scale.

Thus, the end of the Cold War happened during the intensification of the neo-liberal challenge in the global economy, and this increased the distance between Western and Eastern Europe. Western European countries slowly began a transformation, which allowed them gradually to face the global change of capitalism, by means of a stronger integration of the European market, which aimed to achieve greater autonomy as a global actor. Eastern Europe in contrast had to experience a more dramatic change which required not only the dismantling of the socialist state and its bureaucratic structures, but also the universal social guarantees it was able to offer. The interrelationship between Western and Eastern economies increased, particularly from the late 1990s onwards as a consequence of private investments from West to East which put Eastern European countries in a situation of dependence vis à vis the West. But there was also state support for Eastern countries through the EU which favoured the redevelopment of the social capital in Eastern European societies, and which paved the way to the formal entry of the first Eastern members into the EU in 2005. In this way, the post-1989 period was the longest postwar period in the twentieth century.

Competing cultures of consumption

One of the main factors which determined the crisis of the Eastern bloc was the irresistible attraction exerted by the Western consumer society on the people who lived in socialist countries. This means that the consumer issue in the years following 1989 related directly to the two previous postwar periods, since the socialist consumer culture originated in the aftermath of the first postwar period and the Western European one after the second postwar period. In this section, I will therefore present a genealogical sketch of the socialist consumer culture – rooted in the first postwar period – and in the following I will place the birth of the Western European consumer society in the context of the second postwar period.

After the Second World War, countries in the Eastern bloc tried to build their own image as egalitarian 'labour societies' as an alternative to individualistic capitalist societies grounded on social inequalities. This image implied a completely different understanding of consumption than was the case in the Western economies. Consumptions were not deemed to be the realm of individual choice through which desires could be fulfilled and identities could be built, but it was considered the answer to social and physiological needs by means of a centralized system of distribution of goods.

This idea had its origins in the Marxian theory of consumption,[4] but its more specific historical roots lay in the First World War and in the experience of War Communism. The Bolshevik leaders did not examine in depth the issue of consumption; they thought that the most important thing was production. The distribution of goods therefore had to reverse capitalist social hierarchies in order to ensure adequate provisions for the working class, which had to receive more than their so-called class enemies. What to produce and, consequently, what to consume was decided by the state according to a vague notion of 'needs' which was thought to be inscribed in the physiological constitution of human beings.[5] Even Trotsky, who among the Bolshevik leaders was the figure most attentive and interested in the anthropological aspect of the revolution, did not develop a systematic cultural analysis of consumption in the socialist society.[6] By the middle of the 1920s, the economic situation seemed to allow some hopes for improvement in the material daily life, but with the definitive ascendancy of Stalin, the end of the New Economic Policy (NEP) and the beginning of forced industrialization – which imposed a strict containment even of basic forms of consumption – shortages became a constant feature of the socialist society.

There was no market mediation between demand and supply, and this made it difficult to meet the needs of the population: A dramatic confirmation of this failure was the great famine of 1932–33. If the war against the kulaks caused many deaths and forced migrations, the attacks against artisans and shopkeepers – considered to be obsolete social classes – made the production and distribution even of small everyday objects difficult and thus scarcity became a central experience of social life under communism.[7] This sort of permanent war economy was coherent with the Stalinist vision of world history anchored in the Leninist theory of imperialism. Sooner or later – it was believed – the final war against imperialist capitalism had to be fought, and this required that the Soviet economy had to be ready to provide adequate armaments and basic sustenance for the masses. Everything else was a luxury. After the Second World War, the implementation of the Soviet system forcibly expanded to include the Eastern European countries, and this resulted in a worsening of their level of consumption between the end of the 1940s and the beginning of the 1950s. This cut short the weak recovery they had experienced during the first postwar years.

After 1953, the harsh pressure on private consumption was relaxed and the legitimization of the socialist countries began to rest not solely on ideological mobilization but also on the material well-being of population. Thus, it was only in the post-Stalin era that a real competition regarding consumption began with Western capitalism. The so-called kitchen debate between Khrushchev and Nixon, which occurred in 1959 at the American National Exhibition held in Moscow, was emblematic of this new phase.[8] This was an occasion for Americans to show the richness of their consumer society epitomized by the modern kitchen well equipped with every sort of technology ready to prepare plenty of food. The irony of Khrushchev who asked if there was even a machine that 'puts food into the mouth and pushes it down' could hardly hide the enormous distance between the two economies in terms of living standards and private consumption. Nevertheless, Khrushchev was confident that the Soviet system could develop the potential to win this competition, and he had just launched a massive building programme which was intended to satisfy the basic social need for housing as well as demonstrating the superiority of the Soviet model in responding to the needs of the masses.

Khrushchev claimed that the Soviet system would provide things of substance and not of luxury, and his housing programme was based on a pattern which recalled the debates of the 1920s on the building of a modern social space and a rational private sphere. In fact, rather than Soviet constructivism, the cultural background of this new housing programme was more reminiscent of the Weimar Modern movement and its ambition to pursue the rationalization of production and society, such as the case of the famous 'Frankfurt kitchen' designed by Ernst May and Margarete Schütte-Lihotzky, from which it also took its pedagogic purposes: that is, to teach how to live in a modern and correct way. There was no research and experimentation on new lifestyles based on houses within which facilities could be shared and aimed at modifying gender roles and family structure – as theorized in the first years of the Soviet revolution by Alexandra Kollontai – or to pursue a collective utopia – as in the constructivist research epitomized by the Narkofim building. Instead, the new housing projects of the 1960s and 1970s in effect recognized family and private housing as the fundamental social and spatial cell of Soviet society.

In the following years, the socialist regimes did not develop an alternative or a distinctive private consumer culture; rather they followed a similar pattern as in the West albeit at a slower pace and with poorer results.[9] Thus, the phase of Détente with the West was not limited only to the geopolitical level, but also involved an approach to lifestyle and material culture which regarded Western goods no longer just as the mystification of a commodified society, but were evaluated for the use value that they embodied. In this way, the judgements they made on Western consumer culture continued to be defined by the principles of the socialist society. Thus, Western durable goods were appreciated, while other products of the Western consumer society were rejected and condemned, such as rock music – at least in the first phase of its success – which not by chance became a milieu of cultural resistance against the regime within the socialist countries.[10]

The outcome of this long competition regarding material culture between West and East had anyway become blatantly clear in the 1980s. The socialist system was able to guarantee full employment, but had failed in the field of consumption because it could not satisfy the desire of the population for better standards of living. The idea of so-called natural needs, or of needs ascertained through a superior social rationality grounded on a scientific basis, was inadequate. This idea could provide basic food and decent housing, but it was unable to respond effectively to pressures towards consumption as an expression of subjective desires.

Due to pervasive low labour productivity and the absence of the regulatory action of market and prices, the socialist countries were not able to provide the same volume and diversity of Western capitalist consumer goods. Washing machines, refrigerators and similar appliances entered the houses of eastern Europeans in the same period as in the West, or a bit later, but at a much slower pace and with a more modest technological standard. Sometimes these differences were the result of a deliberate choice as in the case of the public transport system which was deemed to have priority over private car ownership, which was usual in the West. But with the new wave of consumer goods in the 1980s, differences with the West were doomed to widen.

These differences solidified the image of the Eastern labour society as a 'shortage economy' which implied social practices in which a specific anthropological attitude towards consumer goods was rooted.[11] To some extent, this attitude would survive the collapse of the socialist states. While the Western capitalist economies increasingly relied on a rapid turnover in sales and on a consumerist attitude, which shortened the social life of products through fashion and innovation, in the labour society, goods were repaired, resold and recycled in order to prolong their social life. But in the short term, in the immediate aftermath of the fall of Berlin's Wall, the exciting and colourful Western consumer society exerted an irresistible appeal. The multitude of East Berliners swarming towards the *KaDeWe* department store in West Berlin after the fall of the Berlin Wall was the most immediate and visible image of the power of seduction exerted by the Western consumer society. Those goods which had been always dreamed of were finally accessible.

However, after the first euphoria, a more reflexive and critical attitude emerged. Even a scholar who convincingly maintains that 'what took place in Central Eastern Europe … [after the fall of the Berlin Wall] is an unparalleled success story'[12] must recognize that a deep disappointment swiftly followed. There were several reasons for that: First of all – as we have seen – the turmoil generated by the economic transition caused a long phase of stagnation and depression; secondly, the recovery after the stagnation phase involved a severe social polarization which was a new phenomenon for the former socialist countries. There was an emerging very rich ruling class as well as a young middle class who could now access new forms of consumption while wide strata of the population had to struggle in order to make ends meet. Moreover, the former socialist societies discovered unemployment which had been a totally unknown phenomenon in their own past, and finally, as explored by recent research, there was also a sort of cultural reaction against the material culture of the West. After the first 'colorful' impact of the consumer society, 'there is a strong indication of resistance and resentment to today's consumption standards'.[13] A throwaway mentality and hyperconsumption were at odds with a socially rooted commitment to the value of frugality and a longing for durable, high-quality products. This did not imply a rejection of capitalism and a nostalgia for socialism, but rather a rejection of the Western material culture which produces social polarization and fragmentation, a waste of resources and ephemeral satisfaction.

It is difficult to evaluate how widespread these feelings were. Nevertheless, linear convergence towards a Western liberal capitalist way of life seems to have been more difficult than expected, and the widespread nostalgia demonstrated for the old material culture seems to be the symptom of an estrangement from the Western consumer culture.[14]

The Marshall Plan and the reinvention of the West

When did a Western consumer pattern take shape, and what is actually a Western consumer pattern? The European consumer pattern after the Second World War was heavily influenced by the American one, as has been convincingly argued by Victoria De Grazia. However, one can be sceptical as to whether this was the result of the irresistible force of attraction exerted by that model. The American business and consumer pattern – as De Grazia shows in her book – had already tried unsuccessfully to conquer Europe in the interwar period, but it succeeded only after the Second World War as the United States acquired a dominant military and political position in the Atlantic world. This does not mean that the success of the mass consumer society in Europe after the Second World War was the result of American imperialism, but rather that it happened in the specific historical context created by the outcome of the Second World War. The defeat of fascism, the military occupation of a large part of Europe, the democratization processes which took place in Italy and West Germany and which contributed to the erosion of long-lasting social hierarchies, were all decisive elements in creating the conditions for the definitive establishment of a new mass consumer society.

Although the role of the United States in all these processes was crucial, the idea of an Americanization process, intended as the transfer of a consumer culture from one shore of the Atlantic to the other, would be misleading. Indeed, the ways through which new marketing techniques and consumer cultures changed European society were very differentiated, and the inputs which came from beyond the Atlantic were adapted in a peculiar way in every country. More than an Americanization process, it would be more correct to speak of a reinvention of the West born out of the encounter between the postwar hegemonic American strategy and the various national political contexts characterized by the heterogeneous democratic antifascist movements and political coalitions which ruled Western Europe after 1945.

During the war, an enormous growth in the productive capacity of European industry had occurred. Wartime destruction did not seriously undermine this potential, because bombings mostly hit housing, infrastructure, transportation and communication lines rather than industrial plants. Thus, the main obstacle to the recovery lay more in market efficiency rather than productive capacity.[15] What was most urgently needed was a project of redesigning the international market. Towards the end of the war, the United States put pressure on the UK government in order to open the British Commonwealth market in order to ease the building of a multilateral international trade system. At the same time, the Americans aimed at containing the German economy in order to scale down its role in Europe, and thereby opening up a space in central Europe in which they could expand. This had major consequences because in 1946 the German economy almost came to a halt, and this prevented them from beginning to make the reparation payments due to the Allies. Moreover, the consumption levels remained so low that the demoralizing effects of the war economy at the daily life level persisted well beyond 1945. Thus, the role of the state in providing basic levels of consumption remained crucial, and this solidified the state–citizen relationship. This relationship increasingly developed in universal forms because unlike in the First World War – during which there had remained a clear distinction between the military and the home fronts – in the Second World War the entire population was directly involved. Air bombing directly hit civilians who needed the help of the state, as did the mass of refugees, who were displaced by the war.

Thus, in this democratic context, as was the case in the United Kingdom, the war strengthened the universal character of the welfare state, whereas in fascist Europe, the distribution of resources was determined by the racial segmentation of the population. This conflict between two patterns of consumption – a system of racialized management on the one hand and a universal model on the other – was one of the conflicts resolved by the outcome of the war, with the consequence that in its aftermath the universal pattern of citizenship was implemented throughout Europe. In Britain, state control and intervention in food provision, healthcare and public housing by means of different tools such as price controls, subsidies and rationing became very popular, because it testified to the common national sacrifice required by the war effort. Moreover, these measures were not simply technical responses to the needs of wartime but they assumed the coherent character of a social project which aimed at distributing more equally the resources of the nation.[16] The Beveridge Report of 1942 provided a general framework, giving these individual measures a universal meaning. Indeed, fiscal reform promoted during the war, in conjunction with price controls, allowed a redistribution of income of which the principal beneficiaries were the labouring classes. This project of redistribution went on well beyond the end of the war, inspiring the Labour government in the second half of the 1940s.

Thus, a specific legacy of the war was the idea that state intervention was necessary in order to implement some principles of redistribution (of income, though not of wealth). But in order to overcome these wartime scarcities, it was necessary to go beyond the narrow limits of the autarchic order of the war economy. The market fragmentation created by the war was moreover a fundamental obstacle to the effort of rebuilding a multilateral system of trade. Europe in 1946 and 1947 experienced an acute food crisis because of the severe destruction of European agriculture during the last war years, including the depletion of the number of cattle, the absence of fertilizer and other effects. This resulted in a booming international demand for food and other staple goods, which were mostly provided by the United States and by the colonies of the major empires so that France and the United Kingdom became debtors to their own colonies. However, in order to make this system run, a recovery of the European economy was necessary along with an integrated system of trade able to strengthen the overall productive capacity. The European internal market was further depressed by the exit from international circuits of exchange of the eastern European states, which fell into the new Soviet sphere of influence. The damage caused by this withdrawal was twofold: On the one side, Western European markets which relied on the staples produced in Eastern Europe no longer had access to those producers; on the other side, the USSR did not absorb the export potential of Eastern European states to an extent comparable to that of Western states, and this provoked further stagnation in the Eastern European economy. In Western Europe, the war had created strict commercial ties under German occupation, but at the end of the war the whole area needed imports in order to survive and was unable to balance external trade since the American market – from north to south – had become increasingly self-sufficient during the war.

The Bretton Woods system and the creation of international financial institutions helped to stabilize the financial situation but this was not sufficient in order to stimulate multilateral trade. The situation radically changed with the Marshall Plan, the origins of which lay more in a political strategy than in an economic strategy. Thus, one can conclude that the feature characterizing the second postwar period, compared with the first postwar period, was that its end coincided with the initial arrangements for a new war economy: that of the Cold War. At the end of the war, the European governments were mostly expressions of the political coalitions permeated by the political culture of the anti-fascist popular fronts of the 1930s. They thought that the failure of liberal capitalism in the 1930s – with its devastating social and political consequences – had to be overcome through economic regulation and social planning. The idea of public control of the economy in order to defend less-privileged social strata from the dangers of the free market was widely accepted. National policies were different according to multiple combinations of technical choices and political background. In Britain, the government pursued a huge programme of nationalization of the major industries and pursued full employment as its fundamental goal. In Italy, the institutional architecture of Italian capitalism designed by fascism in the 1930s – in which the state had a fundamental role – was maintained as the basis of the policies of economic reconstruction. In Germany, negotiation between the trade unions and management occurred at the level of the major industrial sectors according to a specific institutional system. In France, the Monnet Plan resulted from wide cooperation and consultations among trade unions, private companies and public administrations; a similar pattern was also adopted in Czechoslovakia. Most of the states had substantial control of the principal national industries: a fifth in France, around half in Italy and even three-quarters in Czechoslovakia prior to the Soviet putsch.

These planning policies privileged the reconstruction of basic industries and infrastructures at the expense of private consumption and they concerned both Western and Eastern Europe where they had even harsher effects on consumption levels. These policies created dangerous social tensions in the short term because the material conditions of the European masses reached a critical point in 1947. The most basic forms of consumption – food, housing and fuel were scarce – and states were considered responsible for this extreme poverty: The war had finished two years earlier, but the war economy did not seem to have any end.

The American administration was well aware of the economic and political implications of this critical situation with regard to consumption. The misery of the postwar period seemed likely to last indefinitely, bringing with it dangerous social consequences. In response, the Marshall Plan became the fundamental instrument through which the American administration was able to face both the immediate crisis and the pursuit of a stable international economic order grounded on an effective hegemonic political influence. This occurred through the reinvention of the West, which gradually ceased to be associated with colonial empires and became a synonym for the democratic, capitalist and most prosperous area of the world.

The Marshall Plan was both an instrument and a symbol of this successful strategy. The plan was initially presented as a generous American offer open to all countries, included the Eastern European countries. This was a deliberate attempt to break the Eastern bloc by involving Czechoslovakia – and perhaps Poland and Hungary – within the American-led project of European stabilization. Indeed, Czechoslovakia expressed the will to participate, but it was forced by Stalin to renounce doing so. As a result, the Marshall Plan accelerated the division of Europe – and particularly of Germany – into two separated and opposing spheres of influence. In this respect, it represented a first successful step into the Cold War.

If the Marshall Plan was certainly a tactical move within the context of the initial phase of the Cold War, it was also designed to bring about the relaunching of American economy within an international order aimed at preventing the ruinous mismanagement of previous decades. Thus, the defensive side of the plan – namely the containment of Soviet expansion into the empty space created by the defeat and destruction of Germany and Italy – was coupled with a strategic view, which pursued a political hegemony by means of economic stability and increases in consumption. This certainly meant the exportation of a model of economic governance but also of a social and cultural pattern.

The attempt to establish a stable economic and political international order had already begun – from the American side – after the First World War. The transition from the nineteenth-century free-market regime to one of corporate capitalism had required a reorganization of the internal market in the United States which was pursued by Republicans in the 1920s, notably during the Hoover presidency. They had tried to regulate capitalism without an intrusive bureaucratic state intervention, relying instead on private elites and the associations of civil society, which were deemed to have the necessary competence to resolve industrial and practical problems. In this way, associationism seemed to represent the real alternative to socialism.

At the international level, there were also attempts to bring about a new order in a similar way. To achieve this, it would be necessary to overcome nationalism, which entailed the closure and fragmentation of markets, and to build a regulated and open international market. According to Hogan, the Marshall Plan owed much to this approach that had been already developed during the first postwar period; the Dawes plan was an example of this mentality as was the Anglo-American cooperation for the regulation of some global markets, particularly with regard to energy and communication.[17] According to this interpretation, the New Deal represented a development of earlier experiences and a field in which progressive capitalism and liberal politicians could collaborate in order to promote social policies, new patterns of industrial relations and multilateral trade. As Hogan put it, in advocating the continuity of the American approach to the international order between the first and the second postwar periods:

> During both postwar periods, then, American recovery planners forged an uneasy partnership with the British, gave Germany's revival parity with France's security, and sought to promote both European integration and German reintegration. In addition, they urged the Europeans to stabilize currencies, fix realistic exchange

rates, reduce reparations, and eliminate other barriers to the flow of goods and capital. They said that measures of this sort would permit individual initiative and market incentives to have full play in Europe. But they also tempered their faith in free-market forces by stressing the need for American assistance, for new frameworks of public private cooperation, and for new institutions of economic coordination and control.[18]

By stressing the continuity in American policy, this interpretation underestimates the role that the New Deal played in legitimizing state interventionism in the economy as well as the emergence of a Keynesian macroeconomic philosophy, particularly with regard to financial credit. Nevertheless, since it establishes a strict relationship between the first and the second postwar periods, this interpretation stimulates a reflection on the different conditions which characterized the two historical contexts, and which I shall discuss later in this chapter.

How did the Marshall Plan work and what was its impact? Its aim was to revitalize the most advanced European industrial centres in order to make them the engine of the overall economic recovery. This had to happen in a business environment open to the international market and with the pursuit of a rapid increase in mass consumption. There was an American apparatus appointed to oversee the distribution of the funds and to provide assistance in their utilization. However, each country was largely able to decide how to employ the American aid according to its strategic priorities. Thus, it was difficult to represent the plan as an instrument of American imperialism – as communist propaganda tried to do – because the European Recovery Program (ERP), as it was termed, appeared to be the instrument of a friendly cooperation which left European countries free to decide how to use the funds. In this way, the United States ensured the achievement of the two fundamental aims of their political strategy: to push European countries which benefited from the aid to plan a medium-term economic strategy and to do this within the framework of an open Atlantic market economy, that is, within the new West composed of the United States and Western Europe.

Although the implementation of the plan was flexible and able to recognize the specific needs of different countries, the idea of Europe as a united field of intervention was at the core of the philosophy of the plan. Indeed, the necessity to overcome the market fragmentation created by the crisis of the 1930s and exacerbated by the war was one of the main aims of the programme. A fundamental tool of this strategy was the creation of the European Payments Union (EPU), which allowed a multilateral payment system to emerge, and prevented bilateral commercial restrictions between European countries. The EPU served to guarantee the balance payments at a European level, allowing for the compensation of bilateral unbalances. In implementing the plan, bankers and private industrialists cooperated with the public bureaucracy. This was deemed necessary in order to pursue the currency stability and a regulated enlargement of the market, and it represented a model of planning significantly different from those developed in the 1930s. A huge propaganda apparatus also took care of the ideological effects of the plan and created the basis for public approval of American intervention as a way out of the misery of the wartime period and towards a future of prosperity.

The debate on the economic effects of the plan still remains open. It was taken for granted for decades that the plan had a crucial effect in starting up the European boom of the 1950s – a postulate that was partly a consequence of the effective propaganda strategy associated with the plan; but the revisionist interpretation of Alan Milward raised many doubts as to the real economic impact of the ERP.[19] More than a quarter of the value transferred by the plan was constituted by food, which was important for the hungry population, but did not represent the real bottleneck for the economic recovery; it was rather a crucial issue for social and political reasons. The plan also provided fuel and cotton, but these were also not decisive for bringing about economic recovery. Instead, according to Milward, the main contribution of the plan and of the EPU – created thanks to its funding – was the creation of a stable international order.

Charles Maier attributed a fundamental role to the Marshall Plan in institutional terms because it fostered a politics of productivity, pushing labour and capital to find a corporatist agreement, in a way which had failed after the First World War.[20] His view has been supported by Ellwood, who stresses the ideological effect of the plan in changing the political culture of the European labour movement.[21] The shift of the strategy of the labour movement from the pursuit of redistribution to the politics of productivity eased the inflationary effects of salary growth, thereby contributing to twenty-five years of flourishing material stability in Europe.[22]

The plan also had a positive psychological effect because it reassured Europeans that they could count on the American support and because it pushed them to overcome national market boundaries creating the basis of the Western European economic integration.[23] Furthermore, the Marshall Plan helped to overcome the mistrust of the market as the engine of economic growth which had been discredited during the crisis of the 1930s.[24] In this way, the Marshall Plan pushed Europeans to dismantle gradually the structures of state control of the economy which stemmed from the economic policies of the 1930s and had been reinforced during the war years, while a complete opening of the European market occurred from the 1960s onwards and was the effect of economic growth rather than a political choice. Only the economic miracle gave the necessary confidence for opening up of the market, which was then perceived as an opportunity rather than a threat.

Whatever the reality of the effects of the plan, the fact remains that the Marshall Plan marked the end of the postwar period and introduced a new phase in which Europe experienced a long-lasting stability and increase in consumption. From 1947 onwards, two main patterns of consumption regulation began a long competition. On one side, there was the Soviet system which was extended to other Eastern European countries. This developed a legacy of the first postwar period in which the idea of the state as the supplier of basic material needs of the population has been definitively affirmed. On the other side, in Western Europe, there developed an economic, social and cultural system which had the market at its centre, although it maintained some differences from the American pattern since in Western Europe the state – and this was connected with a long-lasting war experience – maintained a greater influence on the sphere of consumption. Nevertheless, what is clear is that the material success of the postwar Western democracies was fundamental in the legitimization of the political system[25] as well as in the building of individual and collective identities.

This does not mean that Western Europe was simply 'Americanized', since European countries developed peculiar cultures of consumption. However, the success of a social system based on increasing mass consumption mediated by the institutional and semiotic system of a market economy brought to Europe some aspects of the commercialization process which had already affected American society in the first decades of the twentieth century. This was certainly the result of the increased American political influence on Western Europe, but the success of this process also depended on the popularity of the image of an American lifestyle built by the cultural industry in the 1920s and 1930s, in particular through cinema, music and dancing. The direct contact that took place with American occupation troops since 1944 had reinforced this image of America as a land of plenty.

Mass consumption and political legitimization: the legacy of the First World War

The continuity of American strategy towards Europe between the first and the second postwar periods cannot serve to disguise a fundamental historiographical question: namely, why the first postwar was a story of failure and the second a story of success. The difference in the end results is undeniable, and demands an explanation. To look just at the different patterns of economic governance and regulation can be misleading because it undervalues the overall conditions in which the two patterns operated. After the Second World War, the United States was obliged to play a hegemonic global role, and the escalation of the Cold War required prompt action in order to establish this hegemony on a solid basis. Thus, it was necessary to build a political and economic order able to win the competition with the Soviet pattern of society, and this stopped any isolationist inclinations on the American side, because the stabilization of Western Europe was clearly essential to such a goal.

Charles Maier has proposed to look at the two post–World War periods, both as two steps in a single path as well as two parallel processes.[26] Indeed, they can be seen as two steps in a single effort to find a new economic and social organization within a well-established international order after the turmoil of the First World War. But they can be also considered comparatively in order to highlight similarities and differences. In fact, some conditions did not change very much: There were similar political divisions and social conflicts as well as some basic common assumptions, which inspired government action. In both historical contexts, the first steps implemented by economic policies were aimed at quickly stabilizing the currency. Nevertheless, in the second postwar period, this aim was pursued in a more flexible way in order to avoid a stalling of economic growth combined with a Keynesian economic mentality – which was now shared by the majority of the Western ruling class – with the building of a multilateral trade system. The second main difference concerned the role played by the US state. US financial support was essential to Europe both after the First and the Second World Wars, but while after 1918 the promoters of financial flows were the private banks – with the consequence that these flows were vulnerable to capital market fluctuations – in the 1940s, they were the results of a political strategy pursued directly by the state, which guaranteed their continuity. There were significant differences on the side of labour too. After the First World War, a large part of the European working class radically challenged the capitalist system, under the influence of the Soviet example or inspired by social democratic ideas. This meant that the issue of power, that is, of who commanded within society, was at stake. After the Second World War, in contrast, the large majority of the labour movement accepted the need to pursue a politics of productivity, namely to negotiate salaries and working conditions within the framework of the capitalist system and of its power structure. This slowed down salary increases and contributed to the acceleration of capital formation which nurtured further investments.

Public spending served as a very good indicator of this altered relationship. On the eve of the First World War, public spending in the United Kingdom and Germany was around 15 per cent of GDP. This figure rapidly increased as a consequence of wartime expenditures and went well beyond 50 per cent, but after the end of the war it did not return to the pre-war level and in the interwar period it amounted to around 25 per cent in the United Kingdom, between 25 per cent and 30 per cent in Germany and 30 per cent in Italy. This had the effect that public spending almost doubled in order to support the new functions taken on by the state, in pensions, healthcare, food provision and education.[27]

The war produced deep changes in agriculture too since the most advanced industrial countries – such as Germany and the United Kingdom – depended on importation from abroad for their food supplies. During the twenty years preceding the outbreak of the First World War, the global integration of the food market of mass-consumed staples such as cereals, meat and sugar quickly developed and hence on the eve of the First World War food accounted for 27 per cent of world exports. This occurred because advanced countries developed their investments in high added-value industrial sectors while profiting from the fall of global prices of agricultural goods which covered their food consumption needs. On the eve of the war, about 19 per cent of calories consumed in Germany came from abroad, 27 per cent of protein and 42 per cent of fat.[28]

Because of the economic blockade imposed during the war, it was necessary to reorientate agriculture in order to maximize the outcome of internal production. At the same time, the state had to intervene in food consumption, rationing distribution in order to prevent the starvation of the population. Accordingly, the state segmented the population into three main categories: soldiers at the front, rural populations and the urban population. The first two categories were mostly better fed than the urban population, because the state concentrated its effort upon feeding the soldiers at the front, whereas in rural areas, people could rely upon their own sources of food. Price control was a necessary tool in order to prevent inflation which could have reduced the poor to starvation. However, fixing prices too low – as happened in Germany – could also discourage peasants from delivering their production for public distribution. Furthermore, there were not many industrially produced goods available, and consequently peasants often decided to feed their families rather than selling products to the state. Thus, agricultural production was significantly depressed and the policies of war mobilization had further damaging consequences: Almost two-thirds of the male labour force was drawn away from the countryside, horses were confiscated and it was difficult to find fertilizers since the substances for producing them were needed by the military sectors of industry. As a consequence, the countryside regressed towards a sort of fragmented autarchic subsistence economy, which continued after the end of the war since the blockade was maintained in order to force Germany to accept the conditions of the Versailles Treaty. In this way, consumption pressure was a fundamental tool for determining the outcome of the war as well as the terms of the peace.

One long-lasting effect of the war was the disruption of the European market following the dismantling of old empires and the birth of a number of new national states, each with different currencies and customs duties. At the end of the war, Europe consisted of thirty-eight states, twelve more than the case in 1914. This fragmentation depressed internal European trade because new states erected burdens in order to defend their own weak industries. This was particularly clear in the former area of the Habsburg Empire, which since the 1890s had represented a region of efficient unified customs and a common currency area. Moreover, the trade between Europe and Russia was interrupted by the revolution, the civil war and the birth of Soviet Union, and this further contributed to the depression of the internal European trade. Only the unification of Poland represented a partial counter-effect within this general trend. This protectionist environment also damaged the most advanced industrial economies of Eastern Europe such as Czechoslovakia and – to a lesser extent – Poland which lost their former export markets within the Habsburg Empire. Fragmentation also hit the financial market since the banking system contracted, as banks were unable to count on larger territories within which to collect private savings.

A fragmented market and a narrow financial system were confronted with the most problematic consequences of the war: inflation and unemployment. These two phenomena were interrelated because inflation was the consequence of the way in which the war had been funded – that is, more through printing paper money and increasing indebtedness rather than by resorting to taxation (which in turn determined another long-lasting effect of the war, namely the intergenerational burden of the war debt) – and unemployment was the result of the difficult transition from a wartime to a peace economy. Inflation had almost eliminated the savings of the middle classes who could have boosted consumption after a long period of scarcity. Thus, with the middle classes damaged by inflation and the working class hit by unemployment and poverty, consumption management continued to be a central task of state policies in the postwar period.

This also brought about institutional consequences. Post–First World War Europe was characterized by the increasing influence of mass organizations such as trade unions, consumer associations and political parties, as well as cartels and industrial syndicates. States maintained their control of foreign trade, prices and salaries, and had to negotiate their policies with the principal social organizations. To put it another way, the management of society and economy relied more upon negotiation between large social aggregates than upon market mechanisms, and this was the result of the fundamental change in power relationships between classes which had occurred during the war which brought about also the extension of the suffrage in most

European countries. Under these circumstances, a new pattern of relationship between consumption and citizenship arose from the war. Food and fuel were considered to be basic items of consumption, which states had to guarantee, and this determined a radical politicization of the daily life. The language of the premodern moral economy resurfaced in entirely new political circumstances,[29] and the state presented itself as a defender of consumers against war speculators, profiteers and middlemen who were considered to be responsible for food scarcity. Sometimes this propaganda was inflected with anti-Semitic features, and it reinforced the unity of the national community necessary in order to sustain the war effort.

The different forms of market regulation – or even market substitution – were usually dismantled in the postwar years. However, in the wake of the war experience, the idea of the state as the guarantor of basic consumption became a fundamental element in the legitimization of the political system. In Germany, for instance, food riots had a fundamental impact on the establishment of a new relationship between state and society, which continued after the war. The war economy went on – de facto – until the summer of 1919 and the administrative apparatus which managed food and coal distribution did not change greatly, although after the November Revolution there was a greater influence of consumer associations and councils.[30] The Weimar Republic constitutionalized the material basis of this political community: Food and citizenship became strictly related and the state was in charge of guaranteeing the material daily life of its citizens. If in the German case the postwar management of basic consumption resulted in the constitutionalization of social rights, in other cases, the politicization of consumption took different forms. Despite these national variations, they all shared two elements: the new role of the state as a guarantor of basic consumption for the masses and the greater influence of consumer associations at the political level. Consumer associations could sometimes use a language, which recalled the old rhetoric of the moral economy, but now they operated continuously – and not simply periodically – as a political actor within the new framework of the interventionist state that had been born out of the war.

Even in Britain, where the free market had traditionally been a cornerstone of popular progressive consumer policy,[31] a new paradigm emerged following the First World War, which had at the centre consumers' organizations and later on evolved into a social-democratic pattern of consumption regulation. By the end of the war, for example, milk in Britain was recognized as a basic essential consumer product, for which the people had a right and that the state had to guarantee its provision, in terms of quality and adequate quantities.[32] Although after 1920 market regulation was gradually dismantled, the role of consumer cooperatives remained very important for basic popular food consumption and this entailed a new arrangement of the market economy.

Thus, in the first postwar period, the politicization of consumption took different forms which varied from the complete nationalization carried out by War Communism to a social democratic perspective which aspired to a gradual socialization of the economy, as well as to solutions compatible with capitalism, but which sought a so-called civilization of capitalism which would temper its harsher effects on living conditions. The common grounds on which these very different positions rested was that the sphere of basic consumption had to be taken away from free-market mechanisms because consumption constituted the material basis on which social and political communities could be constructed. However, this principle could be implemented using a diverse range of tools and took different institutional forms: a public role for consumer associations, public control over prices, retail regulation, municipal socialism, consumer cooperatives and so on.

Conclusion

In the field of consumer policies, there was no strict linkage between the post-1989 and post-1945 periods, but there certainly was between the post-1945 and the post-1918 periods. On the Soviet side, the linkage took the form of continuity since the post-1945 recovery was based on the socialist management of consumption borne out by the Soviet revolution that occurred in the first postwar period. On the Western side in contrast, the catastrophic results of the first postwar settlements acted as a stimulus to explore new directions after the Second World War in order to establish a stable international order within which the restructuring of international capitalism could develop on both shores of the Atlantic. It is hard to see how this could have been achieved in any way other than through war. The policies implemented after the Second World War could only be brought to fruition because fascism had been fought and defeated on the battlefield. If we look at the Spanish case – a country which managed to stay outside the war and where fascism lasted until the 1970s – we can see that nothing similar to the rest of Western Europe happened in the period of post-1945 reconstruction. Spanish economy experienced a severe depression in the 1940s and early 1950s; it benefited by a first injection of American capitals in 1953 but moved towards a substantial economic growth only in the late 1950s and early 1960s after the removal of commercial boundaries, which allowed a flow of foreign investments attracted particularly by the tourist sector.

In the field of consumer cultures, there was certainly an increasing influence of the American mass commercial culture which developed throughout the century; thus, commercialization became a fundamental process in building social identities. In contrast, the lack of a lively consumption dynamic in Eastern Europe was a decisive element in the delegitimization of socialist regimes in Eastern Europe and influenced the terms of transition after 1989. But it is more doubtful if the force of commercialization played a similar role in the other two postwar periods. After the First World War, the management of consumption was deemed to be primarily the responsibility of the state, and this idea found socialist, democratic and fascist forms of expression. Indeed, in some cases, these developments were expressions of a progressive politics, which aimed at managing consumption in order to overcome social inequalities. After the Second World War, the superiority of the market system over state-managed consumption gradually became undeniable over the course of the 1950s. However, in the immediate aftermath of the war, the American pattern of a commercial society seemed to be too far removed from the European social situation to be imitated. Moreover, even in Western Europe, the notion of a 'commodified society' remained a contested arena, and became even more so from the 1960s onwards as the social, ecological and ethical factors inherent in processes of consumption increasingly became the target of political campaigns.

From this, it can be seen how the wars and the postwar periods played a fundamental role in defining twentieth-century European consumption regimes. This was particularly so in two respects: the material basis of citizenship and the dimension and regulation of the European market. In fact, it was through the two war experiences that the state acquired a fundamental role in providing food and other basic forms of consumption, and this function lasted well beyond the end of the two world wars, becoming a fundamental factor in the legitimization of governments. Even in Western Europe after the Second World War – as a fully successful market economy developed – the role of the state remained very influential as the supplier of collective and private forms of consumption, which in the United States were fully in the domain of the market economy.

The European market broke apart following the First World War, and the subsequent two postwar arrangements can be seen as successful attempts to reconstruct a united European market. This cannot however be seen as some form of teleological development since the different steps in this process occurred in the changing contexts of global capitalism. The two postwar periods following 1918 and 1945 occurred in the same era within the history of global capitalism that was characterized by the decline of the colonial empires and the emergence of American hegemony in the Western World. The third postwar period in contrast occurred within an entirely new phase. The increasing liberalization of the global market within a fragmented institutional framework made it difficult to arrange an international agreement for public investment in Eastern Europe. Nobody in the West was available to support the financial burden implied by such a project, which moreover was considered completely outdated because of its Keynesian inspiration. Thus, there was no Marshall Plan for Eastern Europe in the 1990s, and rather a flow of private investments, which took advantage of good opportunities for profit, but did not plan the building of a stable pan-European economic order.

Thus, while there has been certainly a trend towards a larger unified European continental market, which developed through the three postwar periods, in the last decades of the twentieth century, this market became increasingly permeated by global flows which narrowed the space for implementing effective regulatory policies. Therefore, the unification of the European market cannot be embraced within a single narrative, because the conditions within which the market operated depended to a significant degree on external conditions. This means that it is necessary to locate European market and consumption processes during the twentieth century in a global entangled history of capitalism and of its institutions.

Notes

1   See the well-known denounce of Keynes in John Maynard Keynes, *The Economic Consequences of the Peace* (New York: Harcourt Brace, 1920)

2 See Victoria De Grazia, *Irresistible Empire: America's Advance through Twentieth-Century Europe* (Cambridge, MA, and London: Belknap Press of Harvard University Press, 2005).

3 See Silvio Pons, *The Global Revolution: A History of International Communism, 1917–1991* (Oxford: Oxford University Press, 2014), chapter VI.

4 See Karl Marx, *Zur Kritik des sozialdemokratischen Programms von Gotha; der 'Gothaer Programmbrief'*, ed. and foreword Karl Kreibich (Reichenberg: Volksbuchhandlung Runge, 1920).

5 On the debate on consumptions during the War Communism, see Antonella Salomoni, *Il pane quotidiano: Ideologia e congiuntura nella Russia sovietica (1917–1921)* (Bologna: Il Mulino, 2001).

6 In a series of articles published in 1923 – and then collected in a volume rapidly translated into English – Trotsky presented his view of the daily life in the socialist society; see Leon Trotsky, *Problems of Life* (London: Methuen & Co., 1924).

7 See Sheila Fitzpatrick, *Everyday Stalinism: Ordinary Life in Extraordinary Times. Soviet Russia in the 1930s* (Oxford and New York: Oxford University Press, 2000).

8 See Susan Reid, 'The Khrushchev Kitchen: Domesticating the Scientific-Technological Revolution', *Journal of Contemporary History* 40 (2005): 289–316.

9 Stephan Merl, 'Staat und Konsum in der Zentralverwaltungswirtschaft. Rußland und die ostmitteleuropäischen Länder', in *Europäische Konsumgeschichte, Zur Gesellschafts- und Kulturgeschichte des Konsums (18.-20. Jahrhundert)*, ed. Hannes Siegrist, Hartmut Kaelble and Jürgen Kocka (Frankfurt-am-Main and New York: Campus Verlag, 1997), 205–41.

10 See Uta G. Poiger, *Jazz, Rock, and Rebels: Cold War Politics and American Culture in a Divided Germany* (Berkeley: University of California Press, 2000).

11 János Kornai, *Economics of Shortage* (Amsterdam and New York: North-Holland Pub. Co, 1980).

12 János Kornai, 'The Great Transformation of Central Eastern Europe Success and Disappointment', *Economics of Transition* 14, No. 2 (2006): 207–44.

13 Pia A. Albinsson, Marco Wolf and Dennis A. Kopf, 'Anti-consumption in East Germany: Consumer Resistance to Hyperconsumption', *Journal of Consumer Behaviour* 9 (2010): 412–25.

14 Paolo Capuzzo, '"Good bye Lenin". La nostalgia del comunismo nella Germania riunificata', *Studi Culturali* 1 (2004): 151–65.

15 See Alan S. Milward, *War, Economy and Society, 1939–1945* (Berkeley: University of California Press, 1977).

16 See Ina Zweiniger-Bargielowska, *Austerity in Britain: Rationing, Controls and Consumption, 1939–1955* (Oxford: Oxford University Press, 2000).

17 See Michael J. Hogan, *The Marshall Plan: America, Britain and the Reconstruction of Western Europe, 1947–1952* (Cambridge: Cambridge University Press, 1987)

18 Hogan, *The Marshall Plan*, 21.

19 See Alan S. Milward, *The Reconstruction of Western Europe, 1945–51* (London: Routledge, 1984).

20 Charles S. Maier, 'The Two Postwar Eras and the Conditions for Stability in Twentieth-century Western Europe', *American Historical Review* 86 (1981): 327–52.

21 David Ellwood, *Rebuilding Europe; Western Europe, America and Postwar Reconstruction* (Harlow: Longman, 1992).

22 J. Bradford DeLong and Barry Eichengreen, 'The Marshall Plan: History's Most Successful Structural Adjustment Program', in *Postwar Economic Reconstruction and*

Lessons for the East Today, ed. Rudiger Dornbusch, Wilhelm Nölling and Richard Layard (Cambridge, MA: MIT Press, 1993), 189–229.

23 See Raymond Vernon, 'As the Twig is Bent. The Marshall Plan in Europe's industrial structure', in John Agnew and J. Nicholas Entrikin (eds), *The Marshall Plan Today: Model and Metaphor* (London: Routledge, 2004), 155–170.

24 Barry Eichengreen and Marc Uzan, 'The Marshall Plan: Economic Effects and Implications for Eastern Europe and the Former USSR', *Economic Policy* No. 14 (1992): 13–75.

25 Paolo Pombeni, 'La legittimazione del benessere: nuovi parametri di legittimazione in Europa dopo la seconda guerra mondiale', in *Crisi, legittimazione e consenso*, ed. Paolo Pombeni (Bologna: Il Mulino, 2003), 357–417.

26 Maier, 'The Two Postwar Eras'.

27 Stephen N. Broadberry and Mark Harrison, *The Economics of World War I* (Cambridge: Cambridge University Press, 2005).

28 Avner Offer, *The First World War: An Agrarian Interpretation* (Oxford: Clarendon Press, 1989), 25.

29 Thierry Bonzon, 'Consumption and Total Warfare in Paris, 1914–18', in *Food and Conflict in Europe in the Age of the Two World Wars*, ed. Frank Trentmann and Just Flemming (Houndmills: Palgrave Macmillan, 2006), 49–64.

30 See Belinda J. Davis, *Home Fires Burning: Food, Politics, and Everyday Life in World War I Berlin* (Chapel Hill and London: The University of North Carolina Press, 2000).

31 Frank Trentmann, *Free Trade: Commerce, Consumption, and Civil Society in Modern Britain* (Oxford: Oxford University Press, 2009).

32 Frank Trentmann, 'Consumption and Citizenship in Twentieth-Century Britain', in *The Politics of Consumption: Material Culture and Citizenship in Europe and America*, ed. Martin Daunton and Matthew Hilton (Oxford and New York: Berg, 2001), 129–63.

9

Pasts

Péter Apor and Henry Rousso

This text raises a question that opens the door to many others: Do the arguments used to identify the post-1989 era as a postwar period take into account the different ways European countries, both in the East and the West, have dealt with the past in the last two decades? This question differs slightly from simply asking what kind of historical narratives were produced after the fall of the Soviet system in various European countries or in the European Union as such. In this context, historical narratives should be taken as having a very broad meaning: that is, representations manifested in testimonies, historical works, novels and films; actions taken by civil society through survivors, activists and politicians and national or local policies of the past, such as commemorations, reparations, apology speeches, museums, school programs and the like. The nature of historical consciousness – an old concept recently reactivated to replace more or less the dilute notion of 'collective memory'[1] – can be seen as an indicator to identify a postwar sequence, and to distinguish it from other historical episodes. The way in which a given nation or group deals with recent or remote history is particularly significant during and after a major historical catastrophe, such as a war.[2] It is an important component of mobilizing and demobilizing minds, because history is both a weapon used to build the image of the enemy and national legitimacy and a tool to exit the conflict and to give meaning to the death and destruction.

In the post-1989 context, this kind of analysis focuses primarily on the legacy and memory of communism in its various dimensions – keeping in mind, of course, the tremendous differences between the East and the West. In the founding states of the European Union, despite the fact that European integration was largely based on the rejection of totalitarian experiences, the memory of communism never reached the status of a major political issue. As such, discussion of the past or 'pasts' – from the perspective of post-1989 – must include the memory of older major events as well, beginning with the two world wars. Meanwhile, if we want to be exhaustive, we should also take into account how European history as a whole changed after 1989, as reflected in many major historical accounts, such as those of Eric Hobsbawm or Mark Mazower.[3] For the purposes of our project, we will limit our scope to the question of the postwar concept, and will take the lead provided by Tony Judt, who considered the whole history of Europe after 1945 as a postwar period.[4] To what extent did the fall of the Berlin Wall change the representation of historical sequences prior to 1945 and the creation of the European Soviet system? Should the post-1989 period be considered, for instance, a major step, a historical turning point in the long-term perception of the Nazi era? Finally, according to historians like Reinhart Koselleck or François Hartog, and philosophers like Francis Fukuyama or Giorgio Agamben, contemporary societies are going through a major change in their 'regime of historicity', that is, the way they conceive the links among past, present and future. After having lived since the eighteenth century with a conception of time based on expected progress or a movement forward (including utopian conceptions), around the last third of the twentieth century, thinkers entered a new age, one based on the prominence and even the 'triumph' of the present and the immediate.[5] They passed from 'futurism' to 'presentism', a shift that has had significant consequences on issues like history and memory. To what extent, then, did the rupture of 1989 play a role in this evolution?

We will sum up these various questions in a general hypothesis about the place of the past(s) in the three postwar periods we deal with. Since the 1980s, there has obviously been a huge investment in Western Europe (and in other parts of the Western world, namely Israel and the United States) in coping with the legacy of the Holocaust. By focusing on a single event – whatever its magnitude and alleged singularity – this process played a major role in the evolution of European, and probably global, historical consciousness as a whole. Remembering the Holocaust has changed our conception of history, regardless of whether we see it as a cause or a consequence of a deeper phenomenon. Among many other elements, this process put the notion of 'memory' at the heart of any kind of representation of the past. Meanwhile, this process began *before* the fall of the Berlin Wall, and is primarily a belated effect of the aftermath of the Second World War. It influenced a comparable need to cope with the communist past, and led to significant political and moral pressure for Eastern and Central European States and institutions to face the issue in the same framework as that used in the West. At the same time, the end in 1989 of a historical sequence that had started in 1945 led to a reassessment of the First World War and the first postwar period of the twentieth century, similarly in the historical field, in politics and in popular culture. Today, 1918 is no longer analysed simply as a prelude to 1939, just as the violence of the Second World War is no longer seen as the climax of the age of extremes. Conversely, the recent historical perspectives on the First World War have influenced the way we now consider the history of the Second World War and its aftermath. The same is true for post-communist historiography, which still influences the rewriting of the history of Europe as a whole. Our own network and the present project belong to this specific historiographical and political context: This is partly because historians look differently at the temporality of wars and postwar episodes now that it has been possible to propose the hypothesis that 1989 was comparable to 1945 or 1918. As a kind of a paradox, the fact that the fall of the Berlin Wall reinforced peace within the continent (except in the former Yugoslavia and now Ukraine) has also led many historians to reassess the history of the whole twentieth century in terms of a long sequence of successive wars, with concomitant pre-war and postwar periods.

The regressive method applied here is at once both complex and natural because analyzing the state of historical consciousness at a given moment means dealing with past and present at the same time: the past as it was represented or commemorated, and the contemporary cultural or political framework used to read it. Meanwhile, what follows should be taken as an intellectual and speculative exercise.

Post-1989: history continues

The end of the Cold War and the collapse of communism as a political alternative raised different questions in the West and in the East, respectively, in terms of history and memory, depending on the level of the need to make sense of the communist past. Despite such undeniable differences, however, the methods for approaching the past were strikingly similar all over Europe: 1989 opened up new ways to address histories of oppression and emancipation on a global scale, helped to turn 'trauma' into a global concept for framing the understanding of recent dictatorial pasts and reopened many issues related to the Second World War. These processes occurred in different locations and in different political and cultural contexts, but they were basically interconnected and inherently transnational.

As a political alternative, the end of communism created space for other kinds of political fights for emancipation. The relative success of the Holocaust memory policies all over Europe led explicitly to other similar issues. New claims emerged about the legacy of slavery or the colonial past, especially in France, Belgium and the Netherlands. In a certain sense, these claims had deeper social dimensions than the question raised by the Holocaust because they expressed the resentment felt by minorities as a result of their contemporary social situations, rather than simply their historical background. The 'demobilization' of parties or groups who had been fighting for a utopian future opened the way to a 'remobilization' aiming for a new identity and a new place in their respective countries based on a postcolonial, revised past.

Postcolonial criticism and the modes of Holocaust remembrance made a strange, but important, impact on how to make sense of the communist past in at least two ways: These templates seemed to support a focus on violence and tyranny, and they helped to rewrite the history of the socialist dictatorships as the rule of external forces alien to the respective, suppressed indigenous nations. Immediately following 1989, the history of communism and the past of the Soviet-ruled part of Europe appeared to be a burdensome legacy of crime, mass executions, torture and illegality. From the perspective of rather inglorious failure, however, communism was also ridiculed as an overambitious, megalomaniacal attempt to transform the world that, at the end, proved to be nothing more than a mean, miserable and desperate attempt to hinder the inevitable collapse. From the perspective of the seemingly inevitable failure, the pre-1989 period suddenly appeared as an incomprehensible, alien and nonsensical world populated by strange, obscure and exotic persons, objects, rituals and customs. These three varieties of post-1989 perception generated three approaches to representing the pre-1989 past: one dominated by tragic and gloomy visions, an ironic one observing communism from an aristocratic distance and a third one that establishes the pre-1989 past as the object of nostalgic contemplation of a forever lost world.

Many examples of popular memory related to the history of communism in East-Central European National Museums represent an apparently nostalgic display of everyday objects, as shown in the famous German movie, *Good Bye, Lenin!* (2002) or in many exhibitions like the Internet Museum of People's Poland, started in 1999, the 'Golden Sixties' in Prague (2009–10) and the 'Golden Era: Between Propaganda and Reality' in Bucharest (2007). The nostalgic character of representations of communism is not a contemplation of the innocent 'good old days' of youth. Rather, nostalgia in this case represents a deliberate attempt to create a temporal distance from the period of socialist dictatorships, and to turn that period into a different, curious, but still familiar era.[6]

The immediate post-1989 interest in constructing the communist past as obscure and full of secrets waiting to be revealed had important consequences. The history and memory of the period were considered to consist of previously untold and suppressed stories. In many ways, a history of communism was thought to be attainable by correcting previous official narratives, by adding missing information, and by retelling and revealing unknown stories. The correct history of communism appeared possible through the liberation of a previously suppressed counter-memory.[7] Related to this development, the history of communism was broadly considered to be a traumatic past: It was perceived as a period that had negatively impacted both individuals and national communities. In a context of globally circulating histories of oppression and atrocities, the Holocaust and Slavery, however, rendered communism as but one of the many 'traumatic pasts' having global relevance.[8]

Discussions about and revelations of the hidden side of communism had already started around 1988. Such attempts at recovering an allegedly lost past were encouraged by Soviet – particularly Russian – politicians and historians who began to reveal and openly debate the Bolshevik crimes committed during the civil war and collectivization, in the Stalinist repression of the Great Terror, during the Second World War and in the camp systems of the Gulag.[9] Other East-Central European public had their own symbolically relevant cases to demonstrate the theretofore unspoken tragedies of their respective national communities, such as the Katyn massacre ordered by Stalin in Poland, or the trial and execution of Imre Nagy, the prime minister of Hungary during the 1956 revolution.

The rule of the communist parties thus appeared alien to these societies, a result of outside or foreign forces for which the respective nations bore no responsibility. It follows that the dictatorships contradicted the true spirit of these nations, since the regimes were imposed on them by means impossible to resist. More importantly, interpreting communism as one of the traumas of the twentieth century is the basis of one of the most striking aspects of understanding the communist past: the comparison or, more precisely, the strange unification of fascism and communism. The depiction of communism as a terror regime conspicuously next to the already established icon of violence, nazism, is an attempt to transform the Gulag into a counter-Auschwitz, to construct an understanding of the history of communism as the twin of the ultimate horror of nazism, and thus as the Eastern double of the ultimate catastrophe of European civilization. As evidenced by the *Black Book of Communism*, such ideas have gone on to obtain broader credibility beyond post-communist Eastern Europe.[10]

The post-1989 framing of communism as an alien, colonial rule furthered a more revisionist reopening of issues related to the Second World War. Following the dissolution of the erstwhile understanding of the war against fascism as the prelude to the communist-led global anti-imperialist struggle, those pro-German politicians and regimes that had been allied with Nazi Germany could be retrospectively cast as predecessors of the global anti-communist freedom struggle. The post-communist anti-communist revisionism now tried to remember individuals such as Marshal Antonescu or Admiral Horthy not as collaborators of Nazi Germany responsible for the deportation of Jewish citizens of their respective countries and for the catastrophe of war, but rather as heroic resisters to the advance of Bolshevism.[11] One can observe similar trends in the Baltic States or the Ukraine,[12] and one is also reminded of what happened in the Western countries after 1945, that is, the framing of former collaboration with the Nazis as an exceptional and very limited phenomenon, indeed, as an aberration incompatible with the true essence of the nation.

On a global scale, the end of the Cold War contributed directly or indirectly to many transitions to democracy, such as in South Africa or Latin America. These transitions immediately raised the question of what to do with the legacy of traumatic pasts, what place to give to the victims' voices and how to manage the legacy of the previous authoritarian regimes. Despite having these questions in common, most of the countries facing democratic transition found their own distinctive paths. Many of them adopted a new concept for coping with the past: the truth and reconciliation commission, a concept simply impossible to imagine at the end of the Second World War. In Eastern Europe, the perception of 'collective trauma' contributed to the idea that in the wake of communism, a general regeneration was needed that was achievable through coming to terms with, overcoming and then closing the book on the past. These examples likewise confirm that post-communist politics and societies developed a similar confidence in the fact that the most adequate means of shaping the history of communism were legal measures and the recording of survivors' memories. For example, the Czech Republic, Poland and Hungary each passed lustration laws and rehabilitated former political convicts, and early oral history research in many countries focused on stories of suffering and victimization.

'Trauma', as a global concept to commemorate atrocity and dictatorship, was instrumental in the development of 'memory' as a major attitude towards the past. Around 1989 and during the early 1990s, an influential body of scholarship established that the construction of images and interpretations of the past normally occurred beyond the borders of professional historiography. Political-ideological implications, social and collective institutions and the legacy of cultural codes were studied to understand the emergence and persistence of various historical narratives. As the past has become the object of less conscious and controllable sociocultural processes instead of technical rational expertise, terminology – collective, social or cultural memory – that reflected the psychological understanding of individual remembering was crafted in scholarship.[13]

The 'memorial attitude' towards the past played an important role in the emergence of the truth commissions, which were seen as institutions that could effectively reveal and repair 'traumas of the past'. Meanwhile, the first example of such a commission did not emerge in the post-1989 context, even if most of the thirty commissions created all over the world to date were established in the 1990s. The first one was implemented in

Argentina, in 1983, after the end of the military dictatorship, and was partly related to the debates over the impunity of former Nazis who had taken refuge in this country or in the region. In the West, while the end of the Cold War did not immediately create any new pressure on democratic states to deal with the Nazi past and the legacy of the crimes committed during the Second World War – which was already on the agenda for most – it nonetheless allowed for scrutiny of historical policies and practices, for example, by giving access to new documents for pending judicial processes.

One may ask whether the know-how accumulated for the memory of the Second World War in Europe, in the United States or at an international level in the last two decades played a role in the various debates about democratic transition. Without pretending that all the new democratic states imported the Western 'Holocaust model', debates over the necessity of remembrance versus the 'criminal' temptation of oblivion (like amnesty laws) nonetheless look very familiar. Be it in former European communist countries or elsewhere in the world, the precedent of the Holocaust as a traumatic past to master provided a rather successful example.[14] Many lawyers and human rights activists from non-governmental organizations (NGOs) had been trained to grasp new criminal definitions like genocide or crime against humanity, first used in trials linked to the Nazi past. Debates on collective memory, oral history, public history and the ethics of humanities and social sciences when facing crime on a mass scale had an echo all over the world. In other words, the end of the Cold War did not create a new model of dealing with the past, but rather fostered global circulation of notions that had appeared before in the longer shadow of the end of the Second World War.

Post–Second World War: the invention of memory

When people talk today about the past, especially when evoking the recent European past, they mainly use the notion of 'memory' instead of the word 'history'. The concept or the metaphor of 'memory', in the contemporary sense, has a peculiar dimension: It combines a representation of a specific historical event with not only a moral issue, but also a political agenda about what to do with its remembering or its echo in the present. Discussing the memory of Auschwitz – and now, likewise, the memory of the Gulag or Verdun – means providing an active representation of the past which has to serve many purposes in the present: paying tribute to the victims; delivering a broad lesson in history; implementing political actions to prevent any repetition of such horrors and fostering specific ethnic, religious, national or universal identities.

In the same way, most scientific, political or popular recent historical narratives have increasingly been using two other expressions or metaphors. Indeed, we spontaneously used the first one at the beginning of this text: 'to deal with the past' or 'to cope with it'. Similar expressions exist in other languages, such as in French: *'faire face au passé', 'regarder son passé en face'*. In this formula, the past is strangely *before* us, and not behind. It is no longer a set of remote or ancient traditions to perpetuate, or a lost continent to discover again, or a reservoir of experiences which can help us to cope with the present and the future, as in the old tradition of the *historia magistra est*. The past, today, is a problem to confront, an issue to solve, even a war to win against oblivion. The second common, current metaphor is directly linked to this. Most contemporary discourses about the past refer to a state of conflict: 'conflicted memories', 'battles' or 'clashes' of memory, or, in the same vein, 'divided' or 'competing' memories. This trend and these particular common expressions are rather recent. They emerged in the West in the last three decades, during the anamnesis of the Nazi past and the Holocaust memory, and they have had a great influence on how we write and represent history as a whole in many parts of the world.

This is not the place to return in detail to the history of the memory of the Second World War, but let us nonetheless sum up a few key elements, which we can then compare with the two other postwar periods, and which seem, in fact, easier to observe given that the memory of the Second World War became a kind of a model applied to other historical episodes. Due to the magnitude of human and material destruction, the need for remembering and the desire to keep as many traces as possible – both of the crimes committed and of the victims, their culture, their names – began during the war itself, in the ghettos, in the underground, in the everyday lives of millions of people, whether it took the form of archives, artifacts or personal diaries. In the East as well as in the West, despite the respective levels of violence and annihilation, the need to build a memory *for the future* began in the core of the catastrophe. This element is often underestimated. As such, the war period itself constituted the first step in the history of its memory.

In the immediate aftermath, especially in the countries that suffered from military occupation, there was significant production of various historical narratives.[15] The purges, the international or national trials, the policies of denazification and all those processes that sought to define in political and juridical terms what had happened before and during the war produced specific and contradictory interpretations of the past, and not only from the perspective of the winners as it is often claimed. At the same time, a number of testimonies were collected by private or state initiatives, and many were published, even if there is an ongoing debate about their real influence on public opinion.[16] Everywhere in Europe, new institutions appeared to collect sources and to produce the first historical accounts on the war: in West Germany, France, Belgium, the Netherlands, Poland and in the USSR.[17] The period from 1945 to the early 1950s (depending on respective national situations) saw a partial 'demobilization' of the minds and the progressive abandonment of the 'war culture'. Nevertheless, there remained a kind of continuity with the war itself: gathering traces, pointing the devilish nature of Nazi Germany and the other defeated systems, showing the superiority of democracy and communism, respectively. But above all, there was a need for a better comprehension of what happened. Writing history became an urgent task to provide the first articulated and distanced explanations of the inconceivable. After 1945, Europeans needed both bread and meaning.

In the late 1950s and in the 1960s, there was more or less a brief period of oblivion or, at least, official silence. It did not pertain to the whole history of the war, for that event was very thoroughly and quickly documented, mainly due to the trials underway and the availability of myriad official and private sources. Only some aspects were covered up: support to puppet regimes, collaboration, indigenous complicity in the Holocaust – if not the Holocaust as such. At the same time, many countries tried to re-establish a historical continuity with their respective '*romans nationaux*', and to fill the gap caused by political divisions of the Second World War. This was the time for heroic myths, be they based on patriotism, antifascism or moral and spiritual values.

It is true that the production of historical evidence and interpretation in combination with demobilization was a broad European process. Nonetheless, the afterlife of the war showed somewhat divergent tendencies in the Soviet occupation zones, where certain elements of remobilization were almost immediately present. This was the consequence of the reshaping of ideological struggles, this time encouraged by Soviet officials and local communist activists, but it was also fed by the various strong, various traditions of anti-Bolshevik nationalism. East-Central European societies constructed their own versions of the myths of anti-fascism and resistance. These myths were based on the consensus that responsibility for the war fell on the Germans, citizens of a country that had practically ceased to exist in 1945. This interpretation could claim the most considerable authenticity in Yugoslavia, where indigenous partisan troops had defeated the occupying German army by 1945. Nonetheless, Tito and his leadership promoted an interpretation of the war as a united people's war of liberation, thereby ignoring the intense interethnic conflicts between Croats and Serbs, and various intra-Yugoslav pro-German movements. The anti-German narrative could also obtain certain credibility in Poland, which had been the country first attacked by Hitler and where sizable anti-German armed resistance groups had, in effect, operated. Still, the anti-German narrative in Poland was embedded in the traditions of Polish martyrology that in many ways cast Poles as the natural victims of (German) aggression, all the while downplaying the fact that it had been a Polish territory where death camps had seen the extermination of many millions of Jews.[18]

In other societies, particularly Czechoslovakia, Hungary, Bulgaria and Romania, this myth was less tenable. Hungary, Romania and Bulgaria as well as the independent post-Munich Slovakia had been Hitler's allies, and even in the Czech regions there had been little anti-German resistance; in fact, much of society had benefited economically from German occupation. As such, the postwar trials of war criminals played an immense role in the process of myth creation. These legal procedures identified and, hence, personified the abstract theory of pro-German collaboration as the major culprit for the war and its consequences.[19] The purpose of the trials of war criminals in East-Central Europe was, from the beginning, the creation of historical narratives. The foundations of such peculiar representations of the recent past were laid down in communist or leftist political attempts to discredit the constructed history of the interwar political elite in order to bolster the legitimacy of the new political system.

Subsequent to the establishment of communist-ruled states in the region, the anti-Nazi narrative was appropriated by the Communist parties and turned into an interpretation that highlighted the communist anti-fascist resistance, and concomitantly downplaying the role of non-communists and the importance of Jewish and other victims of Nazi genocide.[20] In many ways, this appropriation was based on the official Soviet interpretation of the war, where commemoration, while ubiquitous, was also selective in concentrating on military victory, military loss, the role of the Communist Party and Stalin as well as the men at the front.[21] The process was spectacular in Germany, where the establishment of the Socialist Unity Party of Germany (Sozialistische Einheitspartei Deutschlands, SED) dictatorship resulted in the suppression of the variety of public interpretations of the pre-war past and promotion of an official narrative about East Germany as the successor of anti-fascist – meaning communist – resistance, and West Germany as a place where Nazi personnel supposedly continued to prosper.[22]

These anti-fascist myths, contrary to what eventually happened in the West during the 1950s and 1960s, had little integrative purpose. On the contrary, they served to aggressively reject all non-communist alternatives as potential fascism. These historical constructions suggested that the only purpose of the Nazis had been the elimination of communists and that all anti-communist regimes were actually fascist. Party historians constructed a rigid interpretation of history that consisted exclusively of two factors: fascism and communism.

In the 1970s, two decades before the fall of the Berlin Wall, Western Europe began to experience a long process of anamnesis, that is, a specific focus on – and even obsession – the Nazi past and the question of the Holocaust. Many countries – Germany, France, Belgium and even neutral countries like Switzerland or Sweden – had to face a general reassessment of their behavior during the war. Thirty to forty years after the end of the war, there was a new political and cultural *mobilization* to fight a new invisible enemy: oblivion. This process gave the impression that the war had not completely come to an end in 1945, or at least that an important part of the postwar job remained unfinished. Many judicial cases were reopened, including in Germany, France and Italy. Most of the Western European countries, under international (or, more accurately, American) and national pressure, launched new kinds of policies of the past that aimed to redress crimes committed and to provide compensation to the last survivors of the Holocaust. This process began before 1989 (indeed, it began in the immediate aftermath of the war) but it continued afterwards: Many major achievements in terms of reparation were realized in the 1990s, at a time when another historical trauma was on the agenda. Firmly linked to the attempts to uncover allegedly anti-communist pasts and to the mutual intersections of the transnational culture of Holocaust memory and the emerging transnationalized memory culture of communism, the concept of memory became a global political and cultural tool that profoundly altered the traditional conception of historical time. Among many other elements, one could point to the end of the ancestral necessity to forget or to close the book after a period of internal conflict; the idea that all crimes and wrongdoings of the past, even a remote past, can and should be repaired in the present; the importance given to narratives based on personal experience (testimonies) rather than distant historical knowledge (historical writings) and the emergence and domination of contemporary history as an institutionalized subfield within the historical profession.

Post–First World War: the unachieved memory

One of the consequences of the regressive perspective on the history of postwar periods is to emphasize the renewal of interest in the First World War, not only among historians, but also among the public and in politics all over Europe. We can see it in the rather spectacular impact of the centenary. But here again, the movement began long before 1989, and initially, in the historical field with works focusing on cultural and social dimensions of the conflict. To take but one example, Jean-Jacques Becker published his first study on how the French entered the war in 1977. Until the early 1990s, the interest in the First World War was limited to a cohort of specialists who were mainly working on the history of the event itself. The legacy of the conflict began to attract significant attention in popular culture afterwards: Jean Rouaud was awarded the prestigious Prix Goncourt in 1990 for *Les Champs d'honneur*, the international museum of the Historial de Péronne opened in 1992 and Jay Winter published the first influential study on the history of memory of the First World War in 1995. In the years that followed, there were many books on the comparative or entangled history of the two world wars, as if a generation of scholars was just discovering how intimately the two events were linked together. This probably affected some trends in the historiography of the Nazi era and the Second World War as well, giving, for example, more attention to the impact of the first postwar period: George Mosse's work on *brutalization*, published in 1990, exerted tremendous influence ten years later. The comparison or the affiliation between the two conflicts led to the 'reinvention' of the historical sequence that began in 1912 or 1914, rather than in 1933 or 1939, as well as to the study of forms of violence other than those focusing only on the Holocaust, such as the influential works of Stéphane Audoin-Rouzeau and Annette Becker, or John Horne and Alan Kramer.[23] Obviously, it is difficult not to see this evolution as a direct consequence of 1989, and the consequent rebirth of a continental structure that was supposed to have vanished with the Second World War and the Soviet 'freezing'. Suddenly, in order to understand contemporary politics, it was more relevant to go back to 1918 than to 1945.

There was a huge investment in understanding the context of the postwar period not only in terms of political or diplomatic change, but also by focusing on the place of the past. Born in the context of post–Second World War, the question of memory was raised a few years later in the context of post–First World War. Many historical works insisted on the mass phenomenon of mourning all over Europe, demonstrating to what extent the experience of loss, born at the very beginning of the war, was prolonged throughout the interwar years. The remembrance of the First World War changed or even created what could be seen as a modern model of commemoration. The 1920s saw the invention of the monument of death, the minute of silence, the Unknown Soldier and large military cemeteries, including those for former enemies established on national soil and at the place of the murderous battles (la Somme, Verdun, etc.). Veterans' associations began to play a major role in everyday life as well as in politics. For the first time in history, due to the large number of combatants, there was a huge production of testimonies of all kinds about the war, and emerging from all sections of the society rather than simply from the elites (officers, writers, public intellectuals). Mourning practices invoked common cultural resources and mobilized conventional religious forms, ideas of military heroism and national sacrifice and glory and avant-garde literature and art to reflect the new modern experience of industrial warfare.[24] Often, these interpretations of the war confirmed nationalist passions: either revanchism and frustration or the rigid insistence on positions of ethnonationalist rule and territorial expansion that in the long run proved to be conducive to the emergence of authoritarian-nationalist historiographies. In other words, memories of the First World War were probably as strong in the bodies and minds of people after 1918 as they were after 1945. After all, it is not by chance that the concept of 'demobilizing the minds', understood as the slow process of exiting war, has been articulated to describe the first postwar period.

Nevertheless, there is an important difference between 1918 and the two other postwar periods. Observing what happened after 1945, we know now that memory obeyed specific cycles, as we have seen earlier. The perception of the immediate aftermath changed completely twenty years later, and yet again twenty years after that. Apart from the singularity of the Second World War and the question of the Nazi legacy, there was 'enough' time between 1945 and 1989 – if we consider the last change as a new major change – to observe the difference between generations, the evolution of memory in different contexts and the consequences of time elapsed. For instance, anyone who has worked for a long time on the memory of the Holocaust could have seen how the sensitivity about the past was more and more vivid despite the growing distance from the event, both in survivors' reactions or in those of their grandsons and granddaughters.[25] With respect to 1989, the question is still unanswered: How long will Europeans have to face the legacy of what happened in the Cold War era? Regardless of the answer, it seems safe to predict that, due to the weak involvement in establishing an official and consensual memory of the communist crimes at a European level, the issue will remain unresolved for a while yet.

There is, however, nothing comparable for the memory of the First World War. If we admit that remembering a war means generally remembering losses, violence, destruction, martyrdom, heroic behaviors, hunger and despair, then the memories of the First World War were partly cut short by the traumatic experiences of the Second World War. It is strikingly clear in the case of Russia, where the Bolshevik takeover first imposed October 1917 as the focal point of public commemorations, and hence discouraged and even suppressed individual memories of fallen soldiers who fought for the Tsarist Russian imperial army. Subsequently, as the Great Patriotic War, Soviet Russia's efforts in the Second World War then began to dominate the public sphere, and the commemorations of and memorials to the fallen of the anti-fascist war started to serve as sites where the memory of the dead from the previous Great War could also be taken care of. Nonetheless, due in part to the enormous significance of the Second World War, in Russian history, the conflict between 1914 and 1918 has never become as crucial a period as it has in European historical thinking more generally.[26] This fact notwithstanding, the absorption of the memory of the First World War by cultures of commemoration after the Second World War was a broad pan-European trend. Not only was the second Great War seen as a repeat performance that occurred in the same places, involving practically the same generations of combatants, but the level of violence, destruction and loss – especially involving civilians – was also much higher. As a result, 1939 or 1945 signaled the end of a cycle of memory, or better still, the proof of an 'unachieved' memory of the First World War. After 1945, the First World War would be still commemorated of course, and November 11 has always been a day of major celebration in many European countries; however, the social and cultural memories of this war were relegated to the background, secondary to the legacy of the Second World War and the Holocaust, at least until 2014. The fall of the Berlin Wall recreated a place for a specific memory of the First World War, and it is only recently that writers, historians and politicians have taken the singular legacy of the First World War into account. After all, does anyone really remember the fiftieth anniversary of 1918?

Although post-communist Eastern Europe is certainly part of the major tendencies of broader European framings of the past, 1989 created a specific current of rediscovering 1918 that has brought aspects of the 'unachieved memory' of the First World War to the surface once again. The dismantling of the communist ideological framework of interpreting the recent past was often understood as a return to the 'normal' course of national history, once the accident of the socialist dictatorships had been bracketed. As East-Central European societies struggled to understand what national identities could mean following the dissolution of the frameworks provided by communism, the spectacular and manifest statements about the meaning of the 'nation' that had emerged in the post-1918 period began to have a massive impact on various public representations of the past. In historical cultures of those societies that had achieved nation-state status as the consequence of the war – be they new states such as Poland or Czechoslovakia or expanded pre-war states such as Romania or postwar Yugoslavia – the First World War was generally considered a period of heroic sacrifice in the service of the national cause and was widely celebrated as the culmination and fulfillment of respective national projects. Indeed, even in the case of Hungary, the understanding of the war was framed in similar terms of national sacrifice, despite a radically different outcome of the war: In this case, however, the sense of sacrifice resulted in betrayal and disappointment rather than the realization of the national cause, involving as it did the dismemberment of the old kingdom seen by the Hungarian political and cultural elite as a natural nation state, and the dispersion of a large proportion of ethnic Hungarians under the authority of foreign states. Hungary, as such, with its obsession of Trianon, either in its radical nationalist or moderate critical historical version, is an eloquent example of how difficult it is to 'achieve' a memory of the First World War. At the same time, the similar emergence of the myth of Greater-Romania can quickly parallel the Hungarian case.

As a provisional final word, one may underscore that analyzing the different ways of coping with the legacy of a recent catastrophe, whether it is in a regressive order (from 1989 to 1918) or in a normal chronological order (from 1918 to 1989), highlights how war and postwar period change the perception of the past, how they deeply modify the writing of history as a whole as well as the writing of national histories. Post–First World War saw at the same time the development of a mass collective mourning all over Europe and in other parts of the world, the birth of new kinds of national and local commemorations as well as the beginning of a new historiographical culture. Post-1945 led to new conceptions of transitional justice that changed the relationships between past and present, for example, with belated trials. It led also to the implementation of 'memory' as a new concept, a new understanding of human rights and a new component of democratic societies. The post-1989 period demonstrated that these evolutions were not only the consequence of the Holocaust, seen as a unique moment in history, but they became rather a norm, a standard to be applied to remote events, like the colonial past, or to recent history, like the legacy of communism and other authoritarian experiences all over the world.

Notes

1   Peter Seixas (ed.), *Theorizing Historical Consciousness* (Toronto: University of Toronto Press, 2004).
2   Henry Rousso, *The Latest Catastrophe: History, the Present, the Contemporary* (Chicago: The Chicago University Press, 2016 [2012]).
3   Eric Hobsbawm, *Age of Extremes: The Short Twentieth Century, 1914–1991* (London: Michael Joseph, 1994); Mark Mazower, *Dark Continent: Europe's Twentieth Century* (London: Allen Lane, 1998).
4   Tony Judt, *Postwar: A History of Europe since 1945* (London: William Heinemann, 2005).
5   Reinhart Koselleck, *The Practice of Conceptual History: Timing History, Spacing Concepts* (Stanford: Stanford University Press, 2002); François Hartog, *Régimes d'historicité. Présentisme et expériences du temps* (Paris: Éditions du Seuil, 2003); Francis Fukuyama, *The End of History and the Last Man* (London: Hamish Hamilton, 1992); Giorgio Agamben, 'What Is the Contemporary?', in Giorgio Agamben, *What Is an Apparatus? and Other Essays* (Stanford: Stanford University Press, 2009).
6   Oksana Sarkisova and Peter Apor (eds.), *Past for the Eyes: East European Representations of Communism in Cinema and Museums after 1989* (Budapest and New York: Central European University Press, 2008).
7   Rubie S. Watson (ed.), *Memory, History, and Opposition under State Socialism* (Santa Fe: University of Washington Press, 1994).
8   Paul Williams, *Memorial Museums: The Global Rush to Commemorate Atrocities* (New York & Oxford: Berg, 2007).
9   Arfon Rees, 'Managing the History of the Past in the Former Communist States', in *A European Memory? Contested Histories and Politics of Remembrance*, ed. Małgorzata Pakier and Bo Stråth (New York & Oxford: Berghahn, 2010), 219–32.
10 Stéphane Courtois (ed.), *The Black Book of Communism: Crimes, Terror, Repression* (Cambridge, MA, and London: Harvard University Press, 1999 [1997]).
11 Dietmar Müller, 'Strategien des öffentlichen Erinners in 'Rumänien nach 1989: Postkommunisten und postkommunistische Antikommunisten', in *Zwischen Amnesie und Nostalgie: Die Erinnerung an den Kommunismus in Südosteuropa*, ed. Ulf Brunnbauer and Stefan Troebst (Cologne, Weimar and Vienna: Böhlau, 2007), 47–69.
12 James Mark, *The Unfinished Revolution: Making Sense of the Communist Past in Central-Eastern Europe* (New Haven: Yale University Press, 2010).
13 Pierre Nora, 'Between Memory and History: *Les Lieux de Mémoire*', *Representations* 26 (1989), 7–25; Jan Assmann, *Das kulturelle Gedächtnis: Schrift, Erinnerung und politische Identität in frühen Hochkulturen* (Munich: C. H. Beck, 1992); Iwona Irwin-Zarecka, *Frames of Remembrance: The Dynamics of Collective Memory* (New Brunswick and London: Transaction Publishers, 1994); David Middleton and Derek Edwards (eds.), *Collective Remembering* (London, Thousand Oaks and New Delhi: Sage, 1990).
14 Daniel Levy and Natan Sznaider, *Holocaust and Memory in the Global Age* (Philadelphia: Temple University Press, 2006); Henry Rousso, *Face au passé: Essais sur la mémoire contemporaine* (Paris: Belin, 2016).

15 Richard Ned Lebow, Wulf Kansteiner and Claudio Fogu (eds.), *The Politics of Memory in Postwar Europe* (Durham & London: Duke University Press, 2006).

16 Hasia Diner, *We Remember with Reverence and Love. American Jews and the Myth of Silence after the Holocaust, 1945–1962* (New York: New York University Press, 2009); François Azouvi, *Le Mythe du grand silence. Auschwitz, les Français, la mémoire* (Paris: Fayard, 2012).

17 Pieter Lagrou, *The Legacy of Nazi Occupation: Patriotic Memory and National Recovery in Western Europe, 1945–1965* (Cambridge: Cambridge University Press, 2000).

18 Annamaria Orla-Bukowska, 'New Threads on an Old Loom: National Memory and Social Identity in Postwar and Post-Communist Poland', in Lebow, Kansteiner and Fogu (eds.), *The Politics of Memory in Postwar Europe*, 178–96.

19 Tony Judt, 'The Past is Another Country: Myth and Memory in Postwar Europe', *Daedalus* 121 (1992): 83–97.

20 Ingo Loose, 'The Anti-Fascist Myth of the German Democratic Republic and Its Decline after 1989', in *Past in the Making: Historical Revisionism in Central Europe after 1989*, ed. Michal Kopeček (Budapest and New York: Central European University Press, 2008), 59–73; Heike Karge, 'Practices and Politics of Second World War Remembrance: (Trans-) National Perspectives from Eastern and South-Eastern Europe', *A European Memory?*, ed. Pakier and Stråth, 137–46.

21 Catherine Merridale, *Night of Stone: Death and Memory in Twentieth Century Russia* (London: Granta Books, 2000).

22 Alan L. Nothnagle, *Building the East German Myth: Historical Mythology and Youth Propaganda in the German Democratic Republic, 1945–1989* (Ann Arbor: University of Michigan Press, 1999); Herfried Münkler, *Die Deutschen und ihre Mythen* (Berlin: Rowohlt, 2009); Mary Fulbrook, *German National Identity after the Holocaust* (Cambridge: Polity Press, 1999).

23 George Mosse, *Fallen Soldiers: Reshaping the Memory of the World Wars* (Oxford: Oxford University Press, 1990); Stéphane Audoin-Rouzeau and Annette Becker, *14–18: Understanding the Great War* (New York: Hill and Wang, 2002 [2000]); John Horne and Alan Kramer, *German Atrocities, 1914: A History of Denial* (New Haven: Yale University Press, 2002).

24 Maria Bucur, *Heroes and Victims: Remembering War in Twentieth-Century Romania* (Bloomington: Indiana University Press, 2009).

25 Rousso, *The Latest Catastrophe*.

26 Nina Tumarkin, *The Living and the Dead* (New York: Basic Books, 1994).

Conclusion

Martin Conway and Pieter Lagrou

This book is based on a number of choices, many of which can be challenged. Most obviously, it is based on the assumption that the shape of the history of Europe in the twentieth century can be approached through a comparative history of the three postwar moments of 1989, 1945 and 1918. To talk about these postwar periods is to assert also, and inevitably, the centrality of wars, and more particularly in this book the experience of three wars: the First and Second World Wars and the Cold War. As many of the contributors are at pains to show, these were not the only wars that Europe experienced during the twentieth century, nor were they necessarily the most important ones, especially at the level of individual national experiences. It was not the First World War but the subsequent war of Irish independence that was central to Ireland's early twentieth-century experience; just as it was the Russian Civil War, rather than the First World War, which shaped much of Poland and Finland's subsequent development. But, while making allowance for these forms of national difference, this book argues that the three major conflicts on which we concentrate were European experiences, and that they provided a defining framework for the shape of the century.

The concept of postwar moments is a rather flexible one, and one which is addressed with different emphases in the chapters by different contributors. The central starting point for the way in which we write about these postwar moments is that, more than the conflicts themselves, in the postwar periods, the consequences of war became clear and choices were made, which in turn led to new relations of power. How one might delimit such a postwar moment is a matter for debate. It might be regarded as a specific transitional period that followed the end of a conflict – 1918–19 for example – but in this book we have adopted a more capacious formula which sees postwar moments as distinctive periods stretching over a number of years, when new structures of power and of organization became apparent.

How long those postwar moments lasted depends not only on the nature of the wars, but also on the angle from which one approaches the subject. In this volume, there are four chapters which address the immediate consequences of war. The chapter Demobilizations addresses the pressing challenges of the transition from a wartime to a peacetime society, the consequence of the unprecedented mobilizations generated by warfare during the twentieth century. In this regard, we argue that 1989 does indeed qualify as a postwar moment, as demonstrated by the sheer size of manpower and resources demobilized at the end of the Cold War. In a similar way, the chapter Borders deals with what, for most Europeans, was the most immediately felt consequence of war. After the First World War, millions of Europeans found themselves to be living in new states as a consequence of changed or invented borders. That often took the form of the imposition of borders from above, but borders were also remade by people themselves, who either rejected state authority and migrated or were ejected. Those new authorities, as well as many pre-existing ones, had to address the question of the choices made during wartime. As the Justice chapter demonstrates, the issue of war crimes, and of collaboration, was most obviously visible after the Second World War, when the establishment of a regime of justice (including international courts of justice, imposed notably on a defeated Germany) formed part of the urgent legacies of war, but similar challenges had also arisen after 1918 and would do so again after 1989. Finally, the defeat of former regimes raised the question of planning for the future. As the chapter Futures argues, it was during these postwar moments that rulers, and also populations, set about adopting forms of planning intended to fix the future trajectory of their societies. They used the window of opportunity provided by postwar settlements to implement modernizing visions that had often been stalled in more normal times.

These four chapters are therefore focused on relatively short time periods, even if their consequences and their full implementation (especially in the case of judicial processes) would take much longer. Other chapters adopt a more medium-term chronology. One of the central themes of the chapter States is that there was a certain inertia between the sudden ruptures produced by war and the more gradual changes in the practices and ambitions of state authority. States struggled to catch up with how societies had changed. Conversely, state structures often outlived the processes which had led to their existence. Thus, Habsburg forms of rule survived into mid-twentieth-century Europe, and communist regimes lived on after the parties and movements that had brought them into existence in Central and Eastern Europe after 1945 had lost much of their energy and credibility. The chapter Democracy, too, looks beyond the immediate events of war to explore how rulers and ruled set about (not always collaboratively) creating particular models of democracy during the eras which followed war, stretching the concept of postwar into a more medium-term framework of political adaptation.

Finally, there are three chapters in this volume that threaten to escape from any conventional definition of postwar periods. In the chapter Empires, European postwars often become instead the start of new wars – in North Africa on the symbolic date of 8 May 1945 or in Central Africa after 1989 – which defy a Eurocentric chronology. But, as we have been conscious throughout this project, not all aspects of European history of the twentieth century can be constrained within the framework of specific postwar moments. Thus, the chapters Markets and Pasts show how long-lasting the consequences of war might be: at once influenced by previous experiences, but also stretching forward over an almost indeterminate period. In the case of Pasts, for example, every new conflict durably transformed the way in which previous conflicts were regarded. However, in the case of all three of these chapters, the focus on postwar moments has the benefit of demonstrating how, even in these domains, the postwar was often a decisive period when expectations and opportunities changed substantially. For example, the end of the Cold War raised short-lived hopes of a democratic revolution in many areas of Africa, while within Europe, it provided the possibility for the eastward expansion of market-led policies of liberalization. So, even here, the postwar emphatically mattered.

The second assumption on which this book is based is that to examine these postwar moments in reverse order provides an effective, and at times disconcerting, methodology. Thus, the chapters take 1989 as their starting point, and then work their way backwards across the previous two postwar moments. This approach is conceived as an experiment, and not one which we would advocate as a generally valid methodology for the history of Europe in the twentieth century, and still less for the history of other places and periods. However, in this specific case, the merit of this collective choice has been to make 1989 the starting point of our reflection, and not simply the contemporary terminus of the railway line of twentieth-century European history. The regressive approach is intended in this way to prevent the narrative history of the twentieth century from becoming too fixed in its chain of causes and consequences. We hope therefore that the book will help historians to think afresh about the shape of the twentieth century, using 1989 as a creative means of analysing the previous postwar periods.

One of the reasons we adopted this methodology was also to counter what we feel to be too great a divide between an overly familiar twentieth century and an unknown present. The year 1989 was, in many respects, the last moment when, however unexpected the events themselves proved to be, the patterns of European history appeared to be following a preordained course of regime collapse and liberation. The problem with this approach was that 1989 became defined by previous history. It is most often seen as a moment of closure – the mere end of the twentieth century, if not of history *tout court* – and not as a postwar moment, a defining moment of settlement of things to come. By defining 1989 largely in terms of what it came after, historians fail to contribute to the understanding of the much-changed shape of Europe in the twenty-first century. Instead, it can all too easily encourage historians to explain the events of the present in terms of the return of a past. The limits of such an approach are well demonstrated by the attempts to explain the electoral success of the populist right in the early twenty-first century as a return to the fascism of the interwar years and by the preoccupation with centenaries which encourages comparisons between the events in 2018–19 and those which occurred 100 years earlier. In contrast, we hope that by problematizing the three postwar moments, we have been able to emphasize the contingent and open-ended nature of the history of Europe in the twentieth century, and afterwards. In this way, we wish to emancipate the present from the past, but also the past from the present, each deserving to be understood in its own terms and not just in terms of superficial analogies.

Unless addressed explicitly as a subject in its own right, 1989 will continue to linger under the shadow of its more illustrious predecessors, 1945 and 1918. Inserting 1989 in the 1945–18 sequence forces us to re-evaluate the sheer scale of change that has taken place since 1989 and of the challenge presented by the need to invent once again a postwar settlement adapted to the circumstances of the time. But the regressive methodology also, we believe, allows historians to appreciate more fully what was distinctive about the postwar moments of 1945 and 1918. Each was not the prequel or the sequel of the others. Viewed regressively, they reveal their alterity, and become autonomous but comparable moments of transition, deprived of their sometimes too self-evident nature. If that makes European history appear less predictable, we see that too as an advantage.

One of the unexpected consequences of writing the history of twentieth-century Europe through the prism of these postwar moments has been the way in which it has brought certain regions and issues to the fore while marginalizing others. Thus, the reader of this volume will often encounter the history of Germany, or more precisely of German lands, as well as the impact of the Soviet Union and Russia on European history. We are conscious that there is much less in this volume on post-Ottoman and Balkan history, as well as more surprisingly on the history of France and Britain. These imbalances are in part the consequence of our choice of certain postwar moments. If we had taken the Treaty of Lausanne in 1923 and the consequent reshaping of the south-eastern borders of Europe as one of our case studies, then the history of that region would have come more to the fore. The relative marginalization of the influence of France and Britain is, however, more difficult to explain. This may in part be the consequence of the fact that these states had, with the important exceptions of Alsace-Lorraine and Ireland, achieved their nationhood and territorial definition prior to the twentieth century. Therefore, much that changed in the history of both states was related more to external forces, and more especially to the rise and decline of their imperial power. Even so, it does also highlight the extent to which the three postwar moments were processes that had their centre of gravity in Central and Eastern Europe. France and Britain had been prime movers in these three wars, but the impacts of the postwar settlements were felt most substantially by other states.

As the cases of France and Britain demonstrate, the European focus of this book also risks prioritizing forces internal to Europe at the expense of those which might be more external or indeed global. The most obvious such factor is that of decolonization from the 1950s to the 1970s. This could very well be regarded as a fourth postwar moment, dividing in two the otherwise disproportionately long second European postwar period from 1945 to 1989. As the chapter Empires demonstrates, the process of decolonization had consequences for many of the themes analysed in this volume: borders and state authorities changed; imperial regimes had to demobilize; democratic revolutions took place both in the former colonies and in the metropole, such as in Portugal; and the imperial experience left a bitter legacy of judicial issues to be resolved. In the same way, the influence exerted by the United States over the European continent is not always sufficiently visible in this volume. The impact of 'the American century' on Europe was considerable, and never more so than at the times following the two world wars and the Cold War, when key decisions were often made as much in America as in Europe. However, as the chapter on markets well illustrates, this American influence was not limited to certain moments of transition. Throughout the twentieth century, the shadow effect of the United States on Europe, and especially on its structures of economic and social organization, was pervasive.

In these ways, the conception of the book, and more especially the decision to focus on the three postwar moments, has led the authors to prioritize certain themes at the expense of others. Indeed, it would be easy to imagine a list of other themes that would fully deserve to be included. This applies particularly to a number of fields of social and cultural history, most notably changes in gender relations and the emergence of social-welfare structures. Both of these processes were intimately related to postwar moments. In the case of gender, it was during the first two postwar periods that the majority of women were enfranchised, while, for social welfare, the second postwar period was decisive in East as well as in West for the creation of new frameworks of welfare provision. However, the incremental nature of these changes makes it impossible to limit them to particular postwar moments. As always, the answers are defined in large part by the questions one poses, and our intention in this volume has been to focus on three moments rather than on more medium-term processes of change. In a similar spirit, some of the most profound transformations which occurred in European societies during the twentieth century, such as secularization and the large-scale rural exodus, were ones that happened largely independent of the impact of wars and their consequences and are therefore absent from this volume.

The third, and final, assumption that underpins this book is perhaps the most obvious one. It is that, in common with many other collective history projects conceived since 1989, it seeks to tear down the Iron Curtain in mental representations of Europe's twentieth-century past. The Cold War division of Europe was a tangible reality for only four decades of the twentieth century, from 1948 to 1989, and even then served to disguise substantial commonalities between the two halves of Europe. However, too often this divide between East and West is applied anachronistically to preceding and subsequent decades. There was nothing inherent in the first postwar settlement that implied a division between East and West, just as the post-1989 settlement has too often been regarded as exclusively or primarily limited to Eastern Europe.

This is therefore a volume that is emphatically about the East as well as the West, and which seeks to accord them equivalence in the making of Europe's twentieth century. In that respect, we hope that we have succeeded, but here again there are obvious, and less obvious, dangers. There is of course no essential or core history of Europe in the twentieth century, and any attempt to emphasize the European over the regional, the national and the local risks prioritizing certain forces over others. The writing of European history of the twentieth century has often contained its own unstated forms of imperialism. Especially after 1945, there was a tendency for European history to be written from the West and by Westerners. The consequence after 1989 was to subordinate the history of Central and Eastern Europe to Western-led narratives, or indeed to impose Western norms on the work of East European historians. However, in recent years, the writing of European history has also come from the East and has challenged these Westernizing and at times patronizing narratives. In particular, this historical work has demonstrated the profound and brutalizing impact of Soviet occupation and methods of rule in Central and Eastern Europe which cannot be dismissed as a by-product of the victory over Nazism.

In sum, there is a need for the writing of European history to avoid all forms of triumphalism, including the claim that Europe has ever possessed a history. Soviet rule in Central-Eastern Europe after 1945 and the parallel way in which the history of Western Europe after 1945 was profoundly marked by both American influence and the continuing engagement of many European states in colonial rule outside of Europe demonstrate the inevitable truth that Europe was less sovereign in the twentieth century than it often claimed to be. Its history cannot therefore be studied in isolation from these external forces. Indeed, in so far as there was a common European experience of the twentieth century, it lay not in victory and triumph, but in defeat, division, death and displacement.

The necessary modesty which such perspectives impose demonstrates the need to avoid the lure of Eurocentric narratives, be they explicit or implicit. In this respect, the focus on three postwar periods, studied regressively rather than progressively, does, we believe, offer a correction to assumptions of a forward momentum of the history of Europe in the twentieth century. In particular, it enables historians to juxtapose different moments without seeking to transform them into a linear narrative. Too often the history of twentieth-century Europe is presented as a learning curve, whereby the lessons learned from the errors of the two first postwar settlements were then used to create a unified European structure after 1989. This is not entirely misleading. Europeans at all levels of society sought to learn from previous postwar moments, but they rarely did so with any lasting success. Instead, each of these postwar moments was dominated by internal and external constraints which defined their outcomes. This also explains our reluctance in this volume to adopt the language of a 'refounding' of Europe in each postwar settlement. A teleological narrative by which Jacques Delors completed the task began by Robert Schuman in 1950 and by Aristide Briand in the 1920s neglects the contingencies and discontinuities inherent to each postwar moment. Above all, the history of Europe's twentieth century cannot be reduced to a genealogy of the European Union (EU) that emerged in its final decade. The EU was not preordained by prior history, but the consequence of a particular constellation of primarily political, diplomatic and economic factors.

This recognition of the discontinuous and less-than-sovereign character of the history of Europe in the twentieth century stands as the principal lesson of our twenty-first century present. Whether we are indeed living, in Ivan Krastev's influential formula 'after Europe', will no doubt remain a lively subject of debate.[1] But, as a means of capturing both the diminished sense of Europe's autonomy and the contingent nature of all attempts to provide Europe with a political definition, it serves as a clear lesson for those who would wish to study its twentieth-century past.

Note

1   Ivan Krastev, *After Europe* (Philadelphia: University of Pennsylvania Press, 2017).

Bibliography

Abrams, Bradley F. *The Struggle for the Soul of the Nation: Czech Culture and the Rise of Communism*. Lanham, Boulder, Toronto, New York and Oxford: Rowman and Littlefield, 2004.

Adas, Michael. *Machines as the Measure of Men: Science, Technology, and Ideologies of Western Dominance*. Ithaca: Cornell University Press, 1989.

Adelman, Howard, and Elazar Barkan. *No Return, No Refuge: Rites and Rights in Minority Repatriation*. New York: Columbia University Press, 2011.

Adler, Max. *Neue Menschen: Gedanken über sozialistische Erziehung*. Berlin: E. Laub, 1924.

Agamben, Giorgio. 'What Is the Contemporary?' In *What Is an Apparatus? and Other Essays*, edited by Giorgio Agamben, 39–53. Stanford: Stanford University Press, 2009.

Akçam, Taner, and Vahakn N. Dadrian. *Judgment at Istanbul: The Armenian Genocide Trials*. Oxford and New York: Berghahn, 2011.

Albinsson, Pia A., Marco Wolf and Dennis A. Kopf. 'Anti-consumption in East Germany: Consumer resistance to hyperconsumption', *Journal of Consumer Behaviour*, 9 (2010): 412–425.

Alexievitch, Svetlana. *La Fin de l'homme rouge*. Arles: Actes Sud, 2013.

Anderson, Malcolm. *Frontiers: Territory and State Formation in the Modern World*. Cambridge: Polity Press, 2004.

Andersson, Jenny. 'The Great Future Debate and the Struggle for the World', *American Historical Review*, 117 (2012): 1411–1430.

Applebaum, Anne. *Iron Curtain: The Crushing of Eastern Europe, 1944–1956*. New York: Doubleday, 2012.

Aron, Raymond. *La révolution introuvable: réflexions sur la révolution de mai*. Paris: Fayard, 1968.

Assmann, Jan. *Das kulturelle Gedächtnis: Schrift, Erinnerung und politische Identität in frühen Hochkulturen*. Munich: C. H. Beck, 1992.

Audoin-Rouzeau, Stéphane, and Annette Becker. *14–18: Understanding the Great War*. New York: Hill and Wang, 2002.

Audoin-Rouzeau, Stéphane, and Christophe Prochasson. ed., *Sortir de la Grande Guerre: le monde et l'après 1918*. Paris: Tallandier, 2008.

Azouvi, François. *Le Mythe du grand silence. Auschwitz, les Français, la mémoire*. Paris: Fayard, 2012.

Bachmann, Klaus. 'The Polish Paradox: Transition from and to Democracy'. In *Transitional Justice and Memory in Europe (1945–2013)*, edited by Nico Wouters, 327–350. Antwerp and Cambridge: Intersentia, 2014.

Baron, Nick, and Peter Gatrell. *Homelands: War, Population and Statehood in Eastern Europe and Russia, 1918–1924*. London: Anthem Press, 2004.

Bartolomew, John. *The Times Atlas of the World*. London: The Riverside Press Cambridge, 1959.

Baruch, Marc-Olivier. *Des lois indignes? Les historiens, la politique et le droit*. Paris: Tallandier, 2013.

Bauman, Zygmunt. *Liquid Modernity*. Cambridge: Polity Press, 2000.

Behan, Tom. *The Long-Awaited Moment. The Working Class and the Italian Communist Party in Milan, 1943–1948*. New York: Peter Lang, 1997.

Beissinger, Mark R. *Nationalist Mobilization and the Collapse of the Soviet State*. Cambridge: Cambridge University Press, 2002.

Bell, Wendell. *Foundations of Futures Studies: Human Science for a New Era*. New Brunswick, NJ: Transaction Publishers, 1997.

Benot, Yves. *Massacres coloniaux: 1944–1950: la IVe République et la mise au pas des colonies françaises*. Paris: La Découverte, 2013.

Berend, Ivan T. *Decades of Crisis: Central and Eastern Europe before World War II*. Berkeley: University of California Press, 1998.

Blanchet, Dider, and Olivia Ekert-Jaffe. 'The Demographic Impact of Fertility Benefits: Evidence from a Micro-Model and from Macro-Data'. In *The Family, the Market and the State in Ageing Societies*, edited by John Ermisch and Naohiro Ogawa, 79–104. Oxford: Clarendon Press, 1994.

Bloxham, Donald. *Genocide on Trial: War Crimes Trials and the Formation of Holocaust History and Memory*. Oxford: Oxford University Press, 2003.

Boehling, Rebecca. *A Question of Priorities. Democratic Reform and Recovery in Postwar Germany*. New York and Oxford: Berghahn, 1996.

Bonzon, Thierry. 'Consumption and Total Warfare in Paris, 1914–18'. In *Food and Conflict in Europe in the Age of the Two World Wars*, edited by Frank Trentmann and Just Flemming, 49–64. Houndmills: Palgrave Macmillan, 2006.

Borgwardt, Elizabeth. *A New Deal for the World: America's Vision for Human Rights*. Cambridge Mass: Belknap Press of Harvard University Press, 2005.

Bradley, Mark Philip. 'Decolonization, the Global South, and the Cold War, 1919–1962'. In *The Cambridge History of the Cold War*, vol. 1, edited by Melvyn P. Leffler and Odd Arne Westad, 464–485. Cambridge: Cambridge University Press, 2010.

Branche, Raphaëlle. *La Guerre d'Algérie: une histoire apaisée?* Paris: Editions du Seuil, 2014.

Brandt, Willy. *My Life in Politics*. Harmondsworth: Penguin, 1993.

Bratton, Michael, and Nicholas van de Walle. *Democratic Experiments in Africa: Regime Transitions in Comparative Perspective*. Cambridge and New York: Cambridge University Press, 1997.

Brier, Robert. 'From Civil Society to Neoliberalism and Armed Intervention? Human Rights and the Legacies of "1989"', *Remembrance and Solidarity Studies*, no. 3 (June 2014): 157–188.

Broadberry, Stephen N., and Mark Harrison. *The Economics of World War I*. Cambridge: Cambridge University Press, 2005.

Brocheux, Pierre. *Ho Chi Minh: A Biography*. Cambridge: Cambridge University Press, 2007.

Brogi, Alessandro. *Confronting America. The Cold War between the United States and the Communists in France and Italy*. Chapel Hill: University of North Carolina Press, 2011.

Brubaker, Rogers. 'Nationhood and the National Question in the Soviet Union and Post-Soviet Eurasia: An Institutionalist Account', *Theory and Society*, 23 (1994): 47–78.

Brubaker, Rogers. 'Aftermaths of Empire and the Unmixing of Peoples: Historical and Comparative Perspectives', *Ethnic and Racial Studies*, 18 (1995): 189–218.

Brubaker, Rogers, and David D. Laitin. 'Ethnic and Nationalist Violence', *Annual Review of Sociology*, 24 (1998): 423–452.

Bruchez, Anne. 'La fin de la présence française en Syrie: de la crise de mai 1945 au départ des dernières troupes étrangères', *Relations Internationales*, 122 (2005): 17–32.

Buchanan, Tom. 'Anti-fascism and Democracy in the 1930s', *European History Quarterly*, 32 (2002): 39–57.

Bucur, Maria. *Heroes and Victims: Remembering War in Twentieth-Century Romania.* Bloomington: Indiana University Press, 2009.

Cabanes, Bruno, and Guillaume Piketty. 'Sortir de la guerre: jalons pour une histoire en chantier', *Histoire@Politique*, no. 3 (2007): 1–8.

Capuzzo, Paolo. ' "Good bye Lenin". La nostalgia del comunismo nella Germania riunificata', *Studi Culturali*, 1 (2004): 151–165.

Carsten, Francis L. *Revolution in Central Europe, 1918–1919.* London: Maurice Temple Smith, 1972.

Cassese, Antonio. *Self-Determination of Peoples: A Legal Reappraisal.* Cambridge: Cambridge University Press, 1995.

Cattaruzza, Marina. ' "Last Stop Expulsion" – the Minority Question and Forced Migration in East-Central Europe: 1918–49', *Nations and Nationalism*, 16 (2010): 108–126.

Chernev, Borislav. 'The Brest-Litovsk Moment: Self-Determination Discourse in Eastern Europe before Wilsonianism', *Diplomacy and Statecraft*, 22 (2011): 369–387.

Clark, Geoffrey, Gregory Anderson, Christian Thomann and J.-Matthias Graf von der Schulenburg. ed., *The Appeal of Insurance.* Toronto: University of Toronto Press, 2010.

Clarke, Jackie. *France in the Age of Organization: Factory, Home and Nation from the 1920s to Vichy.* New York and Oxford: Berghahn, 2011.

Clavin, Patricia. *Securing the World Economy: The Reinvention of the League of Nations, 1920–1946.* Oxford: Oxford University Press, 2013.

Collingwood, Robin G. *The Idea of History.* Oxford: Clarendon Press, 1946.

Commercial Atlas of America. Chicago: Randy McNally and Co., 1924.

Conan, Eric, and Henry Rousso. *Vichy, an Ever-Present Past.* Hanover: University Press of New England, 1998.

Condé, Pierre-Yves. 'Causes de la justice internationale, causes judiciaires internationales', *Actes de la recherche en sciences sociales*, 174 (2008): 24–33.

Connelly, Matthew, Matt Fay, Guilia Ferrini, Micki Kaufman, Will Leonard, Harrison Monsky, Ryan Musto, Taunton Paine, Nicholas Standish and Lydia Walker. ' "General, I Have Fought Just as Many Nuclear Wars as You Have": Forecasts, Future Scenarios, and the Politics of Armageddon', *American Historical Review*, 117 (2012): 1431–1460.

Conway, Martin. 'The Age of Christian Democracy. The Frontiers of Success and Failure'. In *European Christian Democracy: Historical Legacies and Comparative Perspectives*, edited by Tom Kselman and Joseph Buttigieg, 43–67. Notre Dame: Notre Dame University Press, 2003.

Conway, Martin. 'The Rise and Fall of Western Europe's Democratic Age, 1945–1973'. *Contemporary European History,* 13 (2004): 67–88.

Conway, Martin. *The Sorrows of Belgium: Liberation and Political Reconstruction, 1944–1947.* Oxford: Oxford University Press, 2012.

Conway, Martin, and Robert Gerwarth. 'Revolution and Counter-Revolution'. In *Political Violence in Twentieth-Century Europe*, edited by Donald Bloxham and Robert Gerwarth, 140–175. Cambridge: Cambridge University Press, 2011.

Cooper, Frederick. *Citizenship between Empire and Nation: Remaking France and French Africa, 1945–1960.* Princeton, NJ: Princeton University Press, 2014.

Corner, Paul. *Fascism in Ferrara, 1915–1925.* London: Oxford University Press, 1975.

Courtois, Stéphane. ed., *The Black Book of Communism: Crimes, Terror, Repression*.
      Cambridge, MA, and London: Harvard University Press, 1999.
'The Covenant of the League of Nations', available on The Avalon Project website of the
      Yale law school library (http://avalon.law.yale.edu/20th_century/leagcov.asp), last
      accessed 4 June 2018.
Craiutu, Aurelian. 'Raymond Aron and the Tradition of Political Moderation in France'.
      In *French Liberalism from Montesquieu to the Present Day*, edited by Raf Geenens and
      Helena Rosenblatt, 271–290. Cambridge: Cambridge University Press, 2012.
Crampton, Richard J. *Eastern Europe in the Twentieth Century*. London: Routledge, 1994.
Crouch, Colin. *Post-Democracy*. Cambridge: Polity, 2004.
Dahrendorf, Ralf. *Reflections on the Revolution in Europe*. Piscataway, NJ: Transaction,
      1990; new ed., 2004.
Davis, Belinda J. *Home Fires Burning: Food, Politics, and Everyday Life in World War
      I Berlin*. Chapel Hill and London: The University of North Carolina Press, 2000.
De Grazia, Victoria. *Irresistible Empire: America's Advance through Twentieth-Century
      Europe*. Cambridge, MA, and London: Belknap Press of Harvard University Press,
      2005.
De Haan, Ido. 'Paths of Normalization after the Persecution of the Jews: The Netherlands,
      France and West Germany in the 1950s'. In *Life after Death: Approaches to a Cultural
      and Social History of Europe during the 1940s and 1950s*, edited by Richard Bessel and
      Dirk Schumann, 65–92. Cambridge: Cambridge University Press, 2003.
de Zayas, Alfred-Maurice. *A Terrible Revenge: The Ethnic Cleansing of East European
      Germans*. London: Palgrave Macmillan, 2006.
Deák, István. 'Introduction'. In *The Politics of Retribution in Europe*, edited by István Deák,
      Jan T. Gross and Tony Judt, 3–14. Princeton, NJ: Princeton University Press, 2000.
Deák, István, Jan T. Gross and Tony Judt. ed., *The Politics of Retribution in Europe*.
      Princeton, NJ: Princeton University Press, 2000.
Dębski, Sławomir. *Między Berlinem a Moskwą: Stosunki niemiecko-sowieckie 1939–1941*.
      Warszawa: PISM, 2007.
DeLong, J. Bradford and Barry Eichengreen. 'The Marshall Plan: History's Most Successful
      Structural Adjustment Program'. In *Postwar Economic Reconstruction and Lessons for
      the East Today*, edited by Rudiger Dornbusch, Wilhelm Nölling and Richard Layard,
      189–229. Cambridge, MA: MIT Press, 1993.
Diner, Hasia. *We Remember with Reverence and Love. American Jews and the Myth of
      Silence after the Holocaust, 1945–1962*. New York: New York University Press, 2009.
Doering-Manteuffel, Anselm. 'Ordnung jenseits der politischen Systeme: Planung im 20.
      Jahrhundert. Ein Kommentar', *Geschichte und Gesellschaft*, 34 (2008): 398–406.
Douglas, Lawrence. *The Memory of Judgment: Making Law and History in the Trials of the
      Holocaust*. New Haven and London: Yale University Press, 2001.
Doumanis, Nicholas. 'Europe and the Wider World'. In *Twisted Paths: Europe 1915–1945*,
      edited by Robert Gerwath, 355–380. Oxford: Oxford University Press, 2007.
Duby, Georges. *Grand Atlas Historique*. Paris: Larousse, 1997.
Duchen, Claire, and Irene Bandhauer-Schöffmann. 'Introduction'. In *When the War Was
      Over: Women, War and Peace in Europe, 1940–1956*, edited by Claire Duchen and
      Irene Bandhauer-Schöffmann, 1–9. London and New York: Leicester University Press,
      2000.
Dullin, Sabine. 'L'invention d'une frontière de guerre froide à l'ouest de l'URSS (1945–
      1949)', *Vingtième siècle. Revue d'histoire*, no. 102 (2009): 49–63.

Durant, Sam. ed., *Black Panther: The Revolutionary Art of Emory Douglas*. New York: Rizzoli, 2007.

Eghigian, Greg. *Making Security Social: Disability, Insurance, and the Birth of the Social Entitlement State in Germany*. Ann Arbor: University of Michigan Press, 2000.

Eichengreen, Barry, and Marc Uzan. 'The Marshall Plan: Economic Effects and Implications for Eastern Europe and the Former USSR', *Economic Policy*, no. 14 (1992): 13–75.

Eichmüller, Andreas. 'Die Strafverfolgung von NS-Verbrechen durch westdeutsche Justizbehörden seit 1945. Eine Zahlenbilanz', *Vierteljahrshefte für Zeitgeschichte*, no. 56 (2008): 621–640.

Eisner, Marc Allen. *From Warfare State to Welfare State. World War I, Compensatory State Building and the Limits of the Modern Order*. University Park: Pennsylvania State University Press, 2000.

Eley, Geoff. *Forging Democracy: The History of the Left in Europe, 1850–2000*. New York and Oxford: Oxford University Press, 2002.

Elisa, Achille. ed., *Aristide Briand. Discours et écrits de politique étrangère*. Paris: Plon, 1965.

Ellwood, David. *Rebuilding Europe; Western Europe, America and Postwar Reconstruction*. Harlow: Longman, 1992.

Ellwood, David. *The Shock of America: Europe and the Challenge of the Century*. Oxford: Oxford University Press, 2012.

Engerman, David C. 'Introduction: Histories of the Future and the Futures of History', *American Historical Review*, 117 (2012): 1402–1410.

Erichsen, Casper W., and David Olusoga. *The Kaiser's Holocaust: Germany's Forgotten Genocide and the Colonial Roots of Nazism*. London: Faber, 2011.

Fejtö, François. *Histoire de la destruction de l'Autriche-Hongrie: requiem pour un empire défunt*. Paris: EDIMA/Lieu Commun, 1993.

Findlay, Ronald, and Kevin H. O'Rourke. *Power and Plenty: Trade, War, and the World Economy in the Second Millennium*. Princeton, NJ, and Woodstock: Princeton University Press, 2007.

Fink, Carole. *Defending the Rights of Others: The Great Powers, the Jews and International Minority Protection 1878–1938*. Cambridge: Cambridge University Press, 2004.

Fitzpatrick, Sheila. *Everyday Stalinism: Ordinary Life in Extraordinary Times. Soviet Russia in the 1930s*. Oxford and New York: Oxford University Press, 2000.

Florian, Dierl, and Alexa Stiller. 'Von Generälen und Partisanen. Die Verbrechen der Wehrmacht in Südosteuropa und der "Geiselmord-Prozess" im Kontext des Kalten Krieges'. In *NMT. Die Nürnberger Militärtribunale zwischen Geschichte, Gerechtigkeit und Rechtschöpfung*, edited by Kim C. Priemel and Alexa Stiller, 230–254. Hamburg: Hamburger Edition, 2013.

Foa, Vittorio. *Il Silenzio dei communisti*. Turin: Einaudi, 2002.

Foner, Eric. *A Short History of Reconstruction, 1863–1877*. New York: Harper and Row, 1990.

Foot, Rosemary. 'The Cold War and Human Rights'. In *The Cambridge History of the Cold War*, vol. 3, edited by Melvyn P. Leffler and Odd Arne Westad, 445–465. Cambridge: Cambridge University Press, 2010.

Frank, Leonhard. *Der Mensch ist Gut*. Zurich: Europäische Bücher, 1918.

Frank, Matthew. 'Fantasies of Ethnic Unmixing: "Population Transfer" at the End of Empire in Europe'. In *Refugees and the End of Empire: Imperial Collapse and Forced*

Migration in the Twentieth Century, edited by Panikos Panayi and Pippa Virdee, 81–101. New York: Palgrave Macmillan, 2011.

Franzki, Hannah, and Carolina Olarte. 'The Political Economy of Transitional Justice. A Critical Theory Perspective', in *Transitional Justice Theories*, edited by Susanne Buckley-Zistel *et al.*, 201–221. London: Routledge, 2013.

Fraser, Nancy. *Justice Interruptus: Critical Reflections on the 'Postsocialist' Condition*. London and New York: Routledge, 1997.

Frei, Norbert. ed., *Transnationale Vergangenheitspolitik: Der Umgang mit deutschen Kriegsverbrechern in Europa nach dem Zweiten Weltkrieg*. Göttingen: Wallstein, 2006.

Frei, Norbert. 'Nach der Tat. Die Ahndung deutscher Kriegs- und NS-Verbrechen in Europa – eine Bilanz'. In *Transnationale Vergangenheitspolitik: Der Umgang mit deutschen Kriegsverbrechern in Europa nach dem Zweiten Weltkrieg*, edited by Norbert Frei, 7–36. Göttingen: Wallstein Verlag, 2006.

Frevert, Ute. *Women in German History: From Bourgeois Emancipation to Sexual Liberation*. Oxford: Berg, 1993.

Fritzsche, Peter. *Rehearsals for Fascism: Populism and Political Mobilization in Weimar Germany*. New York and Oxford: Oxford University Press, 1990.

Fromkin, David. *A Peace to End All Peace: The Fall of the Ottoman Empire and the Creation of the Modern Middle East*. New York: Owl Books, 2001.

Fukuyama, Francis. 'The End of History?', *National Interest*, 16 (Summer 1989): 3–18.

Fukuyama, Francis. *The End of History and the Last Man*. London: Hamish Hamilton, 1992.

Fulbrook, Mary. *German National Identity after the Holocaust*. Cambridge: Polity Press, 1999.

Futter, Andrew. *The Politics of Nuclear Weapons*. London: Sage, 2015.

Gaddis, John Lewis. *The Cold War*. London: Penguin, 2005.

Garapon, Antoine. *Peut-on réparer l'histoire? Colonisation, esclavage, Shoah*. Paris: Odile Jacob, 2008.

Garton Ash, Timothy. *We the People: The Revolution of 89*. London: Granta, 1990; new ed., Penguin, 1999.

Garton Ash, Timothy. 'Trials, Purges and History Lessons: Treating a Difficult Past in Post-Communist Europe'. In *Memory and Power in Post-War Europe. Studies in the Presence of the Past*, edited by Jan-Werner Müller, 265–282. Cambridge: Cambridge University Press, 2002.

Garton Ash, Timothy. '1989!', *New York Review of Books*, 5 November 2009.

Gatrell, Peter. 'Introduction: World Wars and Population Displacement in Europe in the Twentieth Century', *Contemporary European History*, 16 (2007): 415–426.

Gatrell, Peter. 'Trajectories of Population Displacement in the Aftermaths of Two World Wars'. In *The Disentanglement of Populations: Migration, Expulsion and Displacement in Post-War Europe, 1944–49*, edited by Jessica Reinisch and Elizabeth White, 3–26. Basingstoke: Palgrave Macmillan, 2011.

Gatrell, Peter, and Nick Baron. *Warlands: Population Resettlement and State Reconstruction in the Soviet-East European Borderlands, 1945–50*. Basingstoke: Palgrave Macmillan, 2009.

Gatrell, Peter, and Nick Baron. 'Violent Peacetime: Reconceptualizing Displacement and Resettlement in the Soviet-East European Borderlands after the Second World War'. In *Warlands: Population Resettlement and State Reconstruction in the Soviet-East European Borderlands, 1945–50*, edited by Peter Gatrell and Nick Baron, 255–268. Basingstoke: Palgrave Macmillan, 2009.

Gauthier, Anne Hélène. *The State and the Family: A Comparative Analysis of Family Policies in Industrialized Countries*. Oxford: Oxford University Press, 1996.

Gerwarth, Robert. 'The Central European Counter-Revolution: Paramilitary violence in Germany, Austria and Hungary after the Great War', *Past and Present*, no. 200 (2008): 175–209.

Gerwarth, Robert. *The Vanquished. Why the First World War Failed to End*. London: Allen Lane, 2016.

Gerwarth, Robert, and John Horne. ed., *War in Peace: Paramilitary Violence in Europe after the Great War*. Oxford: Oxford University Press, 2012.

Gienow-Hecht, Jessica. 'Culture and the Cold War in Europe'. In *The Cambridge History of the Cold War*, vol. 1, edited by Melvyn P. Leffler and Odd Arne Westad, 398–419. Cambridge: Cambridge University Press, 2010.

Ginsborg, Paul. *Italy and Its Discontents: Family, Civil Society, State, 1980–2001*. London: Allen Lane, 2001.

Glenny, Misha. *The Balkans, 1804–1999: Nationalism, War and the Great Powers*. London: Granta, 1999.

Good bye, Lenin! [film] Dir. Wolfgang Becker, Germany, 2002.

Gordon, Margaret S. *Social Security Policies in Industrial Countries: A Comparative Analysis*. Cambridge: Cambridge University Press, 1988.

Gosewinkel, Dieter. 'Zwischen Diktatur und Demokratie. Wirtschaftliches Planungsdenken in Deutschland und Frankreich: Vom Ersten Weltkrieg bis zur Mitte der 1970er Jahre', *Geschichte und Gesellschaft*, 34 (2008): 327–359.

Graff, Rüdiger. *Öl und Souveränität: Petroknowledge und Energiepolitik in den USA und Westeuropa in den 1970er Jahren*. Berlin: De Gruyter Oldenbourg, 2014.

Graff, Rüdiger, and Kim Christian Priemel. 'Zeitgschichte in der Welt der Sozialwissenschaften. Legitimität und Originalität einer Diziplin', *Vierteljahresheft für Zeitgschichte*, 594 (2011): 479–508.

Grayling, Anthony. *Democracy and Its Crisis*. London: Oneworld, 2017.

Grieves, Keith. *The Politics of Manpower, 1914–18*. Manchester: Manchester University Press, 1990.

Griffin, Roger. 'Tunnel Visions and Mysterious Trees: Modernist Projects of National and Racial Regeneration, 1880–1939'. In *Blood and Homeland: Eugenics and Racial Nationalism in Central and Southeast Europe, 1900–1940*, edited by Marius Turda and Paul J. Weindling, 418–445. Budapest and New York: Central European University Press, 2006.

Gross, Jan. *Neighbors: The Destruction of the Jewish Community in Jedwabne, Poland*. Princeton, NJ, and Oxford: Princeton University Press, 2001.

Grossmann, Atina. *Reforming Sex: The German Movement for Birth Control and Abortion Reform, 1920–1950*. New York: Oxford University Press, 1995.

Guilhot, Nicolas. *The Democracy Makers: Human Rights and International Order*. New York: Columbia University Press 2005.

Gundle, Stephen. 'Visions of Prosperity: Consumerism and Popular Culture in Italy from the 1920s to the 1950s'. In *Three Postwar Eras in Comparison: Western Europe 1918–1945–1989*, edited by Carl Levy and Mark Roseman, 151–172. Basingstoke: Palgrave, 2002.

Gupta, Partha Sarathi, and Anirudh Deshpande. ed., *The British Raj and Its Indian Armed Forces, 1857–1939*. New Delhi and Oxford: Oxford University Press, 2002.

Habermas, Jürgen. *The Lure of Technocracy*. Cambridge and Malden: Polity, 2015.

Hall, John E. ed., *States in History*. Oxford: Blackwell, 1987.

Halmai, Gábor, and Kim Lane Scheppelle. 'Living Well is the Best Revenge: The Hungarian Approach to Judging the Past'. In *Transitional Justice and the Rule of Law in New Democracies*, edited by James A. McAdams, 155–184. Notre Dame: University of Notre Dame Press, 1997.

Hammerstein, Katrin, et al. ed., *Aufarbeitung der Diktatur – Diktat der Aufarbeitung? Normierungsprozesse beim Umgang mit diktatorischer Vergangenheit.* Göttingen: Wallstein, 2009.

Hankel, Gerd. *Die Leipziger Prozesse: Deutsche Kriegsverbrechen und ihre strafrechtliche Verfolgung nach dem Ersten Weltkrieg.* Hamburg: Hamburger Edition, 2003.

Hannum, Hurst. *Autonomy, Sovereignty, and Self-Determination: The Accommodation of Conflicting Rights.* Philadelphia: University of Pennsylvania Press, 1996.

Harkavy, Robert E. *Bases Abroad: The Global Foreign Military Presence.* Oxford and Stockholm: Oxford University Press, 1989.

Harris, Stephen. *Communism on Tomorrow Street: Mass Housing and Everyday Life after Stalin.* Baltimore: Johns Hopkins Press, 2013.

Hartog, François. *Régimes d'historicité: Présentisme et expériences du temps.* Paris: Éditions du Seuil, 2003.

Hasegawa, Tsuyoshi. *Racing the Enemy: Stalin, Truman and the Surrender of Japan.* Cambridge, MA: Harvard University Press, 2005.

Hatzfeld, Jean. *Dans le nu de la vie.* Paris: Seuil, 2005.

Heathcote, T.A. *British Admirals of the Fleet: 1734–1995.* London: Pen and Sword, 2002.

Hecht, Jacqueline and Henri Leridon. 'Fertility Policies: A Limited Influence?' In *The Changing Population of Europe*, edited by Daniel Noin and Robert Woods, 62–75. Cambridge, MA, and Oxford: Blackwell, 1993.

Heilbroner, Robert. *Visions of the Future: the Distant Past, Yesterday, Today, Tomorrow.* New York: New York Public Library, 1995.

HenkeKlaus-Dietmar, and Hans Woller. ed., *Politische Säuberung in Europa: die Abrechnung mit Faschismus und Kollaboration nach dem Zweiten Weltkrieg.* Munich: DTV, 1991.

Herbert, Ulrich. *Geschichte Deutschlands im 20. Jahrhundert.* Munich: C. H. Beck, 2014.

Herf, Jeffrey. *War by Other Means: Soviet Power, West German Resistance and the Battle of the Euromissiles.* New York: Free Press, 1991.

Herf, Jeffrey. *Divided Memory: The Nazi Past in the Two Germanys.* Cambridge, MA: Harvard University Press, 1997.

Hewitson, Mark. 'Inventing Europe and Reinventing the Nation-State in a New World Order'. In *Europe in Crisis. Intellectuals and the European Idea, 1917–1957*, edited by Mark Hewitson and Matthew D'Auria, 63–81. New York and Oxford: Berghahn, 2012.

Himmelfarb, Gertrude. *The Demoralization of Society: From Victorian Virtues to Modern Values.* New York: Knopf, 1995.

Hirsch, Francine. *Empire of Nations: Ethnographic Knowledge and the Making of the Soviet Union.* Ithaca: Cornell University Press, 2005.

Hobsbawm, Eric. *Nations and Nationalism since 1780: Programme, Myth, Reality.* Cambridge and New York: Cambridge University Press, 1990.

Hobsbawm, Eric. *Age of Extremes: The Short Twentieth Century 1914–1991.* London: Michael Joseph, 1994.

Hobsbawm, Eric. 'Marx and Labour: The Long Century'. In Eric Hobsbawm, *How to Change the World: Marx and Marxism 1840–2011*, 411–419. London: Little Brown, 2011.

Hogan, Michael J. *The Marshall Plan. America, Britain and the Reconstruction of Western Europe, 1947–1952.* Cambridge: Cambridge University Press, 1987.

Holden, Ken, David A. Peel and John L. Thompson. *Economic Forecasting: An Introduction.* Cambridge: Cambridge University Press, 1990.

Hölscher, Lucian. *Die Entdeckung der Zukunft.* Frankfurt a/M: Fischer Taschenbuch Verlag, 1999.

Horáček, Milan. 'Die Aufarbeitung der kommunistischen Diktatur in Tschechien – Eintrittskarte in die "europäische Wertegemeinschaft"?' In *Aufarbeitung der Diktatur – Diktat der Aufarbeitung? Normierungsprozesse beim Umgang mit diktatorischer Vergangenheit,* edited by Katrin Hammerstein *et al.,* 215–222. Göttingen: Wallstein, 2009.

Horn, Gerd-Rainer. *The Spirit of '68: Rebellion in Western Europe and North America, 1956–1976.* Oxford and New York: Oxford University Press, 2007.

Horne, John. 'Locarno et la politique de la démobilisation culturelle, 1925–30', *14–18 Aujourd'hui-Heute-Today* (Paris), 5 (2002): 73–87.

Horne, John. 'Kulturelle Demobilmachung 1919–1939. Ein sinnvoller historischer Begriff?' In *Politische Kulturgeschichte der Zwischenkriegszeit, 1918–1939,* edited by Wolfgang Hardtwig, 129–150. Göttingen: Vandenhoeck & Ruprecht, 2005.

Horne, John. 'Demobilizing the Mind: France and the Legacy of the Great War, 1919–1939', *French History and Civilization,* 2 (2009): 101–119.

Horne, John. 'Guerres et réconciliations européennes au 20e siècle'. In *Les 27 leçons d'histoire,* edited by Jean-Noël Jeanneney, 137–145. Paris: Le Seuil, 2009. Also published in *Vingtième siècle. Revue d'histoire,* no. 104 (2009): 3–15.

Horne, John, and Alan Kramer. *German Atrocities, 1914: A History of Denial.* New Haven: Yale University Press, 2002.

House, Jim, and Neil MacMaster. *Paris 1961: Algerians, State Terror and Memory.* Oxford: Oxford University Press, 2006.

Hull, Isabel V. *A Scrap of Paper: Making and Breaking International Law during the Great War.* Ithaca: Cornell University Press, 2014.

Human Security Centre. *Human Security Report 2005.* Oxford: Oxford University Press, 2006.

Irwin-Zarecka, Iwona. *Frames of Remembrance: The Dynamics of Collective Memory.* New Brunswick and London: Transaction Publishers, 1994.

Isaac, Jeffrey C. '1989 and the Future of Democracy'. In *Between Past and Future. The Revolutions of 1989 and Their Aftermath,* edited by Sorin Antohi and Vladimir Tismaneanu, 39–60. Budapest and New York: Central European University Press, 2000.

Israël, Liora, and Guillaume Mouralis. 'Introduction'. In *Dealing with Wars and Dictatorships. Legal Categories and Concepts in Action,* edited by Liora Israël and Guillaume Mouralis, 1–20. The Hague: Asser Press and Springer, 2014.

Jacoby, Russell. *The End of Utopia: Politics and Culture in an Age of Apathy.* New York: Basic Books, 1999.

Jarausch, Konrad. *After Hitler: Re-civilizing the Germans, 1945–1995.* New York: Oxford University Press, 2006.

Jarausch, Konrad. *Out of Ashes: A New History of Europe in the Twentieth Century.* Princeton, NJ: Princeton University Press, 2015.

Jaspers, Karl. *Vom Ursprung und Sinn der Geschichte.* Munich: R. Piper, 1949.

Jean, Jean-Paul, and Denis Salas. ed., *Barbie, Touvier, Papon …: des procès pour la mémoire.* Paris: Autrement, 2002.

Johnson, Douglas. 'France's German Question, 1918–1945–1989'. In *Three Postwar Eras in Comparison: Western Europe 1918–1945–1989*, edited by Carl Levy and Mark Roseman, 237–256. Basingstoke: Palgrave, 2002.

Jones, Mark. *Founding Weimar. Violence and the German Revolution of 1918–1919*. Cambridge: Cambridge University Press, 2016.

Judah, Tim. *The Serbs: History, Myth and the Destruction of Yugoslavia*. New Haven and London: Yale University Press, 1997.

Judt, Tony. 'The Past Is Another Country: Myth and Memory in Postwar Europe', *Daedalus*, 121 (1992): 83–97.

Judt, Tony. 'The Past Is Another Country: Myth and Memory in Postwar Europe'. In *The Politics of Retribution in Europe*, edited by István Deák, Jan T. Gross and Tony Judt, 293–323. Princeton, NJ: Princeton University Press, 2000.

Judt, Tony. *Postwar: A History of Europe since 1945*. London: William Heinemann, 2005.

Judt, Tony (with Timothy Snyder). *Thinking the Twentieth Century*. London: William Heinemann, 2012.

Jünger, Ernst. *Der Kampf als inneres Erlebniss*. Berlin: E. S. Mittler & Sohn, 1922.

Kallis, Aristotle A. 'Racial Politics and Biomedical Totalitarianism in Interwar Europe'. In *Blood and Homeland: Eugenics and Racial Nationalism in Central and Southeast Europe, 1900–1940*, edited by Marius Turda and Paul J. Weindling, 389–415. Budapest and New York: Central European University Press, 2006.

Kalyvas, Stathis. *The Logic of Violence in Civil War*. Cambridge and New York: Cambridge University Press, 2006.

Kamaras, Ferenc, Jirina Kocourkova and Hein Moors. 'The Impact of Social Policies on Reproductive Behaviour'. In *Population, Family and Welfare: A Comparative Survey of European Attitudes*, vol. 2, edited by Rossella Palomba and Hein Moors, 242–261. Oxford: Clarendon Press, 1998.

Kanya-Forstner, Alexander Sydney. 'The War, Imperialism, and Decolonization'. In *The Great War and the Twentieth Century*, edited by Jay Winter and Geoffrey Parker, 231–262. New Haven and London: Yale University Press, 2000.

Karge, Heike. 'Practices and Politics of Second World War Remembrance: (Trans-) National Perspectives from Eastern and South-Eastern Europe'. In *A European Memory? Contested Histories and Politics of Remembrance*, edited by Małgorzata Pakier and Bo Stråth, 137–146. New York and Oxford: Berghahn, 2010.

Kaufmann, Chaim D. 'When All Else Fails: Ethnic Population Transfers and Partitions in the Twentieth Century', *International Security*, 23 (1998): 120–156.

Kenéz, Péter. *A History of the Soviet Union from the Beginning to the End*. Cambridge: Cambridge University Press, 2006.

Kennedy, Paul, and William Hitchcock. ed., *From War to Peace: Altered Strategic Landscapes in the Twentieth Century*. New Haven and London: Yale University Press, 2000.

Kenney, Padraic. *A Carnival of Revolution – Central Europe 1989*. Princeton, NJ: Princeton University Press, 2002.

Kepel, Gilles *Jihad: The Trail of Political Islam*. London: I. B. Tauris, revised edition 2006.

Keynes, John Maynard. *The Economic Consequences of the Peace*. New York: Harcourt Brace, 1920.

King, Alexander, and Bertrand Schneider. *The First Global Revolution: A Report by the Council of the Club of Rome*. New York: Pantheon Books, 1991.

Kopecek, Milan. 'Human Rights Facing a National Past. Dissident "Civic Patriotism" and the Return of History in East Central Europe, 1968–1989', *Geschichte und Gesellschaft*, 38 (2012): 573–602.

Koreman, Megan. *The Expectation of Justice: France, 1944–1946*. Durham and London: Duke University Press, 1999.

Kornai, János. *Economics of Shortage*. Amsterdam and New York: North-Holland Pub. Co, 1980.

Kornai, János. 'The Great Transformation of Central Eastern Europe Success and Disappointment', *Economics of Transition*, 14 (2006): 207–244.

Korobkov, Andrei V., and Zhanna Zaionchkovskaia. 'The Changes in the Migration Patterns in the Post-Soviet States: The First Decade', *Communist and Post-Communist Studies*, 37 (2004): 481–508.

Koselleck, Reinhart. *Futures Past: On the Semantics of Historical Time*. Cambridge, MA: MIT Press, 1985.

Koselleck, Reinhart. *The Practice of Conceptual History: Timing History, Spacing Concepts*. Stanford: Stanford University Press, 2002.

Koskenniemi, Martti. *The Gentle Civilizer of Nations: The Rise and Fall of International Law, 1870–1960*. Cambridge and New York: Cambridge University Press, 2002.

Kott, Sandrine. 'Une "communauté épistémique" du social? Experts de l'OIT et internationalisation des politiques sociales dans l'entre-deux-guerres', *Genèses*, no. 71 (2008): 26–48.

Kowalczuk, Ilko-Sascha, and Stefan Wolle. *Roter Stern über Deutschland: Sowjetische Truppen in der DDR*. Berlin: Links, 2001.

Kramer, Alan. *The West German Economy, 1945–1955*. Oxford: Berg, 1990.

Kramer, Alan. 'The First Wave of International War Crimes Trials: Istanbul and Leipzig', *European Review*, 14 (2006): 441–455.

Kramer, Alan. 'Combatants and Noncombatants: Atrocities, Massacres, and War Crimes'. In *A Companion to World War I*, edited by John Horne, 188–201. Chichester: Wiley-Blackwell, 2010.

Krastev, Ivan. *After Europe*. Philadelphia: Pennsylvania University Press, 2017.

Kreitner, Roy. *Calculating Promises: The Emergence of Modern American Contract Doctrine*. Stanford: Stanford University Press, 2007.

Krogulski, Mariusz Lesław. *Okupacja w imię sojuszu. Armia Radziecka w Polsce, 1956–1993*. Warsaw: von Borowiecky, 2001.

Kuhlman, Erika. *Of Little Comfort: War Widows, Fallen Soldiers, and the Remaking of the Nation after the Great War*. New York: New York University Press, 2012.

Kuisel, Richard. *Capitalism and the State in Modern France*. Cambridge: Cambridge University Press, 1981.

Kuisel, Richard. *Seducing the French: The Dilemma of Americanization*. Berkeley: University of California Press, 1993.

Kulischer, Eugene M. *Europe on the Move: War and Population Changes, 1917–47*. New York: Columbia University Press, 1948.

Kurth, James, and James Petras. *Mediterranean Paradoxes. Politics and Social Structures in Southern Europe*. Oxford: Berg, 1993.

Kurunmäki, Jussi, and Johan Strang. ed., *Rhetorics of Nordic Democracy*. Helsinki: Finnish Literature Society, 2010.

Lagrou, Pieter. *The Legacy of Nazi Occupation: Patriotic Memory and National Recovery in Western Europe, 1945–1965*. Cambridge: Cambridge University Press, 2000.

Lagrou, Pieter. 'Between Europe and the Nation: The Inward Turn of Contemporay Historical Writing'. In *Conflicted Memories: Europeanizing Contemporary Histories*, edited by Konrad Jarausch and Thomas Lindenberger, 69–80. New York and Oxford: Berghahn, 2007.

Lagrou, Pieter. '1945–1955: The Age of Total War'. In *Histories of the Aftermath*, edited by Frank Biess and Robert Moeller, 287–296. New York and Oxford: Berghahn, 2010.

Lagrou, Pieter. 'De l'histoire du temps présent à l'histoire des autres: Comment une discipline critique devint complaisante', *Vingtième Siècle. Revue d'histoire*, no. 118 (2013): 101–119.

Lagrou, Pieter. 'Poor Little Belgium? Belgian Trials of German War Criminals, 1944–1951'. In *Dealing with Wars and Dictatorships: Political and Legal Categories in Action*, edited by Liora Israël and Guillaume Mouralis, 123–143. The Hague: Asser Press and Springer, 2014.

Lampe, John R. *Yugoslavia as History: Twice There Was a Country*. Cambridge: Cambridge University Press, 1996.

Landes, David. *The Unbound Prometheus: Technological Change and Industrial Development in Western Europe from 1750 to the Present*. New York: Cambridge University Press, 1969.

Lauren, Paul G. *The Evolution of International Human Rights: Visions Seen*. Philadelphia: University of Pennsylvania Press, 2011.

Lauwerys, Joseph A. ed., *Scandinavian Democracy: Development of Democratic Thought and Institutions in Denmark, Norway and Sweden*. Copenhagen: Danske selskab, 1958.

Lazar, Marc. *Le Communisme: une passion française*. Paris: Perrin, 2002; new ed., 2005.

Le Cour Grandmaison, Olivier. *Coloniser, Exterminer: Sur La Guerre et l'État Colonial*. Paris: Fayard, 2005.

Lebow, Richard Ned, Wulf Kansteiner and Claudio Fogu. ed., *The Politics of Memory in Postwar Europe*. Durham and London: Duke University Press, 2006.

Lee, Carol. *Talking Tough: The Fight for Masculinity*. London: Arrow Books, 1993.

Leffler, Melvyn P., and Odd Arne Westad. ed., *The Cambridge History of the Cold War*. Cambridge: Cambridge University Press, 2010, 3 vols.

Lefranc, Sandrine. 'La professionnalisation d'un militantisme réformateur du droit. L'invention de la justice transitionnelle', *Droit et société*, 73 (2009): 561–589.

Lengwiler, Martin. 'The Rise of Mixed Welfare Economies in Europe, 1850–1945'. In *The Appeal of Insurance*, edited by Geoffrey Clark, Gregory Anderson, Christian Thomann and J.-Matthias Graf von der Schulenburg, 173–200. Toronto: University of Toronto Press, 2010.

Lepenies, Wolfgang. *The Seduction of Culture in German History*. Princeton: Princeton University Press, 2006.

Levene, Mark. 'The Tragedy of Rimlands, Nation-State Formation and the Destruction of Imperial Peoples, 1912–1948'. In *Refugees and the End of Empire: Imperial Collapse and Forced Migration in the Twentieth Century*, edited by Panikos Panayi and Pippa Virdee, 51–80. New York: Palgrave Macmillan, 2011.

Levy, Carl. '1918–1945–1989: The Making and Unmaking of Stable Societies in Western Europe'. In *Three Postwar Eras in Comparison: Western Europe 1918–1945–1989*, edited by Carl Levy and Mark Roseman, 1–38. Basingstoke: Palgrave, 2002.

Levy, Carl, and Mark Roseman. ed., *Three Postwar Eras in Comparison: Western Europe 1918–1945–1989*. Basingstoke: Palgrave, 2002.

Levy, Daniel, and Natan Sznaider. *Holocaust and Memory in the Global Age*. Philadelphia: Temple University Press, 2006.

Lewis, Mark. *The Birth of the New Justice: The Internationalization of Crime and Punishment*. Oxford: Oxford University Press, 2014.

Lewis, Mary Dewhurst. *Divided Rule: Sovereignty and Empire in French Tunisia, 1881–1938*. Berkeley: University of California Press, 2014.

Lewis, Paul G. *Political Parties in Post-Communist Eastern Europe*. London: Routledge, 2001.

Lindqvist, Sven, and Linda Haverty Rugg. 'Bombing the Savages', *Transition*, no. 87 (2001): 48–64.

Loose, Ingo. 'The Anti-Fascist Myth of the German Democratic Republic and Its Decline after 1989'. In *Past in the Making: Historical Revisionism in Central Europe after 1989*, edited by Michal Kopeček, 59–73. Budapest and New York: Central European University Press, 2008.

Louis, William Roger. *Great Britain and Germany's Lost Colonies, 1914–1919*. Oxford, Clarendon Press, 1967.

Löwith, Karl. *The Meaning of History*. Chicago: University of Chicago Press, 1949.

Lumley, Robert. '1968/1989: Social Movements in Italy Reconsidered'. In *Three Postwar Eras in Comparison: Western Europe 1918–1945–1989*, edited by Carl Levy and Mark Roseman, 199–215. Basingstoke: Palgrave, 2002.

Luyten, Dirk. 'Dealing with Collaboration in Belgium after the Second World War: From Activism to Collaboration and Incivism'. In *Dealing with Wars and Dictatorships: Political and Legal Categories in Action*, edited by Liora Israël and Guillaume Mouralis, 59–76. The Hague: Asser Press and Springer, 2014.

Mack, Andrew. 'Global Political Violence: Explaining the Post-Cold War Decline'. In *Strategies for Peace: Contributions of International Organisations, States, and Non-State Actors*, edited by Volker Rittberger and Martina Fischer, 75–107. Opladen and Farmington Hills: Budrich Verlag, 2008.

Macmillan, Margaret. *Peacemakers: The Paris Conference of 1919 and Its Attempt to End War*. London: John Murray, 2001.

Maier, Charles S. 'The Two Postwar Eras and the Conditions for Stability in Twentieth-century Western Europe', *American Historical Review*, 86 (1981): 327–352.

Maier, Charles S. *Dissolution: The Crisis of Communism and the End of East Germany*. Princeton: Princeton University Press, 1997.

Maier, Charles. 'Empires or Nations? 1918, 1945, 1989…'. In *Three Postwar Eras in Comparison: Western Europe 1918–1945–1989*, edited by Carl Levy and Mark Roseman, 41–66. Basingstoke: Palgrave, 2002.

Mann, Michael. *Fascists*. Cambridge and New York: Cambridge University Press, 2004.

Manuel, Frank E., and Fritzie P. Manuel. ed., *Utopian Thought in the Western World*. Cambridge, MA: Belknap Press of Harvard University Press, 1979.

Mark, James. *The Unfinished Revolution: Making Sense of the Communist Past in Central-Eastern Europe*. New Haven: Yale University Press, 2010.

Markovits, Inga. 'Selective Memory: How Law affects What We Remember and Forget about the Past: The Case of East Germany', *Law and Society Review*, 35 (2001): 513–563.

Marrus, Michael. *The Unwanted: European Refugees in the Twentieth Century*. New York: Oxford University Press, 1985.

Marrus, Michael R. *The Nuremberg War Crimes Trials 1945–46: A Documentary History*. Boston and New York: Bedford, 1997.

Martin, Terry. *The Affirmative Action Empire: Nations and Nationalism in the Soviet Union, 1923–1939*. Ithaca: Cornell University Press, 2001.

Marx, Karl. *Zur Kritik des sozialdemokratischen Programms von Gotha;* der 'Gothaer Programmbrief', edited and foreword by Karl Kreibich. Reichenberg: Volksbuchhandlung Runge, 1920.

Mazower, Mark. *Dark Continent: Europe's Twentieth Century.* London: Allen Lane, 1998.

Mazower, Mark. 'Violence and the State in the Twentieth Century', *The American Historical Review,* 107 (2002): 1158–1178.

Mazower, Mark. 'The Strange Triumph of Human Rights, 1933–1950', *The Historical Journal,* 47 (2004): 379–398.

Mazower, Mark. 'Reconstruction: The Historiographical Issues', *Past and Present,* 210, no. 6 (2011): 17–28.

Mazower, Mark, Jessica Reinisch and David Feldman. ed., *Post-War Reconstruction in Europe: International Perspectives, 1945–1949.* Oxford: Oxford University Press, 2011.

McCauley, Martin. *The Origins of the Cold War: 1941–1949.* London: Pearson Education, 2008.

McDougall, James. 'No, This Isn't the 1930s – But Yes, This Is Fascism', *The Conversation* 16 November 2016. Available online: http://theconversation.com/no-this-isnt-the-1930s-but-yes-this-is-fascism-68867

McMahon, Robert J. ed., *The Cold War in the Third World.* Oxford: Oxford University Press, 2013.

Meadows, Donella H., Denis L. Meadows and Jørgen Randers. *Beyond the Limits: Confronting Global Collapse, Envisioning a Sustainable Future.* Post Mills, VT: Chelsea Green Publishers, 1992.

Melber, Henning. 'How to Come to Terms with the Past: Re-Visiting the German Colonial Genocide in Namibia', *Africa Spectrum,* 40 (2005): 139–148.

Merl, Stephan. 'Staat und Konsum in der Zentralverwaltungswirtschaft. Rußland und die ostmitteleuropäischen Länder'. In *Europäische Konsumgeschichte, Zur Gesellschafts- und Kulturgeschichte des Konsums (18.-20. Jahrhundert),* edited by Hannes Siegrist, Hartmut Kaelble and Jürgen Kocka, 205–241. Frankfurt-am-Main and New York: Campus Verlag, 1997.

Merridale, Catherine. *Night of Stone: Death and Memory in Twentieth Century Russia.* London: Granta Books, 2000.

Middleton, David, and Derek Edwards. ed., *Collective Remembering.* London, Thousand Oaks and New Delhi: Sage, 1990.

Middleton, Stuart. '"Affluence" and the Left in Britain, c. 1958–1974', *The English Historical Review,* 129 (2014): 107–138.

Milder, Stephen. *Greening Democracy: The Anti-Nuclear Movement and Political Democracy in West Germany and Beyond, 1968–1983.* Cambridge: Cambridge University Press, 2017.

Millan, Matteo. 'The Institutionalisaton of *Squadrismo*: Disciplining Paramilitary Violence in the Italian Fascist Dictatorship', *Contemporary European History,* 22 (2013): 551–573.

Millward, Robert. *Private and Public Enterprise in Europe: Energy, Telecommunications and Transport, 1830–1990.* Cambridge: Cambridge University Press, 2005.

Milward, Alan S. *War, Economy and Society, 1939–1945.* Berkeley: University of California Press, 1977.

Milward, Alan. *The Reconstruction of Western Europe, 1945–51.* London: Routledge, 1984.

Milward, Alan (with Federico Romero and George Brennan). *The European Rescue of the Nation-State.* London: Routledge, 1992.

Mink, Georges, and Laure Neumayer. ed., *History, Memory and Politics in Central and Eastern Europe: Memory Games*. Basingstoke: Palgrave Macmillan, 2013.

Mirowski, Philip, and Dieter Plehwe. ed., *The Road from Mont Pèlerin: The Making of the Neoliberal Thought Collective*. Cambridge, MA, and London: Harvard University Press, 2009.

Mitchell, Maria. *The Origins of Christian Democracy: Politics and Confession in Modern Germany*. Ann Arbor: University of Michigan Press, 2012.

Moeller, Robert. *Protecting Motherhood: Women and the Family in the Politics of Postwar West Germany*. Berkeley, Los Angeles and London: University of California Press, 1993.

Moeller, Robert. 'The Bombing War in Germany, *2005–1940*: Back to the Future?' In *Bombing Civilians: A Twentieth Century History*, edited by Yuki Tanaka and Marilyn B. Young, 46–76. New York: The New Press, 2009.

Moll, Peter. *From Scarcity to Sustainability – Future Studies and the Environment: The Role of the Club of Rome*. Frankfurt – Bern: Peter Lang, 1991.

Moll, Peter. 'The Discreet Charm of the Club of Rome', *Futures*, 25 (1993): 801–805.

Moore, David Chioni. 'Is the Post- in Postcolonial the Post- in Post-Soviet? Toward a Global Postcolonial Critique', *Publications of the Modern Language Association of America*, 116 (2001): 111–128.

Moran, Daniel, and Arthur Waldron. ed., *The People in Arms: Military Myth and National Mobilization since the French Revolution*. Cambridge: Cambridge University Press, 2003.

Morawska, Ewa. 'Intended and Unintended Consequences of Forced Migrations: A Neglected Aspect of East Europe's Twentieth Century History', *International Migration Review*, 34 (2000): 1049–1087.

Mosse, George. *Fallen Soldiers: Reshaping the Memory of the World Wars*. Oxford: Oxford University Press, 1990.

Mosse, George L. *The Image of Man: The Creation of Modern Masculinity*. New York, Oxford: Oxford University Press, 1996.

Mouralis, Guillaume. *Une épuration allemande. La RDA en procès. 1949–2004*. Paris: Fayard, 2008.

Mouralis, Guillaume. 'Lawyers versus Jurisconsults. Sociography of the Main Nuremberg Trial'. In *Justice in Wartime and Revolutions. Europe, 1795–1950*, edited by Margo de Koster *et al.*, 325–336. Brussels: Archives Générales du Royaume, 2012.

Mouralis, Guillaume. 'The Invention of "Transitional Justice" in the 1990s'. In *Dealing with Wars and Dictatorships. Political and Legal Categories in Action*, edited by Liora Israël and Guillaume Mouralis, 83–100. The Hague: Asser Press and Springer, 2014.

Moyn, Samuel. *The Last Utopia: Human Rights in History*. Cambridge, MA: Belknap Press of Harvard University Press, 2010.

Moyn, Samuel. 'A Powerless Companion: Human Rights in the Age of Neoliberalism', *Law and Contemporary Problems*, 77 (2014): 147–169.

Müller, Dietmar. 'Strategien des öffentlichen Erinners in 'Rumänien nach 1989: Postkommunisten und postkommunistische Antikommunisten'. In *Zwischen Amnesie und Nostalgie: Die Erinnerung an den Kommunismus in Südosteuropa*, edited by Ulf Brunnbauer and Stefan Troebst, 47–69. Cologne, Weimar and Vienna: Böhlau, 2007.

Müller, Jan-Werner. 'What Did They Think They Were Doing? The Political Thought of (the West European) 1968 Revisited'. In *Promises of 1968: Crisis, Illusion and Utopia*, edited by Vladimir Tismaneanu, 73–102. Budapest and New York: Central European University Press, 2011.

Müller, Jan-Werner. *Contesting Democracy: Political Ideas in Twentieth-Century Europe.* New Haven and London: Yale University Press, 2011.

Müller, Jan-Werner. *What Is Populism?* Philadelphia: University of Pennsylvania Press, 2016.

Münkler, Herfried. *Die Deutschen und ihre Mythen.* Berlin: Rowohlt, 2009.

Naimark, Norman. *Fires of Hatred: Ethnic Cleansing in Twentieth Century Europe.* Cambridge, MA: Harvard University Press, 2001.

Neumann, Iver B. *Russia and the Idea of Europe: A Study in Identity and International Relations.* London: Routledge, 1996.

Nicholls, Anthony J. *Freedom with Responsibility. The Social Market Economy in Germany 1918–1963.* Oxford: Oxford University Press, 1994.

Nicolson, Harold. *Peacemaking 1919.* London: Constable, 1933; new edition, 1943.

Niethammer, Lutz. *Die Mitläuferfabrik. Die Entnazifizierung am Beispiel Bayerns.* Berlin: Dietz, 1982.

Nolan, Mary. 'Human Rights and Market Fundamentalism in the Long 1970s'. In *Toward a New Moral World Order? Menschenrechtspolitik und Völkerrecht seit 1945*, edited by Norbert Frei and Annette Weinke, 172–181. Göttingen: Wallstein Verlag, 2013.

Nora, Pierre. 'Between Memory and History: *Les Lieux de Mémoire*', *Representations*, 26 (1989): 7–25.

Nord, Philip. *France's New Deal: From the Thirties to the Postwar Era.* Princeton: Princeton University Press, 2010.

Noskova, Albina F. 'Zwycięstwo i zniewolenie'. In *Białe plamy – czarne plamy: Sprawy trudne w polsko-rosyjskich stosunkach, 1918–2008*, edited by Adam Daniel Rotfeld and Anatolij Vasil'evič Torkunov, 439–480. Warsaw: PISM, 2010.

Nothnagle, Alan L. *Building the East German Myth: Historical Mythology and Youth Propaganda in the German Democratic Republic, 1945–1989.* Ann Arbor: University of Michigan Press, 1999.

Offer, Avner. *The First World War: An Agrarian Interpretation.* Oxford: Clarendon Press, 1989.

Okey, Robin. *The Demise of Communist East Europe: 1989 in Context.* London: Arnold, 2004.

Orla-Bukowska, Annamaria. 'New Threads on an Old Loom: National Memory and Social Identity in Postwar and Post-Communist Poland'. In *The Politics of Memory in Postwar Europe*, edited by Richard Ned Lebow, Wulf Kansteiner and Claudio Fogu, 178–196. Durham and London: Duke University Press, 2006.

Osiel, Mark. *Mass Atrocity, Collective Memory, and the Law.* New Brunswick, NJ: Transaction Publishers, 1997.

Paige, Arthur. 'How "Transitions" Reshaped Human Rights: A Conceptual History of Transitional Justice', *Human Rights Quarterly*, 31 (2009): 321–367.

Panayi, Panikos. 'Imperial Collapse and the Creation of Refugees in Twentieth-Century Europe'. In *Refugees and the End of Empire: Imperial Collapse and Forced Migration in the Twentieth Century*, edited by Panikos Panayi and Pippa Virdee, 3–27. Houndmills and New York: Palgrave Macmillan, 2011.

Passmore, Kevin. *From Liberalism to Fascism: The Right in a French Province, 1928–1939.* Cambridge: Cambridge University Press, 1997.

Patel, Kiran. *The New Deal: A Global History.* Princeton and Oxford: Princeton University Press, 2017.

Pauer, Jan. 'Die Aufarbeitung der Diktaturen in Tschechien und der Slowakei', *Aus Politik und Zeitgeschichte*, 56, no. 42 (2006): 5–32.

Pavone, Claudio. *A Civil War: A History of the Italian Resistance*. London and New York: Verso, 2013.

Paxton, Robert. *French Peasant Fascism: Henri Dorgères' Greenshirts and the Crises of French Agriculture, 1929–1939*. New York and Oxford: Oxford University Press, 1997.

Pedersen, Susan. *Family, Dependence, and the Origins of the Welfare State: Britain and France, 1914–1945*. Cambridge: Cambridge University Press, 1993.

Pellet, Alain. 'The Opinions of the Badinter Arbitration Committee: A Second Breath for the Self-Determination of Peoples', *European Journal of International Law*, 3 (1992): 178–185.

Peyroulou, Jean-Pierre. *Guelma, 1945: Une subversion française dans l'Algérie coloniale*. Paris: La Découverte, 2009.

Poiger, Uta G. *Jazz, Rock, and Rebels: Cold War Politics and American Culture in a Divided Germany*. Berkeley: University of California Press, 2000.

Pombeni, Paolo. 'La legittimazione del benessere: nuovi parametri di legittimazione in Europa dopo la seconda guerra mondiale'. In *Crisi, legittimazione e consenso*, edited by Paolo Pombeni, 357–417. Bologna: Il Mulino, 2003.

Pons, Silvio. *The Global Revolution: A History of International Communism, 1917–1991*. Oxford: Oxford University Press, 2014.

Porter, Theodore M. *Trust in Numbers: The Pursuit of Objectivity in Science and Public Life*. Princeton: Princeton University Press, 1996.

Priban, Jiri. 'Reconstituting Paradise Lost: Temporality, Civility, and Ethnicity in Post-Communist Constitution-Making', *Law and Society Review*, 38 (2004): 407–432.

Priban, Jiri. 'Political Dissent, Human Rights, and Legal Transformations: Communist and Post-Communist Experiences', *East European Politics and Societies*, 19 (2005): 553–572.

Priban, Jiri. 'Oppressors and Their Victims: The Czech Lustration Law and the Rule of Law'. In *Justice as Prevention: Vetting Public Employees in Transitional Societies*, edited by Alexander Mayer-Rieckh and Pablo de Greiff, 308–346. New York: Social Science Research Council, 2007.

Priemel, Kim C., and Alexa Stiller. ed., *Reassessing the Nuremberg Military Tribunals: Transitional Justice, Trial Narratives, and Historiography*. New York and Oxford: Berghahn Books, 2012.

Priemel, Kim C. *The Betrayal: The Nuremberg Trials and German Divergence*. Oxford and New York: Oxford University Press, 2016.

Prunier, Gérard. *Africa's World War: Congo, the Rwandan Genocide, and the Making of a Continental Catastrophe*. Oxford: Oxford University Press, 2009.

Prusin, Alexander V. *Nationalizing a Borderland: War, Ethnicity, and Anti-Jewish Violence in East Galicia, 1914–1920*. Tuscaloosa: University of Alabama Press, 2005.

Prusin, Alexander V. *The Lands Between: Conflict in the East European Borderlands, 1870–1992*. Oxford: Oxford University Press, 2010.

Putzger, Friedrich Wilhelm. *Historicher Weltatlas*. Berlin: Cornelsen, 1995.

Ratner, Steven R. 'Drawing a Better Line: Uti Possidetis and the Borders of New States', *The American Journal of International Law*, 90 (1996): 590–624.

Rees, Arfon. 'Managing the History of the Past in the Former Communist States'. In *A European Memory? Contested Histories and Politics of Remembrance*, edited by Małgorzata Pakier and Bo Stråth, 219–232. New York and Oxford: Berghahn, 2010.

Reid, Susan. 'The Khrushchev Kitchen: Domesticating the Scientific-Technological Revolution', *Journal of Contemporary History*, 40 (2005): 289–316.

Reinecke, Christiane. 'Localising the Social: The Rediscovery of Urban Poverty in Western European "Affluent" Societies', *Contemporary European History*, 24 (2015): 555–576.

Reinisch, Jessica, and Elizabeth White. ed., *The Disentanglement of Populations: Migration, Expulsion and Displacement in Post-War Europe, 1944–49*. London: Palgrave Macmillan, 2011.

Reyntjens, Filip. *The Great African War: Congo and Regional Geopolitics, 1996–2006*. Cambridge: Cambridge University Press, 2009.

Rich, Roland. 'Recognition of States: The Collapse of Yugoslavia and the Soviet Union'. *European Journal of International Law*, 4 (1993): 36–65.

Richards, Michael. *After the Civil War: Making Memory and Re-making Spain since 1936*. Cambridge: Cambridge University Press, 2013.

Rieber, Alfred J. *The Struggle for the Eurasian Borderlands*. Cambridge: Cambridge University Press, 2014.

Riḥanī, Amīn, *Mulūk al-ʿArab: au riḥlah fī al-bilād al-ʿArabīyah muzayyanah bi-al-kharāʾiṭ wa-al-rusūm*. Beirut: al-Maṭbaʿah al-ʿIlmīyah, 1925.

Roberts, Mary Louise. *Civilization without Sexes: Reconstructing Gender in Postwar France, 1917–1927*. Chicago: University of Chicago Press, 1994.

Romsics, Ignác. 'Regime Change in Hungary', *Remembrance and Solidarity Studies*, no. 3 (June 2014): 111–140.

Roseman, Mark. 'Defeat and Stability: 1918, 1945, and 1989 in Germany'. In *Three Postwar Eras in Comparison: Western Europe 1918–1945–1989*, edited by Carl Levy and Mark Roseman, 257–275. Basingstoke: Palgrave, 2002.

Roshwald, Aviel. *Ethnic Nationalism and the Fall of Empires: Central Europe, Russia, and the Middle East, 1914–1923*. London and New York: Routledge, 2001.

Rothschild, Joseph. *Return to Diversity: A Political History of East Central Europe since World War II*. New York: Oxford University Press, 1989.

Rousso, Henry. *The Vichy Syndrome: History and Memory in France since 1944*. Cambridge, MA, and London: Harvard University Press, 1991.

Rousso, Henry. *Vichy, l'événement, la mémoire, l'histoire*. Paris: Gallimard, 2001.

Rousso, Henry. *The Latest Catastrophe. History, the Present, the Contemporary*. Chicago: The Chicago University Press, 2016.

Rousso, Henry. *Face au passé: Essais sur la mémoire contemporaine*. Paris: Belin, 2016.

Runciman, David. *The Confidence Trap*. Princeton and Oxford: Princeton University Press, 2013.

Sachse, Carole. 'Rationalizing Family Life – Stabilizing German Society: The "Golden Twenties" and the "Economic Miracle" in Comparison'. In *Three Postwar Eras in Comparison: Western Europe 1918–1945–1989*, edited by Carl Levy and Mark Roseman, 173–195. Basingstoke: Palgrave, 2002.

Sacriste, Guillaume, and Antoine Vauchez. 'Les "bons offices" du droit international: la constitution d'une autorité non politique dans le concert diplomatique des années 1920', *Critique internationale*, 26 (2005): 101–117.

Salomoni, Antonella. *Il pane quotidiano. Ideologia e congiuntura nella Russia sovietica (1917–1921)*. Bologna: Il Mulino, 2001.

Saragat, Giuseppe. *Socialismo democratico e socialismo totalitario: Per l'autonomia del Partito Socialista*. Milan: Critica sociale, 1946.

Sarkisova, Oksana, and Peter Apor. ed., *Past for the Eyes: East European Representations of Communism in Cinema and Museums after 1989*. Budapest and New York: Central European University Press, 2008.

Schivelbusch, Wolfgang. *The Culture of Defeat: On National Trauma, Mourning and Recovery*. London: Granta, 2003.

Schöpflin, George. *Politics in Eastern Europe, 1945–1992*. Oxford: Blackwell, 1993.

Schumann, Dirk. *Political Violence in the Weimar Republic, 1918–1933. Fight for the Streets and Fear of Civil War*. New York and Oxford: Berghahn, 2009.

Schwengler, Walter. *Völkerrecht, Versailler Vertrag und Auslieferungsfrage: Die Strafverfolgung wegen Kriegsverbrechen als Problem des Friedensschlusses 1919/20*. Stuttgart: DVA, 1982.

Segesser, Daniel. *Recht statt Rache oder Rache durch Recht? Die Ahndung von Kriegsverbrechen in der internationalen wissenschaftlichen Debatte 1872–1945*. Paderborn: Schöningh, 2010.

Seidman, Michael. *The Imaginary Revolution: Parisian Students and Workers in 1968*. New York: Berghahn, 2004.

Seixas, Peter. ed., *Theorizing Historical Consciousness*. Toronto: University of Toronto Press, 2004.

Sellars, Kirsten. *The Rise and Rise of Human Rights*. Stroud: Sutton, 2002.

Serlin, David. *Replaceable You: Engineering the Body in Postwar America*. Chicago: University of Chicago Press, 2004.

Seton-Watson, Christopher. 'The Nationalist Challenge to Stability in Eastern and Central Europe: 1918–1945–1989'. In *Three Postwar Eras in Comparison: Western Europe 1918–1945–1989*, edited by Carl Levy and Mark Roseman, 86–96. Basingstoke: Palgrave, 2002.

Shaw, Malcolm N. 'Peoples, Territorialism and Boundaries', *European Journal of International Law*, 8 (1997): 478–507.

Shennan, Andrew. *Rethinking France: Plans for Renewal 1940–1946*. Oxford: Oxford University Press, 1989.

Shepard, Todd. *The Invention of Decolonization: The Algerian War and the Remaking of France*. Ithaca and London: Cornell University Press, 2006.

Simonin, Anne. *Le déshonneur dans la République: une histoire de l'indignité 1791–1958*. Paris: Grasset, 2008.

Sluga, Glenda. *Internationalism in the Age of Nationalism*. Philadelphia: University of Pennsylvania Press, 2013.

Smith, Stephen. *Red Petrograd: Revolution in the Factories, 1917–18*. Cambridge: Cambridge University Press, 1983.

Snyder, Timothy. 'The Causes of Ukrainian-Polish Ethnic Cleansing 1943', *Past and Present*, no. 179 (2003): 197–234.

Snyder, Timothy. *The Reconstruction of Nations: Poland, Ukraine, Lithuania, Belarus*. New Haven and London: Yale University Press, 2004.

Snyder, Timothy. *Bloodlands: Europe between Hitler and Stalin*. New York: Basic Books, 2010.

Soucy, Robert. *French Fascism: The First Wave, 1924–1933*. New Haven and London: Yale University Press, 1986.

Spengler, Oswald. *Der Untergang des Abendlandes*. Vol. 1: *Gestalt und Wirklichkeit*. Vienna: Braumüller, 1918.

Spengler, Oswald. *Der Untergang des Abendlandes*. Vol. 2: *Welthistorische Perspektiven*. Munich: C. H. Beck, 1922.

Srogosz, Tomasz. 'Geneza zasady "Uti Possidetis" w prawie międzynarodowym publicznym: kilka uwag o kształtowaniu granic państwowych w Ameryce Łacińskiej w XIX i XX wieku', *Czasopismo Prawno-Historyczne*, 63 (2011): 329–342.

Staley, David J. 'A History of the Future', *History and Theory*, 41 (2002): 72–89.

Steiner, André. *The Plans That Failed: An Economic History of the GDR*. New York and Oxford: Berghahn, 2010.

Steiner, Zara. *The Lights That Failed: European International History, 1919–1935*. Oxford: Oxford University Press, 2005.

Sternhell, Zeev. *Neither Right nor Left: Fascist Ideology in France*. Berkeley: University of California Press, 1986.

Stola, Dariusz. 'Forced Migrations in Central European History', *International Migration Review*, 26 (1992): 324–341.

Stola, Dariusz. *Kraj bez wyjścia? Migracje z Polski 1949–1989*. Warszawa: IPN, ISP PAN, 2010.

Stone, Norman. 'Germany? Maggie Was Absolutely Right', *The Sunday Times*, 23 September 1996, republished at https://www.margaretthatcher.org/document/111048.

Streeck, Wolfgang. *Buying Time. The Delayed Crisis of Democratic Capitalism*. London: Verso, 2014.

Süss, Winfried. 'A "New Social Question"? Politics, Social Sciences and the Rediscovery of Poverty in Post-Boom Western Germany'. In *Poverty and Welfare in Modern German History*, edited by Lutz Raphael, 197–224. New York: Berghahn, 2016.

Tambor, Molly. ' "An Essential Way of Life": Women's Citizenship and the Renewal of Politics in Italy'. In *After Fascism: European Case-Studies in Politics, Society and Identity since 1945*, edited by Matthew Berg and Maria Mesner, 205–219. Vienna and Berlin: Lit, 2009.

Taubes, Jacob. *Abendländische Eschatologie*. Berne: A. Francke Verlag, 1947.

Taylor, Peter J. 'The State as Container: Territoriality in the Modern World-System', *Progress in Human Geography*, 18 (1994): 151–162.

Teitel, Ruti G. *Humanity's Law*. Oxford and New York: Oxford University Press, 2011.

Telo, Mario. *Le new deal européen: la pensée et la politique sociales-democrates face à la crise des années trente*. Brussels: Editions de l'Université Libre de Bruxelles, 1988.

Ther, Philipp. '1989 – eine verhandelte Revolution', *Docupedia-Zeitgeschichte*, 11 February 2010. Available online: http://docupedia.de/zg/1989?oldid=108803

Ther, Philipp. *Die dunkle seite der Nationalstaaten: 'Ethnische Säuberungen' im modernen Europa*. Göttingen: Vandenhoeck and Ruprecht, 2011.

Therborn, Göran. *European Modernity and Beyond: The Trajectory of European Societies 1945–2000*. London: Sage, 1995.

Tishkov, Valery, Zhanna Zayinchkovskaya and Galina Vitkovskaya. *Migration in the Countries of the Former Soviet Union*. Geneva: Global Commission on International Migration, 2005.

Tismaneanu, Vladimir, and Bogdan Jacob. *The End and the Beginning: The Revolutions of 1989 and the Resurgence of History*. Budapest and New York: Central European University Press, 2012.

Todorov, Tzvetan. *A French Tragedy: Scenes of Civil War, Summer 1944*. Hanover: University Press of New England, 1996.

Todorova, Maria. *Imagining the Balkans*. New York and Oxford: Oxford University Press, 1997.

Tomka, Béla. *A Social History of Twentieth-Century Europe*. London and New York: Routledge, 2013.

Tompkins, Andrew. *Better Active than Radioactive: Antinuclear Protest in France and West Germany*. Oxford: Oxford University Press, 2016.

Toynbee, Arnold J., and Veronica M. B. Toynbee. ed., *Hitler's Europe* (London: Oxford University Press, 1954.

Trachtenberg, Marc. *A Constructed Peace: The Making of the European Settlement, 1945–1963*. Princeton: Princeton University Press, 1999.

Traverso, Enzo. *Fire and Blood: The European Civil War, 1914–1945*. London: Verso, 2016.

Trbovich, Ana S. *A Legal Geography of Yugoslavia's Disintegration*. Oxford: Oxford University Press, 2009.

Trentmann, Frank. 'Consumption and Citizenship in Twentieth-Century Britain'. In *The Politics of Consumption. Material Culture and Citizenship in Europe and America*, edited by Martin Daunton and Matthew Hilton, 129–163. Oxford and New York: Berg, 2001.

Trentmann, Frank. *Free Trade. Commerce, Consumption, and Civil Society in Modern Britain*. Oxford: Oxford University Press, 2009.

Troebst, Stefan. 'The Discourse on Forced Migration and European Culture of Remembrance', *Hungarian Historical Review*, no. 3–4 (2012): 397–414.

Trotsky, Leon. *Problems of Life*. London: Methuen & Co., 1924.

Tumarkin, Nina. *The Living and the Dead*. New York: Basic Books, 1994.

Turda, Marius, and Paul J. Weindling. 'Eugenics, Race and Nation in Central and Southeast Europe, 1900–1940: A Historiographic Overview'. In *Blood and Homeland: Eugenics and Racial Nationalism in Central and Southeast Europe, 1900–1940*, edited by Marius Turda and Paul J. Weindling, 2–12. Budapest and New York: Central European University Press, 2006.

Uitz, Renáta. 'The Incomplete Transition in Hungary'. In *Transitional Justice and Memory in Europe (1945–2013)*, edited by Nico Wouters, 289–326. Antwerp and Cambridge: Intersentia, 2014.

Ullrich, Sebastian. *Der Weimar-Komplex: Das Scheitern der ersten deutschen Demokratie und die politische Kultur der frühen Bundesrepublik 1945–1959*. Göttingen: Wallstein, 2009.

United Nations High Commissioner for Refugees. *The State of the World's Refugees, 2000*. Oxford: Oxford University Press, 2000.

Urwin, Derek. *The Community of Europe: A History of European Integration since 1945*. Harlow: Longman, 1991.

van der Wee, Herman. *Prosperity and Upheaval: The World Economy, 1945–1980*. Berkeley: University of California Press, 1986.

van Laak, Dirk. 'Planung. Geschichte und Gegenwart des Vorgriffs auf die Zukunft', *Geschichte und Gesellschaft*, 34 (2008): 305–326.

Verdery, Katherine. 'Nationalism and National Sentiment in Post-Socialist Romania', *Slavic Review*, 52 (1993): 179–203.

Vernon, Raymond. 'As the Twig is Bent. The Marshall Plan in Europe's Industrial Structure'. In *The Marshall Plan Today: Model and Metaphor*, edited by John Agnew and J. Nicholas Entrikin, 155–170. London: Routledge, 2004.

Vickers, Adrian. *A History of Modern Indonesia*. Cambridge: Cambridge University Press, second edition, 2012.

Vincent, Marie-Bénédicte. 'Punir et rééduquer: le processus de dénazification (1945–1949)'. In *La dénazification*, edited by Marie-Bénédicte Vincent, 9–88. Paris: Perrin, 2008.

Vinen, Richard. *Bourgeois Politics in France*. Cambridge and New York: Cambridge University Press, 2010.

von Puttkamer, Joachim. *Ostmitteleuropa im 19. und 20. Jahrhundert*. Munich: Oldenbourg, 2010.

Voutira, Eftihia. 'Ethnic Greeks from the Former Soviet Union as "Privileged Return Migrants"', *Espace populations sociétés/Space populations societies*, no. 2004/3 (2004): 533–544.

Wagar, W. Warren. *A Short History of the Future*. Chicago: University of Chicago Press, 1989.

Waldstein, Maxim, and Sanna Turoma. 'Introduction: Empire and Space. Russian and the Soviet Union in Focus'. In *Empire De/Centered: New Spatial Histories of Russia and the Soviet Union*, edited by Maxim Waldstein and Sanna Turoma, 1–30. Burlington: Ashgate Publishing, 2013.

Wardhaugh, Jessica, Ruth Leiserowitz and Christian Bailey. 'Intellectual Dissidents and the Construction of European Spaces, 1918–1988'. In *Europeanization in the Twentieth Century: Historical Approaches*, edited by Martin Conway and Kiran Klaus Patel, 21–43. New York: Palgrave Macmillan, 2010.

Warner, Geoffrey. 'Allies, Government and Resistance: The Belgian Political Crisis of November 1944', *Transactions of the Royal Historical Society*, Fifth Series, 28 (1978): 45–60.

Watson, Rubie S. ed., *Memory, History, and Opposition under State Socialism*. Santa Fe: University of Washington Press, 1994.

Weber, Eugen. *Peasants into Frenchmen: The Modernization of Rural France, 1870–1914*. Stanford: Stanford University Press, 1976.

Weinke, Annette. 'Der Umgang mit der Stasi und ihren Mitarbeitern'. In *Vergangenheitsbewältigung am Ende des zwanzigsten Jahrhunderts*, edited by Helmut König et al., 167–191. Opladen: Springer Verlag, 1998.

Weinke, Annette. 'Alliierter Angriff auf die nationale Souveränität? Die Strafverfolgung ovn Kriegs- und NS-Verbrechen in der Bundesrepublik, der DDR und Österreich'. In *Transnationale Vergangenheitspolitik: Der Umgang mit deutschen Kriegsverbrechern in Europa nach dem Zweiten Weltkrieg*, edited by Norbert Frei, 37–93. Göttingen: Wallstein Verlag, 2006.

Weinke, Annette. *Eine Gesellschaft ermittelt gegen sich selbst: die Geschichte der Zentralen Stelle Ludwigsburg 1958–2008*. Darmstadt: Wissenschaftliche Buchgesellschaft, 2009.

Weinke, Annette. *Gewalt, Geschichte, Gerechtigkeit. Transnationale Debatten über deutsche Staatsverbrechen im 20. Jahrhundert*. Göttingen: Wallstein, 2016.

Weiner, Amir. *Making Sense of War: The Second World War and the Fate of the Bolshevik Revolution*. Princeton: Princeton University Press, 2001.

Weitz, Eric D. 'From the Vienna to the Paris System: International Politics and the Entangled Histories of Human Rights, Forced Deportations, and Civilizing Missions', *The American Historical Review*, 113 (2008): 1313–1343.

Wejnert, Barbara. *Diffusion of Democracy. The Past and Future of Global Democracy*. Cambridge: Cambridge University Press, 2014.

Wertheim, Stephen. 'The League of Nations: A Retreat from International Law', *Journal of Global History*, 7 (2012): 210–232.

Westad, Odd Arne. *The Global Cold War: Third World Interventions and the Making of Our Times*. Cambridge: Cambridge University Press, 2005.

White, Benjamin Thomas. *The Emergence of Minorities in the Middle East: The Politics of Community in French Mandate Syria*. Edinburgh: Edinburgh University Press, 2011.

Wieviorka, Olivier. 'Les mécanismes de l'épuration', *L'Histoire*, no. 179 (1994): 44–51.

Williams, Paul. *Memorial Museums: The Global Rush to Commemorate Atrocities*. New York and Oxford: Berg, 2007.

Willis, James F. *Prologue to Nuremberg: The Politics and Diplomacy of Punishing War Criminals of the First World War*. London and Westport: Greenwood, 1982.

Wilson, Trevor. 'Lord Bryce's Investigation into Alleged German Atrocities in Belgium, 1914–1915', *Journal of Contemporary History*, 14 (1979): 369–383.

Wimmer, Andreas, and Yuval Feinstein. 'The Rise of the Nation-State across the World, 1816 to 2001', *American Sociological Review*, 75 (2010): 764–790.

Wimmer, Andreas, and Brian Min. 'From Empire to Nation-State: Explaining Wars in the Modern World, 1816–2001', *American Sociological Review*, 71 (2006): 867–897.

Winter, Jay, and Jean-Louis Robert. *Capital Cities at War: Paris, London, Berlin, 1914–1919*. Cambridge and New York: Cambridge University Press, 1997.

Wittner, Lawrence. *Resisting the Bomb: A History of the World Nuclear Disarmament Movement, 1954–1970*. Stanford: Stanford University Press, 1997.

Woodward, Susan L. *Balkan Tragedy: Chaos and Dissolution after the Cold War*. Washington, DC: Brookings Institution, 1995.

Wright, Quincy. 'The Bombardment of Damascus', *The American Journal of International Law*, 20 (1926): 263–280.

Wright, Quincy. *Mandates under the League of Nations*. Chicago: University of Chicago Press, 1930.

Zahra, Tara. *The Lost Children: Reconstructing Europe's Families after World War II*. Cambridge, MA, and London: Harvard University Press, 2011.

Zaremba, Marcin. *Komunizm, legitymizacja, nacjonalizm: Nacjonalistyczna legitymizacja władzy komunistycznej w Polsce*. Warsaw: Trio, 2001.

Zelizer, Viviana A. Rotman. *Morals and Markets: The Development of Life Insurance in the United States*. New York: Columbia University Press, 1979.

Zubok, Vladislav M., and Constantine Pleshakov. *Inside the Kremlin's Cold War: From Stalin to Khrushchev*. Cambridge, MA, and London: Harvard University Press, 1996.

Zweiniger-Bargielowska, Ina. *Austerity in Britain: Rationing, Controls and Consumption, 1939–1955*. Oxford: Oxford University Press, 2000.

Index